St. Louis Community College

Forest Park
Florissant Valley
Meramec

Instructional Resources
St. Louis, Missouri

INSTRUCTIONAL DESIGNS FOR MICROCOMPUTER COURSEWARE

Edited by

DAVID H. JONASSEN
University of Colorado at Denver

LEA LAWRENCE ERLBAUM ASSOCIATES, PUBLISHERS
1988   Hillsdale, New Jersey   London

Lawrence Erlbaum Associates, Inc., Publishers
365 Broadway
Hillsdale, New Jersey 07642

Library of Congress Cataloging in Publication Data

Instructional designs for microcomputer courseware.

Includes bibliographies and indexes.
1. Computer-assisted instruction.   2. Interactive
computer systems.   3. Intelligent tutoring systems.
I. Jonassen, David H., 1947–
LB1028.5.I538   1988   371.3'9445   87-33200
ISBN 0-89859-813-3
ISBN 0-8058-0086-7 (pbk.)

Printed in the United States of America
10   9   8   7   6   5   4   3   2

Contents

Preface

Computer software which is designed to create some sort of instructional environment for the purpose of facilitating learning is known as *courseware*. Courseware is computer software that has an instructional purpose. Courseware is a relatively recent appelation for *computer assisted instruction,* which refers to the use of computers for the delivery of instruction in an interactive mode. In computer assisted instruction, the learner responds to queries presented by the computer which then individualizes instruction by varying the rate, amount, sequence, or type of instructional presentation. An important premise of most of the chapters in this book is that too frequently, the only instructional component which is varied is the rate of presentation.

Computer assisted instruction (courseware) is only one of many educational applications of computers. In fact, Roecks (1981) has identified thirteen educational uses of computers, including

- administrative (accounting, attendance, and scheduling)
- curriculum planning
- professional development
- library applications
- research tool
- guidance, counseling, and special services
- test construction, administration and scoring
- instructional aid
- instructional management
- computer awareness and literacy
- computer science and programming

- institutional coordination and networking, and of course,
- computer assisted instruction

Computer assisted instruction (courseware) often includes both instructional components and learning management systems. The point is clear, however. Courseware is only a piece of the educational computing pie. Now that I have established CAI and courseware in the broadest educational computing context, I should focus on some more detailed analogies and distinctions regarding courseware.

Teaching About/With Computers

An important distinction that is often made when discussing educational applications of computers is between teaching about computers and teaching with computers. Teaching about computers includes the amorphous concept of computer literacy and the teaching of programming languages and principles. Computer literacy may include anything from how to ''boot a disk'' to the social, economic, and anthropological analysis of the uses and effects of computers on our lives, work, leisure and so on. In all of these topics, however, the computer is the object of instruction. The microcomputer and its effects are the content or subject matter of instruction.

Teaching with computers, on the other hand, does not focus on the microcomputer as an object of instruction. Rather, teaching with computers assumes that it is an instructional tool or vehicle which may deliver and/or manage instruction. The role of the computer is to support the existing curriculum. That might entail using the microcomputer to deliver the same curriculum as through traditional delivery media using the enhanced presentational capabilities of the computer. The computer may also cause the curriculum to be modified to accommodate new topics or approaches made possible by the computer. For instance, word processing and database management have altered the ways in which we record and access information in many instructional settings. Many of the chapters of this volume are concerned with such approaches to altering the curriculum or the way in which it is delivered. Clearly, computer assisted instruction and courseware are examples of ''teaching with computers.''

Computer: Tutor, Tool, and Tutee

Perhaps the most useful and lasting taxonomy of educational computer applications is that suggested by Taylor (1980), which classifies computer uses as tutor, tool, or tutee. The computer as a tutor describes its role as a device for delivering electronically programmed instruction. Tutorial uses involve the learners interactively and record and manage their progress. It permits the adaptation of the instructional sequence to fit the needs of the learner, most often in terms of pace and content. The computer in the tutorial mode is in control of the human-computer interaction. The computer as a tutor is best instantiated by computer assisted instruction (courseware). Most existing courseware uses the computer as a tutor, but the trend in new courseware is toward the tool function.

The computer as a tool describes a wide range of utility functions, in which the computer is a tool or extension of man (in McLuhan's terminology) which helps the user accomplish a task quicker, more efficiently, or more effectively. Data processing applications are tool functions. Microcomputer tools, such as spread sheet, database systems, and statistical utilities are examples of the computer as a tool. In education, administrative applications such as scheduling, payroll, and inventorying lead the list of tool functions. Instructional management, test construction, and grading are other classroom tool applications. When the microcomputer is functioning as a tool, it is not teaching, at least not in the sense of the computer as a tutor. However, users may learn from tool uses through modeling the action of the tool. In the tool mode, the user initiates the activity and remains largely in control throughout the user-computer interaction. The tool poses constraints.

Instructional applications of traditionally tool-oriented applications are growing, such as the use of database management systems and spreadsheets being used as learning strategies (Jonassen, 1987). Courseware is adding intelligence in the form of rule systems (expert systems) which are tools. In fact, computer tools are being used to free the learner from traditional conceptions of learning. Additionally, computer assisted instruction and courseware are adding more and more tool uses to their packages. So the distinction between tutor and tool uses, especially with regard to instructional courseware, is not as clear as it was in the days of computer assisted instruction.

In the tutee mode, the computer no longer is used to teach the user. Nor does it control the sequence or type of operations engaged in by the user. In the tutee mode, the user controls the computer. Most tutee functions rely on programming languages or translators which enable the user to command the computer to accomplish some desired task. In doing so, the learner uses the computer to solve a problem or create some useful environment. In so doing, many claim that learners become better problem solvers and thinkers. The computer becomes a "microworld" for exploring not only ideas but also the way in which we come to know those ideas (Papert, 1980). While the effects of such epistemological claims have not been strongly supported, numerous computer environments exist to support exploration in virtually every curriculum. Most scientists, pure, applied, and social, rely so heavily on those environments that they would be unable to conduct their research without them. As indicated in Table 1, courseware primarily represents a tutorial application of computers. However, many of the components of current courseware are adding tool functions and even tutee functions, particularly artificial intelligence applications (see Part IV of this volume). In most cases, courseware is used to teach *with* and not about comput-

TABLE 1

	Tutor	*Tool*	*Tutee*
Teaching about computers			
Teaching with computers	Courseware	New courseware	Future courseware

ers. Courseware, if it follows the principles espoused in this book, will focus less and less on the tutor mode, shifting decidedly toward tutee applications.

Types of Courseware

Courseware has been traditionally classified by its instructional form: drill and practice, tutorial, and simulation. These primarily represent the computer as a tutor, controlling the nature and sequence of instruction for the learner. Drill-and-practice courseware uses the computer to store and randomly present practice items to support specific instructional objectives. Most drill programs provide for different levels of difficulty and for record keeping. Many employ aspects of gaming in order to extrinsically motivate performance by the learner. Tutorial programs, from a types-of-course perspective, purport to teach learners in an interactive dialog by presenting information, providing practice, and then adapting instruction and/or feedback based on the learner's response. Simulations present real-world problems in the computer environment that require integration and synthesis of subject matter knowledge into a course of action. The consequences of any actions simulate the consequences of such an action on the real world. The realistic nature of these activities provides a level of relevance that intrinsically motivates learner involvement (see the fifth section of this volume for a discussion of motivation). Other types of courseware, such as problem solving, are tool- and tutee-oriented rather than tutorial. Problem-solving courseware may assume a variety of forms but are intended to help learners successfully complete some problem situation. As courseware continues to evolve based on newer conceptions of learning, these conceptions of courseware (drill, tutorial, and simulation) are less descriptive of how learner-computer dialogs will occur and therefore less useful for classification purposes.

Approaches to CAI

Hofmeister (1984) subsumes both the drill-and-practice and tutorial conceptions of computer assisted instruction or courseware under the concept of programmed-instruction-based CAI. Traditional drill and tutorial courseware are indeed based on programmed learning instructional designs. Programmed instruction evolved as a print technology which manifested behavioral psychological principles of instruction (stimulus-response-feedback). Drill courseware, by design, recapitulates linear programmed instruction. Tutorial courseware represents branching programmed learning principles. Although branching principles assume a greater degree of learner mental involvement with the material, the process remains largely stimulus-response-feedback. Hofmeister distinguishes programmed-instruction-based CAI from simulation-oriented and tool applications, which have already been discussed. He alludes to artificial-intelligence-based CAI as an optional conception. Truly, the future of courseware lies somewhere in the milieu of artificial intelligence. AI-based courseware seeks to model the knowledge and thought processes of the learner in the means of instruction. AI designs are presented more extensively in the fourth section of this book.

EFFECTIVENESS OF COURSEWARE

A number of meta-analytic studies (Kearsley, Hunter, & Sidel, 1983; Kulik et al., 1980, 1983, 1984) have shown significant improvements in learning from computer assisted instruction when compared with traditional instruction. Computer assisted instruction, as a new technology, remains popular among educators and students. That enthusiasm has doubtlessly contributed much to its relative effectiveness. When the hundreds of studies on which these meta-analyses are based are scrutinized, a variety of confounding effects emerge which compromise the results reported in the literature (Clark, 1986). The reasons that Clark cites for confounding are largely methodological. The amount of instruction, method, and content were uncontrolled in most of the studies. The reason that no effects occurred in the first place is the lack of power in the instructional designs used to construct the CAI. Clark (1983) points out that there is no theoretical reason for comparing computer and traditionally delivered instruction. There are, however, many reasons for comparing instructional designs for creating courseware. As a field, we have finally accepted that technologies do not mediate learning. Rather, knowledge is mediated by the thought processes engendered by technologies. So, we must look for the instructional designs that result in the most productive thought processes which in turn result in the greatest learning. Learning then is more directly affected (mediated) by the instructional designs (soft technologies) than it is by the microcomputer (hard technology). So, this book is dedicated to a comparison of instructional designs for creating courseware. If courseware is to have a significant impact on learning, it must be constructed using truly powerful instructional designs.

INSTRUCTIONAL DESIGNS FOR COURSEWARE

Process vs. Product

Instructional design is a professional activity. It is "the process of deciding which methods of instruction are best for bringing about desired changes in student knowledge and skills for a specific student population'' (Reigeluth, 1983, p. 7). Based on an analysis of learning needs, learner characteristics, and situational factors, the instructional designer ''designs'' instructional sequences based on knowledge about instruction and methods. Instructional design is clearly a process—a variable sequence of design activities. Reigeluth (1983) adds to our conception of instructional design the notion of a discipline of study—the knowledge base on which designers make decisions about methods. We study instructional design as a process; so it becomes an academic entity—a field of study. Through our studying, we refine our models of instruction that we use to make decisions about methods. So instructional design has become more than a process.

The title of this book avers a broader conception of instructional design, one that includes the models resulting from the process. The metaphor that Reigeluth uses to discuss instructional design is that of an ''architect's blueprint.'' This is a useful metaphor, since architecture also represents a design process. The results of the architectural process is a blueprint for an edifice, while the instructional design process results in a blueprint for instruction. The blueprint represents the synthesis of principles and concepts that define the field of architecture, as well as a statement of the architect's creativity and vision. The blueprint is a unique communication not only to the contractor about how to build the edifice but also to the owner and the world about his or her conception of a house, office building, or shopping center. Its uniqueness and the statement that it makes represents a *design* or model for the building. The design may be reused, as in the case of a housing subdivision, or it may remain unique, as in the case of an art museum. Likewise, instructional designers produce *designs,* which are also statements about how instruction ought to be provided. Instructional designs as such are models of the instructional process, however, any given design may synthesize a variety of instructional models to achieve the desired blueprint for instruction. The result of the instructional design process, then, is not merely a blueprint from which the instructional developer produces an instructional product, it is also a statement about how instruction ought to occur in a given class of instructional situations. Instructional designs, then, are certainly *not* the instructional product, but they are more than a blueprint. They are a statement, a unique model as it were, by the designer about how instruction ought to occur. Instructional designs, like architects' blueprints, may be transferable or generalizable to a class of instructional problems, or they may remain unique. Just as artists and architects talk about good designs or bad designs, instructional designers too can be responsible for good designs and bad designs. So the conception of instructional design that has guided the development of this book is that instructional designs are the individual statements of instructional designers about how instruction ought to proceed. In this book, the authors make distinct and unique statements about how microcomputer courseware ought to be developed. The design for courseware that each promotes is based on his or her synthesis of appropriate instructional models and the principles that define the discipline of instructional design.

What makes an instructional design powerful? It must first be based on an instructional design theory—that is, it must be instructional rather than learning oriented, and it must be based on a theory as opposed to models, principles, or propositions (Reigeluth, 1983). It should be consistent, limited in scope, empirically supported, and parsimonious according to Reigeluth. Above all, instructional design theories should be useful, comprehensive, the best model to use, and generalizable to a range of problems. The designs for courseware development that are recommended in this book should possess all of those attributes.

Instructional Designs for Designing Courseware

This book applies instructional design theories and models to courseware development. The courseware designs described in the chapters are all theory-based. The authors explicate their theoretical assumptions before applying them. When applying instructional design theories to courseware design, you are necessarily constraining the theory. Yet, probably no other instructional technology has more consistently applied instructional design theory than courseware, and no other technology has produced as consistently positive results, especially those resulting from the theory-based work reported in this volume. The courseware designs prescribed in this volume are made very useful with examples and prescriptions, and they are generalizable across a range of content. I hope that you, the reader, will agree after reading the book, that they represent the best and most powerful designs available for designing courseware.

What are the components of courseware that are manipulable by instructional design? That is, which components of courseware make a difference in learning? In this book, we investigate five major design components:

- instructional design model
- nature of learner interaction
- adaptation of instruction to the learner or the content
- level of intelligence exhibited by the courseware
- motivational aspects of the design.

These represent the soft design technologies that are used to drive the hard computer technologies. These will ultimately account for more learning variance, since they exert the most direct control over the thought processes which mediate the learning process.

The topics (listed above) around which this book is organized focus on the interactive nature of the computer technology. Computer assisted instruction or courseware are implicitly interactive technologies. Courseware is designed to permit the learner to interact with the computer, i.e., to exert some control over

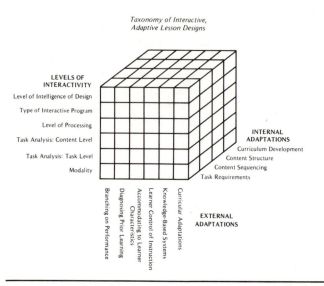

FIG. 1. A Taxonomy of Interactive Adaptive Lesson Designs. From Jonassen (1985). Reprinted by permission of *Educational Technology.*

the technology when acquiring knowledge from it. The more control that is exerted by the user, the more dynamic the interaction can be. Interactive lessons are those in which the learner overtly responds (determined, of course, by some previous covert, mental response) to information and queries presented by the hard technology, and the design adapts the sequence or nature of the technology's response prior to providing the feedback to the learner. Interactive lessons, in classical communication terms, represent a two-way or cyclical communication process. But, is bilateral processing enough? Anyone who has previewed any amount of courseware realizes that the level and type of interaction engaging the learner by different courseware varies considerably. The type and nature of the interaction though determine what and how much is learned from the courseware. It is the interaction which engenders the thought processes necessary for learning. So, like its programmed learning antecedents, microcomputer courseware enables the learner to be an active participant in the learning process. The second section of the book, Interactive Designs for Courseware, examines the nature of the user-courseware interaction.

How can we vary the nature of the learner's interaction with the courseware? Two components of interactive designs emerge: the nature and processing requirements of the interaction, and the nature and extent of the adaptation of lesson content afforded by the courseware design. Interactive lesson designs, then, necessarily entail adaptation. That is, they are necessarily "adaptive, interactive lesson designs" (Jonassen, 1985). So, in analyzing interactive lesson designs, we must analyze both the interactive and the adaptive dimensions of interactive designs. Those dimensions are illustrated in Fig. 1 (Jonassen, 1985).

Interactive Designs

The nature of the learner's interaction may vary in an interactive lesson (see Fig. 1). At the lowest level of interaction, the modality of the learner's response may be varied. Normally, courseware provides visual output and requires kinesthetic input (keypresses). Next, the nature of the processing required by the interaction may be varied, both in terms of the task and the content level of the learner's response. The level of processing required by the learner's response determines the degree to which prior knowledge is accessed and the amount of integration of new material with that prior knowledge. These variables combine to form types of interactive programs (drill, tutorial, simulation, knowledge-based) which require varying levels of task and content. The second section of this book, as previously mentioned, is concerned with the nature and level of learner interactions mediated by microcomputer courseware. Finally, interactive lessons vary in the degree of intelligence that they exhibit. They may be frame-based, node-link, or knowledge-based and intelligent tutors. The depth and meaningfulness of processing afforded by these latter systems represent the goal of contemporary courseware designers. Intelligent courseware, as a technique, is still in its developmental stage. The chapters in the fourth section of this book illustrate the approaches being taken by courseware developers in their attempt to make courseware more intelligent.

Adaptive Designs

What really makes courseware behave like a human tutor is its ability to adapt the presentation of material to meet the needs of the learner or the curriculum. An accomplished tutor can alter, at a moment's notice, the style, substance, or rationale for a presentation to accommodate to what the learner knows or doesn't know, to the way the learner best interprets material or reasons, or to the changing nature of the material. This flexibility of instruction implies pedagogical power. Adaptive instructional designs can be implemented in two ways. First, during instruction, courseware may assess some aspects of a learner's performance or ability to perform and then adapt the strategy, sequence or modality of instruction to best fit the learner's characteristic. These adaptations are based on factors that are external to the presentation, such as learner characteristics. Courseware may also adapt internally, based on the nature of the task requirements or the content being presented to the learner at any time. Courseware may adapt the lesson based on the task requirements of the lesson. For instance, in the first section, David Merrill applies "component display theory" to courseware by prescribing the presentational components required by lessons at different task/content levels. The sequence in which information is presented may also be varied to accommodate different task requirements. Courseware may adapt to varying content structures. For instance, Wallace Hannum's chapter in the third section describes bases for sequencing content based on different content structures. Finally, internal adaptations include those that accommodate to differences in the curricular approach. These are the broadest level of adaptations. Adaptation is a fundamental part of interactive courseware development. The third section of this book presents chapters that analyze some of the best supported heuritics for adapting courseware.

Scope of the Book

This volume presents a variety of instructional designs for designing courseware. These designs are based on the process and discipline of instructional design, which implies a particular perspective to the courseware design process. This book represents what instructional designers have to say about designing courseware, but by no means does it purport to be an exhaustive guide or a beginner's guide to courseware design. You will not see chapters on screen design, graphics, user interfacing, or human factors. Those are very important components of the courseware design process, but they are clearly outside the discipline of instructional design and therefore beyond the scope of this work. The volume is intended for practicing courseware developers, that is, those with some prior knowledge of the process. This book is concerned only with what a very distinguished collection of instructional designers have to recommend to courseware designers. We believe that that is an important message.

The book's title indicates that the authors present principles for designing microcomputer courseware. Although this is true, most of the instructional design principles are generalizable to mini- and main-frame based courseware as well. They are for the most part generic principles for courseware design. The concept of microcomputer was added to the title and thereby the design principles as a constraint. The authors were instructed to include only those principles that could be implemented in a microcomputer environment, with its limitations in memory space and processing speed. If a principle can be implemented on a microcomputer, it can be generalized easily to a larger environment. Since most courseware is currently being developed for microcomputers, the microcomputer orientation (limitation) is justified. What should be obvious by now, though, is that this book is not about computers per se. Rather, it is about instruction. It represents the application of state-of-the-art instructional design theory to contemporary computer technology. If this technology is going to be used to deliver instruction, the instruction ought to be as effective as possible. That is perhaps the most important assumption of this book.

REFERENCES

Clark, R. E. (1983). Reconsidering research on learning from media. *Review of Educational Research, 53,* 445–460.

Clark, R. E. (1986). Research on student thought processes during computer-based instruction. *Journal of Instructional Development, 8*(3), 2–6.

Clark, R. E. (1986). Evidence for confounding in computer-based instruction studies: Analyzing the meta-analyses. *Educational Communications and Technology Journal, 31.*

Hofmeister, A. (1984). *Microcomputer applications in the classroom.* New York: Holt, Rinehart & Winston.

Jonassen, D. H. (1987). Improving recall using database management systems: A learning strategy. *AEDS Journal, 19*(2–3), 189–123.

Jonassen, D. H. (1985). Interactive lesson designs: A taxonomy. *Educational Technology, 25*(6), 7–17.

Kearsley, G., Hunter, B., & Sidel, R. J. (1983). Two decades of computer based instruction: What have we learned? *THE Journal, 10,* 88–96.

Kulik, J., Bangert, R., & Williams, G. (1983). Effects of computer based teaching on secondary school students. *Journal of Educational Psychology, 25,* 19–26.

Kulik, C., Kulik, J., & Bangert-Drowns, R. (1984, April). *Effects of computer based education on secondary school pupils.* Paper presented at the annual meeting of the American Educational Research Association, New Orleans.

Kulik, J., Kulik, C., & Cohen, P. (1980). Effectiveness of computer-based college teaching: A meta-analysis of findings. *Review of Educational Research, 50,* 525–544.

Papert, S. (1980). *Mindstorms: Children, computers, and powerful ideas.* New York: Basic Books.

Reigeluth, C. M. (1983). Instructional design: What is it and why is it? In C. M. Reigeluth (Ed.), *Instructional design theories and models: An overview of their current status.* Hillsdale, NJ: Lawrence Erlbaum Associates.

Roecks, A. L. (1981). How many ways can the computer be used in education? A baker's dozen. *Educational Technology, 21*(9), 16.

Taylor, R. (1980). *The computer in education: Tutor, tool and tutee.* New York: Teachers College Press.

INSTRUCTIONAL DESIGN AND COURSEWARE DESIGN

While the future viability and form of instructional courseware remains an unresolved issue, virtually every discussion on courseware contains some obligatory lamentations on the quality of existing courseware. If you peruse a broad range of existing courseware, those complaints are often justified.

What is the reason for this overall lack of quality? The authors in this book would provide unanimous support for Roblyer's (1981) claim that the poor quality results from the development methods, or lack thereof, used to produce the courseware. Their recommendation is that courseware designers employ a systematic method of instructional design to develop the courseware before the courseware is ever produced, marketed, or used. Systematic design procedures provide a useful methodology for producing any instructional materials, including microcomputer courseware. They would claim that courseware produced without using instructional design procedures based on instructional design theories and models is probably not instructional. Its intention may be instructional, but the result, as evidenced by the universal complaints about courseware, may not be truly instructional.

Instructional Design Theories into Models

Instructional design is a process and a discipline that derives from instructional theory. Reigeluth and Merrill (1979) have proposed that a theory of instruction must consist of methods, conditions, and outcomes. Instructional *conditions* describe the existing, situational factors (e.g., learner characteristics) which impact on learning. Instructional *outcomes* are the predetermined effects produced by instruction, that is, the learning effects which are to be produced by the instruction. Instructional *methods* are the means used to achieve the outcomes. These components are consistent with general systems theories which state that systems are goal-oriented, interactive, interdependent components, which adapt to maximize their output. Any theory of instruction, according to instructional design principles, needs to reflect those beliefs. An instructional design theory must therefore consist of "a set of principles that are systematically integrated and are a means to explain and predict instructional phenomena" (Reigeluth, 1983, p. 21). The instructional methods that derive from those principles comprise instructional design models. Instructional design models are manifestations of instructional design theories and are the means by which the theories are implemented. The models are important to designers who make decisions about the methods which should be used to produce instructional outcomes in given situations. However, the instructional theories on which the models are based are also important, because fallacious theories result in fallacious models which in turn result in ineffective instruction.

Instructional Design Models

Andrews and Goodson (1980) compared forty instructional design models. While they found a good deal of disparity between the models (some of which are not really models), there is general agreement on the major components of the instructional development process. Figure I.1 illustrates the organization and arrangement of those components in a generic instructional design model. The instructional design process consists of three separate stages or phases. The first (Fig. I.1a) is the analysis phase, in which the instructional conditions and outcomes are identified and preliminary decisions about instructional methods are made. In the second, development or synthesis phase (Fig. I.1b), methods decisions are completed and enacted, through either the selection or production of instructional materials or sequences. In the final evaluation phase (Fig. I.1c), the methods decisions are evaluated in light of the conditions and outcomes and may be ammended accordingly. While instructional design models vary, most engage the designer in these three phases. This first section of the book, in fact, provides an interesting contrast between the two most prominent instructional design models in use today.

INTRODUCTION TO PART I

Peggy Roblyer sets the tone for this first overview chapter with some well-documented lamentations, asserting that if CAI is to have a significant impact on education, more systematic design and development methods are essential. She

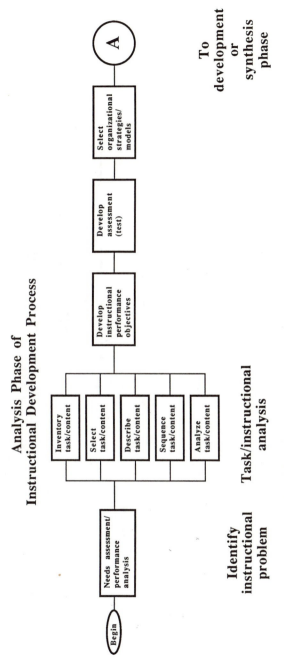

FIG. l.1a. Analysis phase of instructional development process.

3

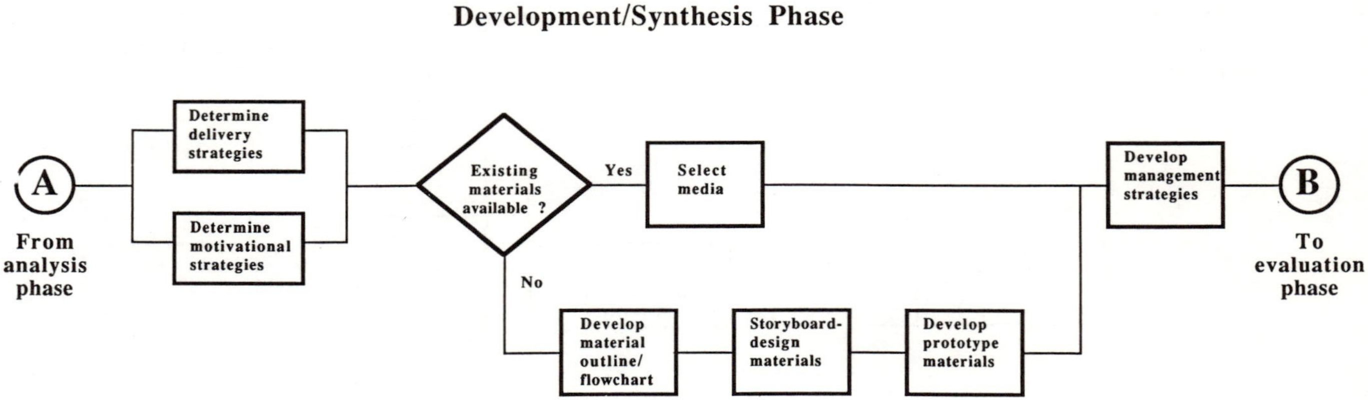

Development/Synthesis Phase

FIG. I.1b. Development/synthesis phase.

4

Evaluation Phase

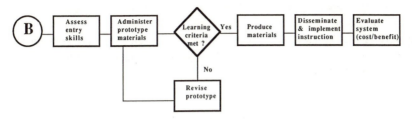

FIG. I.1c. Evaluation phase.

education, more systematic design and development methods are essential. She identifies the specific problems in poor quality courseware (e.g., no objectives, lack of field testing), and the reasons for their occurence, which are, of course, a result of a lack of systematic design effort. She concludes by presenting and illustrating a process model for designing and developing courseware.

The next two chapters provide a useful comparison of the application of the two most prominent instructional design models in use—the events of instruction and component display theory. Walter Wager and Robert Gagné present the Gagné/Briggs model. They establish the context for the model by reviewing and exemplifying Gagné's taxonomy of learning outcomes and next relating instructional events to internal learning processes. After a brief review of courseware authoring, they illustrate the courseware development process by identifying the instructional components required for different learning outcomes. Although this design model is probably the best known, the fresh examples and courseware orientation make this a most useful contribution.

Finally, David Merrill presents the implications of component display theory (CDT) for courseware design. CDT is certainly one of the most coherent and cohesive micro-instructional design models available. As Merrill points out, when combined with elaboration theory or learner control, it provides one of the most comprehensive design systems available. After describing component display theory, Merrill provides a variety of excellent examples of how it can be applied directly to the courseware design process. These first three chapters function as an organizer, setting the stage for the remainder of the book. Instructional design is the context for considering the components of the courseware design process presented in the succeeding chapters.

Limitations of Instructional Design Models

Although it is the contention of the authors in this first section that instructional design models are useful in designing and producing microcomputer courseware, these models are not foolproof (nor would the authors suggest that they were).

The quality of microcomputer-based instruction depends on careful design, we all agree. In addition to the variability in systematic design procedures, the best designs don't compensate for the lack of skills needed to develop quality instruction (Montague, Wulfeck, & Ellis, 1983). Inadequate designers, despite the quality of the design models, will produce inferior quality instruction. Instructional design models function best as heuristics for designing courseware or any other form of instruction.

REFERENCES

Andrews, D. H., & Goodson, L. A. (1980). A comprartive analysis of models of instructional design. *Journal of Instructional Development, 3*(4), 2–16.

Montague, W. E., Wulfeck, W. H., & Ellis, J. A. (1983). Quality CBI depends on quality instructional design and quality implemnetation. *Journal of Computer-Based Instruction, 10*(2), 90–93.

Reigeluth, C. M. (1983). Instructional design: What is it and why is it? In C. M. Reigeluth (Ed.), *Instructional design theories and models: An overview of their current status.* Hillsdale, NJ: Lawrence Erlbaum Associates.

Reigeluth, C. M., & Merrill, M. D. (1979). Classes of instructional variables. *Educational Technology, 18*(3), 5–24.

Roblyer, M. D. (1981). Instructional design versus authoring courseware: Some crucial differences. *AEDS Journal 14*(4), 173–181.

1 Fundamental Problems and Principles of Designing Effective Courseware

M. D. Roblyer
Florida A & M University

INTRODUCTION

The first wave of the so-called microcomputer revolution in education, a period of unchecked enthusiam for computers in the classroom, appears to be at an end. Although school microcomputer purchases continue unabated, there are signs that educators are beginning to question the usefulness of computer-assisted instruction as the primary activity for this technology. Recent microcomputer usage surveys indicate that, while CAI still constitutes about half of all computer-related activity, there has been a substantial decrease in the number of teachers who perceive that this should be the primary role for computers (Becker, 1986). In secondary schools, from 10–30% more teachers than in the last survey see the computer's most important role as that of tools for applications such as word processing, data analysis, and problem solving.

Dissatisfaction with the quality of most available instructional software may be a catalyst responsible for these changing perceptions of CAI. Although Becker's study found that "poor quality of software" ranked below other problems such as money for computer resources and teacher training, it may be that courseware quality has ceased to be the most critical issue in light of decreasing dependency on CAI. It may also be that poor quality software has been instrumental in bringing about other frequently cited problems such as "teachers lacking interest in learning about computers." Observers and practitioners alike (Bell, 1985; Bialo & Erickson, 1985; Futrell & Geisert, 1985) confirm that poor courseware quality continues to be a critical concern.

Certainly, it is becoming more difficult to make a case for increased across-the-board implementation of CAI on the basis of research results. A review of past CAI uses from 1965–85 (Roblyer, 1985) indicates that effects on learning vary widely depending on product design and implementation, and that CAI may often not be as effective in raising student performance as other, less expensive nontraditional methods. The impact of computer courseware on education is especially disappointing in light of the tremendous expectations voiced for it when microcomputers first began to appear in schools. This disenchantment has brought about a second wave of the microcomputer revolution in education, one which stresses analysis and accountability. As Becker's study indicates, educators are expressing concern about the most efficient and effective uses of microcomputers and whether or not we can continue to justify large-scale development and purchases of CAI products.

Now, as educators become more critical and discerning in their product selections and uses, it is time to address these crucial issues. If the outlook on CAI is to improve substantially, in terms of both teacher perceptions and research results, raising courseware quality must become a central focus in the field. That few agreed-upon standards exist for what constitutes high-quality courseware (Cohen, 1983) is most likely due to the lack of agreed-upon design and development strategies. Futrell and Geisert (1985) observe that "the most basic concepts of curriculum design are not being employed" and that the "situation is counterproductive to the maintenance of a healthy growth of microcomputer use in schools." Better design and development methods are an essential component in improving the impact of CAI on education. Without this emphasis, the microcomputer is destined to end up as primarily a tool for computer literacy, word processing, and administrative support. "Making best use of the medium," an often talked about concern of computer educators, is dependent on well-designed courseware.

The purposes of this chapter are two: (1) to cite some of the problems with current software and design methods, and (2) to recommend some overall design and development strategies to address these problems. Some sample products from several of the courseware design steps are offered as examples of how more systematic design methods can improve courseware quality and usefulness.

It should be noted that the emphasis in this chapter is on design problems and methods for use in educational, rather than military and industrial training settings. While there are problems in the latter areas, they are fewer than in education and of dramatically different types. Issues in designing training materials are also less difficult to address due to the top-down management structure of many such organizations. Computer use problems for educators are less clearcut and solutions more difficult to attain. The systematic methods discussed here have already been implemented with demonstrated success in training, and, with proper modification, could yield similar benefits for education.

Problems with Current Software

In a review of 163 microcomputer courseware programs by the Educational Products Information Exchange (EPIE), Bialo and Erickson (1985) report severe design flaws in the majority of the products. The following kinds of problems were observed:

1. Defined objectives—Over two-thirds of the software "either had no objectives stated or had objectives that were unclear or developmentally inappropriate." They stated that this problem was especially prevalent in so-called problem-solving programs or those which purport to teach logic skills.

2. Goal/content/instructional approach match—About one-half of the programs did not have instruction which supported the stated goals, although mathematics software tended to be better in this area. Furthermore, a majority of the courseware failed to use an effective delivery methodology or a presentation which clarified or enhanced content.

3. User appropriateness—Mixed results were reported on the match between software and intended users. Bialo and Erickson were not specific about their criteria for judging this aspect, but it may be assumed that inappropriate reading levels and skills for the grade level were central concerns.

4. Tests and evaluation—About 60% of the programs included no form of evaluation to measure mastery of objectives.

5. Support materials—Almost 70% of the software had no support materials of any kind to help teachers with implementation, and when support materials were provided they were generally found not to be useful or appropriate.

6. Field-testing evidence—Approximately 80% of the software surveyed provided no results of formative evaluation use before the product was marketed.

As Futrell and Geisert (1985) observe, courseware producers still seem to stress more "bells and whistles" than features which have been shown to be instructionally effective. It is also clear that most software is being designed based on marketing priorities, rather than to meet identified needs of specific students. As it is often unclear what instructional problem courseware addresses, it is predictable that there should be a high degree of uncertainty over its effectiveness.

The design flaws found by Bialo and Erickson (1985) may also be seen as contributors to the problems teachers are having integrating software into other classroom activities. Software is rarely identified by objective and is most often not accompanied by other components to form a complete instructional system. The teacher is left to figure out both the purpose of the software and where to use it in the curriculum in order to make best use of its capabilities.

A Rationale for Continued CAI Use

In light of these design and integration problems, reasons for continuing to use CAI are coming into question. It is possible, indeed essential, to distinguish between present courseware effects and potential ones which could be realized if more effective design strategies are employed. Although it may not be fruitful to envision CAI methods taking over a great proportion of teacher roles as some have predicted, it seems likely that courseware could be used to raise the quality of education by making teachers more productive and effective in their instructional activities. This support role for computers will not bring down the costs of education, but it could help assure that present funds are being more productively used.

With effective software, the following kinds of activities are feasible:

• Tutorials may be useful for review after initial teacher instruction, especially for those students who need to spend more time on the topic than the rest of the class. Such self-paced experiences could also be useful as a makeup mechanism for those who missed the teacher's original presentation, or as a substitute for human instruction where no teacher is available.

• Drill and practice software can be used in place of labor-intensive (for teachers) homework and in-class worksheet activities. Since it is automatically scored and feedback is given the student immediately, practice activities take fewer resources and can often yield more effective results.

• Simulations have been shown to be instructionally practical to teach concepts that require graphic displays or role-playing on the part of students in order to clarify or expand on teacher presentations. Although it is frequently preferable to do actual role-playing and experiments, simulations are useful when expense, danger, or lack of time or materials make it impossible to do so.

• Learning tools—Many courseware products that have no stated objectives or which seem to promote unsystematic learning could be made effective adjuncts to teacher presentations if they were part of a complete instructional system. These unstructured products, which range from adventure games to logic puzzles, can help students become systematic problem solvers, if the instructional system surrounding them is designed with this goal in mind.

As Hazen (1985) notes, the computer is an expensive medium and must be implemented where it can resolve an identified instructional problem. The emphasis in all these activities is on making best use of teacher time and using resources where they can enhance educational experiences and address known problems. All these potential uses are dependent, however, on software which meets two primary criteria: (1) it must be proven effective in accomplishing its particular instructional role, and (2) it must be able to be implemented by teachers. Design methods must be implemented which can help assure that these criteria are met.

Systematic design methods have been successful in addressing many of the problems which current software exhibits. The concept underlying such methods has been attractive to many teachers, developers, and researchers in the past. Andrews and Goodson (1980) found some 40 different design models in use at the time of their review. However, most successful applications of design methods have been in training, rather than in education (Gustafson, 1983). Any widespread use of these proven-effective strategies has yet to be realized in education, and especially in microcomputer courseware for education. To arrive at appropriate design methods for education-specific applications, it is helpful to review the problems that have inhibited adoption of such methods to date.

PROBLEMS INHIBITING SYSTEMATIC DESIGN OF COURSEWARE

Perhaps the single greatest impediment to the adoption of systematic design methods has been that courseware products can sell (at least temporarily) regardless of their effectiveness. Many courseware producers may have gotten an unintended message that good courseware design is not of paramount importance to educators. The bandwagon effect has been responsible for unanalytical purchases of CAI products in the past, but it seems to be on the decline now. As educators begin to review costs of CAI and its record of courseware in meeting their instructional problems, they no longer seem to be as impressed by flashy graphics, handsome packaging, and publisher claims. If software purchases decline, publishers may begin to have a more vested interest in improving the quality control of their design methods.

Futrell and Geisert (1985) voice hopes that we may progress from our "national chaos" in courseware quality toward some kind of national design and development guidelines for software producers. They feel that a cooperative exchange among educators and publishers could assist such an effort. However, even if major courseware producers are willing to cooperate in this kind of endeavor (a large step in itself), other problems remain to be addressed if systematic methods are to be used.

Efficiency/Feasibility Issues

In many ways, conditions in industrial and military settings are ideally suited to employing systematic methods (Roblyer, 1983). Learning outcomes are usually clearly defined since they are based on specific job descriptions or known management needs. These are clarified even further through job analysis and task analysis. In addition, these organizations are able and willing to make the substantial resource investment necessary to employ in-depth instructional design methods, especially since the costs can be justified by increased worker productivity and amortized over a large population of potential users.

Clearly, the situation in education is very different. Rather than training for specific jobs, the goals of education are to provide a general liberal arts background, usually as a step to higher education or vocational training, and to make students into "good citizens." It is frequently difficult to get a few teachers to agree on goals or objectives for a given content area, let alone members of an educational organization of the size which could make large-scale design projects cost-effective. Gagné and Briggs (1974) note that there may also be some resistance to systematic methods among educators because of early experiences with poorly applied systems methods which resulted in trivial objectives and overly simplified forms of learning. But probably just as significant a factor is the fact that educational organizations simply do not have the time, personnel, and other resources to invest in design of courseware.

If systematic methods are to be used for courseware design in education, they must be modified considerably from those employed in military/industrial settings. The most time-consuming and (for many educators) frustrating part of instructional design is "front-end analysis," in which exact statements of learning outcomes and sequences are generated. Although it is important to address these items, it seems more practical to require less detail for them and spend more time on defining learner characteristics and other design steps such as formative evaluation. Errors of sequence and skill statements will be caught during built-in revision cycles and as a result of field test data.

A greater emphasis on formative evaluation and field testing is essential. This is the step in which designers test their assumptions about the learners and what will work well with them. Without this activity, any perceptions of the courseware's effectiveness are pure speculation. With smaller, one-or-two-skill packages, it may suffice to make an observation of a few students using the product, along with a review of their responses on the microcomputer, their reactions during an interview, and a teacher review. For larger, more comprehensive packages, a field test with one or more classes of students is an appropriate addition to the other evaluation activities.

Divergent Instructional Philosophies

More difficult to resolve than issues about design strategies are those concerning the reasons for using systematic methods at all. As Gagne and Briggs (1984) point out, such methods aim to identify skills to be taught and arrange instructional conditions such that students are most likely to learn the skills. The product of a systematic approach is a sequence of instruction designed to teach skills efficiently and effectively for a specified target population. If designed appropriately, the instruction plans to build on prior learning and transfers to the learning of later skills.

However, in recent years, the use of the computer as "tutor" (Taylor, 1980) has been roundly criticized by those who object to education which "programs" the students to give correct answers (Papert, 1980). They prefer the student to "teach" the computer, which Taylor refers to as a "tutee" role. Usually, such activities have students engaged in discovery learning and in quests for creative, divergent responses, rather than supplying any one correct answer. Very often, the courseware products are said to teach general problem-solving or logic skills which are believed to transfer to many other areas of later learning, a phenomenon which Pea (1984) refers to as "wheaties of the mind." The two-part rationale of those computer users who hold this perspective seems to be that (1) self-directed, exploratory activities are the only ones which exploit the unique potential of the microcomputer to enhance the quality of education, and (2) these approaches will result in students who are better equipped to deal with the complex demands of our modern problem-oriented society.

Because those who ascribe to the "unsystematic learning" school of thought often do not accept the need for quantitative data to support their beliefs, it is difficult to find very helpful evidence to confirm or refute these claims. Although completely learner-directed activities may have much to offer, our existing societal needs and education frameworks make it infeasible to depend exclusively or even primarily on these methods. Several state educational systems have instituted uniform objectives and assessment plans for many areas of the curriculum. Students must pass these tests for promotion and eventual graduation. It is becoming increasingly important to make instruction effective in addressing these skills and as efficient a means as possible for students attaining them and passing the required tests.

As the move toward educational accountability gathers momentum (U.S. Department of Education, 1983), systematic design methods should become more and more important. This does not mean that learner-directed courseware must be set aside. However, to assure that such products are maximally effective in achieving the desired goals, it seems prudent for systematic instructional design to be applied to the problem of determining how structured and exploratory strategies can best be combined.

RECOMMENDED STRATEGIES FOR IMPROVING COURSEWARE DESIGN

If methodological and philosophical barriers to using systems approaches to design can be overcome, the resulting improved courseware can be expected to resolve a number of problems in the instructional computing field. Improvements should include the following:

1. Greater effectiveness with students—Products will not be released without evidence of usefulness with some of the students for which it was designed. Such useful components as objectives and evaluation strategies will be provided, and there will also be a clear match between objectives, instruction, and tests.

2. Improved research results—With improved courseware design and appropriate accompanying instruction, the measurable effects of CAI on student

achievement should be greater in research studies. It should also become easier to identify the actual contribution of the supplemental CAI treatment to a given skill area, since the factor of instructional design quality will be known.

3. Effective integration into classroom activities—Courseware that is part of a complete instructional system will be more easily integrated into the teacher's activities. The purpose of the product will be clear, and where it fits into the overall instructional strategy will be specified.

General Characteristics of a Practical Design Model

A courseware design model developed by Roblyer and Hall (1985) and shown in Fig. 1.1 has three phases, with a number of steps in each phase and several activities to accomplish each step. This model is based on an earlier version by Roblyer (1981) and is similar to one by Alessi and Trollip (1985) in that it specifies certain development activities peculiar to CAI. However, the model shown here also incorporates principles of models by Gagné and Briggs (1974) and Dick and Carey (1978). It includes revision cycles to correct problems with the design as they are identified, and, as Alessi and Trollip (1985) point out, the design steps may not always be done in the exact order shown in the model. For example, instructional strategies currently used in the area might be explored to determine what new instructional goals and materials are needed. It is important,

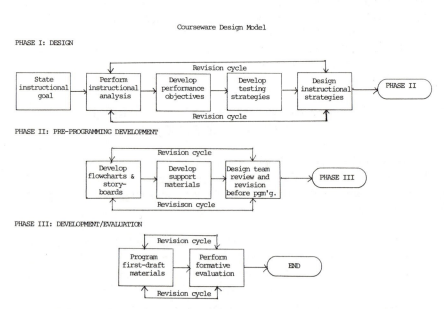

FIG. 1.1. Courseware design model. From Roblyer and Hall (1985). Reproduced by permission.

however, to address each step and to completely design courseware *on paper* before beginning programming.

It is assumed that this model can be most effectively employed by a design team, rather than a designer/programmer working alone. An optimally effective courseware design team consists of at least one person of each of the following types: instructional design expert knowledgable in courseware design and learning theory, content expert who has taught in the area, and a programmer experienced in CAI development. It is not only helpful to have several people involved in creating and reviewing the products, it also helps assure that design will not be limited to what the designer is capable of programming, a common problem in much early courseware.

The documentation produced at each of the steps in the first two phases is an important part of quality assurance during design and development. This written information is the blueprint for the product, and allows everyone on the design team to have a clear idea of what is being planned before it is coded. Examples of some of the documentation for a courseware design project on structural analysis skills (using prefixes, roots, and suffixes to determine word meaning) are included to clarify the purpose and products of each design step.

Phase I: Design

Step 1: State Instructional Goal

Perhaps the most neglected step in most courseware design is a comparison of present needs with available instruction to determine where CAI can be of help. With computer courseware, a decision normally made much later in other models is made very early in the design sequence: the selection of the computer as an instructional medium. This decision is often based not only on instructional presentation factors, but also on such logistical concerns as the need for a self-contained delivery system, or a mechanism for easily collecting data while students work. In any case, there should be some clear indication of what the current problem is and how CAI will help address it. The documentation that results from this step and Step 3 (Develop Performance Objectives) is shown in Fig. 1.2.

Activities to be completed in this step include:

Problem analysis—The design team agrees on the instructional problem to be addressed. For example, a junior high school with a high teacher-to-student ratio and a high percentage of ESL students finds that reading vocabulary test scores are dropping, and a cause seems to be that teachers do not have time to provide the remedial and follow-up work with many students who require more time on language topics. The team determines that a self-paced delivery mechanism for several key basic skills in language arts is required. They agree that a microcomputer tutorial to address each skill and which contains a data collection compo-

Lesson 1: Structural Analysis Skills

Instructional Goal:

Use structural analysis skills to determine word meaning.

Instructional Objectives:

1. Given several different words and their definitions, with each word containing the same root or prefix, or suffix, identify the type of part by entering the correct label into the computer. Criterion: 4/5 posttest

2. Given several words, each containing various roots and affixes, and the labels "ROOT PREFIX SUFFIX," enter into the computer the correctly spelled part(s) of the word under the appropriate labels. Criterion: 4/5 items embedded, 9/10 posttest

3. Given two word/definition combinations:
   -a word containing a root and affix and a definition of the word; and
   -a word containing one part the same and one part different from the first word, and a partial definition of the word,
   supply the missing part of the definition. Criterion: 14/15 posttest
   [Word part definitions must be memorized. Since they are most effectively learned by presenting them a group at a time, this objective will have several sections or modules to cover all the specific word parts required. Each module will cover 15 word parts, and there will be 10 modules, for a total of 150 word parts. Modules will be labeled from easy to difficult based on the selection of word parts. Word parts will be selected based on frequency of introduction at each grade level in textbooks.]

4. Given a word made up of roots and affixes, identify and use the correct sequence of steps to complele the definition of the word based on analysis of word parts. Complete the definition by supplying correctly spelled key words in the definition statement. Criterion: 4/5 embedded, 13/15 posttest.

Target Population:

1) Grade level
   -7-8 grades for students on grade level
   -6-7 grades for high-achieving students
   -8-9 grades for remedial students

2) Prerequisites
   -Instructional reading level of about 5th grade
   -Normal visual perceptual abilities (to be able to see and select out parts within words)
   -Skills in matching words to ap't. definitions
   (Using nonstructural analysis methods)

Instructional Setting:

1) Can be used effectively in classroom or laboratory setting
2) Recommended for individual assignment
3) Should be used as review after teacher presentation, or as remedial review

Type of Equipment/Materials Required:

1) 64K APPLE IIe or IIc with one disk drive
2) B/W or color monitor

Suggestions for Classroom Implementation:

1) Recommended pre-activities - Before computer activities:

   (a) Review concept of compound words
       -Ask them for examples of compound words from their previous lessons
       -Put the parts on separate cards
       -Have students define the parts separately, then define whole word when parts are together
   (b) Introduce concept on non-stand-alone word parts
       -Show examples of words made up of roots, prefixes, suffixes, with parts on separate cards. (Do not use words "root, suffix, prefix" at this time.)
       -Show how they can be put together to make words
       -Show how the same roots can be used with different affixes
   (c) Tell students they will learn that they can use word parts to figure out the meaning of many words.
       -Many words which look long and complicated can be broken down into their component parts. They will become "word spies" when they use these parts to figure out word meanings.

continued...

16

```
(Figure 1.2 continued)

For slower students, teachers may also choose to go through the entire lesson
on identifying roots and affixes BEFORE sending students to computer lessons.
In this case, the computer becomes a review of prerequisite sills and drill-
and practice on the skills.

2) Recommended Follow-up Activities

    (a) Ask students to find exampes of the word parts they covered in news-
        papers, magazines, and their own textbooks. Begin to build a bank of
        words with these parts which are posted in a prominent place in the class-
        room.

    (b) Begin units on using context clues along with structural analysis clues
        to determine word meaning.

    (c) Periodically, give the students a paragraph from published material
        or from student essays containing words with many of the parts they covered.
        Ask them to underline all the roots, prefixes, and suffixes they can find
        in it, and define the words based on context clues and word part meanings.
```

FIG. 1.2. Courseware design documentation—Lesson 1: Structural analysis skills. From Roblyer and Hall (1985). Reproduced by permission.

nent would be a useful supplement to teacher presentations. Data collection would also help diagnose at what points in the skill sequence the problems were occurring.

Identification of student characteristics—The team documents all relevant student characteristics, including grade and reading level. Particular attention is paid to learner characteristics which could have direct impact on the ease of acquiring the skill.

Development of goal statements—General statements of overall goals for each topic area to be covered are written. Like the objectives which will be prepared later in the design sequence, these statements will be in terms of what the student will do as a result of instruction, rather than what the teacher or computer will do.

Definition of instructional setting—Since part of the success of the instruction hinges on implementation variables, the team must specify how and where the courseware might be most effectively used. Two key concerns are whether instruction is to be used on an individual or small group basis, and what kind of microcomputer setting will be needed, e.g., microcomputer lab or classroom.

Step 2: Perform Instructional Analysis

Activities to be completed at this step include:

Development of learning map—The design team members analyze the goal and determine the skills involved in accomplishing it. To document the rela-

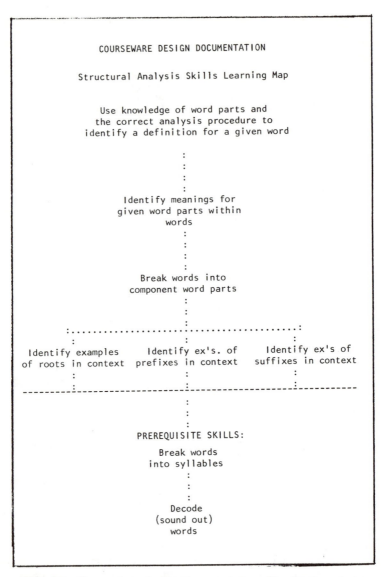

FIG. 1.3. Courseware design documentation—Structural analysis skills learning map. From Roblyer and Hall (1985). Reproduced by permission.

tionships between skills, they prepare a learning map. For verbal information goals, they would develop a content map showing the relationship between the information items. For motor skills, a task sequence would be prepared to show the component tasks in the skill and the order in which they are accomplished. An example learning map is shown in Fig. 1.3.

Determination of prerequisite skills—The team decides at which point in the sequence they will begin designing instruction and which skills they will require as prerequisites for those who will use the materials. This decision is based on knowledge of the students who will use the instruction and the prerequisite skills they can be expected to possess upon entering the instruction.

Determination of skill types/attributes—For those goals that focus on what Gagné (1977) refers to as "intellectual skills," the team must determine whether each skill is discrimination, concept, or rule learning. This has implications for the type of instructional strategy that will be selected to teach each skill. Documentation which may be done on concepts provides both content and structure for the design of instructional sequences. An example of this documentation is shown in Figs. 1.4a–1.4c.

Step 3: Develop Performance Objectives

In this step, an objective statement is matched to each of the learning steps in the sequence. These will not be the same objectives that are given to students

```
                    COURSEWARE DESIGN DOCUMENTATION

                    Lesson 1: Concept Documentation


SUPERORDINATE CONCEPT NAME      Word parts

CONCEPT NAME        Prefix

DEFINITION          A prefix is a word part which precedes a root and which
                    adds meaning to the meaning of a word.

    RELATIONSHIP TO SUPERORDINATE CONCEPT
        A prefix is one of the three kinds of word parts.

    CRITICAL ATTRIBUTES
        -Position before root in word
        -Ability to carry a meaning
        -Ability to expand word meaning when asked

    VARIABLE ATTRIBUTES

EXAMPLES
        trans-              anti-
        post-               circum-
        semi-               hemi-
        super-              sub-
        contra-             pre-
```

FIG. 1.4a. Courseware design documentation—Lesson 1: Concept documentation on roots. From Roblyer and Hall (1985). Reproduced by permission.

```
              COURSEWARE DESIGN DOCUMENTATION
               Lesson 1: Concept Documentation


SUPERORDINATE CONCEPT NAME    Word parts

CONCEPT NAME    Roots

DEFINITION      A root is a word part which supplied the core
                meaning in many different words.

    RELATIONSHIP TO SUPERORDINATE CONCEPT

    A root is one of the three different kinds of word parts.

    CRITICAL ATTRIBUTES

       -Supplies primary meaning for words
       -Can appear at the beginning, in the middle, or at the
       end of words
       -Prefixes and suffixes are added to expand primary meaning

    VARIABLE ATTRIBUTES

       -May have a prefix or a suffix, both affixes at once, or neither
       -Variety of different spellings, lengths
       -Same part can have different meanings

EXAMPLES

       -graph-                 -poly-
       -phobia-                -therm-
       -dic-, -dict-           -aqua-
       -scrib-, script-        -log, -logy-
       -bio-                   -auto-
```

FIG. 1.4b. Courseware design documentation—Lesson 1: Concept documentation on prefixes. From Roblyer and Hall (1985). Reproduced by permission.

before instruction. Rather they are precise statements of what the instruction will enable the student to do and under what conditions.

Step 4: Develop Testing Strategies

Decisions on testing needs—The team must decide what kinds of tests are needed, i.e., pretests for placement or determination of learning readiness, posttests for evaluation and grading, and items embedded in the instruction to ascertain comprehension of key points.

Development of test items—Appropriate response formats must be selected for each kind of test, and actual items must be produced. Items must be written to correspond closely with the performance objectives. An illustration of test items is shown in Figs. 1.5a–1.5c.

20

```
COURSEWARE DESIGN DOCUMENTATION
Lesson 1: Concept Documentation


SUPERORDINATE CONCEPT NAME      Word parts

CONCEPT NAME     Suffix

DEFINITION       A suffix is a word part which comes after a root and
                 whcih adds to the meaning of a word.

    RELATIONSHIP TO SUPERORDINATE CONCEPT

    A suffix is one of the three kinds of word parts.

    CRITICAL ATTRIBUTES

       -Position after root in word
       -Ability to carry a meaning
       -Ability to expand word meaning when added

    VARIABLE ATTRIBUTES

       -Not present in every word
       -Variety of different spellings, lengths
       -Same part can have different meanings depending on use

 EXAMPLES

       -less           -ful
       -er, -or        -ess
       -ee             -ly
       -hood           -itis
```

FIG. 1.4c. Courseware design documentation—Lesson 1: Concept documentation on suffixes. From Roblyer and Hall (1985). Reproduced by permission.

Determination of reliability and validity—For testing systems for use with larger-scale design projects, the team will devise methods of assuring that the test items measure student performance consistently and accurately.

Step 5: Design Instructional Strategies

Based on the documentation created in previous steps, the designers will prepare appropriate strategies matched to each objective. It is at this point that a review of existing materials and media for the skills should be done, if it has not already been done. The team will also prepare descriptions of the media and materials which will be designed or selected to supplement the CAI.

It is helpful to review Gagné's Events of Instruction (Gagné & Briggs, 1974) in order to determine what events of a given lesson the courseware will fulfill.

```
               COURSEWARE DESIGN DOCUMENTATION
Lesson 1:   Test Question Bank - Objective 1

1.  move across              send across          carry across

    (transfer)               (transmit)           (transport)



    Name the KIND of word part common to all these words:


         > ------------


2.  set timepieces to        continuing for       not in keeping with
    the same time            a long time          present times
    (synchronize)            (chronic)            (anachronism)

3.  without fear             without hope         without moving
    (fearless)               (hopeless)           (motionless)

4.  a notation written       holy writing         a series of words that
    below                                         paint a picture
    (subscript)              (Scripture)          (description)

5.  the person being paid    the person attending the person nominated
    (payee)                                       to run for office
                             (attendee)           (nominee)

6.  to speak against         goods imported       to go against;
    (contradict)             against the law      to oppose
                             (contraband)         (contravene)

7.  something written after  after the war        after death
    the main part
    (postscript)             (postwar)            (postmortem)

8.  to say that something    style of speaking    the speaking of a
    will happen                                   curse
    (predict)                (diction)            (malediction)

9.  inflammation of the      inflammation of the  inflammation of the
    appendix                 tonsils              skin
    (appendicitis)           (tonsillitis)        (dermatitis)
```

FIG. 1.5a. Courseware design documentation—Lesson 1: Test item bank for objective 1. From Roblyer and Hall (1985). Reproduced by permission.

These events are: gaining attention, informing learners of objectives, reviewing prerequisite skills, presenting new information, providing learning guidance, eliciting the response, providing feedback, assessing performance, and providing for retention and transfer. Within a lesson for an objective, a tutorial usually covers most or all of the events. Drills mainly provide practice with feedback, and simulations are usually used for learning guidance and/or practice. The design team must develop methods for supplying all the other events in a given lesson which the CAI does not address.

```
            COURSEWARE DESIGN DOCUMENTATION

Lesson 1: Embedded Items - Objective 1

    1.1 Recalling the Terms (Easy-to-difficult):

1.    AUDible        = can be heard
      AUDitor        = "one who hears"
      inAUDible      = cannot be heard

All these words have to do with: HEARING.
They grew out of the word part : -AUD-

        -AUD- is an example of a > --------.

2.    transPORT      = carry across or over
      imPORT         = carry into
      PORTable       = can be carried

All these words have to do with: CARRYING
They grew out of the word part : -PORT-

        -PORT- is an example of a  ---------.

3.    TRACTor        = machine to pull or draw things
      deTRACT        = to draw or pull away
      conTRACTing    = drawing or pulling together

All of these words have to do with: DRAWING or PULLING
They grew out of the word part   : -TRACT-

        -TRACT- is an example of a> ---------.

4.    conSENT        = feel agreement
      SENTsitive     = full of feeling
      reSENTment     = a feeling of hurt, insult

All of these words have to do with: FEELING
They grew out of the word part   : -SENT-

        -SENT- is an example of a> ---------.
```

FIG. 1.5b.   Courseware design documentation—Lesson 1: Embedded
test items for objective 1 (recalling the terms). From Roblyer and Hall
(1985). Reproduced by permission.

Alessi and Trollip (1985) give many helpful suggestions for designing each of
these kinds of courseware. They also give examples of concerns which must be
addressed to make each type meet accepted criteria in the field. The following
are examples of the aspects they emphasize:

1. Some concerns for tutorials (Alessi & Trollip, pp. 132–133)

–Layouts should be attractive and consistent; avoid scrolling
–Don't overprompt and use thematic prompts when possible
–Stress clear transitions between presentations on different topics
–Ask questions about important information

```
            COURSEWARE DESIGN DOCUMENTATIONS

        Lesson 1: Embedded Items - Objective 1

      1.2 Identifying Roots (Easy-to-difficult):

    Choose the word group which contains common roots:

    Item 1 - 1. backWARD, homeWARD, westWARD
             2. UNusual, UNtrue, UNdress
             3. psychoPATH, PATHology, symPATHy

    Item 2 - 1. FINal, deFINite, inFINite
             2. PREpare, PREsent, PRElude
             3. testED, addED, wantED

    Item 3 - 1. SUBtract, SUBdue, SUBmarine
             2. reVERT, VERTical, conVERT
             3. BIcycle, DIenniel, BIlateral

    Item 4 - 1. CIRCUMstanc, CIRCUMvent, CIRCUMference
             2. tireSOME, abERRant, ERRor
             3. ERRatic, AbERRant, ERRor
```

FIG. 1.5c. Courseware design documentation—Lesson 1: Embedded test items for objective 1 (identifying roots). From Roblyer and Hall (1985). Reproduced by permission.

−Provide remediation for repeated poor performance, if only to recommend restudying or seeing the instructor
−Do not put pretests in a tutorial; use only when you know they are needed, and put them in separate programs

2. Some concerns for drills (Alessi & Trollip, p. 160)

−Keep item difficulty consistent in a single drill session
−Consider mixed mode presentations and responses
−Keep feedback short and positive
−Give a short confirmation when the response is correct
−Provide special feedback for discrimination errors

3. Some concerns for simulations (Alessi & Trollip, p. 194)

−Do not use overly detailed graphics; provide just as much detail as is necessary to convey the desired information
−Allow the student to return to initial choices
−Allow internal restarting
−Use modes of presentation a student action that enhance fiedlity
−Use immediate feedback (regardless of fidelity) for beginning students, and natural feedback (regardless of immediacy) for more advanced students

4. Some concerns for games (Alessi & Trollip, p. 238)

–State the rules clearly and allow the student to return to them at any time
–Make the game challenging
–Minimize the use of violence
–Recognize the winner
–At every level of difficulty, allow the student some success
–Reward learning with progress toward winning

5. Some concerns for all courseware types (Alessi & Trollip, pp. 132–133, 160, 194, 238)

–Avoid color in text
–Use a short title page
–Judge student responses intelligently, as a teacher would
–Give complete directions and make them available at any time
–Allow temporary termination at any time

Phase II: Preprogramming Development

Step 1: Develop Flowcharts and Storyboards

The materials developed at this point serve primarily to communicate clearly to the programmer on paper what the instruction is to look like and how it will progress. This sequence may be expected to change many times, but it is still important to have a blueprint from which to work. Storyboards are also essential, but it should be noted that they do not take the place of close interaction between designer and programmer as programming takes place. Examples of an instructional storyboard sequence are shown in Figs. 1.6a–1.6d. An example flowchart sequence if shown in Fig. 1.7.

Step 2: Develop Support Materials

Instructional materials must be developed matched to the needs identified in Step 5 of the design sequence described above. Teacher materials and manuals must be drafted. Working closely with the programmer, the team will also design a management system to collect data, if one is planned, and produce the print materials which will support the management system.

Step 3: Review and Revision Before Programming

In order to avoid as much time-consuming re-programming as possible, it is imperative that the design team take time to review the overall design before actual preparation of the CAI. The team may review the documentation themselves, and may want to ask teachers from the content area to assist them in their review.

COURSEWARE DESIGN DOCUMENTATION

LESSON 1: STRUCTURAL ANALYSIS STORYBOARDS

Lesson Name: __Word Structural Analysis__

Frame Number: __1.1--Segment B__   From Frame Number: __0.2__

```
 1  :                                                              :
 2  :                                                              :
 3  :            There are three kinds of                          :
 4  :                 word parts                                   :
 5  :                                                              :
 6  :        you use as clues to word meaning:                     :
 7  :    ROOTS                                                     :
 8  :                                                              :
 9  :                PREFIXES                                      :
10  :                            SUFFIXES                          :
11  :                                                              :
12  :                                                              :
13  :                                                              :
14  :                                                              :
15  :                                                              :
16  :                                                              :
17  :                                                              :
18  :                                                              :
19  :                                                              :
20  :                                                              :
```

__Response:__ _____
: Feedback   :
:   :
:_____ To Frame Number: __1.2__   :

__Response:__ _____
: Feedback   :
:   :
:_____ To Frame Number: _____   :

__Response:__ _____
: Feedback   :
:   :
:_____ To Frame Number: _____   :

__Response:__ _____
: Feedback   :
:   :
:_____ To Frame Number: _____   :

__Special Instructions to Programmer_____
:   Put "ROOTS" first. wait 2 seconds. then put   :
:   "PREFIXES," wiat, etc.   :

FIG. 1.6a.   Courseware design documentation—Lesson 1: Structural analysis storyboards (Frame 1.1). From Roblyer and Hall (1985). Reproduced by permission.

Lesson Name: Word Structural Analysis

Frame Number: 1.2   From Frame Number: 1.1

```
 1 :
 2 :    ROOT      PREFIX    SUFFIX                          :
 3 :                                                        :
 4 :    Let's look at roots first.                          :
 5 :                                                        :
 6 :    A  root  is a word part which:                      :
 7 :                                                        :
 8 :         *carries the primary meaning                   :
 9 :          for many words, and                           :
10 :                                                        :
11 :         *can appear in any location                    :
12 :          in a word.                                    :
13 :                                                        :
14 :                                                        :
15 :                                                        :
16 :                                                        :
17 :                                                        :
18 :                                                        :
19 :                                                        :
20 :                                                        :
```

Response:
: Feedback   :
:   :
:   To Frame Number: 1.3   :

Response:
: Feedback   :
:   :
:   To Frame Number: :

Response:
: Feedback   :
:   :
:   To Frame Number: :

Response:
: Feedback   :
:   :
:   To Frame Number: :

Special Instructions to Programmer
:   Highlight "ROOT" w/box and/or   :
:   reverse image.   :

FIG. 1.6b. Courseware design documentation—Lesson 1: Structural analysis storyboards (Frame 1.2). From Roblyer and Hall (1985). Reproduced by permission.

Lesson Name: Word Structural Analysis

Frame Number: 1.3   From Frame Number: 1.2

```
 1 :                                                                      :
 2 :              All these words have to do with                        :
 3 :                                                                      :
 4 :                          DISTANCE                                    :
 5 :        They all grew out of the same root.                          :
 6 :                                                                      :
 7 :                                                                      :
 8 :              telegram            telegraph                          :
 9 :                                                                      :
10 :              telephone                                              :
11 :     \\\\\   \\\\\\  )\\)((   ))\((()\\((   )\\/// (\\\\\ //(((/((\)\) )  :
12 :                            -TELE-                                   :
13 :                                                                      :
14 :            -TELE- = distance                                        :
15 :                                                                      :
16 :                                                                      :
17 :                                                                      :
18 :                                                                      :
19 :                                                                      :
20 :                                                                      :
```

Response:_____
: Feedback   :
:   :
:_____To Frame Number: 1.4   :

Response:_____
: Feedback   :
:   :
:_____To Frame Number:_____:

Response:_____
: Feedback   :
:   :
:_____To Frame Number:_____:

Response:_____
: Feedback   :
:   :
:_____To Frame Number:_____:

Special Instructions to Programmer_____
:   :
:   Draw one "branch" and word at a time,   :
:   but draw "root" first.   :

FIG. 1.6c. Courseware design documentation—Lesson 1: Structural analysis storyboards (Frame 1.3). From Roblyer and Hall (1985). Reproduced by permission.

COURSEWARE DESIGN DOCUMENTATION

LESSON 1: STRUCTURAL ANALYSIS STORYBOARDS

Lesson Name: ___Word Structural Analysis___

Frame Number: ___1.4___   From Frame Number: ___1.3___

```
 1 :                                                          :
 2 :          All these words grew out of                    :
 3 :                                                          :
 4 :                 the word part                            :
 5 :        -AUD-      =         hearing                      :
 6 :                                                          :
 7 :     audible       =         can be heard                 :
 8 :   inaudible       =         cannot be heard              :
 9 :                                                          :
10 :     auditor       =         the one hearing              :
11 :             -AUD- is an example of a                     :
12 :                                                          :
13 :                >  _____                            :
14 :                                                          :
15 :                                                          :
16 :                                                          :
17 :                                                          :
18 :                                                          :
19 :                                                          :
20 :_____:
```

Response: ___"Root" or "Root part"___
: Feedback
:   Next 1.4 :
: Correct! Press RETURN.
:   To Frame Number: or 1.6 :
Response: ___"Word part" or "part"___
: Feedback
:   Same   :
:   Yes, but which kind.
:   To Frame Number: 1.4   :

Response: ___General wrong answer___
: Feedback
:   No, it is a ROOT   :
:
:   To Frame Number:_____:

Response: ___After 2 wrong answers on item___
: Feedback
:   :
:   To Frame Number: 1.5   :

___Special Instructions to Programmer___
:   Student must get 2 of these embedded items correct. :
:   See attached for Item 2 content.   :

FIG. 1.6d. Courseware design documentation—Lesson 1: Structural analysis storyboards (Frame 1.4). From Roblyer and Hall (1985). Reproduced by permission.

COURSEWARE DESIGN DOCUMENTATION
LESSON 1: STRUCTURAL ANALYSIS FLOWCHART

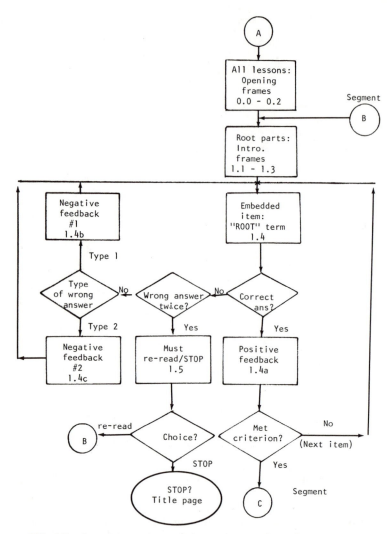

FIG. 1.7. Courseware design documentation—Lesson 1: Structural analysis flowchart. From Roblyer and Hall (1985). Reproduced by permission.

Phase III: Program Development and Evaluation

Step 1: Program First-draft Materials

The programmer prepares screens and sequences according to design. As designer and programer interact, they will develop screen presentation mechanisms to enhance cuing and attention to important details in the instruction, and other devices to maintain motivation and enhance understanding.

Step 2: Perform Formative Evaluation

Finally, the first draft materials are tested with students or classes of students from the target population. Data should be collected on student performance, student attitudes toward instruction, and teacher attitudes. At least one member of the design team should watch students as they go through the instruction to determine any problems they may have with computer use or with understanding what they should do. Students should be interviewed to get their reactions to the materials' ease of use and interest. It is essential that the actual screens be proofread to eliminate any misspellings, incorrect grammar, or typographical errors. Based on this feedback, the team will revise the materials as necessary and finalize them.

SUMMARY CONCLUSIONS AND RECOMMENDATIONS

It should be apparent to courseware producers and educators alike that the design and development approach outlined here differs significantly from those in common use. Systematic design methods require an investment of time and other resources far exceeding what most products on the market have seen. Currently, if a product takes a long time in development, it is usually due to programming or other technical problems, rather than any concentration on instructional design concerns. In systematic design models, the design stage typically takes three-quarters of the total development cycle. The actual programming steps usually, however, go much faster as a result. The time commitment required to implement this model is an investment in product quality. It helps provide a degree of insurance that products will get used and will continue to be useful (and therefore marketable) over time.

A word of caution to those who would implement this model is appropriate. It is easy for the design team to get hung up during front-end analysis steps in disagreements over such issues as prerequisite skills and learning sequences. It is essential to have a team leader who can analyze the problems quickly and make a decision on what will be done. Since this process will go more smoothly if the team members are all compatible and knowledgable in courseware development, the group should be selected with these criteria in mind.

While courseware quality will continue to be a key factor in the continued use of microcomputer-based CAI in the future, it is by no means the only factor. Equally important is a willingness on the part of teachers to alter their traditional methods in order to incorporate CAI. Grossnickle, Laird, Cutter, and Tefft (1982) hypothesized that "faculty may offer excuses such as lack of training, time, and available software, in an attempt to rationalize an overriding lack of desire to change their established teaching routines." However, the availability of courseware within complete instructional systems could help bring about this change. When courseware becomes demonstrably easier to use and more effective, teacher motivation may increase dramatically. It is a hopeful view, and perhaps the only hope left that computers will have a real impact on the quality of classroom instruction.

REFERENCES

Alessi, S. M., & Trollip, S. R. (1985). *Computer-based instruction: Methods and development.* Englewood Cliffs, NJ: Prentice-Hall.

Andrews, D. H., & Goodson, L. A. (1980). A comparative analysis of models of instructional design. *Journal of Instructional Design, 3*(4), 2–16.

Becker, H. J. (1986). Our national report card: Preliminary results from the new Johns Hopkins survey. *Classroom Computer Learning, 6*(4), 30–33.

Bell, M. E. (1985). The role of instructional theories in the evaluation of microcomputer courseware. *Educational Technology, 25*(3), 36–40.

Bialo, E. R., & Erickson, L. B. (1985). Microcomputer courseware: characteristics and design trends. *AEDS Journal, 18*(4), 227–236.

Cohen, V. B. (1983). Criteria for the evaluation of microcomputer courseware. *Educational Technology, 23*(1), 9–14.

Dick, W., & Carey, L. (1978). *The systematic design of instruction.* Glenview, IL: Scott-Foresman.

Futrell, M., & Geisert, P. (1985). A call for action to improve the design of microcomputer instructional courseware. *Educational Technology, 25*(5), 13–15.

Gagne, R. M. (1977). *The conditions of learning.* New York: Holt, Rinehart, and Winston.

Gagné, R. M., & Briggs, L. J. (1974). *Principles of instructional design.* New York: Holt, Rinehart, & Winston.

Grossnickle, D. R., Laird, B. A., Cutter, T. W., & Tefft, J. A. (1982). Profile of change in education: A high school faculty adopts/rejects microcomputers. *Educational Technology, 21*(6), 17–19.

Gustafson, K. L. (1983). About this issue. *Journal of Instructional Development, 6*(2), 1.

Hazen, M. (1985). Instructional software design principles. *Educational Technology, 25*(11), 18–23.

Papert, S. (1980). *Mindstorms: Children, computers, and powerful ideas.* New York: Basic Books.

Pea, R. D. (1984). Logo programming and problem-solving (Technical report No. 12). New York: The Bank Street College of Education, Center for Children and Technology.

Roblyer, M. D. (1981). Instructional design vs. authoring of courseware: Some crucial differences. *AEDS Journal, 14*(4), 173–181.

Roblyer, M. D. (1983). Toward more effective microcomputer courseware through application of systematic instructional design methods. *AEDS Journal, 17*(1–2), 23–32.

Roblyer, M. D. (1985). *Measuring the impact of computers in instruction.* Washington, D.C.: The Association for Educational Data Systems.

Roblyer, M. D., & Hall, K. A. (1985). *Systematic instructional design of computer courseware: A workshop handbook.* Tallahassee, FL: Florida A&M University.

Taylor, R. P. (1980). *The computer in the school: Tutor, tool, and tutee.* New York: Teachers College Press.

U.S. Department of Education (1983). *A nation at risk: The imperative for educational reform.* National Commission on Excellence in Education. Washington, D.C.: U.S. Government Printing Office.

Walker, D. F., & Hess, R. D. (1984). *Instructional software: Principles and perspectives for design and use.* Belmont, CA: Wadsworth.

2 Designing Computer-Aided Instruction

Walter Wager
Robert M. Gagné
Florida State University

As instructional designers we take the position that plans and decisions made in designing computer-aided instruction (CAI) are no different from those that must be made when designing instruction for any other medium. However, media are different in their capabilities of providing stimulus displays and other features that facilitate learning. Accordingly, it is possible to give an account of what can be done in the design process of computer-assisted instruction that might use the medium to best advantage.

One feature of the computer that appears to merit attention is the control it gives the designer over display capabilities that allow for stimulus elaboration (graphic and print devices that have the effect of enhancing learning and retention). Another feature is the possibility it affords for elicitation of responses and the provision of elaborative or adaptive feedback. These two features manifest themselves in many different ways, and may in fact serve different roles at various stages in the learning process; but they do seem to be what sets the computer apart from other media. However, these features must be integrated into an overall design plan for developing instructional materials. In the following pages we present a design plan based on learning theory and associated research. We intend to show how the capabilities of the computer can be taken into account in the systematic development of CAI.

PLANNING FOR THE OUTCOMES OF LEARNING

The general nature of the planned instruction may arise from various sources. Perhaps the designer is highly familiar with what is to be taught, and carries it in memory, as for example, a procedure for making a chocolate cake. Or, the designer may be trying to teach something described to him orally by an expert. More frequently, the designer may be attempting to adapt to CAI form something that appears in print—the description of a piece of equipment, the account of an event, the procedure for a mathematical calculation, or something of the sort. Whatever the sources of these descriptions may be, oral or printed, it is essential to note that they cannot be unquestioningly accepted as valid representations of what is to be learned.

Determining what is to be learned is the first step in instructional design. The goal of instruction cannot be found by simply examining the content of descriptive material about the task to be learned. Instead, an intellectually disciplined step must be taken by the designer to infer the nature of the performance that is expected to be attained as a result of learning. Does one expect the learner to recount the gist of the Preamble to the US Constitution? Or to find the length of the hypotenuse of a right triangle? Or to display an understanding of the idea of *hostage?* Or to behave in ways that indicate valuing an unspoiled environment? Or to tie a bowline knot? Each of these performances represents a *different kind of learning outcome,* and it is important to identify this outcome as a first step. Some are fairly easy to distinguish—tying a knot is obviously a kind of performance differing from recounting an event. Some are less easily distinguished— is stating the equation $E = I \times R$ the same as understanding Ohm's law?

The kind of performance expected of a learner as a result of instruction is called a *learning outcome.* Before thinking about how to instruct, the designer needs to identify the kind of learning outcome he expects the learner to acquire. There are five main kinds of learning outcomes. As is shown later, each of them requires a different instructional treatment in order for learning to be most effectively and efficiently accomplished.

The five kinds of learning outcomes identified by Gagné (1984, 1985; Gagné & Briggs, 1979) are as follows: (1) *intellectual skills;* (2) *verbal information;* (3) *cognitive strategies;* (4) *motor skills;* and (5) *attitudes.* These are listed as *learned capabilities* in Table 2.1, together with examples of each. Note that the category intellectual skill has several subcategories, the most important being *concepts* and *rules.* Each of these categories may be distinguished from the others by its characteristics, and any specific learning objective may accordingly be classified into one of these five types.

Learning outcomes, naturally enough, are the performances made possible by learning—that is, they are what the learner is able to do when learning is completed. The following paragraphs give summary descriptions of each major type (Gagné, 1985).

Intellectual Skill

As the name implies, this kind of learning outcome enables the learner to do something that requires cognitive processing. It is *procedural knowledge.* Sever-

TABLE 2.1
Five Types of Learning Outcomes

Type of Outcome	Examples of Performance
Intellectual Skill	Demonstrating, using symbols, as in the following:
Concrete Concept	Identifying a <u>square</u>; the <u>edge</u> of an object
Defined Concept	Classifying a <u>fortress</u>, using a definition
Rule	Demonstrating the procedure of <u>expressing a mixed number as a fraction</u>
Higher-Order Rule	Generating a rule for <u>finding the length of the diagonal of a rectangle</u>
Cognitive Strategy	Using an efficient method for <u>remembering the contents of a picture</u>
Verbal Information	Stating what happened to the Titanic
Motor Skill	Catching a fly ball
Attitude	Choosing swimming as exercise

al varieties of intellectual skill are usually distinguished: concepts, rules, procedures.

Concrete concept. When they have learned a concrete concept, learners are able to *identify* instances of an object property (*square*), of an object (*keyboard*), of an event (*delete*), or of a spatial direction (*left*). The performance that indicates the attainment of a concrete concept is *identifying* one or more instances of the concept that have not previously been encountered during learning. Identifying may be done by pointing, by selecting; and it is often done by naming, when the name is familiar to the learner as a word. A child's possession of the concrete concept *curved* might be verified by asking the child to pick out object shapes having curves from a group of shapes of varied characteristics. With an adult learner, however, it would be possible to show a group of varied shapes, mark the curved ones with a dot, and ask, "What is common to these marked figures?" Expected answer, "They are curved." It may be noted that identification can always be done by pointing or selecting. However, if naming is required in assessing performance, care must be taken to assure the familiarity of the word; for example, it would be unwise to assume learners' knowledge of a word like *sinusoidal,* even though they might be perfectly able to identify such a shape.

Concrete concepts can be identified by using *definitions,* but this too is a means of verification that places unnecessary literacy demands upon the learner. Thus, possession of the concept *circle* can be verified by requiring the learner to point out shapes of this variety. For many performance purposes, such a means

37

of identifying a circle is fully adequate, and one does not expect the learner to follow a definition such as "locus of points equidistant from a point." For the study of plane geometry, however, the concrete concept is not adequate; learners in this subject must accordingly acquire a *defined concept* of circle.

Defined concept. This kind of intellectual skill is considered to be acquired when the learner is able to demonstrate the application of the rule that defines the concept. For example, it would not be possible to identify a concept like *first cousin* by pointing to instances; nor would this be true of *city,* or *cooking.* Concepts of this defined sort are verified as part of a learner's repertoire by asking that the learner show how the definition applies. In verifying knowledge of the concept *first cousin,* for example, learners must demonstrate that they can identify aunts and uncles (which themselves must be known as defined concepts) and also identify the class of individuals who are children (offspring). By performing in this manner, learners are *demonstrating* that the concept in question accords with a definition ("a first cousin is the child of an uncle or an aunt").

Demonstrating the applicability of a definition needs to be carefully distinguished from *stating* a definition. As science teachers know, some students would be highly prepared to identify Newton's second law by means of the statement: "f = ma." This is verbal knowledge, or *verbal information,* as we describe it later on. But the verbal statement of a definition is an entirely inadequate indicator that the concept of Newton's second law has been learned. In order to convince a teacher of the latter outcome, students would need to identify instances of each of the concepts (force, mass, acceleration) and demonstrate the relationships among them. Of course, if the instructor is willing to make certain assumptions about the prior knowledge of the student, it may be possible to accept a verbal description of a demonstration of the concept's definition. The instructor may say, in effect, "O.K., I'll assume you know what a *force* is, what *mass* is, and what *acceleration* is; now tell me how you would show what Newton's second law is." In this case, students are permitted to use verbal statements to describe *how they would demonstrate* a defined concept. Obviously, this is a very different performance from merely stating a definition.

For purposes of instructional design, it is critically important to maintain this distinction between defining a concept (i.e., *stating* a definition) and *demonstrating* a concept by means of a definition. In any given set of learners, these two performances may be entirely independent. One learner may readily be able to state Newton's second law without having the slightest knowledge of its meaning. Another learner, if given access to suitable equipment, might be able to demonstrate the law without ever having uttered the verbal statement "f = ma." It is the demonstration of the definition that proves possession of the concept. The caution for test designers and teachers who wish to assess whether defined concepts have been learned is clear. In verifying the learning of defined concepts, verbal statements may sometimes be used to describe demonstrations of concept definitions, but verbal statements of the definitions are by themselves inadequate.

Rule.   A rule is a cognitively understood relation between concepts. As noted already, f = ma is a rule relating the concepts of force, mass and acceleration. A rule of English grammar is "A pronoun following a preposition takes the objective case." In the sentence, "Who does what to whom?", the pronoun following the preposition *to* is given the objective form *whom.* In the case of this rule, the component concepts are pronoun, preposition, objective form of pronoun, and the relation is *takes,* or *requires.* A learner shows that this rule has been learned by applying it to some new instance, as in "I consider this the best choice for you and _____."

It may be noted again that the learning of a rule endows the learner with an internally stored capability, that shows itself in a type of performance (using the objective form of pronouns following prepositions). The rule is this capability, but it is not the verbal description of it, which may be called the *rule statement.* A rule statement may be used as a part of instruction, and will likely work if the learner is already able to identify all of its component concepts (pronoun, preposition, etc.). In suitably prepared learners, a verbal rule statement is commonly used as a focal part of instruction. When used in this manner, however, it would be a mistake to infer that the instruction is intended to teach the learner to *say* the rule statement. Whether or not the learner can state the rule, the objective of instruction is *applying* the rule to one or more new instances. Only when the latter kind of performances can be assessed in the learner will it be legitimate to conclude that a rule has been learned.

Higher-order rules in problem solving.   When learners encounter problems to be solved, they make use of previously learned rules. Usually, some combining of these rules occurs in the course of solving the problem, resulting in a more complex or *higher-order* rule. In confronting the problem of finding the length of a diagonal in a rectangle (Table 2.1), students must use the previously acquired skills of (a) identifying the diagonal as the hypotenuse of a right triangle, and (b) finding the length of the hypotenuse of a right triangle, together with the subordinate skills that these imply. In achieving a solution, a new rule is attained, a rule that is of higher order because it can be shown to be composed of these components (Gagné, 1964). When a learner engages in problem solving, one should normally expect the acquiring of a higher-order rule to be one notable outcome.

Cognitive Strategy

The development of a higher-order rule is not the only event that happens during problem solving. A prominent role is also played by *cognitive strategies,* skills by means of which learners exercise control over their own processes of learning and thinking. As applied to the solving of problems, strategies can range from very general rules of self-regulation ("break the problem down into parts") to fairly detailed strategies that pertain to particular problem domains. An example of the latter sort, as applied to the problem of remembering the contents of a picture (Table 2.1), might be: "Form the contents into categories, such as foreground, middle ground, background, and animal, vegetable, mineral." Cognitive strategies enter into the problem-solving process by aiding the learner in the selection of suitable intellectual skills and in the timing of their use.

The use of cognitive strategies can be directly suggested to learners, and their use can also be practiced during the course of instruction (O'Neil, 1978). Strategies included in instruction may be designed to aid the learner to direct attention to features of the learning task, to comprehend printed text, to hold items in short-term memory, to encode learned material efficiently, or to retrieve it from long-term memory, as well as to regulate thinking.

Because of the varied usefulness of strategies in regulating the processing of information, it is a frequent practice for designers of instruction to combine cognitive strategy objectives with those of other types, such as intellectual skills. Thus, a lesson on geometric proofs of relations among triangles may have as its primary purpose instruction in a rule (equality of opposite vertical angles), and may also include one or more cognitive strategies such as "look for an angle in an adjacent triangle that is supplementary" (cf. Greeno, 1978).

Verbal Information

Instruction is often designed to convey systematically organized ideas in various discourse forms such as description, exposition, and narrative. This kind of learned knowledge is *verbal information.* It is sometimes called *declarative knowledge,* to imply that its acquisition makes it possible for the learner to *declare* it, or *state* it.

Examples of verbal information are the following:

a. an account of what is contained in the First Amendment to the US Constitution;
b. the set of events that led to the stock market crash of 1929;
c. a description of the Washington Monument;
d. a biographical sketch of Mahatma Ghandi.

The learner performance, then, that verifies the occurrence of learning is the learner's stating of the knowledge. If we wish to know whether the learner has learned the descriptive features of the Washington Monument, we ask for that description to be stated, orally or in writing. One further condition, applicable to most instances of this sort, is that we ask for the description *in the learner's own words*. That is to say, we try to arrange the situation in a way that will require the learner to employ *constructive* memory, rather than reproductive recall.

When facts or organized knowledge are learned in verbatim fashion, this is a very special kind of knowledge, sometimes given the name of *verbalization* (as opposed to verbal information). Of course, there are special situations that call for verbalization, such as the reciting of poetry, or the pledge of allegiance to the flag, or the lines of an actor in a stage play. But such verbatim recitation does not provide evidence that verbal information, in the sense that we wish to use the phrase, has been learned. In order to qualify as knowledge, verbal information must be *understood*. This means that the ideas (propositions) that comprise it must be capable of being stated in a form that preserves their meaning without having to be reproduced lexically, phonologically, or syntactically.

The exact reproduction of a verbalized word, phrase, sentence, stanza, or paragraph provides nothing except evidence of verbalization. This may be the desired objective of learning, as is true when a simple name for an object is acquired, or the English equivalent of a foreign word. It is a mistake, we believe, to consider the learning of verbalizations as somehow constituting a segment of the domain of verbal knowledge. While verbalizations are a necessary substratum of the repertoire of the learner, they are not legitimately classed as verbal knowledge until it can be shown that they can be generated by the learner in the manner of constructive recall. Thus, quoting "Fourscore and seven years ago . . ." does not in itself provide evidence of the possession of verbal information. To obtain that evidence, we must have an answer to such a question as: "How long ago did Lincolon say our nation was established?"

Verbal information in the form of narrative, description, exposition, or other variety can readily be learned from hearing or reading connected discourse, from viewing pictures, or from both together. Assessing the accomplishment of such learning is done by a number of methods (e.g., free recall, cued recall, sentence completion), each of which is subject to some pitfalls and validity limitations (cf. Anderson, 1972). Verbatim recall which yields verbalizations must always be regarded as being potentially invalid, since it carries no inherent assurance that the observed performance has made use of constructive memory processes. The challenge to the instructional designer is one of developing performance requirements for assessing verbal information that involves constructive memory.

Attitude

Instruction can readily be designed to establish new attitudes or to modify existing ones. An attitude is an acquired internal (motivational) state that influences the learner's choice of personal action (see also Keller Chapter, this volume). A positive attitude toward listening to classical music disposes the learner to choose records of classical music, for example, when confronted with a situation that offers such a choice. An attitude of avoiding fatty foods may determine a person's choices of foods on a dinner menu.

When an attitude has been learned, or modified, the change is observable in the choices made by the learner. Sometimes these can be seen in actual behavior—as when a positive attitude toward reading books is evidenced by a high frequency of library book borrowing. In many cases, though, direct observation of behavior becomes infeasible, and some form of self-reporting is used instead. Various forms of attitude questionnaires are designed to reveal people's choices of personal action.

Motor Skill

Productive actions involving movement controlled by the muscles are refined in timing and smoothness by the learning that occurs during practice. The result of such learning is a motor skill. Examples are the printing of letters by young children, removing and replacing a contact lens, casting a fishing lure, catching a baseball.

The sequence of actions embodied in a motor skill constitutes a procedure (i.e., an intellectual skill), which has been called the *executive subroutine* (Fitts & Posner, 1967). The subroutine of a motor skill is usually learned as an early part of practice, and may in fact be learned before actual motor practice is undertaken. As for the skill itself, this is evidenced by increasing smoothness and precision of timing of the movements involved. Continued improvements in these aspects of motor skills may be observed over long periods of practice.

THE EVENTS OF INSTRUCTION

In designing instruction, the identification of the expected type of learning outcome, as described in the previous section, should be one of the first steps accomplished. Once it is done, the designer can attend to the question of how to arrange events that will make learning readily occur. These arranged external events are collectively called *instruction,* and their purpose is to support the internal processes associated with learning.

The events of instruction, to be most effective, must be differentially designed for each type of learning outcome. Yet they occur in a sequence that is not inflexible, each step of which reflects a particular purpose. To understand these purposes, one must consider the underlying processes that occur in learning.

Learning involves a number of internal processes, each of which transforms information affecting the learner, and brings about a change in state that advances learning (Estes, 1978; Klatzky, 1980). Learning theory and the research flowing from it have identified a number of these processes, as listed in the first column of Table 2.2. This table provides a brief indication of the function served

TABLE 2.2
Internal Processes of Learning, their Functions, and the
Types of External Events that May Support Them

Internal Learning Process	External Instructional Events
1. Alerting the learner to receive stimulation	1. Gaining attention
2. Acquiring an expectancy of the results of learning	2. Informing learner of lesson objectives
3. Retrieval of items in long-term memory to the working memory	3. Stimulating recall of prior learning
4. Selective perception of the patterns that enter into learning	4. Presenting stimuli with distinctive features
5. Semantic encoding of presented material, to attain a form for long-term storage and ready retrieval	5. Providing learning guidance
6. Responding with a performance that verifies learning	6. Eliciting performance
7. Reinforcement, by means of which the results of learning are established	7. Providing feedback
8. Providing cues that are used in recall	8. Assessing performance
9. Generalizing performance to new situations	9. Enhancing retention and learning transfer

by each process, and a final column suggests the general nature of external events that may be used to influence (i.e., enhance) each of the processes. These are deliberately arranged occurrences, called the events of instruction (Gagné & Briggs, 1979). Any complete act of learning involves these nine events of instruction.

There are, of course, conditions in the learners and in the learning situation that modify the particular ways in which these events are delivered. Sometimes, an instructional event may be present in the setting where the learner is located and so may only need to be noted by the designer, rather than being specially constructed. For example, learners who approach CAI with eagerness may not need to have their state of alertness additionally stimulated—their attention has already been gained. Whether or not learners need to be informed of the lesson's objective in some comprehensive manner may depend on whether they already know what the goal of learning is—perhaps by reading the lesson's title, or because it is one in a series having a common or general objective. Event 3, stimulating recall of prior learning, is usually of importance for new learning. However, the nature of the prior learning that is most relevant depends not only on what learners have previously learned, but also on the category of learning outcome intended. An expanded discussion of the latter point is contained in a later section.

The nine different events of instruction need to be considered in every case as potential ways of providing external support to internal learning processes. The displays designed for instruction, however, do not always need to include every one of these events. The designer may decide to omit one or more of the events, either because of particular characteristics of the targeted learners or of the learning task. The nine events constitute a useful checklist that enables the designer to ensure that no essential or helpful source has been neglected.

Different specific forms are taken by the events of instruction, depending on the category of learning outcome intended as an objective. The description of these events in the second column of Table 2.2 is necessarily general to the extent that each applies to any lesson; the specificity of design must come with the consideration of the intended type of learning outcome. For example, event 5, guiding learning, requires quite a different form of external guidance for the learning of verbal information than for the acquiring of an attitude, or for the learning of an intellectual skill.

In examining the description of events of Table 2.2, readers may pose to themselves the question "how?" for each event listed in the second column. The first pointer to the answer to this question is to be found in the corresponding item in the first column. Thus, "4. Presenting stimuli with distinctive features" needs to be accomplished in such a way as to fulfill the *purpose* indicated in the first column, to bring about *selective perception*. Of course, there are many ways to do this, depending on the content of the learning task. If a prose text is being presented to the learner, features may be made distinctive in a number of ways, including block printing, underlining, topic sentences, and others of this sort. If a diagram or map is presented, selective perception may be aided by using certain graphic techniques such as outlining, circling, pointing, and the like. The fact that these many options are available to the designer makes it undesirable to attempt to describe events of instruction in more specific terms for applicability to learning in general. A degree of greater specificity is to be attained when type of learning outcome is taken into account (as described later). However, we contend that prescriptive rules that attempt to specify the content of the events in greater detail have a tendency to confront the designer with too many exceptions, and thus impede the design process.

The planning of CAI instruction needs to consider the requirement for the display of print and diagrams capable of presenting all of the events of instruction. As for the sequence of the events, it is usually from one to nine, although reversals within this order are sometimes desirable. Event 7, providing informative feedback, must inevitably occur following event 6, eliciting performance. Event 1, gaining attention, would likely be reduced in effectiveness if it did not occur first in the sequence. However, events 3, 4, and 5 are sometimes presented in an altered sequence, or in combination, as they all involve the presentation of stimuli employed in enhancing learning.

AUTHORNG CAI

Authoring refers to the process of designing screen displays and preparing specifications to the programmer for the development of a CAI program. But what sort of specifications? What constitutes a CAI program? The answers to these questions depend on what role the program is expected to serve in the learning process. There are three general forms of CAI: Tutorial, Drill and Practice, and Simulations. Each form can be analyzed in terms of the events of instruction it provides, and what additional events must be supplied by the learning environment.

Tutorial Programs

Tutorial programs are the most complete forms of CAI. The purpose of a tutorial program is to teach new skills. To this end tutorial programs should provide as many events of instruction as possible on the computer. One would expect a good tutorial to provide for attention and motivation (Event 1), test or review prerequisite skills (Event 3), and present the learning objective(s) (Event 2) toward the start of the program. This would be followed by presentation of the new content (Event 4), with learning guidance and questions that focused the learner's attention on important details and checked for misunderstandings (Events 5–7). Finally, the lesson would provide practice on the newly learned skill to enhance retention and transfer (Events 8 and 9).

Drill and Practice

Generally drill and practice programs ask questions and provide feedback (Events 6–8). The role these questions and feedback serve depends on how they are used within the total instructional environment. However, they are most often used to enhance retention and transfer (Event 9). Used in this way they are serving a different role than the questions used within a tutorial program that direct attention and check for misunderstandings.

A drill and practice program can be used to strengthen already learned associations and to build skill in concept classification and rule using. For example, a common type of drill and practice program is one in which the learner is provided with a word and asked to supply an associated word (e.g., foreign language vocabulary drill). It is unlikely that having the student approach the drill without first studying the associations would be effective instruction. Instead one would expect that the student has already learned (encoded) the associations.

Simulations

A simulation is a representation of reality. As such, it is a stimulus in the learning environment upon which the learner can act. The learner's action is generally followed by a change in the stimulus, which serves as feedback. This feedback allows the learner to deduce relationships among the variables and formulate hypotheses about the effects of future manipulations.

Learning from simulations is mostly a trial and error or discovery learning process, involving self-generated learning guidance (Event 5), unless additional external events of instruction are provided by either the instructor or the program. For instance, it is unlikely that a student would learn the process of finding the molar weight of an unknown solution from a computerized titration experiment without additional instructional help. Like drill and practice programs, simulations by themselves are seldom an efficient instructional methodology. Most lack important events of instruction like recalling prerequisite skills (Event 3), providing structured learning guidance (Event 5), and giving corrective feedback (Event 7).

Implications for Authoring CAI

The form of CAI is probably not as important as the role that it is serving in the learning environment. Although it is convenient to divide the types of CAI into the categories mentioned, it is helpful only in that it helps us to focus on the events of instruction that they generally provide, and how they fit into the instructional plan.

The implications for developing CAI are to plan how the program will be used, and then to specify the events necessary or appropriate for the situation. That is, if the program is to teach a new skill (a tutorial program) assure that the design includes as many of the external events of instruction as necessary for the task and the target audience. If the program is to enhance proficiency with and/or retention and transfer of a newly learned skill (drill and practice), ensure that it has an adequate number and range of examples. If the program is to represent reality (simulation), assure that there is provision for learning guidance and feedback, either within or external to the program itself.

The next step is to define the content of the events through the development of screen displays that will present appropriate stimuli. This requires consideration of the type of learning outcome.

CAI for Different Types of Learning Outcomes

We have alluded several times to the premise that different types of learning outcomes require different instructional conditions to facilitate acquisition. In the following section we look at the five domains of learning outcomes and their subordinate types, from the viewpoint of what might be included in the events of instruction that would facilitate the particular kind of learning outcome intended.

As applied to the various types of learning outcome, the events of instruction can be understood in a fairly straightforward manner for each type. If one defines an event such as No. 2 "informing the learners of what they will be able to do when learning has been completed," and the learning outcome is verbal information, obviously what is expected is that the learner can *state* whatever particular content is being specified (see Table 2.1), whether it be the names of the states, an account of Paul Revere's ride, or whatever. If an intellectual skill is being taught, it will be expected that the learner will be able to *do* (or *demonstrate*) whatever specific concept or rule is intended. Certain of the events of instruction, however, take on different meanings depending upon the type of learning outcome expected (in addition to their inevitable reflection of the specific content of the learning task). This differentiation by outcome type applies mainly to events 3, *stimulating recall of prior learning;* 4, *presenting the stimulus;* and 5, *providing learning guidance.*

These considerations lead us to adopt the following procedure as we proceed to give examples of the events of instruction for various kinds of learning tasks. We begin with verbal information, and then proceed to defined concepts as a representative type of intellectual skill. For these two kinds of outcome, we describe all nine of the events of instruction. Subsequently, other kinds of outcome are handled in a somewhat briefer fashion: in that events 3, 4, and 5 are particularly distinctive for each type, only these three are described.

Verbal Information

By verbal information we refer here to an objective like "The learner will be able to describe the Washington Monument in terms of its shape, size, and material composition." Notice that this objective identifies the nature of the information to be learned, omitting such descriptive aspects as dates, builders, and costs. The student will be expected to learn the facts specified in the objective from reading a passage (such as might be found in an encyclopedia) about the Washington Monument. An example passage is as follows:

The Washington Monument

This lofty obelisk, the tallest shaft of masonry in the world, was begun in the early summer of 1848 by the Washington National Monument Society, following the designs by Robert Mills. The original foundation of gneiss was 23 feet thick, 80 feet square at the base, and 58 feet square at its top. The shaft was started 55 feet at the base, with 15-foot walls, which had a facing of 15 to 18 inches of white marble. Work progressed slowly till, at the close of 1856, the obelisk had been carried to a height of 156 feet. The expense incurred by the Washington Monument Society up to that time was $300,000. On January 19, 1877, the society conveyed all its property to the United States. No further work was done till 1878, when the first steps were taken to strengthen the foundations in accordance with plans made by Lt. Col. T. L. Casey, U.S. Engineers, who had charge of the building of the monument from 1877 on. The strengthening consisted in enlarging the area of the foundation from 6,400 to 16,000 square feet. This was successfully completed in

May, 1880, and the work of building the obelisk proper was begun in August of the same year, the old shaft having been first reduced to a height of 150 feet. The shaft, which is 55 feet at the base, and 34 feet square at the top, rises to a height of 500 feet and is surmounted by an apex 55 feet high, making the total height 555 feet. The topmost point is 596 feet above the mean level of the Atlantic Ocean at Sandy Hook, and 597 feet above the low-water level in the Potomac. The apex is built of 7-inch marble slabs, and is capped by an aluminum point. The monument was completed in 1884, the capstone being laid on December 6 of that year.

1. *Gaining attention.*   Present a picture of the Washington Monument, with dimensional arrows, and dimensions shown as question marks.

Rationale for the event: Gaining attention is not always necessary, as the learner generally approaches CAI with certain expectations, such as the notion that this is a learning task that will require attention. In this case the event is providing a reason for learning the material that follows. Whether this is a sufficient reason probably has to do with the learner's reasons for learning this information in the first place, but it does provide a setting for the possible use of the newly learned information.

2. *Present the objective.*   For example: ''In this lesson you will learn about the Washington Monument, its size, shape, and material composition.''

Again in this case a formal statement of the objective may be unnecessary depending upon the learner's expectations approaching the task. If the title of the lesson were *The Structure of the Washington Monument* the learner might make a good guess at the objectives for herself.

3. *Recall prerequisites.*   As is often true for verbal information, this task has no formal prerequisites. Obviously the learner must be able to comprehend printed prose, including understanding technical terms applicable to shapes (e.g., rectangular shaft), dimensions (feet) and material (basalt, marble).

4. *Present the stimulus.*   The basic text has been given in a previous paragraph. However, since the purpose of this event is to aid selective perception, special emphasis might be given to certain features of the text. There are several ways to do this, including the use of different size, color, or emphasized type (such as italics, bold print, or highlighting) of the words that pertain to key attributes of the monument.

5. *Provide learning guidance.*   The purpose of learning guidance is to support the process called *semantic encoding*. That is, the information being learned must be made highly meaningful and readily accessible when recall is called for. One way to aid this process is to encourage the learner to embed the new facts into a larger meaningful context. When the word *gneiss* is encountered, for example, an additional frame might appear which describes gneiss and its relation to other rocks. When the word *obelisk* appears, an additional frame might define this term in relation to other geometric shapes.

Another way of enhancing the process of semantic encoding is to use adjunct questions (Rothkopf, 1970) inserted at several points in the text. This particular text gives an opportunity for the employment of questions requiring inferences on the part of the learner. For example, following the second sentence of the text, a question might depict four different drawings of the base of the monument, and ask, "which of these represents the approximate shape of the original base of the monument?"

Other ways can be invented to support the encoding process. Diagrams may help the learner to learn and remember the dimensions of the monument. Certain kinds of mnemonic techniques may be suggested to the learner ("gneiss is nice"). Ingenuity in designing interesting additions to the text, any of which may help the semantic encoding process, is surely to be considered a desirable quality for the instructional designer.

6. *Elicit performance.*   Present questions to be answered by the learner, pertaining to the size, shape, and composition of the Washington Monument. Use questions requiring constructed responses whenever possible. Examples would be:

> The monument's shaft, at its top, is how many square feet? (34)
> What is the total height in feet of the monument, from the ground?

Other questions may need to take a multiple-choice form:

> The apex of the monument is made of:
> A. Gneiss   B. Marble   C. Copper   D. Slate

7. *Provide feedback.*   The feedback here is in terms of knowledge of the correct response, or an indication of the correct answer when an incorrect one is given by the learner.

8. *Assess performance.*   This assessment can be done at a later time off the computer, if desired. Questions presented in CAI will have the form described previously under event 6.

9. *Provide for retention and transfer.*   The student might be asked to recall those parts of the passage that pertain to size, shape, and composition. In addition, questions might be asked that require inference, such as the following:

> The foundation of the monument is approximately how many feet on a side?
> A. 80   B. 92   C. 120   D. 130

> Gneiss is a rock that is most like:
> A. sandstone   B. fluorspar   C. granite   D. marble

Intellectual Skills Learning

Within the intellectual skills domain there are five types of learning outcomes compatible with CAI: (1) discriminations, (2) concrete concepts, (3) defined concepts, (4) rule using, and (5) problem solving. Because intellectual skills relate to each other in a hierarchical sense (Gagné, 1985), it is necessary to classify the nature of the outcome to be demonstrated and to determine what underlying skills support the performance of the new skill.

Concrete Concepts

A concrete concept is a class of objects or object qualities that have similar physical attributes. For example, *dog* is a concrete concept. One recognizes an animal as a dog by distinctive attributes that distinguish it from other classes of objects such as cats, birds, airplanes, etc. Another example of a concrete concept is the *shape* of street signs. One learns that an octagonal sign means STOP, a diamond shaped sign warns of a road hazard, a round sign marks a railroad crossing, and so on. The shape of the sign is a physical attribute that identifies the type of sign.

The learning of concrete concepts is dependent on discrimination skills; in learning to identify a stop sign one must be able to discriminate a diamond from an octagon. Obviously this is a very simple learning task for those who have the prerequisite skills, and impossible for those who do not. One point might be emphasized here. The learner does not have to be able to state that a road hazard sign is "diamond shaped." That is a verbalization of the attributes of the sign, and is not required for learning the skill.

A lesson to teach this objective would probably be paired with other objectives requiring the identification of stop signs, yield signs, railroad signs, and others. The events might be operationalized as follows:

1. *Gaining attention.* Read the headline of a newspaper article that states two people were killed in an accident in which a train hit a car on a railroad crossing. Point out that this tragedy might have been avoided if the driver paid attention to the shape of signs.

2. *Inform learners about the objective.* In this case we will assume that there are multiple objectives. "In this lesson you will learn that the shapes of signs tell you something about the road ahead."

3. *Recall prerequisite.* The prerequisites are discriminations of the sign shapes. These have most probably been well learned long ago. If not (or should mental deficiencies be present), displays could be generated to recall the discriminations to the learner.

4. *Present the stimulus.* Display the sign shapes to be taught (octagonal, diamond, circular, and inverted triangle) along with the respective concept names—STOP, HAZARD, RAILROAD, YIELD. In following frames, show pairs of the shapes with their concept names, and call attention to distinctive features. See Fig. 2.1a. Continue with other shapes, contrasting two at a time, and naming their distinctive shapes (octagon, diamond, circle, upside-down

a)

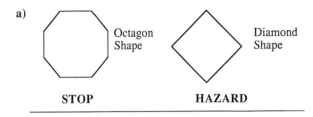

STOP   HAZARD

b)   Which of these signs would
      you stop for?

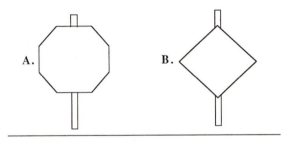

c)   Whoops! Remember a STOP sign
      Looks like this:

STOP

FIG. 2.1. Some events associated with instruction on concepts of shapes of road signs.

triangle). In the case of HAZARD, show several different types of road guides within the diamond shape.

5. *Provide learning guidance.* Present a number of successive frames, each containing two different sign shapes. In random order, show the sign shapes matched with correct and incorrect concept names, and require that the learner respond so as to indicate "correct" (yes) or "incorrect" (no). Alternatively, require that the learner view the two shapes and respond by typing their concept names. Learning guidance here has the purpose of appropriate encoding of the shapes, and is carried out by providing practice in identifying contrasting shapes together with their concept names.

6. *Elicit performance.* Ask the question: "Which of these two signs would you stop for?" (Fig. 2.1b)

7. *Present feedback.* Provide knowledge of results. For a correct result—"Yes, you got it." For a wrong response, with remediation, use a message like that of Fig. 2.1c.

8. *Assess performance.* Performance is assessed by presenting a number of sign shapes and having the learner identify them as one of the types. For example, learners might be asked to circle all the stop signs, put a box around all the railroad signs, put a line under all the road hazard signs, and so on.

9. *Enhance retention.* Retention might be enhanced by presenting the different shapes with a variety of appropriate words and diagrams printed on them (e.g., SLOW, CURVE AHEAD), in several environmental contexts, continuing to provide the learner with practice in identifying their concept names.

Defined Concepts

Defined concepts, like concrete concepts, require the learner to categorize something as an instance of a class of things. The important difference is that the critical attributes for classification are not necessarily physical. The defined concept is actually a *rule* about the relationships among words or other concepts. For example, *female* is a concrete concept. *Mother* is a defined concept. The rule that defines the concept is: *A mother is a female parent.* Notice that the definition contains a concrete concept and another defined concept, parent. In order that as student understand the concept *mother* she must know the concept *parent.*

Critical to the teaching of defined concepts is recall of prerequisite concepts involved in the new concept to be learned, statement of the new rule or definition, and learning guidance that makes the relationships among component concepts clear. The following example shows how this might be accomplished for events 3, 4, and 5.

3. *Recall prerequisites.* "What is a parent? A parent is someone who has children. You have two parents; your mother is a female parent, your father a male parent." (This presentation is designed to recall the meaning of *female* and *parent.*)

4. *Present the stimulus.* "A *female parent* is called a *mother.*" (This is simply a statement of a definition, emphasizing key concepts as distinctive features.)

5. *Provide learning guidance.* "Your mother is female and she is your parent. Your other parent (father) is a male. Not all females are mothers. A female who has never had a child is not a mother." (This guidance has the purpose of emphasizing the distinctions *female, not female, having a child, not having a child.*) Also, additional meaningful context is provided for the newly introduced concept.

Obviously this is a very simple defined concept. A more difficult concept would have been *second cousin*. Even so, these are easy concepts compared to defined concepts such as *love* or *democracy*.

Rules

Rules represent relationships among concepts. Since intellectual skills are hierarchically related, it is often necessary to determine what underlying skills contribute to the learning of the new skill.

Let us use the following example of a rule: Given any color-coded resistor, the student will be able to determine its value in ohms. This is a rule-using task, involving several underlying concepts and relationships among them. As a designer one must ask, What prerequisite skills are related to this rule? What skills does the learner already possess? Which skills do I need to teach?

The prerequisite skills can be placed into a learning hierarchy.

A learning hierarchy for the resistor task is shown in Fig. 2.2. For the rule "determine the value of a color-coded resistor," there are two main prerequisites: the concrete concepts of color value and of position (1st, 2nd, 3rd). The discriminations that are prerequisite to these concepts are likely to be already learned. Learning the positions of bands on a resistor would appear to be a very easy task. So far as prerequisites are concerned, therefore, the main task is learning the values that correspond to colors.

Let's look at the events of instruction 3, 4, and 5 for this rule.

3. *Recall prerequisites.* The learner needs to be able to recall the numerical value of each color: Black = 0; Brown = 2; Orange = 3; Yellow = 4; Green = 5; Blue = 6; Violet = 7; Gray = 8; White = 9. Since the numbers 2 through 7 correspond to the sequence of rainbow colors, it is likely that the learner has a convenient mnemonic for the other four. Or, the student may remember the sentence "Billy Brown Raids Our Young Garden But Violet Gray Waits" to

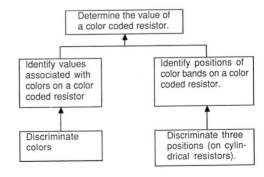

FIG. 2.2. Learning hierarchy showing prerequisite skills involved in the task of determining resistor values.

a.

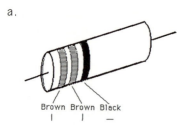

Brown Brown Black
  1   1   —

b.

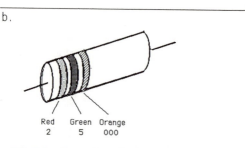

Red   Green Orange
 2   5   000

FIG. 2.3. Examples of color-banded resistors.

provide him with cues to the first letters of the colors in the sequence beginning with 0.

4. *Present the stimulus*. This may be done by stating: "To determine the value of a resistor, record the color value for the first band, the color value for the second band, and the number of zeros for the third band." An accompanying picture is suggested in Fig. 2.3a.

5. *Provide learning guidance*. In this case the rule has been stated and also illustrated. Learning guidance is a matter of communicating the rule once more, along with a different example. This is not a very difficult rule to learn. Students sometimes have trouble dealing with the black band when it occurs in the first position (zero), and when it is in the third position (indicating *no zeros*). For these reasons, learning guidance would emphasize application of the rule under a number of different circumstances to show how potentially confusing examples are resolved. For example:

The first color band on a resistor is given the number value as you learned it from the color-value lesson. If the first band is red, the first number in the value is 2. Likewise, the second color represents the second number in the value. For example, if the second color is green its value would be 5.

However, the third color band on a resistor is a multiplier. Its value is indicated by placing a number of zeros after the first two values. For example, if the color of the third band is orange (3), three zeros would be placed after the first two numbers. The value of the resistor would be depicted as in Fig. 2.3b.

Learning guidance has the purpose of emphasizing key concepts and their relationships, providing elaboration of the rule with varied examples.

Problem Solving and Higher-Order Rules

As distinguished from simple rule-using, in a problem-solving situation the learner has to *generate* an appropriate solution strategy, and apply appropriate rules in the implementation of that strategy. For instance, if students are to design an electric circuit so that it contains two switches, either of which might be used to turn a light on or off, they are going to have to possess a fairly good knowledge of concepts and rules related to electric circuits.

In real life, a person would formulate a hypothesis about what the circuit would do, and lacking any other type of feedback, would try it out. The problem with this approach (discovery learning) is that the hypothesis might be wrong, and so the procedure poses the possibility of injury. This problem has a straightforward solution. In solving it, subordinate rules are combined and integrated into a higher-order rule. The question is, how might problem-solving skills be taught using the computer?

Again, let us look at possible external events of instruction. In this case we might want to promote problem-solving behavior by allowing the computer to simulate reality, but at the same time give corrective feedback. The instructional strategy would be *guided discovery*. The difference between problem solving and other intellectual skill programs is that problem solving cannot be taught in a didactic manner. That is, the student must respond to the problem while being given learning guidance.

3. *Recall prerequisites.* In an actual problem-solving situation the student will have to recall the prerequisite rules for himself. However, in the learning situation learners might be reminded that they will have to use their knowledge about serial circuits and single-pole double-throw switches to solve the problem. (The purpose of the event is to stimulate the learner's recall of appropriate rules.)

4. *Presenting stimuli with distinctive features.* The stimulus in the case of this and most other problem-solving tasks is information about the existing state of affairs. In this case learners might have to list and select the components they wish to use in solving the problem. They might then be directed to use designated keys to construct a circuit on the screen.

5. *Provide learning guidance.* Discovery learning implies minimal learning guidance; the student learns by trying a solution and getting feedback as to how it works. Guided discovery assumes that the computer is capable of monitoring the student's actions and intercepting possible errors before allowing the student to continue. For example, if the student were to attempt to connect a shorted circuit, the computer might respond "are you sure you want to do that?". At that point

the student might be allowed to change his course of action, or to ask for elaboration of the message. The purpose served by this event is to require the learner to investigate his strategy and the applicability of the rules being used.

Instruction as an Iterative Process

An actual lesson may cycle through the event of learning guidance, eliciting performance and providing feedback many times for a single concept or rule. For example, the previous account of rule learning deals with the problem students often have with the third color band. The next sequence might demonstrate what happens when the first color band is black. This cycle can be repeated as often as necessary to teach the entire skill. In fact, Event 3, present the stimulus, might also be included in the cycle if new information is being presented in small steps. Instruction is often an iterative process of providing stimuli, guidance, confirmation of understanding, and then additional presentation of the essential task stimuli.

Attitudes

Although the majority of CAI programs are designed to teach verbal information and intellectual skills, there are now programs aimed at changing attitudes. Recall that an attitude is a predisposition to choose one alternative course of action over another. For example, although smoking involves motor behavior, the smoker must choose to smoke rather than not to smoke. When this behavior is observed, one says that the smoker has a positive attitude toward smoking. It might be argued that the smoker really hates it and wishes he could give it up but for many reasons he can't. At that point we should say that the learner has a related attitude towards smoking which might be described as follows: The learner chooses to believe that smoking is a behavior beyond his personal control rather than under his control. Belief systems are complex, however they are learned, and they can be affected by properly designed instruction.

A choice behavior is generally based on expectancies of consequences for the choice. For example, a smoker might think, "If I smoke my anxieties will be reduced and I will be more relaxed than if I don't; and that is important to me." Any instruction that is to change an attitude-driven behavior must change the expectancies or create new stronger competing expectancies. For instance, it would be ineffective to argue that the individual's anxieties are not reduced by smoking. However, the smoker may never have realized that those anxieties are caused by the smoking. Recognizing the relationship between the behavior and the attitude is the first step in designing instruction to change it. The following scenario is taken from a CAI lesson called "The Smoking Decision" by Sunburst Software. This program attempts to change smoking behavior by educating the student as to the causes and effects of smoking. It does not try to deny what the learner knows to be true but does attempt to provide evidence which will help the learner to make the no smoking decision.

3. *Recall prerequisites*. The student is reminded of the original reasons that may have started the smoking. Peer pressure, tradition, modeling, and so on. Old information is presented that confirms the student's knowledge about the effects of smoking and health. (It will be realized that the student already has a fair amount of knowledge about an attitude-driven behavior.)

4. *Provide the stimulus*. New information is presented. If the student isn't familiar with the latest information about health consequences, these might be presented at this point. In "The Smoking Decision," the new stimulus is information about the circular relationship between smoking and the reduction of anxiety caused by smoking. For example:

> Smokers claim that smoking reduces your anxiety, and this is probably true. However, did you know that smoking causes anxiety? Here is how . . .

The purpose of this event is to illustrate the relationships between the behavior and its determinants. That is, the stimulus presentation reminds learners of the situations in which they might think about these relationships.

5. *Provide learning guidance*. Learning guidance is provided by the modeling by an expert of the desirable choices of thought and action. The model is a physician who is explaining the smoker's dilemma. Although the physician isn't physically present, the referent status is obvious through the use of illustrations that would only be available from a physician (X-rays of lungs, etc.). Since most attitudes are formulated on the basis of information regarding consequences, learners must be provided with credible data from which they can draw conclusions. Learning guidance may be in the form of help in processing data and drawing logical conclusions. (The human model and his presentation of the attitude-driven choices is considered an essential part of learning guidance. This example might be improved in effectiveness by the selection of a more convincing model.)

Motor Skills

The acquisition of motor skills depends upon practice involving kinesthetic feedback. Most motor skills have both procedural and motor components. For example, in order to touch type one must understand which fingers are used to press which keys, and the location of the keys on the keyboard. The actual motor skill in typing, however, comes only after a great deal of practice in pressing the proper keys without looking. Computer-assisted instruction may be used to teach the procedural component of motor performance. It is unlikely that it can teach any motor skill other than those inherent in equipment operation, such as touch typing and eye-hand coordination skills that may be developed in tracking games (such as Pac-Man).

Cognitive Strategies

Cognitive strategies are learned skills by means of which learners control their own processes of information processing. For example, when challenged to learn new history facts a learner might obtain a world globe and attach each piece of new information to a place on the globe. This strategy would be one of associating a visual image with information. Images are often remembered better than verbal information, and can serve as cues for information recall at a later time (Gagné & White, 1978; Levie & Lentz, 1982).

Frequently, cognitive strategies are used in the course of instruction rather than being directly taught. For example, a verbal message may be elaborated with an image to facilitate learning and recall. When strategies are embedded within CAI lessons, the learner has the opportunity to practice their use, and this may be an effective measure for assuring their use in subsequent learning situations. (See Jonassen chapter, this volume, for examples.)

Other CAI lessons may be designed to teach cognitive strategies in a direct manner. Examples are lessons in strategies of time management in learning, anxiety reduction, facts organization, and reading comprehension. Often, the event of learning guidance in this instruction consists of verbal statements of directions, such as "say to yourself the main idea of each paragraph as soon as you have read it." Again in these instances, *practice in using* the strategies in varied situations usually gives the best assurance for later retention and transfer.

SUMMARY

We have described in some detail the process we believe to be involved in making plans for effective computer-aided instruction. Design decisions contained in this process are considered to be essentially similar to those employed when designing for other instructional media. CAI, however, affords the possibility of two important and useful design features: (1) the display of integral content elaborations in graphics and print, and (2) the provision for learning responding and subsequent response-relevant feedback. These features make possible the design of a number of advantageous characteristics for instruction.

As is true of instruction generally, CAI planning begins with a clear identification of learning objectives. The various categories of learning outcomes (verbal information, intellectual skills, cognitive strategies, attitudes, motor skills) differ notably in the expectations of learning results by the designer as well as by the learner. Further, each of these outcomes requires a different content organization for display during the course of instruction.

The suggestions for lesson design that derive from these considerations differ considerably from the many authoring guides (e.g., MECC, CDC, CONDUIT) that provide guidelines for the construction of CAI. These guides address such issues as formatting screen displays, placement of questions and response prompts on the screen, instructions to the user about available options (press H for HELP, C to CONTINUE), and the like. The purpose of these guidelines appears to be that of making the medium as user-friendly as possible, allowing the student desirable options, and to the degree possible, preventing errors in response judging. Although these are important guidelines, following them to the letter will not guarantee that the lesson will teach.

We have proposed a set of guidelines derived from a base of human information-processing theory, and the premise that the presentations made in external displays can support the internal processes of learning. These guidelines take the form of *events of instruction* which provide a suitable framework for designing screen displays. Lessons incorporating events that are appropriate for the type of learning outcomes desired will be more likely to attain the desired learning goals than lessons that do not include them. Our guidelines cannot be more specific than this, since it is the designer who must interpret the function being served by any particular display. To imagine that the design process can be reduced to a set of cook-book prescriptions is wishful thinking.

Different types of CAI serve different roles in the instructional process. They must be designed with the purpose they are to serve firmly in mind. Drill and practice and simulation programs serve important functions in the support of learning, and one should refrain from supposing that any one type of learning program is inherently better delivered by the computer. The suitability of any individual program must be addressed with consideration of its role in the learning environment, and the degree to which it provides the necessary support for the processing of information that results in learning.

REFERENCES

Anderson, R. C. (1972). How to construct achievement tests to assess comprehension. *Review of Educational Research, 42,* 145–170.

Estes, W. K. (1978). The information-processing approach to cognition: A confluence of metaphors and methods. In W. K. Estes (Ed.), *Handbook of learning and cognitive processes. Human information processing* (Vol. 5). Hillsdale, NJ: Lawrence Erlbaum Associates.

Fitts, P. M., & Posner, M. J. (1967). *Human performance.* Monterey, CA: Brooks/Cole.

Gagné, R. M. (1964). Problem solving. In A. W. Melton (Ed.), *Categories of human learning.* New York: Academic Press.

Gagné, R. M. (1984). Learning outcomes and their effects: Useful categories of human performance. *American Psychologist, 39,* 377–385.

Gagné, R. M. (1985). *The conditions of learning* (4th ed.). New York: Holt, Rinehart and Winston.

Gagné, R. M., & Briggs, L. J. (1979). *Principles of instructional design* (2nd ed.). New York: Holt, Rinehart and Winston.

Gagné, R. M., & White, R. T. (1978). Memory structures and learning outcomes. *Review of Educational Research, 48*, 187–222.

Greeno, J. G. (1978). A study of problem solving. In R. Glaser (Ed.), *Advances in instructional psychology* (Vol. 1). Hillsdale, NJ: Lawrence Erlbaum Associates.

Klatzky, R. L. (1980). *Human memory: Structures and processes* (2nd ed.). San Francisco: Freeman.

Levie, W. N., & Lentz, R. (1982). Effects of text illustrations: A review of research. *ECTJ, 30*(4), 195–232.

O'Neil, H. F., Jr. (1978). *Learning strategies*. New York: Academic Press.

Rothkopf, E. Z. (1970). The concept of mathemagenic activities. *Review of Educational Research, 40*, 325–336.

3 Applying Component Display Theory to the Design of Courseware

M. David Merrill
Utah State University

OVERVIEW OF COMPONENT DISPLAY THEORY

Component Display Theory (CDT) has been previously described (See Merrill, 1983) and illustrated (Merrill, 1987). An overview of the complete theory here would be redundant. It is assumed that the reader is already familiar with the theory. This chapter concentrates on the application of CDT to the design of instructional software.

Component Display Theory (CDT) is not a method but rather a theory about those components that comprise every instructional presentation. In order to use CDT, the instructional method (in this case computer based instruction) selected by a designer must incorporate the prescriptions of the theory appropriate for the desired student performance in relationship to the subject matter content to be taught. This chapter first summarizes some of the most important prescriptions from CDT and illustrates how they have been implemented in the TICCIT authoring system and EduWare's Algebra software. The second section illustrates a variety of expository presentations and their use in educational software. A variety of inquisitory presentations and their use in educational software is illustrated in the third section.

BRIEF SUMMARY OF CDT

Component Display Theory is comprised of three parts:a 2-dimensional performance-content classification system, a taxonomy of presentation forms, and a set of prescriptions relating the classification system to the presentation forms.

The Performance Content Matrix

CDT holds that instructional outcomes, represented either by objectives or test items, can be classified on two dimensions: student performance (Remember Instance, Remember Generality, Use, and Find) and subject matter content (Fact, Concept, Procedure, and Principle). As represented in this chapter **CDT** is appropriate only for cognitive outcomes and does not include psychomotor or affective objectives. Except as indicated, the software illustrated will be at the use-concept, use-procedure or use-principle level and the prescriptions cited are for objectives at this level unless otherwise indicated.

Presentation Forms

CDT also assumes that all instructional presentations are comprised of a series of discrete displays or presentation forms. Any presentation can be described as a sequence of such presentation forms together with the interrelationships between such forms. The four Primary Presentation Forms (PPF) are expository generality (*EG*); expository instance (*Eeg*—the little *eg* is the abbreviation for example); inquisitory generality (*IG*) and inquisitory instance (*leg*). A generality (rule) is a statement of a definition, principle or the steps in a procedure. An instance (example) is a specific illustration of an object, symbol, event, process, or procedure.

Primary Presentation Form—Performance Consistency Prescriptions

CDT is based on Gagné's assumption of different conditions of learning for different outcomes. Each of the different performance levels in the content/performance (P/C) matrix is associated with a different combination of primary presentation forms. When the necessary presentation forms are present, student achievement and learning efficiency are increased; when the necessary presentation forms are not present or inappropriate there is a decrement in student achievement and learning efficiency. The most important PPF/performance consistency prescription for the use-level of instruction is the following:

1. PPF Sequence Rule

The presentation should consist of an **expository generality** ("rule" or *EG*) followed by a set of **expository instances** ("Examples" or *Eegs*) consisting of several different examples, followed by a set of previously unencountered **inquisitory instances** ("practice"—*legs*) consisting of several additional instances different from the instances used for *Eegs*. For Concepts practice should consist of choosing (classifying) examples and nonexamples. For processes practice which asks the student to explain a given situation is better than having the student choose between an appropriate and inappropriate application or explanation.

Primary Presentation Form—Content Consistency Prescriptions

Different kinds of content require different manifestations of the four primary presentation forms. To be consistent the primary presentation form must contain the information necessary to present the content. Some of the most important PPF/content consistency prescriptions are the following:

2. PPF Content Rule

For a **concept** *EG* is a definition which includes identification of the superordinate class, the relevant attributes which distinguishes instances of this concept from coordinate concepts within the same superordinate class and the relationship of these attributes to one another. *Eegs* and *legs* are objects, events or symbols comprising the concept. If instances are representations of actual objects or events they must include all of the relevant attributes as defined by *EG*. The practice examples (*legs*) should be different from the examples (*Eegs*).

For a **principle** *EG* is a statement of the proposition(s) which explain the process. This statement should clearly indicate the component concepts of which it is comprised and the causal or correlational relationships between these concepts. *Eegs* illustrate the process. The illustration must enable the student to see the operation of the proposition(s). *legs* ask the student to make predictions or find errors in the process as it occurs in a different situation from the illustration (*Eeg*).

For a **procedure** *EG* indicates the outcome that will result from following the procedure and indicates each of the steps and their order of execution, indicates each of the decisions required and the resulting branches (steps) following the various alternatives from these decisions. *Eegs* demonstrate how to perform each of the steps and how to make appropriate decisions. *legs* ask the student to execute the steps. If the procedure being taught will be used with a variety of objects and materials the student should have an opportunity to practice with different objects and/or materials.

Adequacy Prescriptions: Secondary Presentation Forms

Secondary Presentation Forms (SPF) represent information added to the primary presentation forms to enhance the learning that occurs. A presentation that is more adequate, that is enhanced by the addition of appropriate secondary presentations, will promote an increment in the achievement and learning efficiency of students participating in the instruction. For use-concept, use-principle, and use-procedure objectives some of the most important secondary presentation form prescriptions are the following:

3. Help Rule

The Generality (*EG*) should be elaborated by way of secondary presentation forms which provide **attention focusing information** to help the student identify the relevant attributes (for concepts), see the relationship between component concepts (for principles) and to remember the steps and sequence of execution (for procedures).

The examples (*Eegs*) should also be elaborated by **attention focusing** secondary presentation forms (SPFs) which link the specific attributes of the examples to the labels for these attributes contained in the definition (for concepts); indicate the causal or correlational relationships between the component concepts (for principles); and clearly identify each step as it is being executed and focus the student's attention on the decisions required and the consequences of these decisions (for procedures).

4. Prerequisite Rule

SPFs should also help the student recall **prerequisite** information which should have already been learned. The definition, proposition or procedure should also be restated or represented via some different mode such as a graph, chart or diagram.

5. Fading Rule

The amount of this helping information should be **faded** or gradually decreased during the later stages of the presentation.

6. Alternative Representation Rule

Different examples should also be presented using **alternative modes of representation.** The practice instances (*legs*) should be presented using a **variety of representation** modes.

7. Feedback Rule

Student responses to practice should be followed by **feedback** which shows the student why the instance belongs to the concept class under consideration (for concepts); indicates the causal or correlational relationships involved (for principles); and indicating to the student steps omitted, steps performed incorrectly, decisions omitted or incorrect (for procedures). Where possible the consequences of the student's actions should provide the feedback concerning adequate performance.

This attention focusing help should **not be used prior to the student's response** and the amount of information provided should be **faded** during the later stages of practice.

Adequacy Prescriptions: Interdisplay Relationships

In addition to material that can be added to the primary presentation forms the relationship between these forms also affects the learning that will occur. Some of the most important interdisplay relationship prescriptions are the following:

8. Isolation Rule

Each of the primary presentations should be concise and to the point and separated from elaborative information so that the main ideas and illustrations of these ideas are easily identified by the student.

9. Divergent Rule

Subsequent examples in both *Eegs* and *legs* should be **divergent** from one another so that the student is exposed to a wide variety of specific cases. If the real world, where the procedure will be used, involves different types of equipment and materials then the student should see a **variety** of equipment demonstrated and should have the opportunity to practice on a variety of equipment.

10. Difficulty Rule

In both the example *(Eegs)* and practice *(legs)* stages of the instruction the instances used should represent a **range of difficulty.** This procedure assures exposure to the variety of instances the student is likely to encounter following the instruction. If the process involves both simple and more complex means of execution the **range** of such operations should be illustrated during the demonstrations and the student should have an opportunity to practice both the straight forward and the more complex forms of the procedure. In some situations the application of the principle should be more obvious while in others the application may be more subtle. This procedure increases the student's ability to apply the principle to a wide variety of situations following the instruction.

11. Matching Rule

For concepts, examples that are presented in *Eegs* should be **matched** to potentially confusing nonexamples from coordinate concepts within the same superordinate concept. This matching procedure should be used early in the presentation but faded during the later stages of the presentation.

Matching should not be used during practice *legs*. Both examples and nonexamples should be presented for student classification but they should be presented one-by-one in a random order to minimize unintentional prompts.

For procedures, during the demonstration the student should be shown **common incorrect ways** to perform the steps or make the required decisions. These incorrect paths should be clearly labeled and the student given sufficient warning to avoid these incorrect procedures. Clearly identifying and illustrating incorrect paths helps the student avoid such mistakes during their own practice.

For principles, illustrative explanations presented should include explanations of **common misconceptions.** The student should be shown where the principle does not work or situations to which the principle does not apply. This procedure assists the student to be discriminating in the application of the principle to subsequent situations. In later stages of the presentation and in practice the student should be asked to identify inappropriate applications of the principle.

THE TICCIT CAI SYSTEM

The author has occasionally been asked the question, "Does Component Display Theory apply to computer based instruction?" Simultaneous to the development of CDT, the author was involved in the design of the TICCIT authoring system. It should come as no surprise that the TICCIT authoring system is a hardware/software implementation of CDT. In this chapter TICCIT can only be briefly described. (For additional information see Merrill, 1980; Merrill, Schneider, & Fletcher, 1980 or contact Ford Aerospace Corporation, Reston VA).

The most unique characteristic of the TICCIT philosophy is **learner control** which means that each learner can choose not only which content segment, lesson or unit to study next but can also select which primary or secondary presentation form they would like to have presented next. The TICCIT keyboard contains 15 learner control keys, to the right of the standard typewriter keys, which are used by the student to select the instructional displays she or he would like to study next. Thus each student can select a combination of displays that is most appropriate for his or her own unique combination of aptitudes or prior learning.

The buttons on the TICCIT system keyboard correspond to aspects of Component Display Theory. Figure 3.1 shows a drawing of the learner control keys. The three bottom keys: **rule, example, and practice,** correspond to the primary presentation forms of *EG, Eeg,* and *leg.* There is no key for *IG* because the authoring system was designed for the *use* level of instruction and *IG* is not a prescribed PPF for the *use* level (see rule 1 above). The **help** key enables the student to access attention focusing information and corresponds to the help rule (see rule 3 above). The **hard** and **easy** keys enable the student to see easier and harder versions of *EG* (see rule 6, alternative representation rule) and to see easier or harder *Eegs* or *legs* consistent with the rule 10 (the difficulty rule). The **obj'tive** key enables the student to look at the objective for the current segment. The **map** key enables the student to access a prerequisite hierarchy of the lesson segments and to obtain a report of their progress in the system. **Advice** provides the student with detailed information concerning their progress to date. If the

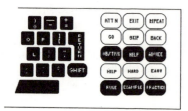

FIG. 3.1. The TICCIT keyboard and learner control keys.

student requests, advice provides a unique prescription indicating which learner control key the student should press next. The advisor function is similar to the coach function in intelligent tutoring systems. There is a model of how the ideal student would use the learner control buttons to learn a lesson. The system keeps a model of the student's activities and performance. This student model is compared to the ideal model and the advisor then provides guidance that would encourage the student to behave more like the ideal student.

Figures 3.2 through 3.7 show drawings of sample displays from an English grammar lesson prepared for the TICCIT system. The displays shown are the lesson map, a rule display, an example display, a practice display, a rule help display, and an advisor display.

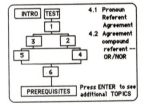

FIG. 3.2.   TICCIT Lesson Map Display.

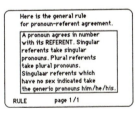

FIG. 3.3.   TICCIT Rule Display.

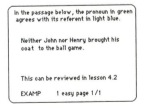

FIG. 3.4.   TICCIT Example Display.

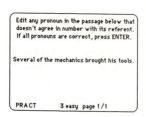

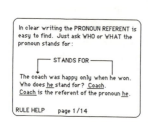

FIG. 3.5. TICCIT Practice Display.

FIG. 3.6. TICCIT Rule Help Display.

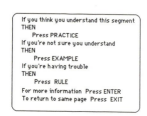

FIG. 3.7. TICCIT Advisor Prescriptions Display.

EDUWARE ALGEBRA

The TICCIT learner control approach to instruction with CDT built in inspired other courseware development efforts. Perhaps one of the most successful serious (as contrasted with Edutainment games) educational programs was the Algebra series produced by Sherwin Steffin and Eduware Inc.[1] Like TICCIT, ALGEBRA is a direct implementation of CDT principles in CAI. Unlike TICCIT this implementation was done independently of the author or his immediate associates. The documentation for ALGEBRA states,

> To make the most of the ALGEBRA series' potential for managing your own learning, each of the units is divided into concepts. Each concept is explained in four distinct learning styles:

---

[1]Eduware was sold to DesignWare a subsidiary of Encyclopedia Britannica. Algebra is available from DesignWare Inc. 185 Berry Street, San Francisco, CA 94107.

[1] **Definition/Discussion Discovery** This mode provides discussion of ideas and definitions of terms and lays the groundwork for understanding a concept before specific problems are presented. {*This is equivalent to the rule frames in the TICCIT system and implements the EG presentation form from CDT.*}

[2] **Rules** This mode provides rules for using each idea presented in a particular concept. {*This mode does not have an exact equivalent in CDT but the content shown here is often part of the rule help or rule easy presentation. The rule is the procedures or algorithms necessary to solve the problem. ALGEBRA thus separates the formal definitions of the concepts from the procedures needed to solve the problems. This mode implements part of the EG presentation form from CDT.*}

[3] **Examples** You may see as many examples as you need to learn how to apply a rule or solve a problem. {*This is equivalent to the example frames in the TICCIT system and implements the Eeg presentation form from CDT.*}

[4] **Sample problems** This style presents problems which test your ability to use the information presented in the other modes. Each time you respond, your answer is confirmed. RIGHT or CORRECT follows a correct answer; an incorrect answer elicits WRONG or NO accompanied by the correct answer. If you are dissatisfied with your performance, you may select any of the other learning styles and then return to the sample problems to retest yourself. {*This is equivalent to the practice frames in the TICCIT system and implements the Ieg presentation form from CDT.*}

ALGEBRA has a map structure similar to TICCIT where the student can select which lesson to study and then within each lesson she or he can select which segment to study. Within each segment the user can select from each of the learning modes previously described. Following are some sample frames from the EDUWARE ALGEBRA.

Each mode may consist of several pages of material following the same format. The content of the second and third pages of the Definition mode presents the following content:

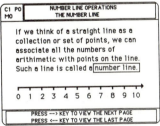

FIG. 3.8. Definition/Discussion/Discovery mode from Algebra.

P2 The number which is associated with a point on the number line is called the coordinate of that point. The point on the number line which is associated with a number is called the graph of that number.

P3 The distance between 0, the origin, and 1 is called the unit length of the line.

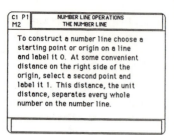

FIG. 3.9.   Rules mode from ALGEBRA.

The content of the second page of the rule mode is as follows:

P2   No matter how close two points may be in the number line, there is always an infinite number of points between them. These points may be graphed by dividing the interval between the points which are associated with whole numbers into more and more equal parts.

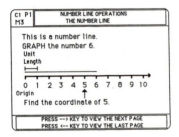

FIG. 3.10.   Example mode from ALGEBRA.

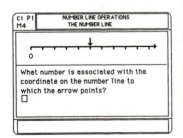

FIG. 3.11. Sample problem mode from ALGEBRA.

EXPOSITORY PRESENTATIONS

One of the criticisms often leveled at the TICCIT system is that is nothing more than a glorified page turner. Often applications of CDT in other media equate

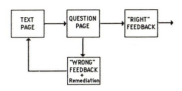

FIG. 3.12. Programed instruction branching model of instruction.

Expository with a static page of information. The examples of TICCIT frames shown and the examples of ALGEBRA shown would seem to support this criticism.

Much of CAI seems to be based on the programed instruction branching model of instruction illustrated in Fig. 3.12. The instruction that results consists of the following events: (1) Present a page of text (which may include graphics) for the student to read. (2) Ask a question. (3) If the student's answer is correct provide feedback saying she or he is correct; if the student's response is incorrect provide feedback plus remedial material (which is sometimes omitted). (4) Repeat this cycle.

The branching programed instruction model is a very limited concept of the instructional interaction. This model does not make use of the unique capabilities of the computer. The model promotes passive student interaction—the "pour it in and check to see if it stuck" theory. The model lends itself to the imitation of the textbook with "Press the Space Bar Please" substituted for "Please Turn the Page." At least with a real textbook the student can skip a few pages or scan for what is important. With computer based programed instruction it is often impossible to skip a page or to even know how many pages are included. (Merrill, 1985).

TICCIT and ALGEBRA at least provide for different kinds of text pages when the user selects a rule vs. an example. Providing text pages for each of the expository primary presentations increases the effectiveness of the instruction when compared with simple branching programed instruction. However, the resulting expository presentations are still passive.

Perhaps we are trapped by our metaphor. The term, *frame,* is often seen as synonymous with page. The CRT screen is seen as the page of a book. Hence, we limit our thinking to putting a book on the screen and branching to different pages depending on the student's response. Perhaps we should change our metaphor. Rather than the frame, as the basic building block of CAI, we should use an **instructional transaction.** According to Webster's unabridged dictionary one definition for a transaction is, "a communicative action or activity involving two parties or two things reciprocally affecting or influencing each other." *Frame* is a passive concept whereas *transaction* is an active concept. It is the mutual, dynamic, real-time give and take which is possible through a computer, and which is not possible through a book, that should characterize computer based instruction. An instructional transaction is a dynamic interaction between the program and the student in which there is an interchange of information.

Can there be an *expository transaction?* Is the word, *expository,* also a passive word like the word, *frame?* According to Webster, *exposition* includes: "a setting forth of the meaning or purpose; an expounding of the sense or intent; an interpretation. The art of presenting a subject matter in detail . . . ." There is nothing inherent in the meaning of the word exposition that would indicate that there can be no student interaction. It is our position that there can and should be *expository transactions* rather than merely *expository frames* in effective CAI.

One of the primary functions of instruction is **to promote and guide active mental processing on the part of the student.** The amount learned and retained is a function of the relevant cognitive processing done by the student when learning the information. Passive frames do little to promote such mental activity. In the next few paragraphs we present some examples of *Expository* presentations including *EG* and *Eegs* which involve transactions that require considerable processing by the student rather than passive frames. While there are many more types of transactions that would fit within our definition of **expository transactions** we have selected a few representatives which show a range of possibilities. These might be characterized as conversational programing, interactive demonstrations and controllable microworlds.

Conversational Programing

Poetic Meter. Figures 3.13 and 3.15 illustrate three expository frames from a pseudo lesson on poetic meter developed by the author to show some of the inappropriate techniques often used for CAI. The following paragraph describes the interaction:

The text shown in Fig. 3.13 is presented to the student.
After reading the text the student presses the RETURN key.
The text shown below the "Press RETURN to continue" message is displayed line by line. As the bottom of the screen is reached the text scrolls up causing the top lines of the previous display (Fig. 3.13) to disappear off the top of the screen.
Pressing the RETURN key causes the text in Fig. 3.14 to scroll and the new paragraph of text shown in Fig. 3.15 to appear.

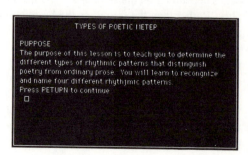

FIG. 3.13.   Inadequate Poetic Meter
—frame 1.

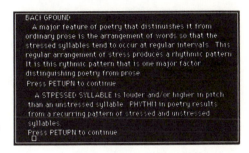

different types of rhythmic patterns that distinguish
poetry from ordinary prose. You will learn to recognize
and name four different rhythmic patterns.

Press RETURN to continue

BACKGROUND:
  A major feature of poetry that distinguishes it from
ordinary prose is the arrangement of words so that the
stressed syllables tend to occur at regular intervals. This
regular arrangement of stress produces a rhythmic pattern.
It is this rythmic pattern that is one major factor
distinguishing poetry from prose.

Press RETURN to continue
  □

FIG. 3.14. Inadequate Poetic Meter —frame 2.

BACKGROUND:
  A major feature of poetry that distinguishes it from
ordinary prose is the arrangement of words so that the
stressed syllables tend to occur at regular intervals. This
regular arrangement of stress produces a rhythmic pattern.
It is this rythmic pattern that is one major factor
distinguishing poetry from prose.

Press RETURN to continue
  A STRESSED SYLLABLE is louder and/or higher in pitch
than an unstressed syllable. RHYTHM in poetry results
from a recurring pattern of stressed and unstressed
syllables.

Press RETURN to continue
  □

FIG. 3.15. Inadequate Poetic Meter —frame 3.

There are a number of violations of effective screen design which make this poor CAI. These include: white letters on a black screen, filling margin to margin with text, and scrolling previous messages off the screen. However, our concern here is with the noninteractive nature of the presentation. This is a classic example of a "book on the screen." The student reads a message then presses the RETURN key for the next message. Furthermore the scrolling causes even the page orientation to be disturbed since the message moves to a new location on the screen everytime the next message is requested. It takes only a few frames presented in this fashion to put the student into a catatonic state of inattention.

Consider a revised example of this material in Figs. 3.16 and 3.18. The following paragraph describes the interaction on these frames.[2]

In Fig. 3.16 the questions appear one by one with a 3 sec pause after the display of the first question before the next question appears. The student does not respond to questions 1 and 2 but after question 3 the cursor appears for the student to enter a response.

---

[2]Based on the program "Introduction to Poetry" by M. David Merrill published by Olympus/MicroTeacher Software Inc., San Diego, CA. These materials are similar to the published program but may have been changed to better illustrate the message of this chapter.

FIG. 3.16. Poetic Meter showing
use of rhetorical questions.

If the student responds with rhyme the message shown in Fig. 3.16 appears. If the student responds with rhythm or meter (or another synonym of rhythm) the message says "RHYTHM or METER is very important." The system recognizes a number of synonyms and spelling errors in the student's answers.

After a short pause of 3 sec the following message appears on the bottom of the screen, "Poetry has two main characteristics:

RHYME And RHYTHM

The turn the page message shown at the bottom of Fig. 3.16 then appears for the student to continue.

Figure 3.17 presents an example of poetry and an example of prose and tries to show the student the difference. The black box appears with the message "Listen to this passage": After a short pause the poem is printed syllable by syllable. Each syllable is accompanied by a beep from the computer speaker. The stressed syllables are accompanied by a high pitched beep and the unstressed syllables are accompanied by a low pitched beep. The effect is a series of sounds which chant the rhythm pattern of the poem.

The next black box now appears with the message "Now listen to this passage": The prose example is presented in the same manner as the poetry passage. However the rhythm pattern of the sound is random in this passage rather than regular.

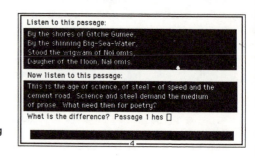

FIG. 3.17. Poetic Meter showing
sound reinforced examples.

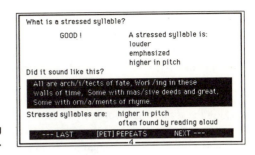

FIG. 3.18. Poetic Meter showing student activity in reading passage.

After the prose passage is presented the student is asked to respond to the question appearing at the bottom of the screen. The answer to the first question is "regular (steady) meter (beat, stress, rhythm)." If the student anticipates one of the correct answers the system displays the message "GOOD" and asks the next question. The student is then asked "Passage 2 has □"? The answer is "irregular (unsteady, random) meter (beat, stress, rhythm)."

Figure 3.18 is then presented. The question at the top is presented first and a cursor appears at the end of the question for the student's answer. The correct answer is louder, emphasized, higher in pitch (and a series of equivalent responses). If the student answers "stressed" a message appears "Can you think of another word?" The word "GOOD!" appears if the student types one of the anticipated answers. If not the message shown still appears but the word "GOOD!" does not.

The black box is displayed with the poem printed in the box and the following message "Read the following passage aloud". After the box the student has a message to press the RETURN key when finished.

When the return key is pressed the poem is removed from the black box and the message "Did it sound like this?" appears. After a pause of 2 sec the poem is then printed syllable by syllable accompanied by sound as in Fig. 3.17. After the poem is "chanted" the message on the bottom of the screen appears.

Note that Figs. 3.16 through 3.18 represent expository frames. Their purpose is to present the definition of poetry as contrasted with prose. However, they are much more interactive and involve the student much more than Figs. 3.13 through 3.15, which merely present text on the screen.

In Fig. 3.16 we used rhetorical questions. A rhetorical question is one used ". . . to emphasize a point, introduce a topic, etc., no answer being expected" (Webster). The purpose of questions 1 and 2 is to make the student think, to involve the student in a mental dialog about the topic, to cause the student to recall what is already known related to the topic. Question 3 is still rhetorical but now we have the student provide an answer. However, we are not concerned about whether or not the answer is correct. This is not practice nor a test but merely a device for involving the student in an "expository" dialog about the topic. This rhetorical conversation is far more effective in helping the student learn the topic than is equivalent information presented in a passive paragraph. The computer is much more like a live teacher tutoring a single student than it is like a book. We should strive for this **conversational tutoring** in our expository presentations.

In Fig. 3.17 we again present some information but we involve the student by asking the student questions to focus their attention on the relevant characteristics of the examples given. The purpose of the question is to engage the student in a conversation that focuses attention on important aspects of the presentation rather than to provide practice or test understanding.

In Fig. 3.18 we use another rhetorical question to reemphasize the idea of stress. Then we use another form of transaction by having the student read a passage aloud. We can't check that they did but if they do their understanding of the idea of stress will be reinforced. This is also not practice but merely an activity to help show the student what is meant by stress.

Figures 3.16 through 3.18 are examples of expository transactions which involve the student in a conversational tutorial, increase the level of mental effort required for the student to interact with the material, and thus increase the probability of learning. These interactive transactions are examples of Expository displays from Component Display Theory.

Writing Skills.   Figures 3.19 through 3.21 show another example of expository presentations using a conversational tutorial. The topic is usage errors frequently made by writers of English. The topic of the lesson shown is the confusion that often occurs between its and it's. The following paragraphs describe the interaction that occurs.[3]

Figures 3.19 through 3.21 show the first few frames of a conversational tutorial on writing skills. In Fig. 3.19 the student is asked to provide a free form answer explaining the difference between its and it's. The answer processing looks for key words such as "sound alike" and "mean different." Whatever the students answer the feedback message in the bottom box presents the message shown.

In Fig. 3.20 the program is looking for the words "it" and "is." The feedback message shows what is displayed if something else is typed.

In Fig. 3.21 an example is presented in the first black box. The student is asked to type in the response in the other two black boxes. The frame shows that the student typed "it" in the first box. The response for the second box is "cat" or "the cat." The feedback would correct the students first response replacing the word "it" with the word "its" in the first response box. The correct information

---

[3]Based on the program "Writing Skills" by Marvin Rosen, Bennie Lowery, and M. David Merrill developed by Olympus/MicroTeacher Software Inc., and published by DesignWare/Eduware Inc. San Francisco. These materials are similar to the published program but may have been changed to better illustrate the message of this chapter.

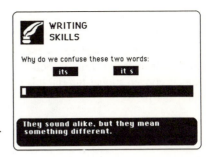

FIG. 3.19. Writing Skills showing conversational tutorial—frame 1.

FIG. 3.20. Writing Skills showing conversational tutorial—frame 2.

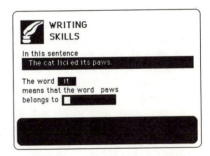

FIG. 3.21. Writing Skills showing conversational tutorial—frame 3.

would be given in the feedback box at the bottom of the screen. The dialog would continue in this manner helping the student see the difference between these two words. Other frames suggest that the student substitute the separate words "it" and "is" in the sentence. The student is allowed to actually make this substitution and then read the sentence to see if it makes sense.

These frames from Writing Skills illustrate expository transactions. The technique is a conversational tutorial which involves the student in a dialog with the teacher. These are not practice. The purpose of the response is not to find out what the student knows, this will come later in an editing exercise. The purpose of the interaction is to increase the level of mental effort on the part of the student by causing the student to interact with the material in a meaningful way that facilitates understanding. It should be apparent to the reader that when expository equals conversational-tutorial it is far more effective than expository equals turn-the-page-please.

Interactive Demonstrations

One of the most difficult curriculum areas for junior high school students is arithmetic story problems. These problems attempt to pose real world situations and have the student apply the principles of arithmetic to these situations. However, the problems posed are often contrived in such a way that while the objects and setting may be familiar the particular manipulations involved are not. The following figure illustrates a simple visual demonstration that allows the student to manipulate the objects in the same way as required by the problem. Hopefully, allowing the student to manipulate the situation will provide the experiential base needed to better understand the story problems.[4]

Figure 3.22 shows an interactive illustration representing the candy counter. The black box contains a particular arithmetic story problem based on this setting. The student is asked to solve the problem but is given the opportunity to manipulate the objects according to the problem and thus find the answer empirically rather than by computation. The student can open either jar and place the contents on the scale one unit (ounces in this case) at a time. As the candy is placed on the scale several counters are activated. The weight and cost counters above the jar indicate the amount (in units) and the total cost of the candy removed from the jar. The counters on the scale show the price per ounce of the combined candy on the scale, the weight of the combined candy on the scale and the total cost of the combined candy on the scale. For example if the student pressed the ← arrow the M&M jar would open and one ounce of candy would be placed on the scale. Above the jar the counters would read: weight = 1 oz, cost = 10¢. On the scale the counters would read: price = 10¢, weight = 1 oz and cost = 10¢. Pressing the ↑ arrow would open the second jar and place one ounce of candy corn on the scale. The counters would change as follows: above candy corn weight = 1 oz, cost = 7¢. On the scale price = 8.5¢, weight = 2 oz, cost = 17¢. The student can continue to add or remove candy from the scale until the conditions of the problem are satisfied. This interactive illustration can be used for a wide variety of mixture problems.

Figure 3.22 may appear to be practice, and in a way it is. But the real practice for word problems is to solve them without the aid of the interactive illustration.

---

[4]Based on a program "Story Problems" by Charlene West, Bennie Lowrey and M. David Merrill developed by Olympus/MicroTeacher Educational Software Inc. San Diego. This program has not yet been published. The display shown is similar to the Olympus/MicroTeacher program but has been changed to better illustrate the message of this chapter.

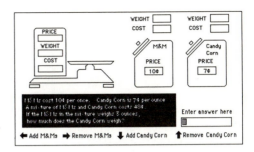

FIG. 3.22. Story Problems showing interactive illustration.

Then what is the purpose of the interactive illustration? It is an expository presentation of a series of examples of the problem with many attention focusing devices built into the illustration which enables the student to *experience* the problem. This experiential representation is far more effective than merely solving the problem for the student. This illustration commands attention by active involvement of the student. It focuses attention by counters and actual changes in the representation of the physical situation. It enables the student to explore correct as well as incorrect strategies. It enables the student to get a *feel* for the problem so that solution algorithms presented later are more meaningful and less rote. Finally, it met the criterion for the expository presentation of examples *Eeg* from CDT.

Controllable Microworlds

Seymour Papert (1980) has advocated the preparation of microworlds which a student explores and which enables the student to learn underlying principles from a base discipline. Logo was developed as such a microworld where the student could explore concepts of geometry and computer programing. Alfred Bork (1981) has suggested that what is needed is controllable microworlds where the student can conduct experiments and experience a simulation of a phenomena in order to learn about the underlying principles.

An Imaginary Science. Figure 3.23 illustrates a controllable microworld which the author and his associates developed as an experimental tool to study student hypothesis forming behavior. The student is told that this screen represents a number of instruments which enable him to observe a special scientific phenomena called a Xenograde System (pronounced Zenograde). Xenograde systems are imaginary and created merely for the purpose of this experimental system. Each of the meters and devices are explained to the student (see the explanation below). The student is challenged to learn enough about the system so that he or she can predict the charge (chrg) and velocity (velo) of each of the two satellites (● and ○) at some specific time in the future measured in alphon seconds. The student can stop the system, change any of the parameters and

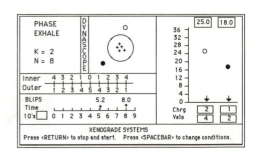

FIG. 3.23. Xenograde System simulation controllable world.

perform a number of other experiments in attempt to learn about the laws that govern the action of the system. This system simulates the process of science in learning about some physical system.[5]

Figure 3.23 shows all of the meters and devices necessary to study a Xenograde system. These devices simulate the Xenograde system in real time. The Dynascope shows a diagram of the system. The particles in the nucleus of the system (+) are called alphons and migrate one by one to the outer edge of the nucleus (called the exhale phase) then they migrate back to the center of the nucleus (called the inhale phase). The time between migrations is called an alphon second and is shown on the time scale in the lower left of the screen. The number of alphons (+) in each region at each time is shown on the scale labeled inner and outer. This scale corresponds to the time scale below. The satellites (● and ○) move toward the nucleus as they rotate until they collide then they move back toward their original orbit. The scale to the right of the screen shows the distance of each satellite from the nucleus and the arrows show the direction of movement. The Blips scale shows when a satellite collides with the nucleus but not which satellite collided. When a satellite collides with the nucleus it can pick up or drop off alphons (+). As the number of alphons increase the velocity of the satellite increases in its inward and outward movement. The student must figure out the laws governing the picking up and dropping off of alphons and then use these laws to predict the distance and velocity of a satellite at some given time in the future.

The student can control the devices by pressing the spacebar. A menu of items is presented and the student is allowed to change the value of any component of the system. For example the student can change the number of alphons in the nucleus, the distance or velocity of either satellite, the constant K or the alphon number N. Having made these changes the student can observe the result on the system. The student can also stop or start the action of the system by pressing the RETURN key. Thus by carefully selecting what to change the student can test various hypotheses about the system and thereby derive the rules by which the system works.

---

[5]Xenograde Systems was invented by Carl Bereiter. The science was expanded by M. David Merrill. The current simulation of the system was programed by Tom Eucker. Please write to the author if you would like to use this material for experimental purposes.

This controllable world may appear to be practice. If the student is given specific problems to solve it could be practice in hypothesis testing, experimentation, and data gathering. However, in exploration mode the system is also an expository presentation of a large number of examples (Eeg). In a way it is just like the scale in the interactive illustration for story problems except that the rules that govern the system are more complex and interact with each other. It may be that exploration alone is not sufficient to teach the student about Xenograde systems. Adequate instruction will probably involve a series of suggested experiments that the student is directed to perform. The simulation then becomes a laboratory where the student can perform the designated experiment. The experiment and its execution may still be considered a demonstration and thus an expository presentation even though there is a considerable amount of control that the student can exercise over the system.

The Psychology Experimenter.   A second example of a controllable world as an expository presentation is *The Psychology Experimenter,* a program developed to accompany introductory psychology texts. It is easy to discuss laboratory experiments and to explain what happens but anyone who has ever conducted an experiment with human subjects knows that the description in the text book has only superficial resemblance to the real activity. On the other hand to design and conduct an experiment from scratch is a very involved effort and class assignments often are inadequate to provide an adequate example of the experimental process. Furthermore a student is lucky to get a single experiment prepared and has only one instance rather than a set of instances. *The Psychology Experimenter* was designed to make it easy to provide experience in psychological experimentation by providing a controllable world which enables the psychology student to set up and conduct experiments with a minimum of effort.

The package allows the student to set up a two group experiment in any of four areas: serial learning, paried word learning, digit span experiments, and comparative size perception experiments. The software provides an experiment editor which enables the student to set up an experimental condition by merely selecting parameter values for a series of variables. The computer screen then presents the stimulus materials to the subjects and automatically collects the data. A data analysis program enables the student to quickly analyze the data with a *t-test*. The following paragraphs show some of the displays and explain how the student sets up and conducts an experiment.[6]

Figure 3.24 shows the experiment editor. The student-experimenter can select the number of treatments (1 or 2), the treatment type (one-by-one or free recall), the

---

[6]*The Psychology Experimenter* by M. David Merrill and Ben R. Lowery was developed by Olympus/MicroTeacher Educational Software Inc. and is marketed by Harcourt Brace Jovanovich, publishers, 1985.

PAIRED WORD EXPERIMENT

INFORMATION (1 of 6): The paired-word experiment allows you to compare the performance of two groups of subjects (Ss) as they learn pairs of words.

[SPACE BAR] to read more

Treatment Menu
Experiment Name: HBJ Pair
Number of Treatments: 2

	Treatment 1	Treatment 2
Treatment Type:	One-by-one	One-by-one
Words:	Meaningful	Nonsense
Number of Pairs:	5	5
Number of Trials:	2	2
Order:	Same	Same
Exposure Time:	2 Sec.	2 Sec.

[↓↑←→] to next choice   [F1] to [F2] to Word list
[TAB] to Response Menu   [ESC] to exit

FIG. 3.24. *The Psychology Experimenter* treatment menu.

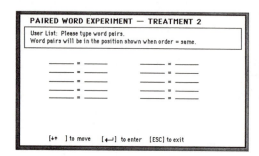

FIG. 3.25. *The Psychology Experimenter* word editor.

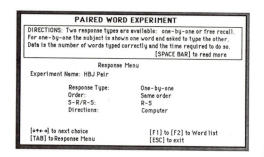

FIG. 3.26. *The Psychology Experimenter* response menu.

type of words (meaningful, nonsense or user defined), the number of pairs (1–26), the number of learning trials (1–10), the order of presentation (same or random), and the exposure time for each word pair in presentation (1–10 sec).

Figure 3.25 shows the paired word list editor which enables the student-experimenter to enter their own word pairs. The computer also has its own list of meaningful or nonsense words should the student-experimenter prefer to use them.

Figure 3.26 shows the response menu where the student-experimenter can select the response mode for the experiment. The variables are response type (one-by-one or free recall), order (same or random), whether the stimulus word or response

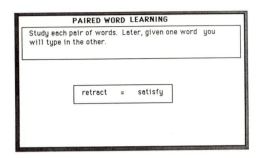

FIG. 3.27. *The Psychology Experimenter* presentation of treatment.

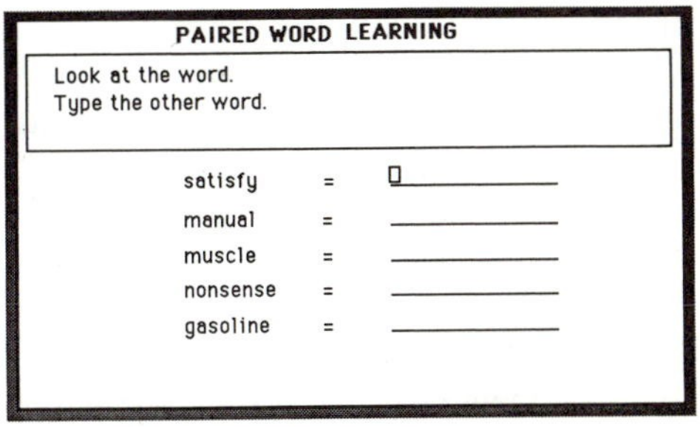

FIG. 3.28. *The Psychology Experimenter* subject response.

word is presented as the stimulus (S-R or R-S) and directions (computer defined or user defined).

Figure 3.27 shows the experiment as it would be presented to the subject in one-by-one treatment mode. In this type of treatment the word pairs are presented one at a time for a given length of time. The subject must learn each word pair as it is presented.

Figure 3.28 shows the experiment as it would be presented to the subject in free recall response mode. The subject is shown a screen showing the stimulus word for each pair of the words in the list. The subject must correctly type each response word next to the correct stimulus word. There is not time limit in this response mode and the response words can be entered in any order. The data that the program collects in free recall response mode is the number of words correct and the time required to complete the list.

The Psychology Experimenter may appear to fall outside the scope of Component Display Theory, however, one way to conceptualize this piece of software is as a series of examples of experiments. If the generality is the procedure for conducting an experiment then this software provides a tool for providing a series of examples which can be explored by the student. The controllable world provided may need additional guidance from the instructor as to what constitutes an adequate experiment and what does not, as to the correct procedure for assigning subjects to treatments, and numerous other items. Nevertheless, the computer based experimenter is a tool used to represent a series of expository examples and perhaps a device for providing practice as well. In this situation the computer program is used as part of the total instructional system rather than as a stand alone tutorial device.

INQUISITORY PRESENTATIONS

The term "inquisitory" has frequently been interpreted to mean, ask a question. The Navy version of CDT, called the *Instructional Quality Inventory* (Ellis & Wulfeck, 1978) substitutes the word *ASK* for the word *inquisitory*. The branching programed instruction model illustrated in Fig. 3.12 substitutes answering questions (often multiple choice or short answer) for practice. The metaphor is a text or work book with questions at the end of the chapter.

We previously suggested that a primary function of instruction is to promote active mental processing and guide cognitive processing. A second primary function of instruction is to **allow the student to engage in a task or a representation of the task which is similar to the "real world" performance being taught. While engaged in this interaction with the task the student should receive feedback concerning the adequacy of his or her performance.**

This activity is frequently called practice and what was intended by the term, *inquisitory presentations* from CDT. The operational word is DO. In planning CAI practice experiences we should ask what will the student be required to do? Then we should ask ourselves how can we allow the student to do this activity with feedback. When planning inquisitory presentations we should strive to make the interaction as functionally similar to the task being taught as is practical.

In the following paragraphs we have presented some examples of practice which attempt to engage the student in activities that resemble the task being taught and which attempt to avoid merely asking questions. These tasks include several different types of tasks including editing, computation, error/detection, assembly/disassembly and hypothesis testing. All of the activities illustrated can be implemented on small computers with common programming languages.

Editing

Poetic Meter. Figure 3.29 illustrates a practice transaction based on the lesson on Poetic Meter previously described.[7] The objective of this lesson is to teach the

---

[7]Based on the program "Introduction to Poetry" by M. David Merrill published by Olympus/MicroTeacher Software Inc., San Diego, CA. The interaction described here is a significant modification of the editor in the published version of the program.

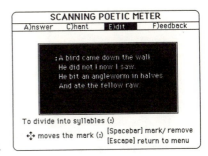

SCANNING POETIC METER
A)nswer   C)hant   E)dit   F)eedback

: A bird came down the wall
He did not know I saw.
He bit an angleworm in halves
And ate the fellow raw.

To divide into syllables (:)
✦ moves the mark (:)   [Spacebar] mark/ remove
                        [Escape] return to menu

FIG. 3.29. Practice in scanning poetry.

SCANNING POETIC METER
A)nswer   C)hant   E)dit   F)eedback

T)rochaic	T)rochaic	S)yllables
I)ambic	I)ambic	F)oot
D)actylic	D)actylic	S(T)ress
A)napestic	A)napestic	

FIG. 3.30. Pull down menus for poetic meter practice.

student to find the type of poetic meter used in a given passage of poetry. This activity is called "scanning poetry" and involves several steps. The student must identify the individual syllables in multiple syllable words, the student must identify which syllables are stressed and the student must divide the lines of the passage into poetic feet. Having accomplished these steps it is relatively easy to recognize the type of poetic meter involved. A tool that is useful to find the stress patterns is to "chant" or read the poem aloud using different stress patterns.

In Fig. 3.29 a passage of poetry is presented in the editing window. Above the editing window is a menu bar consisting of several options for the student. Each item in this command menu calls a pull down menu as shown in Fig. 3.30. The student can select a choice using the key board or by using the spacebar and return key. For example, pressing the keys [A] [D] [Return] would select the answer dactylic. Or the user can select the answer dactylic by pressing the spacebar to move the pointer to A)nswer on the main menu bar. Pressing [Return] shows the pull down menu. Pressing [spacebar] moves through the choices. Pressing [return] again selects the choice. Pressing [escape] returns the user to the main menu.

A)nswer is a multiple choice item which enables the student to select the type of meter involved in the passage. Selecting the type of meter illustrated is usually the last thing the student does as part of the practice. After selecting the answer the system presents a RIGHT or WRONG message (see Fig. 3.31) and instructs the student to press the return key to try again or the spacebar to continue to the next passage.

E)dit allows the student to engage in analysis of the passage prior to answering the question. Selecting S)yllables from the E)dit menu enables the student to move a colon (:) between each set of letters using the arrow keys to move the marker (:) and

85

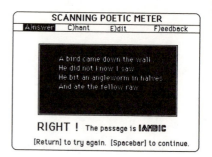

FIG. 3.31. RIGHT/WRONG feedback for poetic meter practice.

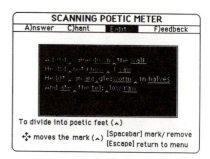

FIG. 3.32 An edited passage from Scanning Poetry Editor.

the spacebar to set or remove a marker. Selecting s(T)ress from the E)dit menu enables the student to move an underline (＿＿＿) from syllable to syllable using the arrow keys to move the marker (＿＿＿) and the spacebar to set or remove the marker. Selecting F)oot from the E)dit menu enables the student to move an up-arrow (ˆ) between each syllable to divide the passage into poetic feet. The [Return] key returns the student to the E)dit menu to change from S)yllables to s(T)ress to F)oot. The [Escape] key enables the user to return to the command menu. The student can modify the editing of the passage as much as he or she wants prior to choosing an answer for the passage. Figure 3.32 shows a passage after the student finished editing to determine the poetic meter involved.

C)hant allows the student to select a type of meter and have the system "chant" the passage by highlighting each syllable as the computer speaker emits a high tone for stressed syllables and a low tone for unstressed syllables. This enables the user to hear various stress patterns to see which one fits.

F)eedback enables the user to have the system check the analysis done with the editor. Selecting F)eedback causes the system to highlight in turn each editing mark (:) for dividing syllables, (_) for underlining stressed syllables, and (▲) for dividing poetic feet). If the student has inserted a mark where one does not belong the system flashes the mark and beeps the speaker. The mark is not removed. If the student has failed to insert a mark where one belongs the computer inserts the

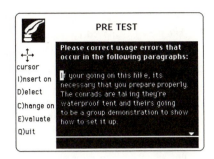

FIG. 3.33. The editor from Writing Skills.

appropriate mark and flashes it while beeping the speaker. The mark does not remain inserted.

The poetic meter scanner enables the student to engage in the careful analysis of a poem that may be required by a teacher in a homework assignment. The commercial product also has a teacher editor which enables the teacher to enter his or her own poems for student analysis. The system has the added advantage that the student's analysis can be checked immediately and the student allowed to redo the analysis until it is correct and the correct classification has been made. While there is a question involved the practice enables the student to engage in much more than merely answering the question. The practice essentially helps the student determine why a given passage has a given poetic meter pattern.

Writing Skills. Figure 3.33 shows the editor from Writing Skills.[8] It would be nice to have a writing exercise where the student uses a word processor to write a composition and the computer then analyses the composition for errors. There are some writing assistance programs, of which Writer's Workbench is one of the most sophisticated, that are able to detect certain writing errors in original compositions (Frase & Diel, 1986). Because *Writing Skills* was an attempt to develop an economical package the authors used an editing approach to the practice. It was assumed that one of the tasks after writing a composition was to edit it and detect errors that the writer may have overlooked. In this software the student is given a number of passages and asked to detect certain classes of errors. After the passage has been edited the system scans the passage and indicates where the student failed to make corrections that were necessary or where the student made corrections which should not have been made.

---

[8]Based on the program "Writing Skills" by Marvin Rosen, Bennie Lowery and M. David Merrill developed by Olympus/MicroTeacher Software Inc., and published by DesignWare/ Eduware Inc. San Francisco. For purposes of this chapter this transaction has been modified from the version in the published software.

Figure 3.33 illustrates the editor from Writing Skills. The operation is very simple. The cursor is moved through the passage via the arrow keys. Moving the cursor beyond the last line or top line scrolls the passage automatically if there is more.

I)nsert enables the student to insert words or punctuation at the cursor. The insert mode is terminated by pressing [Return] to enter the change or [Escape] to cancel the insert. The editor is not like a word processor. The only changes allowed are those anticipated by the authors of the program to prevent the student from completely changing the word structure and thus making evaluation difficult or impossible for this simple analysis program. If the student tries to make a change that is not anticipated an error message appears in a window that is overlayed on the screen stating:

Change not anticipated.

Press [Spacebar] to proceed to the next error.

D)elete enables the student to delete the character under the cursor.

C)hange enables the student to change the character under the cursor. Change is turned off by pressing [Escape].

E)valuate causes the system to highlight each word or punctuation mark in turn. When a correct change is encountered the cursor flashes and a message is shown in the feedback window at the bottom of the screen stating:

Correct change. [Spacebar]

The student presses the spacebar to continue the evaluation. When an incorrect change is encountered the cursor flashes and a message is shown which states:

This was correct. You should not have changed it. [Spacebar]

When an error is missed the cursor flashes and a message is shown which states:

You missed this error. [Spacebar]

The system does not correct the student's errors or omissions but merely points them out as described.

The system can be used in test mode which turns off the evaluation feedback to the student. After the evaluation the student is allowed to return to the editing task or to go to the lesson menu.

Writing skills has a considerable amount of editing practice included. Each disk contains a pretest which includes all of the errors taught in the disk and which does not allow the evaluation to be shown to the student. The results of the pretest are shown on a menu of the lessons together with a recommendation for which the lessons the student must study (see Fig. 3.34). After each lesson the student is required to edit a passage of several paragraphs containing only the type of error taught in the lesson. Feedback is provided as described above. After the student has successfully studied all of the lessons in a set he or she is given another editing opportunity with passages containing all of the errors in each of the lessons in the set. Feedback is provided as described. After all of the lessons on a disk have been successfully studied the student is given a posttest consisting of a number of passages containing all of the errors taught in the disk. Feedback

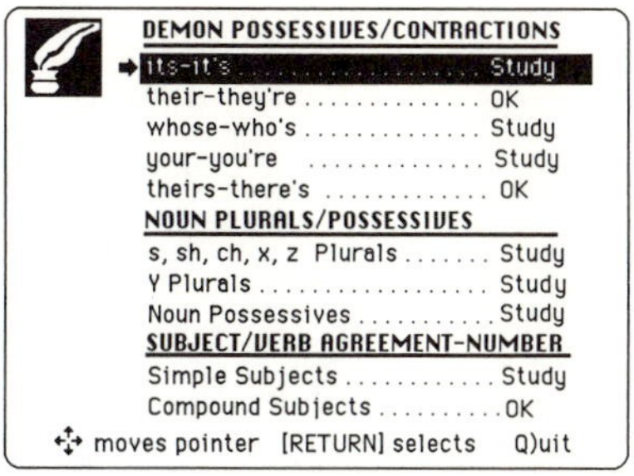

```
   ┌─────────────────────────────────────────┐
   │ 🖋  DEMON POSSESSIVES/CONTRACTIONS        │
   │   ➤ its-it's ................... Study    │
   │     their-they're ............. OK        │
   │     whose-who's .............. Study      │
   │     your-you're  ............. Study      │
   │     theirs-there's ............ OK        │
   │     NOUN PLURALS/POSSESSIVES              │
   │     s, sh, ch, x, z Plurals ....... Study │
   │     Y Plurals .................. Study    │
   │     Noun Possessives .......... Study     │
   │     SUBJECT/VERB AGREEMENT-NUMBER         │
   │     Simple Subjects ........... Study     │
   │     Compound Subjects ......... OK        │
   │   ✛ moves pointer  [RETURN] selects  Q)uit│
   └─────────────────────────────────────────┘
```

FIG. 3.34. Lesson Menu for Writing Skills.

is not provided for the posttest. If the student fails any part of the test he or she is returned to the lesson menu which recommends study of the misunderstood material.

The attempt here is to provide a practice opportunity that resembles the type of editing task the student will encounter in the real world. This is an inquisitory transaction that enables the student to DO the task being taught rather than to merely answer questions about the task.

Computation

Many learning experiences involve the organization of data and computation of intermediate results as well as the final value. Too often asking a series of questions, as in the programed instruction or workbook model, provides too much prompting to the student and does not allow him or her to do the entire process of organizing the data. *General Statistics.*[9] is a program designed to teach the student how to compute common statistics. Figure 3.35 illustrates how to compute a Pearson Product correlation coefficient (r). In this day of high power statistics programs the computer can do these computations from the scores with little or no intervention from the analyst. However, the philosophy of this program is to encourage the user to experience the step by step process of setting up and performing the computation.

Figure 3.35 is based on a display from General Statistics. The display consists of a command line menu on the top line which enables the student to access a number of utilities including a glossary, an on screen calculator, a scattergram of the data and a function to evaluate their work. The second section shows the formula for the calculation to be performed.

---

[9]Based on the program "General Statistics" by Douglas Degelman, Robert M. Hubbard, Bennie R. Lowery and M. David Merrill developed by Olympus/MicroTeacher Software Inc. To be published by DesignWare/Eduware Inc. San Francisco. The display shown has been modified from the original for purposes of this chapter.

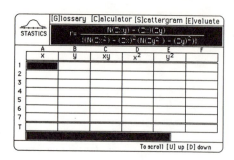

FIG. 3.35. General Statistics correlation computation.

The third window is the work space and for this program consists of a simplified spread sheet. The student is required to enter column headings for intermediate values, to enter data in the appropriate columns, to compute intermediate values or enter formulas for the spread sheet to compute intermediate values, and to compute the value of the statistic using the formula. The system is an assistant into which the user can enter any appropriate data, perhaps that from a text or homework assignment. (The Olympus/Microteacher program also has a demonstration mode with data already supplied which is not described here.) The user moves the cursor with the arrow keys. To enter a value the student types a number in the cell using a minus (−) sign when necessary. To enter a formula instead of a value the user presses the [=] key first and then enters the formula consisting of variables (column-row identifiers e.g., B2) or constants and operators. The formula appears in the black register at the bottom of the spread sheet. The result of the formula appears in the cell of the spread sheet. To copy a formula the user pressed control [D] to fill down or control [R] to fill right. The formulas are automatically adjusted for corresponding rows and columns. To compute the spread sheet the user presses control [=]. The spread sheet has additional rows which the user can scroll to by pressing control [U] or [D]. Pressing the arrow key beyond the upper cell or the lower cell also causes the spread sheet to scroll.

[G]lossary enables the user to get a definition of any technical word in the program. The glossary overlays the workspace and then is removed when the student presses [escape]. The function of the glossary is secondary to our purposes here.

[C]alculator enables the user to call up a simple calculator which operates like most hand held calculators. The user enters a value, an operation, another value, the equal sign. The results appear in the register as shown in Fig. 3.36. The results can be transferred directly to the spread sheet by pressing [return]. Pressing [escape] removes the calculator without transferring the value. Pressing control [C] when the calculator is displayed clears the register.

[S]cattergram enables the user to see the data plotted on a graph. The graph overlays the workspace and is removed when the user presses [escape].

[E]valuate causes the system to check the student's work. This is the unique part of the system that distinguishes it from an ordinary spread sheet. The system first checks to see if all of the necessary intermediate values have been assigned to a

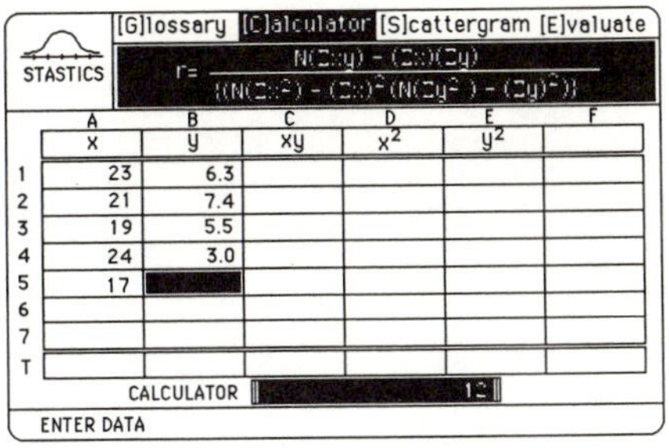

FIG. 3.36. General Statistics computation spread sheet with calculator.

The spreadsheet shows:

	A	B	C	D	E	F
	x	y	xy	x^2	y^2	
1	23	6.3				
2	21	7.4				
3	19	5.5				
4	24	3.0				
5	17					
6						
7						
T						

[G]lossary [C]alculator [S]cattergram [E]valuate

STATISTICS

$$r = \frac{N(\Sigma xy) - (\Sigma x)(\Sigma y)}{\{(N(\Sigma x^2) - (\Sigma x)^2)(N(\Sigma y^2) - (\Sigma y)^2)\}}$$

CALCULATOR

ENTER DATA

column for calculation. If not the value is flashed in the formula. The student must press [spacebar] to continue the evaluation or [escape] to terminate the evaluation and fix the problem identified. The intermediate calculations are checked by either comparing the formulas with the column heads or by checking the actual values filled in by the student. Any errors are flashed but not corrected.

Assembly

In addition to an editor or a spread sheet computation device the computer can also represent devices to be assembled or disassembled. Perhaps one of the most fascinating and imaginative programs released in the past few years is Pinball Construction Set by Bill Budge. Although this is a game the implications for instruction are significant.

Figure 3.37 shows the basic construction screen from the Macintosh version of Pinball Construction Set.[10] The user can use the mouse to drag parts onto the pinball machine at the left. The parts operate like their counterparts in the real world. The user can configure any type of pinball machine imaginable. Other functions represented by the scissors and the soldering iron icons in the command menu enable the user to connect parts so they interact, to assign points to the parts so when the ball hits them they add to the score. The user can use MacPaint to decorate the glass under the balls or the display for the scores. These paintings have no effect on the play.

If Bill Budge can build a pinball construction set then it is possible to build a circuit board construction set, a blue print construction set, etc. In fact any thing for which a plan or diagram can be drawn can be constructed. By coupling this design assembly task with appropriate evaluation and feedback we have the mechanism for very creative practice which far exceeds answering questions at the end of the chapter.

---

[10]Published by Electronic Arts, San Mateo, CA.

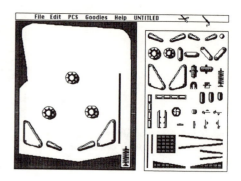

FIG. 3.37.   Pinball construction set.

Panel and Equipment Operation

Many procedural tasks involve operating a control panel consisting of switchs, dials, meters, buttons and even data entry. Another type of experiential practice consists of simulating the interaction of the learner with the panel by drawing a representation of the panel on the screen and asking the learner to press buttons, flip switches, and read dials in sequence thus providing a partial simulation of the task to be performed in the real world. It is relatively easy for the computer to check the learner's sequence of events and to react to the responses of the student.

Figure 3.38 shows a simulation of a multimeter meter and a circuit diagram.[11] The learner must demonstrate the sequence of steps necessary to use the multimeter and show where on the schematic to place the leads to make the reading requested. The user moves the pointer with the arrow keys (or with a mouse if one is available). To change the setting of the meter the user points to the dial. Pressing the spacebar moves the picture of the dial step by step. To attach the leads the user points to the appropriate terminal on the multimeter and presses the spacebar (or clicks the mouse). The lead is attached as shown in Fig. 3.39. Pointing to the schematic the user shows where the lead should be attached. The user continues in this manner until the entire sequence of events necessary to using the multimeter for the requested task has been completed.

The computer program monitors this sequence of actions. Feedback can be given immediately or delayed until after the user has completed the sequence. Inappropriate actions are highlighted and an appropriate message is displayed in the message box at the bottom of the screen.

The above demonstration uses simple graphics and involves very little intelligence on the part of the computer program. Nevertheless, it provides a pro-

---

[11]This program was designed by the author for this chapter and has not been implemented.

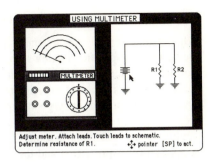

FIG. 3.38. Simulation of the multimeter.

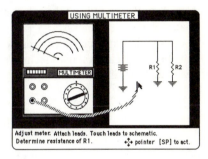

FIG. 3.39. Simulation of the multimeter showing lead attached.

cedural simulation that enables the student to practice an activity similar to the sequence of events required in the actual situation. Far more sophisticated simulations of equipment and panels, which involve artificial intelligence, are being developed. Towne (1986) has developed a program that lets the user create a wide variety of equipment by moving pictures on the screen. The resulting equipment can act like the actual equipment providing a practice environment for operating or monitoring the operation of such equipment.

Error Detection

Another form of experiential practice involves trouble shooting or error detection. Consider the example given in Fig. 3.38. The circuit could contain a defective part. Given the multimeter, which for this program would operate in simulation mode so that actual readings could be obtained from a circuit diagram, the learner could be asked to locate and replace the defective part so that the circuit operates correctly. This type of experiential activity can be quite involved but simple versions are easily implemented using standard programing languages on personal computers. One of the most sophisticated applications of error detection is the work of Bill Johnson and the FAULT system (Johnson, 1986).

Hypothesis Testing and Prediction

When a student really understands a principle he or she should be able to make predictions in specific situations concerning the application of that principle. Consider the Xenograde Science simulation presented in Fig. 3.23. The student could be given a series of experiments to perform or hypotheses to test and this system would provide very good experiential practice in prediction. For example, the student could be asked to predict the velocity and charge of a given satellite at a given point in time. The simulation can then be used to test the accuracy of this prediction and the adequacy of the student's hypothesis.

In a similar way the Psychology Experimenter described in Figs. 3.24 through 3.27 provides a miniature psychology laboratory in which a student can be let to form hypotheses and test these hypotheses by performing experiments on classmates or other students.

A simple experiential environment can be conceived for many prediction situations obvious examples include physics laboratories, chemistry laboratories, mathematical simulations and many others.

SUMMARY

One of the primary contributions of Component Display Theory is the identification of *Primary Presentation Forms* and the rules which prescribe the combinations of primary presentation forms which are most appropriate for promoting specific learning outcomes. Many instructional designers have incorrectly assumed that *Expository Generalities* (*EGs*) and *Expository Instances* (*Eegs*) means the presentation of information without student response. They have also incorrectly assumed that *Inquisitory Instances* (*Iegs*) are best implemented by asking questions. Application of these incorrect assumptions often result in computer based instruction that fails to take advantage of the interactive capabilities of the computer. The resulting instruction is often little more than the work books on the CRT.

One of the primary functions of instruction is to promote active mental processing on the part of the student. There is ample evidence that the amount and quality of the resultant learning is a direct function of the student's appropriate cognitive processing of relevant information. Passive presentation of text-like displays does little to promote the necessary mental activity. However, the appropriate use of rhetorical questions, attention focusing information, and experiential presentations can do much to increase the necessary relevant mental processing and thus increase the level of learning. The interactive nature of the computer makes the implementation of this active involvement much easier than is often possible or practical with other instructional media.

In this chapter we have described several examples of *Expository Presenta-*

tions which more adequately implement the relevant active involvement of the student in the learning process. We have attempted to show that *Expository* does not mean passive. We have attempted to show a variety of ways that carefully orchestrated transactions provide better instruction than passive book-like presentations.

A second purpose of effective instruction is to provide an opportunity for the student to actively DO or practice the activity being learned. We have suggested that merely answering questions is often not sufficiently similar to the real world tasks to be performed. Better practice is provided when the computer provides interactive experiential situations in which the learner can perform a task similar to that which will be required when the skills are applied in the real world. We have provided a number of examples of *Inquisitory Presentations (legs)* which go considerably beyond merely asking questions. Each of the activities described has been, or could easily be, implemented on personal computers with standard programing languages.

Component Display Theory suggests a set of prescriptive principles for more effective instruction regardless of the delivery system by which the instruction is implemented. If the Primary Presentation Forms are interpreted to mean *Primary Presentation Functions,* which are implemented by interactive transactions, then the resulting CAI will be significantly more effective then passive page turning.

REFERENCES

Bork, A. (1981). *Learning with computers.* Bedford, MA: Digital Press.

Ellis, J. A., & Wulfeck, W. H., II (1978). *Interim training manual for the instructional quality inventory* (NPROC TN 78-5). San Diego: Navy Personnel Research and Development Center.

Frase, L. T., & Diel, M. (1986). UNIX Writer's workbench: Software for streamlined communication. *T.H.E. Journal. 14,* 74–79.

Johnson, W. B. (1986). Development and evaluation of simulation-oriented computer-based instruction for diagnostic training. In. W. B. Rouse (Ed.), *Advances in man-machine systems research: Vol. 3.* Greenwich, CT: JAI Press.

Merrill, M. D. (1980). Learner control in computer based learning. *Computers and Education. 4,* 77–95.

Merrill, M. D. (1983). Component Display Theory. In C. M. Reigeluth (Ed.), *Instructional design theories and models.* Hillsdale, NJ: Lawrence Erlbaum Associates.

Merrill, M. D. (1985). Where is the authoring in authoring systems? *Journal of Computer-based Instruction. 14*(4), 90–96.

Merrill, M. D. (1987). An illustration of Component Display Theory. In C. M. Reigeluth (Ed.), *Instructional design theories in action: Lessons illustrating selected theories.* Hillsdale, NJ: Lawrence Erlbaum Associates.

Merrill, M. D., Schneider, E. W., & Fletcher, K. A. (1980). *TICCIT.* Englewood Cliffs, NJ: Educational Technology Publications.

Papert, S. (1980). *Mindstorms.* New York: Basic Books.

Towne, D. M. (1986). The generalized maintenance trainer: Evolution and revolution. In W. B. Rouse (Ed.), *Advances in man-machine systems research: Vol 3.* Greenwich, CT: JAI Press.

II
INTERACTIVE DESIGNS FOR COURSEWARE

Active participation in the learning process is not a new notion. It was, in fact, the basis for Socrates' teaching. However, the relationship between active participation and learning doubtlessly antedates Socratic thinking. It certainly is not original to microcomputer courseware, as some of the marketing promotion would have us believe. Yet, computer-based instruction provides greater potential for truly interactive instruction than any mediated teaching device to date, excluding in many instances, the human tutor. Exactly what does that interactive potential involve?

Interactivity refers to the activity *between* two organisms. In computer-based instruction, it refers to the activities performed by the learner and by the computer. In an interactive communication, they are both active. An interactive computer-based program involves the learner in a true dialog. The conception of interactivity traditionally promoted by instructional technologists is based on the programmed learning model, which entails the presentation of instructional stimuli, followed by some form of question by the technology, which presumably elicits a response by the learner, and finally the rejoinder or feedback to the learner by the technology. This interactive process is iterative, with the same or similar sequence repeated throughout the program. The technology is actively involved in presenting material and rejoining to learner responses. The learner is actively involved in responding to the technology. Both are active, but is mere activity enough?

The quality of the interaction between learner and computer

program is a function of three things: the type of input required of the learner while responding to the computer, the way in which the computer analyzes the learner's response, and the nature of the action taken by the computer in response to the learner (Bork, 1982).

The first criterion, the type of input required by the learner, may be evaluated in a variety of ways. Learner input may be measured by the number of responses. Connectionism predicts that the more responses the learner makes, the more she or he will learn. The type of input might also refer to the modality of the response—oral, kinesthetic, etc. Modality requirements affect the information processing requirements of the program, as discussed later. More importantly, it may also be a function of the depth of information processing required by the response. Meaningful responses by the learner are those that require the learner to access prior knowledge in order to integrate the response.

The second criterion concerns the computer's reply to learner responses, more commonly referred to as feedback. The quality of an instructional interaction is certainly a function of the quality of the feedback. Feedback, as discussed by Schimmel in his chapter, may present confirmation of results, remediation, or supplementary information.

The third criterion, the action taken by the technology in response to the learner, is not, I contend, a part of the definition of the interaction. This third criterion actually refers to the nature of the technology's adaptation of instruction. When we speak of interactive instruction, more often than not we are actually refering to interactive, *adaptive* instruction (Jonassen, 1985). Quality interactive instruction entails not only active roles for the learner and the computer, but also the ability of the technology to adapt its actions based on those of the learner. Socrates was a revered tutor not simply because he presented information and posed questions and problems for the learner, but also because he selected more relevant questions or adjusted the difficulty or content of the question to fit the needs or ability of the learner. He also prompted, cued, and cajoled adaptively to elicit a meaningful response from the learner. Meaningfulness in interactions is provided by establishing the right context for the interaction, that is, by causing the learner to access the appropriate schemata from their memory to use in integrating his or her responses (McMeen & Templeton, 1985). The context may take the form of an advanced organizer, according to the authors. We might also use analogies, comparison-contrasts, or other metaphorical devices. Principles of cognitive psychology contend that in order to be successful, a dialog must access knowledge currently available to the learner.

A number of designers rate the quality of interactivity by the level of learner control, that is, the degree to which the learner controls the content, structure, form, and style of the instructional presentation. Is the content, sequence, or type of activity under learner control or program control? In a review of the learner orientation literature, Hannum and Gleason (in press) found more than four times as many studies that showed that total learner control of various aspects of instruction (difficulty of practice, instructional support, pace, sequence, etc.) was less effective than studies showing it to be more effective than program control. Ross and Rakow (1981, 1982) have found that adaptive control by the computer program using a meaningful algorithm for assigning the level of instructional support to be consistently more effective than learner control. If you are still contemplating learner control, just what level of learner control is most effective.

According to Rhodes and Azbell (1985), there are three levels of interactivity in CAI. At the lowest level, reactive designs, there is little learner control of content or program structure. Reactive interactions feature program-directed options and feedback. In a coactive design, learners have control of program structure or style. They choose the sequence, pace, or style of the presentation or feedback. Proactive designs put the learner in control of both the structure and content of the program. Such programs are inherently more personalized and therefore, as the authors argue, more meaningful to the learner. Learner prerogatives are satisfying. However, making wise choices depends upon the learner knowing what is best for him or her and then exercising choices that will provide the most productive learning environment. Research has shown that prelearning and on-task advisement can improve learners' choices (Johansen & Tennyson, 1983) as well as supplanting learning skills in the learner (Tennyson & Buttrey, 1980). In reality, learners don't usually make the most effective choices, but they can be effectively advised to do so.

Levels of Interaction

The nature of an interactive dialog is determined by the nature of the active processing by the learner and the computer as well as the types of adaptations built into the computer program. This part of the book is concerned with the nature of the interactivity, while Part III examines the adaptations possible with microcomputer courseware. Just how can interactivity vary? Damarin (1982) conceived of six levels of interactivity in courseware—watching, finding, doing, using, constructing, and creating. Table II.1 lists the levels of interactivity presented as part of the taxonomy of interactive, adaptive lesson designs (Jonassen, 1985). The most fundamental level of the interactivity concerns the modality of the learner's response to the computer. Which sensory systems are required of the user by the computer's input and output devices, and to what extent are they compatible and consistent? Microcomputer courseware relies mostly on visual input to the learner from the screen, although the speech synthesis and recognition technologies are changing that rapidly. How consistent are learner input vs. learner output modalities, though? We know that the psychomotor skills involved in keyboarding, while providing the best evidence of learning, constitutes a significant distraction to a large number of learners (Kearsley, 1983). So designers require single keypress responses, which limits the learner's attention

TABLE II.1
Levels of Interactivity

Level of intelligence of design....	
Type of interactive program....	
Level of processing....	
Task analysis: Content level....	
Task level....	
Modality of response....	

(Schwade, 1984) or the learning effectiveness when compared with constructed responses which require more keypresses. Most importantly, the nature of the learner response needs to be appropriate to the task requirements. Barker (1982), for instance, found that a joystick permits a more sophisticated dialog than a light pen, and that keyboards provided for the most advanced types of learner activity. This discussion should be tempered by the fairly consistent findings that overt responses generally produce no more learning than covert responses (Fleming & Levie, 1978).

The next two levels of interactivity refer to the nature of the task, most often operationalized in courseware by questions of different types inserted into the presentation. Instructional design principles insist that the information processing required by the practice task (inserted question) in courseware be consistent with the task level of the objective and the test item. So, identifying the task level (remember, use, generate, etc.) and the content level (fact, concept, procedure, principle, or problem) of all of the tasks and test items embedded in courseware is an essential step in the design process.

Closely allied to task analysis is the depth of processing entailed by the learner responses. As the level of responding increases, so does the amount of learning (Fleming & Levie, 1978), so questions requiring lower levels of (shallower) processing impede deeper, more meaningful processing. Deeper, more meaningful processing entails more semantic processing, requiring the learner to access prior knowledge to relate to new information and the integration of the new with existing knowledge to provide an expanded knowledge base capable of assimilating even more information (see Generative Learning section of Jonassen chapter for a more detailed discussion). It is generally accepted that deeper processing of information is more meaningful and resistant to forgetting. Interactive courseware should establish a meaningful context and require the learner to access what they know about that context in order to integrate the new information presented by the program.

The type of program (the next level of interactivity) also affects the information processing. Generally, drill-and-practice programs involve shallower processing, because they use more recall type questions. Tutorial programs can help by establishing a meaningful context for learning and following through with more relevant processing. Problem-solving programs generally require deeper

100

processing. The most meaningful instruction results from intelligent tutors, which model optimal methods for problem solutions based on a model of the learner's processing (Sleeman & Brown, 1982). These types of programs lead us to the highest level of interactivity—the level of intelligence implied by the interaction. Intelligent tutoring is based on principles of artificial intelligence and is discussed more extensively in the fourth section of this book.

Generally, the quality of the interaction in microcomputer courseware is a function of the nature of the learner's response and the computer's feedback. If the reponse is consistent with the learner's information processing needs, then it is meaningful. The deeper the processing required by the learner in integrating his or her response, the more personally meaningful will be the interaction. However, we already agreed that interactive courseware is a dialog, so we must also be mindful of the nature of the feedback provided by the computer. Is it consistent with the processing requirements of the learner's response? Does it prompt deeper processing? Does it require the learner to monitor and analyze his or her understanding? These are issues addressed in this part of the book.

INTRODUCTION TO PART II

In the first chapter, David Salisbury presents the best conceived and most comprehensive set of strategies for designing drill and practice to date. These strategies focus on providing increasing levels of review, which are designed to further integrate the learner's responses into memory.

William Montague borrows from early principles of vocational education and more recent principles of military training (both of which are recapitulated by current work in the cognitive sciences) to provide a set of heuristics for designing interactive instruction. Meaningful cognitive processing, he claims, is best promoted by learning environments which simulate the conditions and interactions required by the task performance. This functional orientation pervades the excellent examples of CBI that he provides.

In the next chapter, I argue that cognitive learning strategies are intended to produce deeper processing by the learner, so we should replace the shallower responses that are a part of so much existing courseware with learning strategies. The microcomputer is uniquely suited to the embedding of these strategies.

Finally, Barry Schimmel discusses the roles and importance of feedback, the second criterion of the quality of courseware. After reviewing the types and functions of feedback, he provides some principles to the courseware designer for integrating feedback based upon the depth of processing required by the instruction.

These chapters all focus on how to produce good interactive instruction. We know generally that good interactive instruction includes (Gayeski, 1985):

- Good questions
- Meaningful, responsive, human-like dialog
- Ability to catch common errors
- Ability to relate to different learning styles

The chapters in this part present some of the means for producing those qualities in microcomputer courseware.

REFERENCES

Barker, P. G. (1982). Some experiments in man-machine interaction relevant to CAI. *British Journal of Educational Technology, 13*(1), 65–75.

Bork, A. (1982). Interactive learning. In R. Taylor (Ed.), *The computer in the school*. New York: Teachers College Press.

Damarin, S. (1982, April). *Fitting the tool with the task: A problem in the instructional use of microcomputers*. Paper presented at the annual meeting of the American Educational Research Association, New York.

Fleming, M., & Levie, H. (1978). *Instructional message design*. Englewood Cliffs, NJ: Educational Technology Publications.

Gayeski, D. M. (1985). New designs for new media. *Training and Development Journal, 39*(12), 34–35.

Hannum, W. H., & Gleason, J. M. (in press). Learner-courseware interactions in CBI: A review of the literature. *Educational Technology*.

Johansen, K. J., & Tennyson, R. D. (1983). Effect of adaptive advisement on perception in learner controlled, computer-based instruction using a rule-learning task. *Educational Communications and Technology Journal, 31*, 226–236.

Jonassen, D. H. (1985). Interactive lesson designs: A taxonomy. *Educational Technology, 26*(6), 7–16.

Kearsley, G. (1983). *Computer-based training: A guide to selection and implementation*. Reading, MA: Addison-Wesley.

McMeen, G. R., & Templeton, S. (1985). Improving the meaningfulness of interactive dialogue in computer courseware. *Educational Technology, 26*(5), 36–39.

Rhodes, D. M., & Azbell, J. W. (1985). Desiging interactive video instruction professionally. *Training and Development Journal, 39*(12), 31–33.

Ross, S. M., & Rakow, E. A. (1981). Learner control vs. program control as adaptive strategies for selection of instructional support on math rules. *Journal of Educational Psychology, 73*, 745–753.

Ross, S. M., & Rakow, E. A. (1982). Adaptive instructional strategies for teaching rules in mathematics. *Educational Communications and Technology Journal, 30*, 67–74.

Sleeman, D., & Brown, J. S. (1982). *Intelligent tutoring systems*. London: Academic Press.

Tennyson, R. D., & Buttrey, T. (1980). Advisement and management strategies as design variables in computer-assisted instruction. *Journal of Computer-Based Instruction, 5*(3), 63–71.

4 Effective Drill and Practice Strategies

David F. Salisbury
Florida State University

INTRODUCTION

Performance of almost any skill is greatly influenced by practice. Consider the profound influence of practice on such skills as reading, speaking a foreign language, computer programming, typing, or tennis. No matter how effective the initial instruction and guidance on a skill might be, unless learners have sufficient opportunity to practice the skill they may fail to achieve mastery. Some skills require a great deal of practice over a long period of time in order for learners to master the skill to the point that they can perform it readily in the real world situation.

The computer is currently being utilized as a means to optimize the practice process by making practice more interesting, self-motivating, and efficient. However, there is still a need to better utilize this technology to optimize practice activities. Many of the computer-based drills currently available are dry, boring, and unpleasant and do not capitalize on the power of the computer. These bad examples though, should not cause us to underestimate the potential value of computer-based drill and practice. Practice does not have to be an unenjoyable experience. Many kinds of arrangements can be made to make drill and practice an interesting activity. In addition, computers allow instructional designers to incorporate into practice activities psychologically sound techniques and procedures beyond what might be possible otherwise.

This chapter describes computer-based drill and practice strategies for practicing factual information as well as strategies for practicing intellectual skills. The strategies range from relatively simple drill paradigms to very sophisticated and complex drill structures which might be termed "intelligent drills." Each of the drill strategies is evaluated in terms of its effectiveness and theoretical soundness.

THE STAGES OF SKILL LEARNING

Modern cognitive learning theory allows us to explain skill learning in terms of stages (for example, see Fitts & Posner, 1967). These stages are: (a) the cognitive stage, (b) the associative stage, and (c) the autonomous stage. Each of these are described briefly below.

Cognitive stage.   Skill learning usually begins with an instructional or overview phase in which the learner receives or studies information or instructions about the skill. This is referred to as the cognitive stage of skill development. This stage usually results in an internal mental representation of how the skill is performed. Also, the learner is usually able to give a verbal description of how the skill is performed and state the basic facts associated with the skill. For instance, the learner may memorize the names of the controls on a control panel and state briefly how they should be used.

Associative stage.   Next, the learner usually attempts to perform the skill based on the knowledge acquired in the cognitive stage. The initial attempts inevitably reveal errors or inadequacies in the initial understanding. Through additional practice, these errors or inadequacies are generally corrected. A second thing that happens during this stage is that the associations between the various elements in the skill are strengthened as a result of the practice process. The outcome of the stage is a smooth but deliberate execution of the skill.

Autonomous stage.   The third stage of skill acquisition, the autonomous stage, occurs as the performance of the skill becomes more automatic and rapid. Skills that have reached the autonomous stage can usually be performed while simultaneously performing some secondary task, much like most people can read while walking, or talk while driving. Not all skills reach the autonomous stage. For certain skills, a smooth but deliberate execution of the skill is all that is required. For other skills, however, automaticity is a necessity, especially if the skill will eventually need to serve as a component of a more complex, higher level skill and therefore must be executed without much of the attentional capacity devoted to it.

Based on this brief overview of the three stages of skill acquisition one can see the important role that drill and practice plays in the learning process. Practice during the cognitive stage usually involves the learning of factual information which is prerequisite to performing the final skill. During the associative stage, the role of practice is to assist the learner in being able to perform the skill smoothly and accurately. However, at this stage the learner may have to use a great deal of mental concentration to perform the skill. During the autonomous stage, the objective of practice is to allow the learner to perform the skill without a great deal of mental concentration so that some of the learner's attentional capacity will be available to devote to other aspects of the total task. Many skills, however, must be performed at the autonomous stage in order to be useful. This would be true for skills that will ultimately be performed in conjunction with more complex skills. Complex skills like reading, problem solving, computer programming, or speaking a foreign language are examples of skill areas that contain many subskills that must be learned to the autonomous stage. Some factual information also needs to be automatized if the learner will be required to draw upon that factual information as part of a higher level skill.

BASIC DRILL STRUCTURE FOR FACTUAL INFORMATION

Computer drills are often employed for learning information that is factual in nature. Such information includes learning facts, names, labels, or paired associations. Often, this factual information is prerequisite to efficient performance of a more complex, higher level skill. For example, the names and abbreviations of the chemical elements and their atomic weights must be well learned in order to comprehend scientific writing or chemical formulas. The names of stars and constellations must be learned in order to effectively work in the field of astronomy. Other, more simple examples include learning the names of letters, learning sight words, states and capitals, or the parts of an engine.

Cognitive learning research has provided us with useful knowledge about how people learn factual information. Earlier behavioristic theory suggested that factual information was learned strictly through response reinforcement and repetition. More recent cognitive learning research, however, has revealed that people learn factual information by paying attention to the *meaning* of the information and organizing structural representations of the material in their minds. For the learning of factual information, organizing material (such as the entire list of the facts to be learned) should be presented to the learner prior to using the drill. Also, attempts should be made to make the material as meaningful as possible by highlighting any important relationships, sequences, or groups among the items or by providing rhymes, analogies, acronyms, or other devices to give additional meaning and organization to the material and thus aid memory. The objective of a practice drill should not be just to ''burn it into memory'' but to organize material in such a way as to make it more meaningful.

A drill for practicing factual information should involve a series of practice items presented in a repeating cycle. The flowchart in Fig. 4.1 represents the general structure and flow of a drill for factual information.

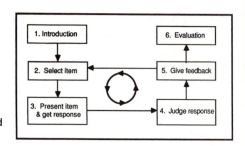

FIG. 4.1. The general structure and flow of a drill for factual information.

The flowchart in Fig. 4.1 depicts the following steps:

1. Introduction	Introductory information about the drill is presented. This may include instructions on how to use the drill, how to temporarily terminate the drill, and scoring criteria.
2. Select item	Items are selected either in a set sequence or in a random sequence.
3. Present an item	An item or question is presented to the learner.
Get Response	The learner enters a response.
4. Judge Response	The response entered by the learner is judged to be correct or incorrect.
5. Give Feedback	Appropriate feedback is given.
Repeat Cycle or,	
6. Evaluation	Provide the learner with an assessment of performance.

STOPPING THE CYCLE

The cycle can be programmed by using a loop structure (such as a for/next loop in BASIC). One of two methods can be employed for ending the cycle: (a) the cycle can continue until all items are presented a certain number of times, or (b) items can be presented until the user stops the drill. A drill structure that allows the learner to stop the drill at any point by typing ''STOP'' as an answer to any item is shown in Fig. 4.2. Other methods for stopping the drill (such as allowing the learner to stop the drill at any point by pressing ESCAPE or some other special key) can also be employed.

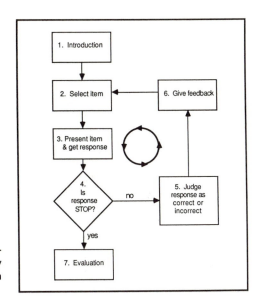

FIG. 4.2. Drill structure which allows learner to stop the drill at any point by typing STOP for an answer.

METHODS FOR SELECTING ITEMS

Some very simple drills are written so that the same items are presented in the same sequence each time through the drill. This strategy is the same as one might employ using flashcards which contain the question or stimulus on one side of the flashcard and the correct answer on the other side of the card. The learner would respond to each flashcard one at a time. After responding to a card and checking the answer, the learner would place the flashcard at the back of the deck. The learner then continues going through the deck of flashcards (without ever altering the sequence) until all items are learned.

This procedure, of course, is not a good instructional strategy and may be detrimental to the learner since going through the items in the same sequence each time may produce a *serial learning effect*. This means that the sequence of the items serves as a "contextual cue" for the next response. There are several strategies for selecting the items to be presented in a drill which can be used to eliminate this serial learning effect. These are (a) shuffling, and (b) random selection of items.

Figure 4.3 shows a drill structure for shuffling 20 items to be presented in a drill. In this drill the numbers 1–20 are randomly assigned to each item. The items are then presented in the sequence indicated by the random numbers. Note that once all the items have been used, a second set of random numbers is

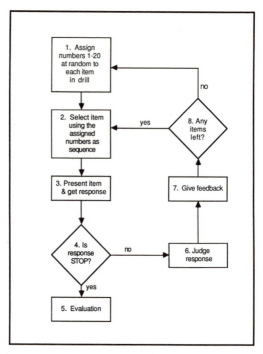

FIG. 4.3. Drill structure for shuffling twenty items.

assigned to the items and the drill continues with a new presentation sequence. The drill will continue until the learner types "STOP."

Another technique for shuffling the items is to simply select the items at random from a list without replacement. Some authoring languages have mechanisms for selecting without replacement, or, this can be done by writing a subroutine which (a) selects an item, (b) checks to see if that item has already been selected, (c) if so, selects another item, (d) if not, presents the item.

Either of these two strategies is better than the nonshuffled strategy presented in Fig. 4.2 in several ways: (a) they present the items in a different sequence each time through the list (no serial learning effect); and (b) they allow the learner to continue using the drill indefinitely. These strategies are still somewhat inefficient, however, because they require the learner to spend the same amount of time on all the items in the drill—the learned items as well as the unlearned ones. The learner is required to respond to all the items each time through the list even if some of the items have already been learned. There is no provision for the learners to concentrate their effort on the unlearned items. Two-pool and three-pool drill structures provide this additional advantage.

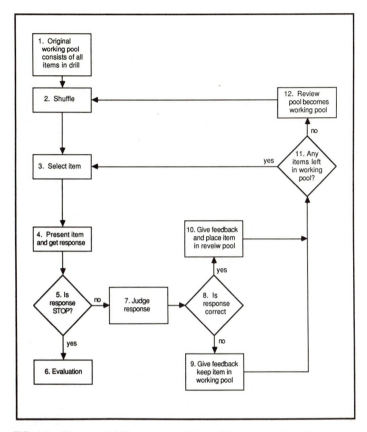

FIG. 4.4.   Two-pool drill structure with working pool and review pool.

TWO-POOL DRILLS

A more efficient drill strategy can be formed by separating the items into two pools as the learner proceeds through the drill. Items to which the learner gives a correct response go into a *review pool*. Items to which the learner gives an incorrect response remain in the *working pool*. Once all items are in the *review pool* the drill begins again. This strategy is shown in flowchart form in Fig. 4.4.

This drill strategy provides for the elimination of learned items so that the learner can concentrate effort on the items not yet learned. One might think of this strategy as it would be employed using flashcards. In this case, each time the learner gives a correct response to a card, the card is placed in a discard pile. Once all the cards have made it to the discard pile, the discard pile is shuffled and the drill begins again.

THREE-POOL DRILLS

Although the two-pool drill is more efficient than the previous ones, it still requires the learner to go through all the items in the list the first time through the drill. Research shows that a person can hold only about 7 (plus or minus 2) new pieces of information in short-term memory. Hence drills that involve more new items than this place an undue memory load on short-term memory. Also, when many items are involved the potential for "interference" is very great. Interference refers to the psychological phenomenon that the learning of one item (stimulus and corresponding response) tends to interfere with the learning of other items. This interference results in what might be called "confusion errors" where the learner becomes confused about which responses go with which items.

To reduce the short-term memory load and presence of interference in drills involving many items, a drill can be structured so that the learner works with only a small subset of the total number of items to be learned. By practicing on a smaller subset of items the amount of interference between items and the short-term memory load is reduced. The subset of items being drilled during a practice session could be referred to as the *working pool* of items. The size of this pool should be about 7 items, depending on the difficulty of the material and the age level of the learners.

Figure 4.5 shows a drill strategy which selects seven items from the total list of items (the *item pool*) to form a *working pool*. The *working pool* is shuffled and the items are presented to the learner. If the learner gives a correct response to an item the item goes into the *review pool*. If the learner gives an incorrect response, the item remains in the *working pool*. Once all seven items in the *working pool* have gone into the *review pool* another seven items are selected from the *item pool*. Eventually, all the items will have gone into the *review pool* leaving no more items in the *item pool*. At this point the *review pool* becomes the *working pool* and the drill begins again.

Note that the drill structure consists of three pools of items—an *item pool* (the original list of items to be learned); a *working pool* (the subset of seven items being used currently in the drill); and, a *review pool* (learned items to be reviewed).

RECORD KEEPING IN A DRILL

Drills that involve a large number of items require some mechanism for keeping a record of student performance from session to session as the drill will probably not be completed in one sitting. This data can then be used as *restart data* to allow learners to pick up in the drill using the same subset of items they were working on during the previous session. In the case of the three-pool drill described above, necessary data to be collected and recorded on a student record would include:

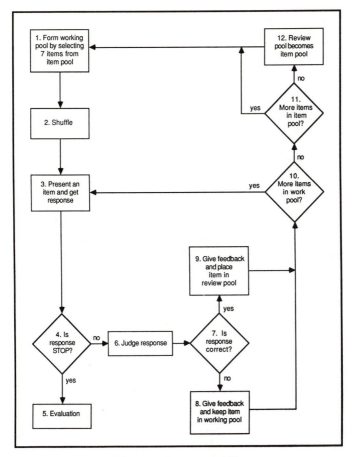

FIG. 4.5.   Three-pool drill.

- items left in the *item pool*
- items in the current *working pool*
- items in the *review pool*
- student's name

To record the data an additional procedure must be included in the drill. When the learner terminates the drill (by typing STOP as an answer), the program would record the data onto a disk before giving the score and ending. Keeping a student record also requires that part of the sign-on procedures include having the student give his or her name, password, etcetera so that the computer can retrieve the student's personal record. Each student will need to keep his or her own data disk which contains that student's record to be used during each session with the drill. Or the student data disks could be stored in a central location and checked out by each student when needed.

COMPLETING THE DRILL

When has a learner completed a drill? Some drills might be structured so that the learner never actually *completes* the drill. For example, a learner may continue to use a typing drill indefinitely to continually strive for a higher level of proficiency. Drills may also be designed so as to require a predetermined level of proficiency at which point the learner would permanently terminate the drill. For example, a drill on associating the names of chemical elements with their abbreviations may be constructed to require that learners can complete one perfect recital before permanently terminating the drill. In the case of the three-pool drill in Fig. 4.5, this would involve getting all items into the *review pool* in one run through the drill. Ideally, drills should be constructed so that a specified level of proficiency must be attained by the learner. Learners should be able, though, to return to the drill from time to time to check their proficiency and if deficient, to use the drill as a review mechanism to again reach the desired level of proficiency.

THREE-POOL DRILLS WITH INCREASING RATIO REVIEW

The three-pool drill described previously can be made more efficient by re-introducing review items from the review pool systematically throughout the drill rather than wai   g until all items have gone into the review pool. This strategy allows the desi ner to incorporate into the drill the concept of *increasing ratio review*. Simply stated, increasing ratio review means that new and review items will be intermixed throughout the drill with the ratio of review to new items increasing as the drill progresses. When the learner first begins the drill, all items will be new items. As the learner masters items, these become review items and are reintroduced systematically into the drill based on time elapsed since the learner was last presented that item. Toward the end of the drill most of the items will be review items with only a few new items being introduced.

Drills that are structured in this way are very useful for the purpose of skill maintenance in addition to initial learning. Learners can work on the drill initially to master the content and then they can continue to use the drill from time to time to review and re-check mastery. Typically, once a person has attained a high level of accuracy and precision on a skill, it can be maintained at that level over a long period of time with only a small amount of practice at regular intervals.

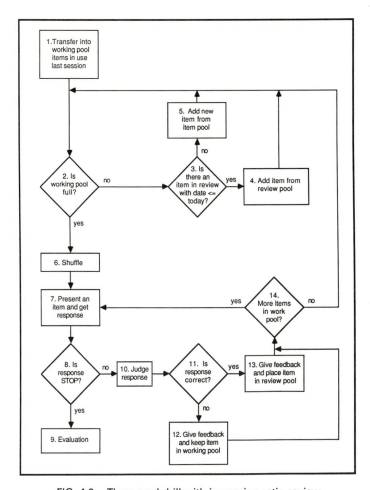

FIG. 4.6. Three-pool drill with increasing ratio review.

In order to construct a drill with increasing ratio review it is necessary that each item in the review pool have a review date associated with it. This review date indicates when the item is next to be reviewed. Figure 4.6 shows a drill structure with increasing ratio review. When the learner begins a practice session, any items left in that learner's working pool from the last session are transferred from the disk to the current working pool. The working pool is shuffled and the items in the working pool are presented to the learner. If the learner gives a correct response to an item the item goes into the review pool. If an incorrect response is given the item remains in the working pool. Steps 3–5 show how the working pool is replenished. The procedure first checks to see if there are any items in the review pool that are ready for review (Steps 3 and 4).

113

An item is ready for review when its review date is equal to or less than the current date. Otherwise, the replacement item is a new item from the item pool (Step 5).

PROGRESSIVE STATE DRILLS

Progressive state drills represent a further expansion of three-pool drills with increasing ratio review. The term *progressive state* is used to describe the drill since items are presented to the learner in a progressive sequence passing from one presentation state to another based on performance criteria for each state. Figure 4.7 shows a flowchart for a progressive state drill. In this drill items are presented in six different states. These are:

1. *Pretest* state—used to determine if the learner already knows the item
2. *Rehearsal* state—presents item and response simultaneously on the screen for a brief moment to allow learner to associate them together. The learner is then asked to type in the correct response.
3. *Drill* state—presents the item and prompts learner for correct response
4. *First Review* state—identical to how item was presented in drill state
5. *Second Review* state—same as first review state
6. *Third Review* state—same as first review state

Each item in the drill has a state number associated with it. This state number indicates the current state of the item and determines the presentation state in which the item will be presented. When the learner begins a practice session any items left in the learner's working pool from the last session are transferred from the disk to the current working pool (Step 1). Review dates and state numbers corresponding to each of the items are also transferred from the disk. If the working pool is not full, then additional items are selected from the review pool if there are any review items which have review dates less than or equal to today's date (Steps 3 and 4); otherwise additional items are selected from the new item pool (Step 5). After the working pool is shuffled (Step 6), the first item is selected and its state noted (Steps 7 and 8). If the item has just entered the drill as a new item, it will be presented as a pretest item (State 1). If the learner responds correctly to the item, it will be deleted from the system. Otherwise, its state will be updated to State 2. The value of the item counter (N) is then incremented, and the second item from the working pool is selected (Step 7 again). This item is presented in accordance with *its* specified state. After all the items in the current working pool have been presented once (N > 7), the working pool is replenished and shuffled (Steps 1–6), and the item counter (N) is set back to 1 (Step 7). This process is repeated until the learner terminates the practice session.

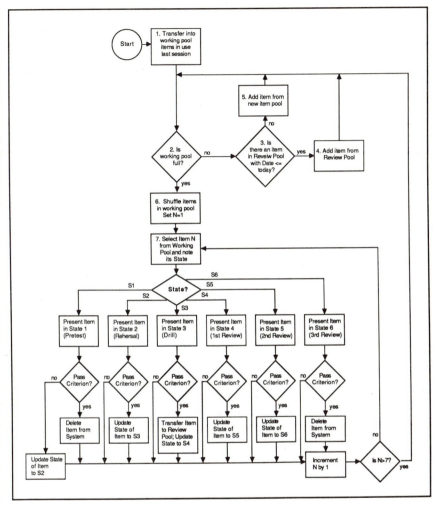

FIG. 4.7. A progressive state drill. Adapted from Atkinson (1974).

Note that after an item is presented in State 3 (drill), it is removed from the working pool and transferred into the review pool. The review pool is divided into three states to provide *spacing of review*. For example, in State 4 the review item may be presented after one day. In State 5, after two days, and in State 6 after a week. The spacing between the reviews is somewhat arbitrary. Spaced review has been shown to be effective (Gay, 1973), but further research needs to be conducted to establish the most effective spacing. The age, ability level of the learners, and the subject matter will influence the spacing decision.

It should also be noted that separate criteria can be established for allowing an

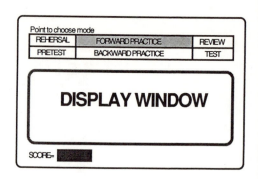

FIG. 4.8. Practice display which allows student to select mode.

item to move from one state to the next. The criteria could be set such that an item would move to the next state after it had been answered correctly a certain number of times or a certain number of times in a row. The most effective criteria would need to be determined empirically through formative evaluation.

Some progressive state drills are structured so that the learner can select the particular state or mode in which to practice the items. All items that have not been mastered in that state are presented until the learner chooses another state. The learner may select the state from a menu such as that shown in Fig. 4.8.

In the display shown in Fig. 4.8, practice items and feedback messages are displayed on the main area of the screen in the area labeled "display window." The practice modes are displayed on the top part of the screen. This allows the learner to change to a new practice mode at any time during the drill. The decision to allow the learner to select the practice mode should be made with caution. Most learners do not choose well when given the opportunity to select strategy unless they receive appropriate advisement (Tennyson & Buttery, 1980).

VARIABLE ITEM INTERVAL DRILLS

Variable item interval (VII) drills (Alessi & Trollip, 1985; Seigal & Misselt, 1984) appear to be another way to effectively provide practice for factual information type items. VII drills begin with a list or queue of items to be learned. If the learner responds incorrectly to an item, the future positions of that item in the queue are altered so that the item will be presented several more items to the learner.

For example, suppose the content to be learned was a list of Spanish/English vocabulary words. At the start of the drill the queue of items might be arranged as shown in column 1 of Fig. 4.9. Notice that in order for the learner to go all the way through the queue, the learner will have to respond correctly to each item

Original Queue of Items	Altered Queue of Items After Learner Commits Error on Item a. (Note that Item a will now reappear at positions 3, 6, and 10).
Item a	Item A
Item b	Item b
Item c	Item a
Item d	Item c
Item e	Item d
Item f	Item a
Item g	Item e
Item h	Item f
Item i	Item g
Item j	Item a
Item a	Item h
Item b	Item i
Item c	Item j
Item d	Item b
Item e	Item c
Item f	Item d
Item g	Item e
Item h	Item f
Item i	Item g
Item j	Item h
	Item i
	Item j

FIG. 4.9. Original and altered item queue for a single missed item. (An uppercase letter represents a missed item.)

twice (since each item appears twice in the queue). Now suppose the learner makes an error on the first item. The item is then re-queued at positions 3, 6, and 10 (see column 2, Fig. 4.9). This will cause the item to appear again after one intervening item, then again after two more items, then again after three items. If the learner were to respond incorrectly to an item the second time, the queue positions would again be altered. The effect of VII queuing is that after an item is missed it is quickly presented again to the learner, and then re-presented less frequently as long as the learner responds correctly to it.

DRILLS FOR INTELLECTUAL SKILLS

In addition to drills for factual information, computer drills are also used to provide practice for intellectual skills such as concept learning, rule using, problem solving, or using procedures. This section describes computer-based drill strategies for intellectual skills.

Drills for learning skills differ from drills for learning factual information in that, in the case of an intellectual skill what is being learned is the ability to perform the skill in response to a variety of problems. This is different than learning particular pieces of factual information. In concept learning, for example, it is not the particular instances of the concept which are to be learned, but rather the ability to identify instances not seen before as examples of the concept. Because of this, a variety of instances must be used in the drill to illustrate each concept. In rule using or in learning procedures, the rule or procedure being learned must be applied successfully to a variety of problems in a variety of situations.

Constructing a drill for concept learning requires that a large number of instances, representing both examples and nonexamples of the concept are included as part of the computer program in order to provide learners with a continuous amount of *previously unencountered* instances of the concept. Previously unencountered means that the instances have not been used previously as part of the initial instruction or in past practice activities.

For any concept there may be countless instances, all of which share the same critical attributes which define the concept even though they may vary in attributes not critical to the concept. The instances presented in a concept learning drill should be selected based on the critical and noncritical attributes they each possess. For example, in a practice drill for the concept *triangle* the learner might be presented with various shaped objects and asked to select the objects which are triangles. Each triangle should differ in nonrelevant attributes so that the learner is forced to focus on the critical attributes of a triangle and not just memorize a particular triangle. The nonexamples presented should be *matched* to the examples to focus on the critical attributes present in the examples but absent in the nonexamples.

Figure 4.10 shows the basic structure of a drill for practicing intellectual skills. The difference between this diagram and the diagram shown earlier in Fig. 4.1 is that the term "stimulus material" is used to refer to the items or problems presented to the learner. In a concept learning drill, the stimulus material presented to the learner is a set of instances and noninstances of the concept or concepts being practiced. These instances and noninstances can be either displayed simultaneously on the screen (i.e., display a set of triangles and nontriangles and ask

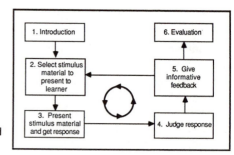

FIG. 4.10.   The general structure and flow of a drill for skill learning.

learner to indicate which are triangles) or they can be displayed one at a time in a series (i.e., present a geometric shape and ask learner to indicate whether or not it is a triangle, then present another shape, and so on).

Similarly, a drill for practicing the application of a rule or procedure must present a continuous number of unique problems or situations to which the learner is to respond. There must be enough problems in the item pool to prevent the learner from getting them right simply by memorizing the answers to those particular problems.

Another difference between drills for factual information and drills for intellectual skills is the type of feedback given to the learner. In factual information drills, learners need only be told the correct answer as feedback for an incorrect response. Drills for intellectual skills need to provide more informative forms of feedback. In the case of concept learning drills, the learner should be informed as to why the instance is or is not an example of the concept. The feedback might include a restatement of the definition or characteristics of the concept for the learner to review. In the case of rule using drills, the feedback might include a restatement of the rule and a demonstration of its correct application showing the learners where they erred in applying the rule.

Rather than giving learners this type of informative feedback each time an error is made, some drills are programmed so that learners are given informative feedback only when they request it. An example of this would be a rule using drill which has been programmed in the form of a game. When learners correctly apply the rule they advance in the game. In this case, it may not be necessary to provide informative feedback except when the learner requests it.

The diagram in Fig. 4.10 described a drill for practicing a single concept, rule, or procedure. What about the case where a number of concepts, rules, or procedures are to be learned and practiced as part of the curriculum? One option is to employ *subdrill grouping* and simply construct separate drills for each concept or rule. Learners can go through the series of subdrills and review old drills in a systematic manner. The various subdrills may be selected by the learner from a menu such as that shown in Fig. 4.11. This menu shows which

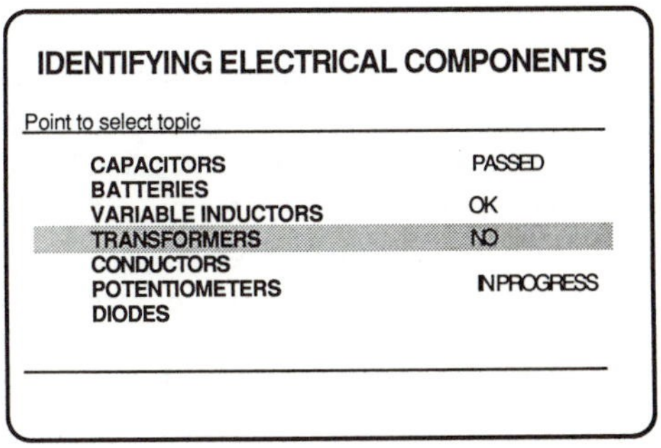

IDENTIFYING ELECTRICAL COMPONENTS

Point to select topic

CAPACITORS	PASSED
BATTERIES	
VARIABLE INDUCTORS	OK
TRANSFORMERS	NO
CONDUCTORS	
POTENTIOMETERS	INPROGRESS
DIODES	

FIG. 4.11. Student menu for selection of subdrills.

subdrills (or topics) are available and also provides a message to the learners about their performance in each subdrill. Five levels of information are provided. "PASSED" means that the learner completed the topic with no errors and in the time limit. "OK" means that the learner completed the topic with no errors but exceeded the time limit. "IN PROGRESS" means that the learner made only 1 or 2 errors on that topic the last time through, and "NO" means that the learner made more than two errors. No message means that the learner has not attempted that topic. When the subdrill grouping technique is used it is valuable to provide a display which shows the subordinate or superordinate relationships between the various subdrills. It may also be advisable to restrict learners from working on drills for which they have not mastered all drills which are at a subordinate level. The advantage of the subdrill grouping technique is that the drills are easier to construct than are drills that attempt to integrate the various topics into a single drill.

Constructing drills that integrate more than one topic, concept, or rule can be done in a variety of ways. One method is to introduce new concepts one at a time in a systematic manner. For example, consider a drill on the concepts of *triangle, square, rectangle,* and *irregular shape.* Learners may be drilled on the concept of *triangle* until they achieve a predetermined level of mastery. At this point the concept of a *square* is introduced along with triangle. Once learners are able to identify instances of triangle and square, the concept of *rectangle* is introduced. These three concepts are then drilled together until learners master them, at which time the concept *irregular shape* is introduced into the drill. At each stage in the drill it is important that the previously mastered concepts continue to be presented for the purpose of review, however they can be presented less often as new concepts are introduced.

Various mathematical models have been employed in order to provide the optimal frequency of review and timing for introduction of new material. Atkinson (1974) prescribed a mathematical optimization technique based on *optimal control theory.* Optimal control theory was used as a means to specify how a given learner's response history should be used to make ongoing adjustments in the drill. Atkinson's mathematical model makes adjustments in the drill based on two factors: (a) the ability of the particular learner, and (b) the difficulty of the particular item, concept, or rule. An estimate of the learners ability is obtained by analyzing that learner's response record on all previous items. An estimate of the item's difficulty is obtained by analyzing performance on that particular item for all learners. As can be seen, use of such a model produces a practice scheme which is much more than a simple branching program based on the last response. Rather, what is produced is a program that continually adjusts the drill based on the student's complete response history.

A different approach to optimizing the drill process has been used by Tennyson (Tennyson, Christensen, & Park, 1984). Tennyson's model, referred to as the Minnesota Adaptive Instructional System (MAIS), uses Baye's theorem of conditional probability as a basis for making ongoing adjustments in a drill. For each individual student, various pretask student learning characteristics (such as ability and performance scores on previous drills), are used to compute a probability for learning a given task or content. This initial probability figure is continuously adjusted during the student's session based on performance data continually being collected during the session. This strategy thus uses both pretask measures and actual performance data to continually adjust future instructional presentations. The presentation of the material is adjusted in four major ways: amount of instruction, sequence of instruction, instructional display time, and difficulty level.

A typical sequence for an adaptive concept learning drill would be as follows: (a) when a correct response is made the next example is randomly selected, (b) when an incorrect response is made, the next selected example is from the concept the student thought the previous example was from. Also, students may be required to respond to items across several levels of difficulty before going on to a new concept.

DRILLS FOR THE AUTONOMOUS STAGE

As mentioned in the first part of this chapter, some skills need to be practiced to the point where they become automatic to the learner. Automatic, in this case, refers to skills that do not require much of the learner's attention and which can be carried out simultaneously with other functions (Bahrick & Shelly, 1958; LaBerge & Samuels, 1974).

The process of skill automatization usually comes about as a result of a great deal of practice over a long period of time (Bloom, 1985, 1986). Attempting to use CAI programs as a means to aid the process of automatization is a relatively new endeavor. Research on this endeavor has been reported in Lesgold (1983), Schneider (1982), and Salisbury, Richards, and Klein (1985). Drills for the autonomous stage basically involve having the learner perform the skill under mild speed stress and under a low, then moderate, then high *secondary task workload*. By secondary task workload is meant a second task which the learner is required to perform while continuing to perform the original task. A performance drop would be expected when the secondary task is initially introduced. Eventually, though, performance of the primary task should return to its original level, even in the presence of the secondary task. The secondary task might be a higher level, more complex skill of which the original skill is a subpart. Or, in some cases, the secondary skill may not be directly related to the original skill, such as a counting task, a digit canceling task, or a computer game.

INTELLIGENT VERSUS NONINTELLIGENT DRILLS

Intelligence in a CAI program refers to the degree to which the computer responds like a expert teacher or tutor might respond in the same situation. The expertise held by the teacher or tutor should not only include expertise about the content, but also expertise about optimal instructional strategies, learning theory, and instructional psychology. An intelligent drill, then, would be one that responds to the learner much like a teacher or tutor who possesses expertise in these various areas would respond (see Section IV of this book for a more elaborate discussion of these issues).

The more sophisticated drill strategies described in this chapter (such as the progressive state drill, the variable item interval drill, and concept learning drills) might be described as "intelligent" drills in that they are constantly adapting future instructional presentations based on a continuous process of collecting and analyzing student performance data. Drills that simply follow the same preset sequence for each learner would be considered "nonintelligent" drills. Much more remains to be done to incorporate additional aspects of intelligence (such as techniques for intelligent understanding of English, speech, pictures, or sketches) into computer-based drills.

WHICH DRILL STRATEGY TO USE

This chapter has described computer-based drill strategies that range from relatively simple drill paradigms to very sophisticated and complex drill structures. In considering the question "Which drill strategy should be used?" several things must be considered. First of all, as has been shown, strategies that are appropriate for practicing information such as facts, names, labels, or associations differ a great deal from strategies that are appropriate for skill learning. The first consideration, then, in selecting the appropriate strategy, is to determine if what is to be practiced is factual information or if it is an intellectual skill.

A second consideration in selecting a drill strategy is the sophistication of the learners in terms of their own learning skills. If the learners in the target population possess good learning strategies of their own, then a simple drill without systematic review and one that uses subdrill grouping may be adequate. In this case, the learners will be left to handle review on their own and to integrate into a coherent whole the material from the various subdrills. On the other hand, if the learners do not possess good learning skills of their own it may be necessary to construct a more sophisticated drill which will provide systematic review, integration of material, and adapt the presentation to individual learners based on student performance data.

An additional consideration will be the amount of programming time and expertise available. Creation of the data storage and analysis routines and sophisticated logic required for the more complex drill structures demand a great deal more programming time and expertise than do the simpler drill strategies. Some programming tools, such as CONDUIT'S *Drill Shell* are available to aid in the development of drill programs.

ADVANTAGES OF COMPUTER-BASED DRILLS

The computer certainly shows great potential as a means to optimize the practice process. Use of the computer as an instructional medium can allow instructional designers to incorporate into the practice process many psychologically sound techniques and procedures such as systematic review, spaced review, and informative feedback. Computer-based drills also can make practice more interesting and engaging through competition, use of graphics, reinforcement, and variations in presentation. Computer-based drills also provide for easy updating of material or representation of equipment that may change rapidly. The various methods of introducing new items in a systematic way, monitoring progress of individual learners, adjusting the instructional presentation based on student performance data, and timing learner responses and other features discussed in this chapter are nearly impossible to implement with other media.

Another reason for using computer-based drills relates to the issue of automaticity discussed in this chapter. The only way a skill becomes automatic is through an extensive amount of practice, usually extending over a long period of time. It is difficult for teachers to provide sufficient practice to assure that all students automatize important subskills. Computer-based drills can provide the type and amount of practice necessary to produce automaticity.

REFERENCES

Alessi, S. M., & Trollip, S. R. (1985). *Computer-based instruction: Methods and development.* Englewood Cliffs, NJ: Prentice-Hall.

Atkinson, R. C. (1974, March). Teaching children to read using a computer. *American Psychologist, 29*(3), 169–178.

Bahrick, H. P., & Shelly, C. (1958). Time sharing as an index of automatization. *Journal of experimental psychology, 56,* 288–293.

Bloom, B. S. (Ed.). (1985). *Developing talent in young people.* New York: Ballantine.

Bloom, B. S. (1986, February). The hands and feet of genius: Automaticity. *Educational Leadership, 43,* 70–77.

Fitts, P. M., & Posner, M. I. (1967). *Human performance.* Belmont, CA: Brooks Cole.

Gay, I. R. (1973). Temporal position of reviews and its effect on the retention of mathematical rules. *Journal of Educational Psychology, 64,* 171–182.

LaBerge, D., & Samuels, S. J. (1974). Toward a theory of automatic information processing in reading. *Cognitive Psychology, 6,* 293–323.

Lesgold, A. M. (1983). A rationale for computer-based reading instruction. In A. C. Wilkinson (Ed.), *Classroom computers and cognitive science.* New York: Academic Press.

Salisbury, D. F., Richards, B. K., & Klein, J. D. (1985, April). *Prescriptions for the design of practice activities for learning: An integration from instructional design theories.* Paper presented at the annual meeting of the American Educational Research Association, Chicago.

Schneider, W. (1982). *Automatic/control processing concepts and their implications for the training of skills.* (Final Report No. HARL-ONR-8101). Washington, DC: U.S. Government Printing office.

Seigal, M. A., & Misselt, A. L. (1984). An adaptive feedback and review paradigm for computer-based drills. *Journal of Educational Psychology, 76*(2), 310–317.

Tennyson, R. D., & Buttrey, T. (1980). Advisement and management strategies as design variables in computer-assisted instruction. *Educational Communication and Technology Journal, 28,* 169–176.

Tennyson, R. D., Christensen, D. L., & Park, S. I. (1984). The Minnesota adaptive instructional system: An intelligent CBI system. *Journal of Computer-Based Instruction, 11*(1), 2–13.

5

Promoting Cognitive Processing and Learning by Designing the Learning Environment

William E. Montague[1]
Navy Personnel Research and Development Center San Diego, CA

BACKGROUND: THE ENVIRONMENT FOR LEARNING IS THE PROPER FOCUS OF DESIGN

The purpose of this paper is to present the view that planning to use computers for instruction is secondary to planning or designing a course of instruction in a broader sense. Important heuristics that can help the design process were generated many years ago. They provide a functional, use context model for instruction. They are consistent with advice for teaching derived from recent research and instructional theorizing. The primary idea is that the instructional environment must represent to the learner the context of the environment in which what is learned will be or could be used. Knowledge learned will then be appropriate for use and students learn to think and act in appropriate ways. Transfer should be direct and strong.

The design of the learning environment thus may include clever combinations of various means for representing tasks and information to students, for eliciting appropriate thought and planning to carry out actions, for assessing errors in thought and planning and correcting them. I take the view that the task of the designer of instruction is to provide the student with the necessary tools and conditions for learning. That is to say, the student needs to learn the appropriate language and concepts to use to understand situations in which what is learned is used and how to operate in them. She or he needs to know a multitude of appropriate facts and when and how to use them. Then, the student needs to learn

---
[1]The opinions and assertions are the author's and should not be construed to represent that of the Navy Department or the Defense Department.

how to put the information, facts, situations, and performance-skill together in appropriate contexts. This *performance-* or *use-orientation* is meant to contrast with formal, *topic-oriented* teaching that focuses on formal, general, knowledge and skills abstracted from their uses and taught as isolated topics. Performance- or use-orientation in teaching embeds the knowledge and skills to be learned in the functional context of their use. This is not a trivial distinction. It has serious implications for the kind of learning that takes place, and how to make it happen. Highly interactive, simulation-like, representations will be important for learning. Obviously, computer-based systems can be used for such simulations.

Competent performance of complicated tasks develops slowly, and requires an environment that supports the development of subskills, knowledge, and their coordination. Anyone who intends to design instruction has a substantial orchestration problem on their hands. It requires consideration of the process and progress of learning, not merely of simple tasks, but of representative complex tasks of a realistic sort. It requires analysis of competence or skill and breaking it into manageable, and appropriate chunks for students to learn. It requires sophisticated techniques for using environmental resources to provide a learning environment. It also requires understanding of the uses to which the competencies will or can be put. This description seems to me to be a fair rendition of the problem faced by anyone attempting to design instruction no matter how it is to be accomplished. Although utilizing computer-based technologies in this effort can help both design of instruction and its delivery, it can provide additional difficulty. What I suggest in this paper is adopting a functional, performance-oriented perspective or framework to guide the design and development efforts and keeps them coherent. Research evidence suggests that this should facilitate student cognition, learning, and transfer.

To accomplish this goal, attention must be given to the design of *learning environments*. Designing learning environments to promote *directly* the appropriate cognitive processes is a somewhat different focus for instruction design from the emphasis on learning abstract bodies of knowledge typical in most schooling. Schooling often leaves it to the learner to infer whether, when, and how to use the knowledge later. The current focus derives from attempts to devise more effective practical instruction in vocational, industrial and military education and training where efficiency and job/task relevance is important (Foley, 1978, Montague & Wulfeck 1986). Furthermore, it receives support from research and modern theories of cognition and learning (Fredericksen, 1984). A similar "cognitive apprenticeship" model for teaching has been recommended recently by Collins, Brown and Newman (1987).

The design process involves a substantial effort in analysis and specification of what must be learned, and decisions, based on experience and educational and psychological knowledge, about how to "best" accomplish the instruction given current constraints in resources. Therefore, the primary issue is specifying the learning environment, content and student interactions. After that come decisions about implementing the design using computer-based and other technologies.

HEURISTICS FOR THE LEARNING ENVIRONMENT

To organize the discussion I use some *heuristics* proposed many years ago to guide instruction (Prosser & Quigley, 1949). They were called "principles for vocational education" and were first published in 1925. I prefer the word *heuristic* to *principle* because they are general guides, not principles that can be validated. They don't always work. Their effectiveness can be overwhelmed by other variables or factors (cf. Schneider, 1985). Practice, for example, does not always yield learning in situations where performance complexity overwhelms a student's attentive capacity.

Table 5.1 represents my distillation of the principles of Prosser and Quigley. Notice the importance placed on the replication of the working or performing environment for teaching. They call for a learning situation that simulates appropriately a "working environment." The environment requires students to actively integrate and use skills and knowledge appropriately. Designing appropriate simulations is not simple, and is probably where computer-based instruction can have a most important role. One problem for designers is the fidelity of the simulation. Instruction needs to be adaptive to the learner, both in terms of what she or he brings to the course, and learns in it. They emphasize the importance, for both development and instruction, of the subject-matter expert. Implicit here is the notion that he or she should know how to communicate the knowledge and how to monitor student progress.

TABLE 5.1
Heuristics for Functional Context

● Replicate working environment in training

--same operations
--same tools
--same machines
--same thinking & manipulations

● Adapt training to trainee

--intelligence, aptitudes
--interests

● Give frequent practive

--enough to develop skill

● Use "expert" trainers who know the job

--to design training
--to teach

From Prosser and Quigley (1949/1925), *Vocational education in a democracy*. Chicago, IL: American Technical Soceity.

Their advice provides an important perspective for contriving learning environments and for evaluating them. Also, the perspective contrasts considerably with that I infer to be typical in schooling from the characteristics of most instruction, including computer-based instruction. Schooling tends to emphasize the basic knowledge and skills taught as abstract material or performance unrelated to situations in which the skills or knowledge might be used. There has been considerable recent concern that a problem in education is the lack of connection between what is learned in school and work and life generally. Schoolroom learning does not transfer straightforwardly. A change in perspective seems necessary.

The heuristics are similar to some recommendations for instruction made recently by cognitive scientists. Cognitive scientists are attempting to understand mental processes involved in learning and in performing important real tasks (e.g., solving algebra or geometry problems, developing complex skills in chess and mental arithmetic, learning to troubleshoot equipment) rather than the oversimplified laboratory tasks used a decade or two ago. In this work scientists suggest that learning involves the development of elaborate mental entities they call: frames, scripts, mental models, or schemas. These mental structures provide the means for organizing and reorganizing memory and in controlling performance (e.g., R. C. Anderson, 1977; Brewer & Nakamura, 1985; Gentner & Stevens, 1983). Whatever we call them, these schemas or mental models naturally evolve through the interaction of the learner in particular environments. They enable the learner to predict the outcomes of his or her actions, or the way devices operate, or decide approaches to problems. One generalization from this work is that it is important to provide a learning environment that promotes the development of appropriate and accurate mental models or schemata. This sounds much like the advice from Prosser and Quigley.

Some cognitive scientists attempt to construct intelligent tutoring systems (e.g., Anderson, Boyle, Corbett, & Lewis, 1986; Sleeman & Brown, 1982). In doing so they must become intricately involved in the design of instruction. They must analyze task content and student knowledge. They devise computer programs for evaluating the development of knowledge and skill, as well as programs for analyzing errors, inferring reasons for the errors, and providing corrective feedback to explain the materials and correct the errors. The attention to the details of the teaching and learning processes provides an improved understanding of tutoring and provides important guidance for designing instruction. In reviewing heuristics for instruction published by several cognitive scientists, I developed a synthesis of their recommendations. These are shown in Table 5.2.

The consonance of their recommendations with those of Prosser and Quigley lend credibility to the perspective. There are recurring themes. Students should learn to perform in a realistic situational context. Systematic analysis of performance is needed to do error analysis and corrective instruction. Teaching should not overload the student. New experiences are built on old. Students need to

TABLE 5.2
Synthesis of Heuristics

- Use a situational context
- Analyze tasks systematically
- Provide realistic practice
- Minimize memory load initially
- Analyze performance errors for causes
- Provide corrective feedback
- Develop students' self-monitoring skills

---

learn what good performance is so they can monitor their own performance. These cognitive and metacognitive processes and strategies are the organizers of competence. These are reasonable recommendations, and they have empirical support. But implementing them in instruction is a formidable job that can be aided by simulating a functional, work context for teaching and learning.

There have been attempts for many years to develop a technology for instructional development that emphasize job- or work-relatedness. For example, military-school course design has been done by using the rules and procedures of Instructional Systems Design (Branson et al., 1975; Montague & Wulfeck, 1986). Although this model, as well as similar models, recognize the importance of good design of instruction, they do not organize complex subject matter well. Training literature, often like its counterpart schooling literature, is topic-oriented, or theory/engineering oriented,not use- or performance-oriented (Foley, 1978; Kern, Sticht, Welty, & Hauke, 1976). For example, it reviews the principles and theory of radar, rather than discussing how to use it. Smith and Reigeluth (1982) suggested that at least part of the inadequacy of the materials developed to teach complex skills and knowledge can be attributed to the choice of subject matter and the *lack of a performance orientation*. They stated that the disorganization is a result of following an exhaustive, detailed, linear presentation, apparently with the objective of conveying stores of detailed information to be memorized so that it can be used at a later time. The approach, like much of schooling generally, ignores relationships among topics, requires a lot of brute-force memorization, overloads processing ability, provides no general context to help student understanding or information retrieval, and demotivates through tedium. Students learning in this kind of course are (implicitly) expected to discover a model to guide their competent performance of the task mostly from verbal descriptions (Bunderson, Gibbons, Olsen, & Kearsley, 1981). What seems to be lacking in the approach is the framework provided by requiring the functional context of the work environment to be used for deriving the teaching environment.

An alternate approach for developing instruction has been developed and tested in military training. It incorporates these recommendations directly. We

TABLE 5.3
Functional Context Training Assumptions[a]

1. All new knowledge is acquired on the foundations of old knowledge.

2. Knowledge can be used to learn new knowledge through "concrete" experiential learning, as in the early stages of the developmental model of literacy, and later through the "abstract" mediation of oral and written language. "Whole-to-part," or "familiar-to-unfamiliar" sequences can build on this developmental sequence, which can be replicated in presenting instruction to adults.

3. Knowledge development can be focused on somewhat restricted domains of learning, and in job-related technical or literacy training, or in multiple domains such as the grade school system. When time is limited, both technical and literacy training for work can be most expeditiously accomplished using knowledge (including processes) objectives closely related to the requirements of jobs.

4. Knowledge development requires active information processing by learners and, for maximum transfer from training to the next environment, information processing should use the contexts, tasks, procedures, and materials of the future in the present training environment. The best way to prepare the cognitive system for the future is to practice in the present. Obviously, to the extent the future is unknown, education and training cannot transfer.

5. Knowledge is used to process information and to comprehend it. Thus, for instance, "reading comprehension" can be improved by improving knowledge in the domain or domains to be read. This is what education in the various content or discipline areas accomplishes (among other things).

[a]From Sticht et al., 1986, pp. 175-176.

turn to it now. A basic tenet is that to facilitate transfer of learning, the learning environment needs to be designed based on environments in which what is learned must function. The environment must be adjusted to student knowledge and skill levels. Such adaptation is done to help learning. An instructional approach found to accomplish these aims is Functional Context Training (FCT) (Foley, 1978, refers to it as Task Oriented Training). Sticht, Armstrong, Hickey, and Caylor (1986) present a detailed review of FCT and several evaluations and attempt to synthesize the FCT approach. This FCT approach is proposed to help guide the development of instruction and to help with decisions about incorporation of computers into the process. In-so-far-as the FCT approach suggests learning environments that simulate the conditions and interactions required for task performance, computer-based instruction can play a significant role in implementation. Table 5.3 provides assumptions that underlie Functional Context Training from Sticht et al.

There are important advantages to be gained by using the functional context approach. It provides a system for developing competence that provides the appropriate framework to aid transfer nearly by default. Initial simplification of the context and tasks is done to make it understandable and to speed learning. The schemas needed for performing are used to provide organization for the knowledge and skills involved, to allow the learner to learn and practice his or

TABLE 5.4
Military Research Projects Evaluating the FCT Approach[a]

Year	Course	Less Attrition	Less Time	Better Achievement
1949	Basic Electricity/Electronics (BE/E)	yes	yes	yes
1954-60	BE/E for Field Radio	--	--	yes
1955-60	Radio Troubleshooting	--	--	yes
1964-66	BE/E for lower aptitude	--	yes	yes
1967-70	Medical Corpsman	--	fixed	yes
1967-70	Radio Operator	yes	yes	yes
1968-72	Field Wireman	yes	yes	yes

[a] Table adapted from Sticht et al. (1986), p. 121.

her roles. It is consonant with the general recommendations deriving from research in cognitive science and artificial intelligence (Table 5.2) but, specific training procedures still need to be elaborated. Modern method and theory often provides much better specification of how teaching should be done (e.g., Collins et al. 1987; Schneider, 1985).

There have been several experimental projects that have compared the performance-oriented, FCT approach with more standard training on training efficiency and transfer to the work situation. These are reviewed in detail by Sticht et al. (1986), and a summary is presented in Table 5.4. Courses were revised using the assumptions shown in Table 5.3 along with particular decisions about implementation that depended on the content and constraints of the course. Abstract theory was omitted, training became primarily hands-on rather than listening to oral lectures, reading materials were simplified and programmed for self-study. The context of the learning environment was modeled after the future work environment. In general, the results were positive. Attrition of students from the course was less where the comparison was possible. Similarly, training time was less where it was examined or allowed to vary. Achievement on-the-job was superior in all cases. Although the evaluation of the effects of the approach is oversimplified by the tabled information, the important point is made: modeling the learning context from the job, and carefully adapting instruction to the learner produces desirable effects on student learning and achievement.

Before continuing the discussion, a word of caution is in order. The tentative nature of the heuristics in the functional context scheme points up the need for more detailed theory about how to instruct particular tasks. Current theories are still tentative. Therefore, empirical evaluation of the decisions about how to instruct is needed continually. Detailed evaluation of the changes in student mental structures, reasoning, and other cognition is needed if a reliable technology is ever going to be developed. The findings from a few experimental projects, and the agreement between theorists regarding general heuristic recommendations is insufficient as technology. The details of instruction are the product of the skill, content knowledge, instruction knowledge, and creativity of the person(s) designing it. Those details and decisions need to be checked against student achievement and perhaps, even against management considerations. In the next section is an example of some materials prepared for an FCT course as an example of what might be done. Then a brief discussion of how computers might be used to help the process and some examples from some existing programs are given.

EXAMPLE OF FUNCTIONAL CONTEXT APPROACH

This section provides a brief outline of a recent small course developed for a beginning electronic technician to provide him or her with the basic competencies to go on into other advanced courses of apprenticeship on-the-job (Sticht et al. 1986). The development was intended to illustrate what a functional context course should look like, and is not a complete technician's course.

The course attempts to ease learning by using three techniques. Upon course entry initial learning is supported by using electrical devices familiar to the student to teach basic principles and concepts of electricity, and of procedures for equipment analysis. Next, for each electric device used, the instruction proceeds from direct manipulation of the device to see how it and its subcomponents work, to examining and devising block diagrams of the device and its components, and then to reading about and calculation of information related to knowledge about the device. This sequencing is viewed as concrete to abstract. The third technique constructs individual lessons and their sequence to directly transfer what has been learned from lesson to lesson. For example, troubleshooting of electrical equipment is taught directly in each module, thereby preparing students for jobs repairing equipment, and/or for advanced courses where such *basic* skills are often assumed.

The course is designed to provide the learning environment in which the students would develop the *mind* of a good technician. A good technician possesses systematic knowledge about how electrical and electronic equipment works, knows how to describe it, and knows equipment needed and procedures for diagnosing equipment failures. Enough theoretical knowledge of electricity is needed to support this reasoning but no more. Thus, the course explicitly aims at developing the appropriate mental models of equipment and analytic procedures for thinking about equipment systematically, to enable transfer to expected troubleshooting tasks. Several domains of knowledge are integrated together in the lessons: problem solving, basic electricity/electronics knowledge, device mental models, language processing, and mathematics. These are taught together and the student learns the appropriate skills of extracting appropriate information from tests on equipment, from manuals, from calculations in the context of realistic problems. Instructor lectures and demonstrations support the hands-on simulation of work environments.

The content and sequence of the course were organized into modules centered around pieces of equipment, and proceed from concrete to abstract, specific to general, from practice to theory, and from familiar to unfamiliar. Lessons within the modules build on and extend a student's knowledge base. Students explore each new device (module) in a hands-on fashion, then hear related discussion and a demonstration, and work with the instructor to learn how to analyze and think about the equipment as a *system* with particular inputs and outputs. Learners are taught that a system has subsystems, and that each of these has its own function. These together must all function for the system to function. A subsystem is composed of individual circuits, and these are made of individual components. Table 5.5 provides a representation of the equipment contexts (modules) concepts from basic electricity and test equipment used for checking function and troubleshooting. The equipment modules were chosen to be generally familiar to entering students, and were ordered, more or less, in familiarity, and for introducing different concepts and test equipment.

The course moves downward through each system and simulates the troubleshooting actions of an expert. Students must understand the function of each element of a system and its interrelation with other elements to be able to hypothesize about the location of faulty elements. Fault isolation logic is pursued to the level at which an element is replaced or repaired. When one module has been completed successfully, the equipment decomposed and fixed, a student moves on to the next system.

The course used no computer-based systems for delivery or management. Resources were unavailable for such implementation. Even with the brief characterization of the course made here, it should be apparent that microcomputers might be used in many ways in such a course. For example, simulations of the different equipment used for the hands-on actions could provide additional rapid practice on a greater range of problems than is easy to carry out using actual devices. Simulated practice in using test equipment could be provided more rapidly to ensure rapid buildup of skill. However, implementing such simulations requires substantial skill. Poor implementation could even interfere with student learning. In addition, students need to learn a considerable amount about physically manipulating the equipment, setting up and using the test equipment, and evaluating the results of tests. It is not clear when and how to best use simulations in courses. They might be used best later in the course after some of the basic concepts and skill with test equipment is assured. Performance testing could then be done, or perhaps rapid practice of troubleshooting could then be accomplished. Considerable development of instructional theory is needed before a principled system to guide the design process will be available. One effort to develop such a system is that by Schneider (1985). Until such guidance is available careful use of computers is recommended, and empirical justification of its use should be required (Montague & Wulfeck, 1984). In the next section, examples of how simulations have been implemented to help in teaching courses are given. These are currently being evaluated.

TABLE 5.5

Equipment Modules for FCT/ET Knowledge Domains[a]

	Basic Strategy for all Equipment				
Device Mental Models	Device as System	Input-Output Functional Analysis	Analysis into Sybsystems, Circuits, and Components		
Knowledge Domain	Flashlight	Table Lamp	Curling Iron	AC Adapter	Soldering Iron
Components/ Circuits	Batteries, Bulbs, Switches	Cords, Switches, Bulbs	Heating elements, Circuit boards, Resistors, Diodes, Switches	Transformer primary-secondary coils, Diodes, Bridge-Rectifiers, Electrolytic capacitors	NOTE: Soldering iron module developed especially to teach mathematics.
Basic Electricity Concepts	Conductance, DC circuits, Voltage, Current, Polarity, Open/Closed Circuits	Insulation, AC circuits, Resistance, Conductance, Polarity, Cycles	Ohm's Law, Tolerance, Cycles, Shorts, Rectification, Power Watts, Ohm's, Peak inverse voltage	Half/Full Rectification Inductance, Filtering, Capacitance, Bridge Rectifier, Ripple	Ohm's Law, Voltage, Current, Resistance, Power (calculations)
Test Equipment/ Procedures	Test Lamp, Continuity Checker, Voltmeter, Substitution, Isolation, Replacement	Continuity Checker, Volt/Ohmeter, Outlet Checker, Trouble-shooting	Oscilloscope (intro.), Volt/Ohmeter, Trouble-shooting	Oscilloscope (Use), Volt/Ohmeter, Trouble-shooting	Volt/Ohmeter, (Math.)

Other knowledge domains: Problem solving, Mathematics, Graphic Language processing

[a]Table adapted from Sticht et al. (1986), p. 218.

USING COMPUTERS FOR FUNCTIONAL, PERFORMANCE-ORIENTED INSTRUCTION

The availability of progressively more powerful microcomputer hardware at an affordable price is tempting industry, the military services, and schools to adopt computers for instruction. However, if one examines available instructional programs, or the ability to develop or author high quality instructional programs using existing systems, that temptation should be tempered by serious planning and evaluation of costs and effectiveness (see, Kearsley, 1983; Zemke, 1984, for discussion about when and why to use CBI). It should be apparent from the earlier discussion that a considerable effort is needed for development of instruction. It seems likely that in schooling, the model of instruction will incorporate teachers, peer interaction where appropriate, and computers in various combinations in the attempt to orchestrate performance-oriented training. Determining how these all go together requires considerable thought, knowledge, guesswork, and artistry. Following the guidance provided in the FCT approach can help the general planning effort, but the details will differ with content domains and resources. Microcomputers can be useful in performance-oriented instruction to help simulate aspects of tasks that need extensive practice, and to provide realism. They can also be used to do performance testing, to keep records and provide graphical demonstrations of system operation. The following sections gives examples of programs that may represent useful, performance-oriented instruction.

Ideally, CBI should provide a flexible and creative learning environment that adapts to student knowledge and understanding (cf. Jonassen, 1985). The computer's capability to simulate tasks and problems, and to carry on an interactive dialog with the student is not seen often in available CBI (Harmon, 1985). Such capabilities are needed to make the learning task like the situations in which what is learned will be used.

EXAMPLES OF INTERACTIVE PERFORMANCE-ORIENTED CBI

The knowledge about how students represent knowledge and solve problems can be combined with the capabilities in hardware and software to develop programs to aid cognitive processing appropriate for a domain and simulation-like interactions for CBI. The use of such simulations is increasing partly because of cost reductions in hardware, and partly because of the face validity of the simulations themselves. These programs are generative or intelligent, in that they produce instruction "on-the-fly," in response to student input.

Generative, intelligent CBI represents a departure from the bulk of instructional programs currently available on computer systems familiar to most people.

The idea is that the instruction is generated through interaction between some content or knowledge base, and programs that incorporate teaching methods, e.g., an instruction manager, and a monitor of the student's progress with the material to be learned. The subject matter and the instructional methods can be in separate programs. The interactions are not prestructured combinations of material and instructional strategy in the usual *Programmed Instruction* sense. Models of the expert allow prediction of problem solutions that can be compared with a student's solution for comment. The tutor model provides for interactive questioning or demonstration as appropriate. Finally, the student model provides a way for the program to compare particular interactions with those expected from students and monitor student progress through the content. Intelligent CBI has the goal of making the instruction resemble the interactions between a tutor and a pupil. In the examples to be discussed, techniques for representing the content or tasks to be learned are separated from techniques that represent the ''theory'' of teaching. The advantages are that programs can be refined independently and the system can be responsive to student idiosyncracies (see, e.g., Sleeman & Brown, 1982, for more extensive discussion).

The first example is the Computer-Based Memorization System (CBMS) under development at our Center (Crawford & Hollan, 1983). It is being developed as a program that can provide practice in learning large, associative databases of information. The programs that present materials and test students are separate from the database of associative information. The particular content in this example is factual information about Naval ships: their class (destroyers, cruisers, carriers, etc.) their characteristics (size, crew size, weapons, functions, etc.), their capabilities (range, speed, etc.). This knowledge base is important fundamental knowledge for Tactical Action Officers. To be able to make rapid tactical decisions, such information must be immediately retrievable from memory. Thus the retrieval needs to be automatic (see Schneider, 1985 for discussion of automaticity). The CBMS programs can be considered as part-task training to ensure that people have learned this information well, before proceeding to learn the higher level tasks that use the information. Therefore, a computer program was developed to be used in part of their course, that can provide extensive practice on the database of information.

Experience with using semantic networks as representations of declarative knowledge, plus the development of programming methods that allow structuring such networks in computer memory led to the development of ways of putting the content into a microcomputer. Then, management programs were constructed to be able to search through the knowledge base for related items. Using these programs, the interface to the student was developed as a variety of games like ''Twenty Questions'' or ''Jeopardy'' or ''Flash-card'' (Crawford & Hollan, 1983; McCandless, 1981).

The modularity of this approach allows the retrieval management programs and the game interfaces to be independent of the particular content. Other content

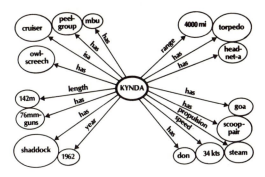

FIG. 5.1.   Example of a node (class: KYNDA) in the semantic network.

can be (and has been) substituted. Authoring programs simplify entry of a database into the system by nonprogrammers.

Knowledge base representation.   The game programs in this software system are designed to use only the information in the data base. No other information is programmed into the games. The information is arranged in the data base as a semantic network in which each object is a node. Figure 5.1 graphically portrays part of the data base. Nodes (objects) are connected by relations. For example, in our data base on ships, a (proposition) ⟨Kynda⟩ ⟨isa⟩ ⟨cruiser⟩ relates two nodes. A node may participate in any number of linkages. All nodes in the database are connected to at least one other object. Thus, a semantic network is created in which any two objects are related by some combination of links. Any content that can be expressed in this form can be substituted, i.e., is a, has a, property of, etc.

Access and retrieval functions.   Various functions and procedures are made available to game writers or instructional designers to retrieve and manipulate the information in the semantic network. For example, a frequently used procedure to find information involves giving the objects and a relation and the search returns a pointer to the link if it exists. Without going into detail, all the objects and relations can be retrieved from the database by the game writer or the user. All objects associated with ⟨Kynda⟩ can be listed. Figures 5.2 and 5.3 show other ways that the information about a particular object in the data base can be shown.

Interfacing to students.   The procedures and retrieval functions are used by several programs that present the learner with a variety of ''games'' to help him or her in learning the database. Figures 5.4 and 5.5 show displays at the beginning of a Twenty Questions game. In *Twenty Questions* the computer may select a list of objects in a category (e.g., cruisers) and from that one object that the student is to guess. The student is given 100 points at the beginning of the game,

137

```
                          KYNDA
                has            : owl screech
                has            : peel-group
                has            : scoop-pair
                has            : head-net
                has            : don
                has            : mbu
                has            : torpedo
                has            : 76mm guns
                has            : goa
                has            : shaddock
                range          : 4000 mi
                speed          : 34 kts
                propulsion     : steam
                length         : 142 m
                year           : 1962
```

FIG. 5.2. Description of a Russian cruiser Kynda retrieved from the data base. The items are characteristics: radars, weapons, etc., taken from the public documents.

and pays for answers to questions about the hidden item (e.g., does it have a xyz radar?). The student has commands to ask questions, see a description of any object, ask the computer for a hint, or a guess, ask for help. All these cost points. The goal is to develop a sufficient description to identify the object while maintaining a high score. The *Flash Card* game is a more straightforward interface with the student. Direct questions are asked about objects and their relations. The

```
LIST = <subject>           <relation>          <object>

<Kynda>                    <has>           : <owl screech>
<Kynda>                    <has>           : <peel-group>
<Kynda>                    <has>           : <scoop-pair>
<Kynda>                    <has>           : <head-net>
<Kynda>                    <has>           : <don>
<Kynda>                    <has>           : <mbu>
<Kynda>                    <has>           : <torpedo>
<Kynda>                    <has>           : <76mm guns>
<Kynda>                    <has>           : <goa>
<Kynda>                    <has>           : <shaddock>
<Kynda>                    <range>         : <4000 mi>
<Kynda>                    <speed>         : <34 kts>
<Kynda>                    <propulsion>    : <steam>
<Kynda>                    <length>        : <142> m
<Kynda>                    <year>          : <1962>
```

FIG. 5.3. All semantic "triangles dealing with ⟨Kynda⟩ ⟨relation⟩ ⟨thing⟩ from the data base.

138

```
PLAYER: You                              POINTS: 100

| Those with    | Those without  | list of relations | y/n |
|---------------|----------------|-------------------|-----|
| kirov         |                |                   |     |
| chapaov       |                |                   |     |
| sverdlov      |                |                   |     |
| sverdlov-cn   |                |                   |     |
| sverdlov-cg   |                |                   |     |
| kara          |                |                   |     |
| kresta-2      |                |                   |     |
| kresta-1      |                |                   |     |
| kynda         |                |                   |     |

Commands: G)uess, S)how, D)isplay, C)omputer guess, H)int, I)s-it-a?
```

FIG. 5.4.   Screen display at the start of a twenty-questions game.

student specifies a category and the computer formulates a question, e.g., "Cruising range of a Kynda is _____?" Again, the student can ask for help or hints, but it costs points. The goal of the game is to provide facility for the advanced student to drill himself about the database. Several other games have been developed as student interfaces to the database. All games record detailed "audit trails" regarding student performance, e.g., session number, student, date, start time, game, items asked, response time, etc. Figure 5.6 shows one of the possible audit trails for the Twenty-Questions game. These records provide the capability for comparing individual and group performance from one session to another. Particularly difficult parts of the database can be identified.

Simulation-based training.   As indicated in the discussion above regarding functional, performance-oriented instruction, computer-based instruction should take the form of simulations. Simulation has always played a role in instruction, and elaborate simulators have been used for training in aviation for many years (see Blaiwes & Regan, 1986). In aviation, tremendous effort has been made to attain high levels of physical fidelity in simulators, e.g., motion, 360° field of view, visual fidelity, etc. That high degree of physical fidelity might not be needed for training many tasks, and may even interfere with learning complicated skills. Another perspective is that cognitive and instructional fidelity may

```
PLAYER: You                              POINTS: 97

| Those with    | Those without  | list of relations   | y/n |
|---------------|----------------|---------------------|-----|
| averdlov-cg   | kirov          | has: tracking-radar | y   |
| averdlov-cn   | chapaov        |                     |     |
| kara          | sverdlov       |                     |     |
| kresta-1      | kresta-2       |                     |     |
| kynda         |                |                     |     |

Commands: G)uess, S)how, D)isplay, C)omputer guess, H)int, I)s-it-a?
```

FIG. 5.5.   Screen display after one guess in a twenty-questions game.

```
------------------- begin session 5 ------------
Name > James Kirk
Date > 2-12-80
Time > 10:15
Session > 5

***** begin game 1 *****

Database > db_cruisers
Player > James Kirk
looking for >            kirov

clock starts

alternatives > 9

Guess >                  has : scoop-pair        dif= 17.4s.

alternatives > 0

Computer guess(2) >   has : tracking-radar    dif= 60.4s.

Comment > Charting unexplored database (crew on edge)
Comment > Find myself becoming confused until number of
Comment > alternatives is reduced to three or less

alternatives > 4

Hint >                   has : fire-control-radar dif= 18.8s.

Show >                   kresta-2

alternatives > 4

Guess >               Is-it-a : kresta-2       dif= 7.3s.

alternatives > 3

Guess >               Is-it-a : kirov          dif= 8.3s.

Final time :  3.92 mins
Total of guesses : 3
Total of regular guesses : 3
Total of hints : 1
Total of computer guesses : 1
Total of shows : 1
Answer > kirov
Final score > 53 points

******* end game 1 *********
------------------- end session 5 ------------
```

FIG. 5.6.   Sample audit trial for a twenty-questions game.

be more important concepts in some instances. Students need to be taught the appropriate cognitive models and processes to enable them to reason about devices or systems. Parts of tasks may need to be broken out and trained separately to reduce complexity and speed learning. Small computers can support interactive representations of tasks and systems that allow the required reasoning processes to occur, or can allow slow development of complex skill, or provide large amounts of time-compressed practice.

140

FIG. 5.7. Drawing of Steamer display screens.

As one example of this approach examine Fig. 5.7. It displays a drawing representing a computer-based training system being developed at our Center called Steamer (Hollan, Hutchins, & Weitzman, 1984). It is a system designed to help students in understanding a steam propulsion system. The system consists of a graphical interface to a simulation (mathematical model) of a 1200 psi propulsion system. The training device provides a variety of abstract views of the propulsion system that are designed to show students representations or mental models that experts use to reason about the steam plant. The idea is that by directly providing the graphical displays, it might be possible to decrease the length of time it takes to understand the system. The graphical interface to the mathematical model provides students with an easy and natural means of inspecting and manipulating the plant simulation. The other display helps the student to select the particular aspect of the simulation he or she wants to view and enables selection of various states. The simulation is displayed as animated diagrams that can be manipulated by the student. Components such as valves, switches, and pumps can be operated and the effects can be observed on plant parameters such as changes in pressures, temperatures, and flows. In Fig. 5.7 the left display shows one of the engineroom displays. The engine lube oil system is shown graphically in Fig. 5.8. The tutorial part of Steamer is being developed piece by piece into the intelligent tutor desired. It currently includes an explanation generator to show how components work, one for teaching basic physics principles, and one to provide guidance on plant operating procedures. The mathematical

BASIC STEAM CYCLE

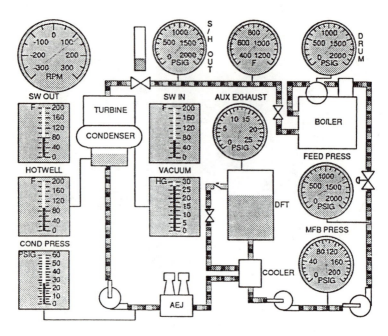

FIG. 5.8. Basic steam cycle schematically portrayed normally in color. This view is a global view of a system distributed throughout the plant. The boxes shown within the pipes are used on the color screen to provide animation of flows.

model (simulation) was translated into LISP and the other components have been developed in that language. The interface is a color graphics terminal that dynamically shows the functioning of the steam plant and an alphanumeric terminal to allow students/instructors to select material to be shown. It runs currently on a stand-alone computer running the LISP programming language.

Another simulation-like program is the Maneuvering Board Trainer that is being used as a classroom trainer to help in training students in the solution of ship navigation problems. In this task, the operator normally receives information from a radar, on which contacts are located by distance and compass angle from his "own" or "reference" ship in the center. Thus, the motion is "relative" to his own ship, and it reveals nothing about movement in geographic space. The operator must translate the relative motion information *in his head* to geographic movement. This is especially important where several ships are maneuvering or where land masses are nearby. The system is designed to teach students to understand the translation between relative and geographic motion. It

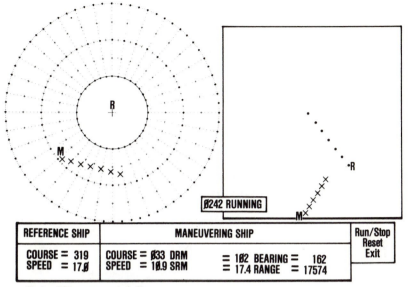

REFERENCE SHIP	MANEUVERING SHIP			Run/Stop Reset Exit
COURSE = 319 SPEED = 17.0	COURSE = 033 DRM SPEED = 10.9 SRM	= 102 BEARING = 162 = 17.4 RANGE = 17574		

Start and Stop movement of ships

FIG. 5.9. Relative motion display of reference ship (R) and maneuvering ship (M) on left with geographic plot shown on the right. Ship movements are plotted dynamically. Student controls the display using the menu on the right.

accomplishes this by showing a side-by-side plot of a simulated radar plot and an absolute geographic plot.

Figure 5.9 depicts a simulation where the reference ship is heading northwest (319°) at 17 knots, and the maneuvering contact is on course 033° at 10.9 knots. The Direction of Relative Motion (DRM) is 102° and relative speed (SRM) is 17.4 knots. The direct bearing and range are shown also, and these figures change as the problem progresses. To the bottom right is the student's menu that controls the simulation; she or he uses up or down arrow keys to choose a line, and selects it by pressing the spacebar.

The program can generate problems by choosing contact angles, actual course and speed, or the student can do so. The system simulates the motion of several ships in a given problem so that the relationship between the two plots is made obvious. The system can be used as an interactive trainer, or as a classroom teaching aid for an instructor. The instructor could set up a problem and allow the computer to run it while he discusses important points of the exercise.

Students also have to learn to solve various navigational problems using a paper and pencil device called the Maneuvering Board. On it they plot the contact, measure distances, predict future positions, etc. Programs have been

143

Closest Point of Approach Problem

At time Ø21Ø, CIC reports a contact bearing 225 (T)
at 182ØØ yards. This same contact is reported bearing 2Ø7
degrees (T) at 158ØØ yards at time Ø22Ø.

	YOUR SOLUTION		SYSTEM SOLUTION
Bearing of CPA	⟩ 2Ø5	Incorrect	191
Range of CPA	⟩153ØØ	CORRECT	
Time of CPA	⟩ Ø222	Incorrect	Ø227

> See ship movements on the relative and geographic plots
> See solution on relative plot
> Get another problem of the SAME type
> Get a DIFFERENT type of problem

FIG. 5.10. Screen shows the presentation of a closest point of approach problem. Student inputs his/her calculated answers using the keyboard. The system then presents correct solution. Menu at bottom allows student to view the problem on the different plots, view the solution on the maneuvering board, or select another problem.

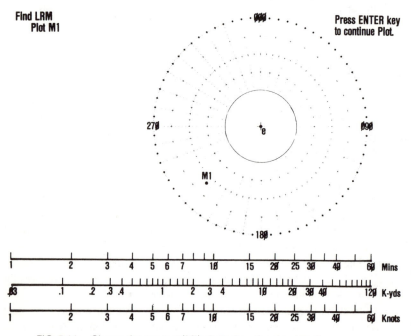

FIG. 5.11. Shows the contact (MI) plotted on the simulated maneuvering board. Note the nomographs at the bottom used for calculating speed and time.

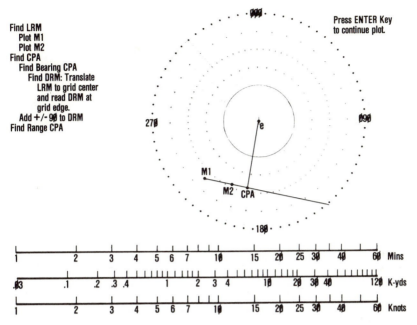

Find LRM
  Plot M1
  Plot M2
Find CPA
  Find Bearing CPA
  Find DRM: Translate
    LRM to grid center
    and read DRM at
    grid edge.
  Add +/- 9Ø to DRM
Find Range CPA

Press ENTER Key
to continue plot.

27Ø

Ø9Ø

ØØØ

18Ø

e

M1

M2   CPA

| Mins | 1 | 2 | 3 | 4 | 5 | 6 | 7 | 1Ø | 15 | 2Ø | 25 | 3Ø | 4Ø | 6Ø |

| K-yds | Ø3 | .1 | .2 | .3 | .4 | 1 | 2 | 3 | 4 | 1Ø | 2Ø | 3Ø | 4Ø | 12Ø |

| Knots | 1 | 2 | 3 | 4 | 5 | 6 | 7 | 1Ø | 15 | 2Ø | 25 | 3Ø | 4Ø | 6Ø |

FIG. 5.12. Shows a view several plots later in the solution of the closest point of approach problem. Each step in the solution is printed in the top-left quadrant, and as points or lines are drawn on the plot they blink.

developed that train students in solving problems of various sorts like those in the regular course. Figure 5.10 shows a "closest point of approach" problem posed by the computer. This type of problem is typical and frequent. If another ship on its course will get too close evasive action is needed. That knowledge is needed in time to get the massive own ship on a safe alternate track to avoid danger.

A student can **either** solve or not solve the problem on the paper and pencil Maneuvering Board, enter the bearing, range and time values, and then the program does the calculations and shows the correct figures. The student can then choose any of the alternatives shown in the menu window. She or he can view the same problem on the relative plot (see Fig. 5.9), or watch the computer solve the problem step-by-step graphically on a relative plot that is similar to the paper Maneuvering Board.

In the step-by-step solution the simulated Maneuvering Board is shown (Fig. 5.11) graphically on the screen and the first contact is plotted (M1). It blinks during the plotting. Then each step in the procedure is plotted in the appropriate sequence and shown in the list at the left, and the lines and points are plotted on the graphic display. Figure 5.12 shows the sequence up to finding the range of the closest point of approach. In Fig. 5.13 the solution is complete, the bearing range and time of the closest point of approach have been found. Now the student

145

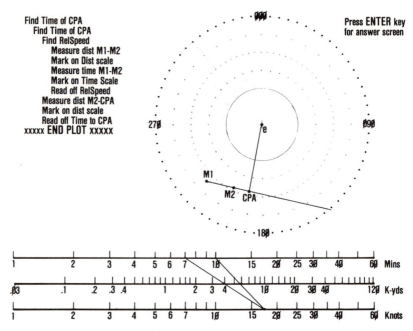

FIG. 5.13. Shows the completed solution of the problem with the use of the nomographs to calculate the time and distance of the closest point of approach.

returns to the answer window, and then can exit or have the computer generate another problem.

DISCUSSION

Adopting a functional context, performance-oriented strategy in instruction provides a strategic advantage in schooling. It should enhance learning and transfer. By starting with the working environment and designing the learning environment to resemble and simulate it, has decided practical advantages. Foremost among these is that what is learned in schools is more relevant, and is perceived by students as relevant. The scheme has obvious utility for practical instruction, but it should not be considered only for vocational or occupational use. Mathematics and science education might benefit substantially from implementation of a more use-oriented framework for instruction (see Abelson & DiSessa, 1981, Bork, 1981, for more discussion). Similarly, Collins et al. (1987) suggest that this sort of approach should be viewed as cognitive apprenticeship, and that they provide detailed examples from reading, writing and mathematics.

The use of computer-based instructional systems as tools to help in implementing instructional programs has obvious value. However, programming interactive instruction to provide students with situations that helps them develop needed subskills is still difficult. Similarly, task simulations are hand crafted and expensive. Therefore, their widespread use will be slow. Programs like the CBMS discussed earlier, can be standardized and distributed for widespread use since they can be used for different content. At NPRDC with the help of computer scientists at the University of Utah, we have been attempting to prepare a library of programs, proper user documentation, and easy methods of authoring new content into the instructional programs. These programs are intended to be used by instructors to develop computer–based instruction for use in their classrooms.

Commercially available programs may or may not fit into the requirements of an instructional program. Only careful analysis of the programs, and/or student's use of programs can determine a program's fitness. Selections are often based on publicity and cosmetics rather than on an analysis of the skills and knowledge imparted by the instruction. At present, there is little performance-based evidence to guide selection of available programs, although some general guidance has been attempted (e.g., Kearsley, 1983).

For constructing microcomputer-based simulation, considerable support for providing graphical representation of systems is necessary. Several workers have developed graphics editors to allow easy preparation of interfaces for instruction (see Hollan, Hutchins, & Weitzman, 1984; Hutchins, Hollan, & Norman, 1986; Towne et al., 1986). Such efforts will lead to important tools for developing performance–oriented instruction. Schneider (1985) at the University of Pittsburgh is also developing tools for instructors to help them build simulation-like instruction.

The thesis proposed in this paper is straightforward. Important positive effects on instruction are possible by changing the orientation used in planning the programs. By adopting a performance orientation rather than a topic orientation, instructional development efforts should provide instruction that is organized appropriately to produce transfer. As long as care is taken to match presentations to students' knowledge levels, learning may be enhanced as well. It seems apparent that considerable skill is needed in analyzing performance and the knowledge required before decisions about teaching can be made with much confidence. There is not yet much of a technology for this. It also takes considerable analytical skill to determine what and how to represent to students using currently popular microprocessors. Their limited graphics capability make a lot of graphic, visual simulations either difficult or impossible. The lack of easy ways for teachers and subject-matter experts to prepare and try out sophisticated representations for teaching, is a serious impediment to the use of CBI. The quality of instruction depends on a combination of factors: the analysis of the need for instruction, and of the performance environment, from which a learning environment and what students are to learn are specified, the care taken in designing instructional interactions that ensure learning, and the capability of computer-based systems to incorporate the needed characteristics. Methods and trained people for carrying out the necessary design, development, implementation, and quality assurance will take time to develop. The use-oriented perspective can help in structuring the learning environment, in pointing out weaknesses in existing instruction, and in instructor training. But, don't expect rapid progress.

REFERENCES

Abelson, H., & DiSessa, A. (1981). *Turtle geometry: The computer as a medium for exploring mathematics.* Cambridge, MA: MIT Press.

Anderson, J. R., Boyle, C. F., Corbett, A., & Lewis, M. (1986). *Cognitive modeling and intelligent tutoring.* (Technical Report No. ONR-86-1) Pittsburgh, PA: Carnegie-Mellon University.

Anderson, R. C. (1977). The notion of schemata and the educational enterprise: General discussion of the conference. In R. C. Anderson, R. J. Spiro, & W. E. Montague (Eds.), *Schooling and the acquisition of knowledge* (pp. 415–431). Hillsdale, NJ: Lawrence Erlbaum Associates.

Blaiwes, A. J., & Regan, J. J. (1986). Training devices: Concepts and progress. In J. A. Ellis (Ed.), *Military contributions to instructional technology,* New York: Praeger.

Bork, A. (1981) Computer based instruction in physics. *Physics Today, 34*(9), 24–30.

Branson, R. K., Rayner, G. T., Cox, J. G., Furman, J. P., King, F. J., & Harnum, W. H. (1975). *Interservice procedures for instructional systems development.* (Technical Report NAVEDTRA 106A). Pensacola, FL: Navy Education and Training Command.

Brewer, W. F., & Nakamura, G. V. (1985). The nature and functions of schemas. In S. Chipman, J. W. Segal, & R. Glaser (Eds.), *Thinking and learning skills, Volume 3.* Hillsdale, NJ: Lawrence Erlbaum Associates.

Bunderson, C. V., Gibbons, A. S., Olsen, J. B., & Kearsley, G. P. (1981). Work models: Beyond instructional objectives. *Instructional Science, 10,* 205–215.

Collins, A., Brown, J. S., & Newman, S. E. (1987). Cognitive apprenticeship: Teaching the craft of reading, writing, and mathematics. In L. B. Resnick (Ed.), *Cognition and instruction: Issues and agendas.* Hillsdale, NJ: Lawrence Erlbaum Associates.

Crawford, A. M., & Hollan, J. D. (1983, January). *Development of a computer-based tactical training system.* (Special Report: SR 83-13). San Diego, CA: Navy Personnel Research & Development Center.

Foley, J. P. (1978). Instructional materials for improved job performance. *Journal of Industrial Teacher Education, 15*(4), 1–15.

Fredericksen, N. (1984). Implications of cognitive theory for instruction in problem solving. *Review of Educational Research, 54*(3), 363–408.

Gentner, D., & Stevens, A. L. (Eds.). (1983). *Mental models.* Hillsdale, NJ: Lawrence Erlbaum Associates.

Harmon, P. (1985, June). Instructional software: A basic taxonomy. *Performance & Instruction Journal, 24*(5), 9–10.

Hollan, J. D., Hutchins, E. L., & Weitzman, L. (1984). Steamer: An interactive inspectable simulation-based training system. *AI Magazine, 5*(2), 15–27.

Hutchins, E. L., Hollan, J. D., & Norman, D. A. (1986). Direct manipulation interfaces. In D. A. Norman & S. Draper (Eds.), *New perspectives on human-computer interaction.* Hillsdale, NJ: Lawrence Erlbaum Associates.

Jonassen, D. H. (1985, June). Interactive lesson designs: A taxonomy. *Educational Technology, 25*(6), 7–17.

Kearsley, G. P. (1983). *Computer-based training*. Reading, MA: Addison-Wesley.

Kern, R. P., Sticht, T. G., Welty, D., & Hauke, R. N. (1976). *Guidebook for the development of Army training literature*. (Special Publication: AD A033935). Arlington, VA: Human Resources Research Organization.

McCandless, T. (1981). *Computer-based tactical memorization system*. (Technical Note 81–8, March). San Diego, CA: Navy Personnel Research & Development Center.

Montague, W. E., & Wulfeck, W. H. (1984). Computer-based instruction: Will it improve instructional quality? *Training Technology Journal, 1*(2), 4–19.

Montague, W. E., & Wulfeck, W. H. (1986). Instructional systems design. In J. A. Ellis (Ed.), *Military contributions to instructional technology*, New York: Praeger.

Prosser, C. A., & Quigley, T. H. (1949). *Vocational education in a democracy*. Chicago, IL: American Technical Society.

Schneider, W. (1985). Training high performance skills: Fallacies and guidelines. *Human Factors, 27*(3), 285–300.

Sleeman, D., & Brown, J. S. (1982). *Intelligent tutoring systems*. New York: Academic Press.

Smith, J., & Reigeluth, C. M. (1982, May). *The structural strategies model*. (Technical Note: TN 82-18). San Diego, CA: Navy Personnel Research & Development Center.

Sticht, T. G., Armstrong, W. B., Hickey, D. T., & Caylor, J. S. (1986, February). *Cast off youth: Policy and training methods from the military experience*. San Diego: Applied Behavioral & Cognitive Sciences, Inc.

Towne, D., Munro, A., Pizzini, Q., Surmon, D., Johnson, M., Johnson, W., Rouse, W., & Hunt, R. (1986). *Development of intelligent maintenance training technology*. Los Angeles, CA: Behavioral Technology Laboratory, University of Southern California.

Zemke, R. (1984, May). Evaluating computer-assisted instruction: The good, the bad and the why. *Training, 21*(6), 22–47.

6

Integrating Learning Strategies into Courseware to Facilitate Deeper Processing

David H. Jonassen
University of Colorado at Denver

THE PROBLEM: SHALLOW PROCESSING IN COURSEWARE

Limitations of Computer Courseware

Presently, the majority of commercially available instructional microcomputer courseware is in the drill-and-practice mode (Cohen, 1983). The combination of tutorial and drill-and-practice represents as much as 85% of all commercially available courseware. The paradigmatic design of this courseware borrows heavily from alternative forms of programmed learning. In drill-and-practice courseware, information or problems, usually though not always in prose form, are presented on the screen, followed immediately by recall or recognition questions about the information. This form of instruction is primarily presentational because the interaction does not result in meaningful learning, but rather only in rote recall of information presented. The sequence of the presentation is usually linear like linear programmed instruction. Instruction proceeds sequentially from one frame to another requiring only minimal attention-level responding—"Press SPACE BAR to Continue" or immediate recall of information from the previous screen.

Based largely on the behavioral principle of connectionism, traditional drill courseware (see Salisbury chapter for more sophisticated drill-and-practice designs) assumes that enough practice ultimately produces correct performance. What should be of concern to the designers of this type of courseware is the level of learner processing produced by the practice embedded in the courseware.

Tutorial courseware allegedly reflects a dialog between the coursewriter and the learners. Tutorial courseware normally is designed to adapt the presentation of information and practice in some way, usually varying the presentation based on a learner's ability to comprehend the material or based on prior knowledge. The most common form of adaptation is remedial, in which learners are branched to remedial practice or recycled through previously presented material if they don't perform well. Such adaptations to learner's comprehension are a reincarnation of branching programmed learning. The nature of the interactivity is still usually recall and repetition of information presented on the previous screen (see Carrier & Jonassen chapter for alternatives to this adaptive design).

Drill-and-practice and tutorial courseware gradually are being supplanted by more sophisticated simulation, problem-oriented, and intelligent modes of tutoring. Designs for such courseware are assuming aspects of intelligence as a direct application of artificial intelligence research (Bregar & Farley, 1980; Weyer, 1984). For the near future, however, the microcomputer will remain a tutor, trapped by the popularity of designs which necessarily constrain the level of interactivity between the courseware and the learner. But why do these designs so constrain the level of interactivity?

Limits of the Programmed Learning/Mathemagenic Model

Tutorial courseware is basically a mis-application of the programmed learning model of instructional design, which has been the dominate paradigm in the field of educational technology for nearly 3 decades. Since the programmed learning model is easily confused with the procedure or technique of programmed instruction, it is better conceptually defined by the mathemagenic hypothesis.

Mathemagenic behaviors are "those student activities that are relevant to the achievement of specified instructional objectives in specified situations or places," that is, those which "give birth to learning" (Rothkopf, 1970). These behaviors, according to the hypothesis, can be controlled or manipulated by specific design attributes of instruction. The form or structure of instruction or the activities stimulated by it induce the necessary cognitive operations to produce desired learning. So, the instructor merely needs to specify the appropriate orienting, acquisition, and translation processes that most efficiently result in the acquisition of a specified skill or body of knowledge and then incorporate those learning activities in instruction. Such an approach presumes that learners will perform the activities, and that such performance will produce learning. The purpose of mathemagenic activities, such as inserted questions (the basis of programmed learning), is to control the way in which information is transformed and encoded into memory. It is therefore a reductive approach to learning (Jonassen, 1984a), which regards learners as active performers whose mental behavior should be strictly controlled by the activities imposed by the lesson.

Three problems with computer applications of the mathemagenic model exist and are discussed briefly: The model is no longer valid with regard to cognitive principles of psychology; the levels of processing normally produced by mathemagenic behaviors (especially in programmed learning) is too low or shallow; and the microcomputer technology has simply outgrown the mathemagenic/programmed learning model of learning.

Cognitive Principles of Psychology.   Based on principles of cognitive psychology that have in the last decade become almost universally accepted, we now make an entirely different set of assumptions about how learners process information than when behaviorism dominated learning theory. Rather than passively responding to instructional controls imposed by the author/designer/teacher while integrating stimuli of any sort, learners actually need to attend to stimuli, access existing knowledge to relate to it, realign the structure of that knowledge in order to accommodate that new information, and finally encode the restructured knowledge base into memory, which then becomes accessible in order to explain and interpret new information. The meaning that is generated by each learner for material they see is individual and cannot be controlled by the author. Rather it is constructed by the learner, using existing knowledge as the foundation for interpreting information and building new knowledge. Learning is not "a passive reception of someone else's organizations and abstractions" (Wittrock, 1974a). Instead, it is an active, constructive process. These cognitive principles of learning are not represented in the programmed instruction model or in the design or nature of learning activities embedded in most tutorial microcomputer courseware.

Levels of Processing.   Craik and Lockhart (1972) proposed that what gets encoded into memory depends on the level or depth of processing of the presented information as it is encoded into memory. Processing deepens on a continuum as one progresses from sensory to semantic processing. Assigning meaning to materials naturally entails semantic processing. Only deeper, semantic processing of information requires the learner to access prior knowledge in order to interpret new material. As the level of processing deepens, then, more information will be recalled because more meaning will be assigned to it. The activities embedded in courseware should begin to reflect deeper levels of processing. It is exactly this level of meaningful learning that is most frequently missing from tutorial types of courseware. The emphasis is on practice of associations in working memory based only on information recently presented in the courseware. In interacting with the tutorial courseware, learners are too seldom required to access prior knowledge in order to interpret the information that is presented.

Matching the Microcomputer.   A third problem with applying the mathemagenic/programmed learning model to instructional courseware design is that virtually all computer technologies, including microcomputers, have outgrown it. These technologies and those now evolving are clearly more powerful than the model can accommodate. Like our understanding of human learning, the capability of microcomputers to manipulate information have already stretched the mathemagenic model to its limits. Drill and tutorial courseware are frame-based. Each and every optional response needs to be anticipated and programmed into the courseware. Computers are capable of representing knowledge in ways that are more consistent with human learners (see Part IV for descriptions of more artificial intelligence designs). So, the use of microcomputers for iterative presentation-feedback cycles is an example of technological overkill. The design model needs to fit the technology.

The Future of Tutorial Courseware

There is little doubt that drill-and-practice and tutorial programs will continue to be published well into the future. Designers of this courseware should expand their conceptions of learning in order to accommodate more constructive conceptions of learning, that is, to include tutorial instruction which is more cognitively oriented, which requires deeper levels of processing, and which matches the capabilities of today's microcomputers.

SOLUTION: GENERATIVE LEARNING STRATEGIES

We accept that learning is an active, constructive process whereby learners generate meaning for information by accessing and applying existing knowledge. An instructional model that manifests these principles is the generative hypothesis. The generative hypothesis (Wittrock, 1974b, 1978) asserts that meaning for material presented by computers or any other medium is generated by activating and altering existing knowledge structures in order to interpret what is presented. The ammended structures are then encoded in memory as distinctive features that may be accessed later to explain or interpret new information. Comprehension, according to the generative hypothesis, requires the proactive transfer of existing knowledge to new material. Although this may sound simple enough, it actually depends on a complex set of cognitive transformations and elaborations which are unique to the learner. These processes are integral to such tasks as generating mental images, making inferences about information from existing knowledge, or retrieving information from memory.

Generative learning activities are those that require learners consciously and intentionally to relate new information to their existing knowledge rather than responding to material without using personal, contextual knowledge (the classic drill-and-practice paradigm). Examples of generative learning activities include generating mnemonic memory aids, notetaking, underlining, paraphrasing, summarizing, generating questions, creating images, outlining, and cognitive mapping. In these activities, information is transformed and elaborated into a more personal form that is more memorable to the learner. This type of cognitive activity is seldom used in tutorial software, which relies rather on short-term recall of presented information to complete constructed or discriminant responses. Such information is not properly integrated with prior knowledge, so it is less meaningful and therefore less memorable. It is the premise of this chapter that this type of activity should be included in courseware to raise (deepen) the level of processing of material by learners interacting with the courseware. The emphasis of instructional activities embedded in courseware should be on facilitating knowledge acquisition by making the learner processing more generative.

Learning Strategies as Generative Activities

The most consistently generative learning activities are learning strategies, which are designed to foster not only learning but also learning-to-learn (Brown, Campione, & Day, 1981). Learning strategies, sometimes referred to as cognitive strategies, are mental "operations or procedures that the student may use to acquire, retain, and retrieve different kinds of knowledge and performance" (Rigney, 1978, p. 165). Learning strategies are intended to increase the number of links between presented information and existing knowledge in order to enhance retention, that is, process information generatively. In presenting her information processing theory of instruction, Brunig (1983) has argued that learning strategies facilitate transfer of information from short-term to long-term memory regardless of whether they are internally generated or externally controlled. The rationale is simple: Learning is an individual, constructive activity, so learning activities need to allow for individual encoding of information rather than constraining the encoding process. Learning strategies are activities that foster the unique interpretation and encoding of information into memory. Because knowledge is mediated through student thought processes and not the medium itself (Clark, 1984), instructional design should focus on the thought processes activated by learning activities. Both research and cognitive theory support the need for training learning skills (learning strategies) directly as well as through instructional materials (Derry & Murphy, 1986). Learning strategies represent a new breed of educational technology, because they mediate learning more directly through their activation of meaningful thought processes (Jonassen, 1985).

Types of Learning Strategies

Learning strategies represent a wide range of cognitive activities that support learning. They include techniques that learners can be taught to use during instruction. The rationale for their use is that good teaching includes teaching students how to learn, remember, and think and how to motivate themselves

(Weinstein & Mayer, 1985). They describe eight categories of learning strategies, including basic and complex rehearsal strategies, basic and complex elaboration strategies, basic and complex organizational strategies, and affective and motivational strategies.

Many other activities may be classified as learning strategies. The graphic organizer in Fig. 6.1 illustrates the breadth of available learning strategies. At the most general level, learning strategies can be classified as primary or supporting strategies. Primary strategies act on the material to be learned directly, that is they represent information processing activities that affect the way learners relate to or process information. Support strategies are used to maintain a suitable learning climate (Dansereau et al., 1979a, 1979b).

Two types of primary strategies exist, material processing strategies and active study strategies. Active study strategies include study systems such as MURDER (Dansereau, 1978) or the popular SQ3R (Robinson, 1946). Material processing strategies include such study strategies as notetaking, underlining, and test preparation. Whereas active study strategies assume certain cognitive processing of materials, information processing strategies specify the processing activities more directly. For that reason, this chapter is primarily concerned with information-processing strategies.

There are four types of information-processing strategies; recall, integration, organization, and elaboration. As indicated in Table 6.1, recall strategies are primarily behavioral, verbal learning practices, such as chunking, organization, and practice. They concentrate on repetitive practice and organizational procedures designed to facilitate list learning, so performance does not generally transfer to other tasks. Although some mnemonic tasks are generative in nature, these strategies are less generative than information-processing strategies, which are more generative and therefore the focus of this chapter.

Integration and organization strategies are also referred to as recall and transformation strategies (Dansereau, 1978; Dansereau et al., 1979a, 1979b). They are processing strategies that facilitate the transformation of information into a more memorable form. Paraphrasing and exemplifying are important integration strategies, which are based on schema theory (Rumelhart & Ortony, 1977). They are intended to help learners integrate new information into existing schemata (accretion), rearrange those schemata (restructuring), or refine them (tuning) (Norman et al., 1976). These strategies are designed to help learners develop better knowledge structures. Exemplifying, paraphrasing, and metaphors are useful strategies for facilitating these processes. Covert and overt practice, if they require meaningful processing of material, can also facilitate it. Practice often tends to be more mathemagenic, though.

Organizational strategies are helpful in structuring and restructuring one's knowledge base, that is, seeing how ideas relate to other ideas. Organizational strategies require learners to manifest what they know and to analyze the relationships between those ideas. Categorization and outlining require learners systematically to compare sets of concepts. Procedures such as cognitive mapping

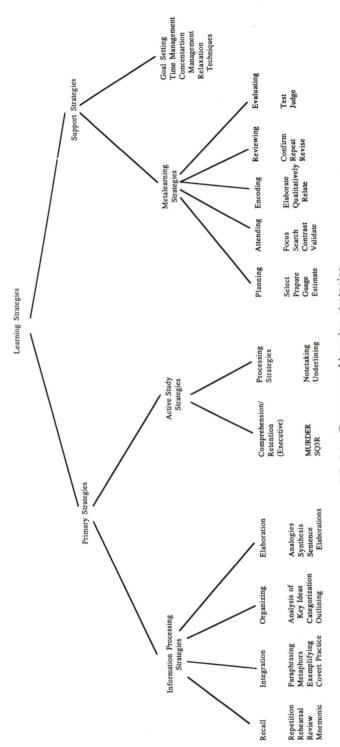

FIG. 6.1. Taxonomy of learning strategies.

157

TABLE 6.1
Information Processing Strategies

Cognitive Processes	Learning Strategy	Learning/Instructional Activity
	RECALL	
Behavioral theory Verbal learning Chunking Connectionism (practice effect)	Repetition Rehearsal Review Mnemonic techniques	Repeat processing, such as re-reading a text passage. Repetitive practice in recalling information without reorganization.
	INTEGRATION	
Schema theory Network memory theories	Paraphrasing Metaphors Exemplifying Covert practice Overt practice	Restate information in your own words. Generate additional examples of an event, objector, idea. Mentally practice learning behaviors. Complete practice activities (exercises).
	ORGANIZATION	
Associative memory Node-link model of long-term memory	Analysis of key ideas Categorization Outlining Networking Pattern noting Cognitive mapping	Identify key concepts, develop definitions, and compare with other concepts. Classify concepts according to taxonomy or class scheme. Develop hierarchical list of concepts found in materials. Identify nodes, classify links, and diagram, linking ideas to each other producing a map of concepts. Pairwise comparison strength of relationships and statistical scaling to produce a map.
	ELABORATION	
Dual encoding Encoding variability Schema theory Problem solving Higher order thinking skills	Imaging Analogies Synthesis Sentence elaboration Implications Drawing inferences	Mental images or create drawings that describe content. Complete analogies or generate own. Add descriptive information to make material more personally meaningful/understandable. State implications for personal fulfillment or for an event. Infer causes for outcomes/events.

or pattern noting require learners to produce spatial maps of what they know. Learning strategy systems, such as analysis of key ideas and networking require learners to do all of the above.

The final type of information-processing strategy is elaboration. In elaborating on presented information, learners add information which makes the material more meaningful. Generating mental or physical images, inferences, implications, analogies or sentence elaboration adds information to schemata being developed as well as relating new or developing schemata to existing ones.

In addition to primary strategies which operate on information directly, learners may also use a variety of support strategies. Support strategies are intended to "support" information processing by helping the learner to maintain a proper learning orientation. These include study system strategies such as goal setting, time management, concentration management, and relaxation techniques. While it is possible to embed some of these strategies in courseware, their general consideration is beyond the scope of this chapter.

Probably the most important support strategies include metalearning—"an individual's awareness, knowledge, and use of the monitoring of cognitive goals, experiences, and actions for the purpose of increasing understanding and retention of learned material" (Brezin, 1980). Metalearning is based on the principles of metamemory (Flavell & Wellman, 1977), which describe the learner's awareness of their ability to store and retrieve information from memory. Metamemory is specific to the trait characteristics of the learner, the nature of the task, and the specific strategy that a learner chooses to improve his memorization of presented information. Another conception of metalearning is a higher level "executive control" mechanism that allows learners to respond to different learning situations by selecting and implementing relevant lower level strategies. Both "executive and non-executive information processing" should be trained (Sternberg, 1983). Flavell and Wellman (1977) have found that more capable and mature learners are more adept at selecting and using appropriate strategies to monitor their storage and retrieval of information. So, in addition to processing information, better learners remain aware of (monitor) their learning more consistently.

Brezin (1980) has identified five classes of monitoring strategies (see Fig. 6.1); planning, attending, encoding, reviewing, and evaluating. Planning strategies include selecting (identifying learning goals), preparing (activating relevant memory schemata), gauging (determining difficulty or depth of processing required), and estimating (predicting the information processing demands of the task). Attending strategies include focusing (attending to material), searching (relating presented information to memory), contrasting (comparing presented information to memory), and validating (reconciling or confirming presented information with existing knowledge). Encoding strategies include elaborating (trying to link new information with existing knowledge) and qualitatively relating (linking new information with deeper levels of existing knowledge). These encoding strategies include many of the information processing requirements of integration strategies discussed earlier. Reviewing strategies include confirming (using new information), repeating (practice recall), and revising (elaborating on them as with elaboration strategies). Finally, learners may use evaluating strategies, such as testing (determining the consistency of new material) and judging (valuing the information). While many of these strategies overlap with information processing strategies, their function as metalearning or monitoring strategies is to monitor learning rather than to produce it. Brezin (1980) believes that they can be embedded into instructional materials to foster monitoring processes, thereby improving memory.

SOLUTION APPLIED TO COURSEWARE: EMBEDDING LEARNING STRATEGIES IN COURSEWARE

I assume, as does Brunig (1983), that learning strategies may be trained, that is, learners may acquire through instruction and practice the strategies presented above. Numerous research studies have verified the effectiveness of learning strategy training systems for improving learning (Dansereau, 1978; Dansereau et al., 1979a, 1979b; Weinstein, 1978). Learning strategies may be explicitly taught study skills (detached) or they may be embedded in the activities in instructional materials (embedded) (Rigney, 1978). When embedded within learning materials, such as courseware, control of the strategies used may vary along a locus of processing continuum (Allen & Merrill, 1985). Strategies may be embedded in the content so that learners must perform the mental operations in order to acquire the subject matter, such as a question that requires learners to relate new material to prior learning in order to solve a problem. Embedded strategies are an example of supplantation matching (Salomon, 1972), where the strategy is supplanted by the material. Learning strategies included in courseware may also be either detached or embedded. Strategies may be detached from the content and assigned by the system, such as explicit instructions to generate a question or form an image. Strategies also may be detached and selected by the student. A potential strength of detached strategies is their generalizability to other tasks, however, strategies training that is detached from subject matter normally does not transfer to learning situations beyond the immediate training environment (Derry & Murphy, 1986). That is, detached strategies do not contribute to the development of executive control. The role or effectiveness of detached metalearning or executive control training is simply not known. Probably the best compromise is limited training of detached strategies, including tactics or executive control training, followed by unobtrusive prompting in the normal course of instruction, an "incidental learning approach" (Derry & Murphy, 1986).

The simplest method for integrating strategies in courseware is to replace the adjunct, mathemagenic activities that are normally included as practice in courseware with specific information processing or perhaps metalearning strategies or prompting—depending, of course, upon the nature of the material, the stated objectives, and the type of learners involved. It is possible to include active study and support study strategies, however, such a discussion is beyond the scope of this chapter. For example, rather than inserting multiple-choice questions to test immediate recall or comprehension of information in a program, you might periodically insert any of the following directions: Summarize in your own words the ideas presented; recall and record key ideas and use them to create analogies, outlines, or cognitive maps; draw a picture or generate a mental image of the subject matter; or list the implications of the material that you are studying. How or where this information is recorded and how it is later used for review or integration are important, researchable design issues. This form of integration would be an example of a system-assigned detached or embedded strategy, depending upon the kinds of activities and directions given.

Microcomputer courseware is particularly amenable to the inclusion of such strategies, because of the accepted abilities of microcomputers to rapidly store, manipulate, and retrieve information. Presenting recall questions to learners and recording the percentage of correct learner responses doesn't exploit the capabilities of computers. Nor does it produce meaningful learning. The literature does not strongly support the effectiveness of adjunct questions in text (Lindner & Rickards, 1985). There is no rationale or empirical support for the belief that they work any better in courseware. The processing capabilities of microcomputers can be used more effectively to individually foster the information processing capabilities through generative learning activities. Strategies integrated into courseware can become an "electronic notebook" for storing, manipulating, and retrieving individual learner constructions as well as providing learners with valuable skills for processing similar information. In this way, the microcomputer can foster not only learning but also learning-to-learn.

INTEGRATING LEARNING STRATEGIES INTO COURSEWARE

A metaphor for considering the integration of learning strategies into courseware is the "electronic notebook," based on a paper notebook analog. The electronic notebook, because of the levels of processing it can generate, is more powerful than its paper analog. While there is "good evidence to suggest that notetaking can aid the learning process in certain situations and that reviewing one's notes can be a useful procedure" (Hartley, 1983, p. 13), notetaking strategies most often employed by learners tend toward rote recording of ideas with little reference to prior knowledge. This approach is clearly not generative. However, embedding generative learning strategies that require learners to integrate material with prior knowledge has been shown to improve comprehension even in paper/pencil tasks, so the principle is here being applied to an electronic notebook, which may be implemented in a microcomputer environment to foster more meaningful learning.

There are three reasons why system-assigned learning strategies should be successful. First, since tutorial-type courseware relies so heavily on rote recall, efforts to raise the levels of processing should produce greater comprehension of material. Second, the courseware can "force" deeper processing by making further presentation of material contingent upon responses of a certain type, length, or modality. It can also provide consistent, unobtrusive prompting or explanations of why strategies are being called in order to model the metacognitive decision making. With print notebooks, few if any constraints on their content or use can be exercised, so learners often employ the strategies that require the least mental effort, i.e., rote recording. Third, it should become obvious from this discussion that computer processing can make the use of these strategies easier for the student by performing many of the mechanical/numerical tasks for them, allowing them to concentrate on meaning. In adaptive courseware, providing for learner control of the amount of instructional stimuli (Park & Tennyson, 1980; Tennyson, 1980; Tennyson & Rothen, 1979) and sequence of instruction (Ross & Rakow, 1981), has generally resulted in less learning. While learner control is philosophically desirable, it depends on a level of metacognitive awareness rarely found in learners. The integration of metalearning strategies or advisement (discussed below) may well improve the self-selection of strategies among learners.

Model for Integrating Strategies

The electronic notebook may assume a variety of forms. A program block diagram for integrating strategies into courseware is shown in Fig. 6.2. Strategy subroutines or procedures are accessed from the main program block in which information or subroutines are being displayed. If strategies are system-assigned, the presentation of information will be interrupted at appropriate intervals and a relevant strategy will be called, requiring learners to respond to a strategy (some described later in the chapter). For learner assigned strategies, the program would activate an interrupt key (similar to a help key) which would interrupt the display, save the location of the display on the stack, and call a strategy subroutine or a strategy menu. The menu would provide the learner with optional strategy selections. The learner's choice would call the strategy subroutine. Metalearning training could be added to both system- or learner-assigned strategies by including advisement. After the display program is interrupted, either by the learner or the program, a strategy menu would be displayed. Advisement about which strategy should be chosen could be made by the system based on the nature of the task being learned or on the basis of characteristics of the learner. The information needed to make this decision (encoded in a procedure in the program (see Ross & Morrison chapter for an example) would need to be input prior to the program and called by the program. Advisement has been shown to improve strategy selection and consequent learning (Johansen & Tennyson, 1983; Tennyson & Buttrey, 1980).

INFORMATION PROCESSING STRATEGIES IN COURSEWARE

Information processing strategies may facilitate recall/rehearsal, integration, organization or elaboration of material presented in courseware. They all facilitate

```
Program block
    Present information, simulation, etc.
    Activate interrupt for strategy use
    Store current location on stack
    Call strategy subroutine (procedure) or strategy menu
    Present information, simulation, etc.

Strategy menu subroutine (procedure)
    Present strategy options available
    Call advisement subroutine
    Accept learner's choice
    Case structure of options
        Call specific strategy subroutine (procedure)

Advisement subroutine (procedure)
    Classify task requirement
    Classify learner characteristic
    Recommend strategies common to task and learner

Strategy subroutine (procedure)
    Present learning strategy task
    Accept responses
    Call disc storage subroutine (procedure)

Disc storage subroutine (procedure)
    Open port to disc drive
    Open file for learner responses
    Write (append) learner responses to file
    Close file and port
    Pull location off stack and return to program

Review subroutine (procedure)
    Open port to disc drive and open file
    Read responses
    Write to screen or printer
    Close file and port
```

FIG. 6.2.   Program block structure for embedding learning strategies in courseware.

recall and comprehension of presented material, so that what is committed to memory is well anchored and therefore more meaningful and memorable.

Integration Strategies in Courseware

Integration strategies require that learners access prior knowledge in order to integrate newly presented material with it. These strategies facilitate the building of personally unique but meaningful schemata for events, objects, and ideas.

Paraphrasing Strategy. Paraphrasing is perhaps the most straightforward integration strategy. It requires learners to recall all parts of the presented information and then to describe it in their own words. In doing so, learners presumably are required to access appropriate existing knowledge in order to interpret the presented material and then generate a description of what it means to them based on their updated knowledge structures.

This strategy can be implemented in courseware in a variety of ways. The simplest means would be to include it in the courseware program as a subroutine. At the end of each block or unit of an instructional presentation (graphics, text, or combination) or at any point in a learner-controlled environment the learner chooses to interrupt the flow, the program would call a paraphrasing subroutine. A simple BASIC language paraphrasing subroutine, written for the Apple II computer, is presented in Fig. 6.3. Essentially the subroutine consists of a simple text file handling sequence and a keyboard routine for constructing text. The

```
100   REM   **ESTABLISH FILE**
110 D$ =  CHR$ (4):R$ =  CHR$ (13)
120   HOME : INPUT "WHAT IS YOUR SURNAME? "; NAME$
130   PRINT D$;"OPEN "NAME$
140   PRINT D$;"CLOSE "NAME$
1000   REM   **PARAPHRASING SUBROUTINE**
1005   HOME :I = 0
1010   PRINT  TAB( 11)"PARAPHRASING MEANING": PRINT
1020   PRINT "YOU JUST SAW SOME INFORMATION ON THE ": PRINT "SCREEN.   TRY
TO REMEMBER ALL OF IT AND": PRINT "THINK ABOUT WHAT IT MEANT. THEN "
1025   PRINT "DESCRIBE WHAT IT MEANT ";: INVERSE : PRINT "IN YOUR OWN WORDS";
: NORMAL : PRINT ".": PRINT : PRINT "PRESS RETURN AFTER EACH THOUGHT."
1030   PRINT : PRINT "WHEN FINISHED, PRESS RETURN ON AN EMPTY": PRINT "LINE."
1100   POKE 34, 12: REM   **SET TOP OF SCREEN TO LINE 12
1110 1 = 1: PRINT 1;"": "::
1120   GOSUB 2000
1130   IF L$(1) = "" THEN VTAB (18): PRINT "YOU MUST REMEMBER SOMETHING. PLEASE
TRY":1 = 0: GOTO 1110
1140   IF L$(1) < > "" THEN GOTO 1110
1145   REM   **WRITE PARAPHRASE TO FILE**
1150   PRINT D$; "APPEND "NAME$
1160   PRINT D$; "WRITE "NAME$
1170   FOR X = 1 TO 1 - 1: PRINT L$(X): NEXT X
1180   PRINT D$; "CLOSE "NAME$
1190   TEXT : GOTO 5000
2000   REM   ** KEYBOARD ENTRY SUBROUTINE **
2005   GET A$: PRINT A$;: REM   **GET EACH CHARACTER AND PRINT IT TO THE SCREEN
2010   IF A$ =R$ THEN GOTO 2040
2020   L$(1) = L$(1) + A$
2030   GOTO 2005
2040   RETURN
5000   PRINT D$;"OPEN "NAME$
5010   PRINT D$;"READ "NAME$
5020 L = 0
5025   INPUT L$:L = L + 1
5030   ONERR  GOTO 5050
5040   GOTO 5025
5050   PRINT D$;"CLOSE "NAME$
5060   PRINT D$;"PR#1"
5070   FOR X = 1 TO L: PRINT L$(X): NEXT X
5080   END
```

FIG. 6.3.   Example of BASIC paraphrasing routine.

program creates a file, enables the learner to type in some text paraphrasing the meaning of some previously presented information, and then, near the end of the routine, prints out his or her paraphrasing on a printer. The learners' paraphrasing is retained on the disc and may be presented for on-line review by the learner or the teacher. These presentation options present some interesting research variables. For instance, the designer could make the paraphrasing which the learner recorded available for on-line review or make a hard copy available for off-line test review.

The directions could be elaborated to include virtually any response contingency the courseware author would want to impose. They could be written in any language normally used for producing courseware, including authoring systems. The primary advantage of the computer for presenting a paraphrasing strategy is that the original material is removed from the screen, which precludes referral to the presented material which occurs so frequently when paraphrasing from print text. The computer forces the learner to read for recall, that is, to access prior knowledge in order to interpret what is being viewed. Such a comprehension strategy is necessarily generative. Another advantage of microcomputer presentation is that learners cannot continue the lesson until they have responded. You could easily add program statements that evaluate the length of the paraphrasing or which look for certain key concepts to be included. The premise is that learners are obligated to process the information in a way that presumably entails more generative processing of the material.

Summary/Question Generating/Exemplifying Strategies. Using a subroutine similar to that in Fig. 6.3, you could easily alter the nature of the strategy employed. Simply by changing the directions (lines 1000–1060), you could direct learners to write a summary of presented material rather than paraphrasing. Whereas paraphrasing specifically requires the learner to relate the information to prior knowledge, writing summaries does not, although it has been shown to be an effective study strategy. Other effective strategies that could be integrated easily into the electronic notebook format would be to have learners generate new examples of or questions about the material rather than memorizing embedded examples or answering inserted questions (Frase & Schwartz, 1975). After presentation of material, learners would generate examples or questions about the material as if they were teaching or writing a test for their peers. These examples and questions could be written off to a disk file to be presented later to the learner for review—prior to rereading the material (as an organizer) or presented without the material as a retrieval aid. These questions provide an overt form of comprehension practice.

Organization Strategies

After ideas are integrated into the learner's memory, organization strategies facilitate the rearrangement or organization of those ideas, the part of the learning process that Norman et al. (1976) refers to as restructuring. Examples of these strategies include analysis of key ideas, categorization and outlining, mapping techniques such as cognitive mapping and pattern noting, and study systems such as networking.

Analysis of Key Ideas.   An important class of organization strategy involves the analysis of key concepts or ideas presented in the material. In such strategies, learners identify the key ideas, then systematically define and elaborate on them, and then interrelate them in some way. Text processing strategies involving analysis of key ideas sometimes use worksheets that specify the types of definitions and comparisons required (e.g., Diekhoff, Brown, & Dansereau, 1982). The worksheet format is easily adaptable to courseware, with the users' responses and interrelationships stored by the computer.

The analysis of key ideas is supported by the teaching strategy of direct, systematic vocabulary instruction (Jones & Friedman, 1983). Theoretical support comes from schema theory and advanced organizer research. Understanding important concepts and their interrelationships is the basis of comprehension. So, rather than including learning activities in courseware which exercise recall of isolated concepts out of context, integrating analysis of key ideas into your electronic notebook should assist learners in understanding and interrelating the important concepts that have been presented.

The first and perhaps most critical step in the analysis of key concepts is to identify them. All network representations of information include nodes which represent key concepts (Diekhoff et al., 1982). A primary decision here is whether learners should be required to select the key concepts from presented information or whether they should be identified by the courseware writer. After working through a unit of information, learners could be directed to recall all of the key ideas presented. Because this is such a critical stage in the learning process, some program assistance may ensure the inclusion of all important ideas. The courseware, for instance, could cue important concepts by presenting them in inverse or flashing (for really important concepts) type. Terms could be set out in headings or included in a special glossary of key terms. The courseware could also allow the learners to mark important terms while working through the presentation, perhaps by moving the cursor over a word which would be marked by the program and presented later (electronic underlining, as it were). Whatever method you choose, it should ensure the identification of the most important concepts. Without some help, learners may identify too few or perhaps too many concepts, which would lead to content structures that are too lean or too tedious and time consuming.

The next critical stage in building a semantic network of concepts, having identified its constituents, is to describe the links between those concepts. A method for doing this, suggested by the Node Acquisition and integration Technique (NAIT) (Diekhoff et al., 1982), is the completion of definition worksheets, which require learners to identify six types of relationships for each key concept; characteristics and descriptors, antecedents, consequences, evidence, subsets, and supersets. As information is encountered during reading, which relates in any of these ways to key concepts, learners fill it in on the worksheets. This could be easily implemented in courseware by using a "definition key," which permits the learner at any response point in the program to activate a procedure that presents a NAIT-like worksheet. This procedure would first set up a worksheet for the appropriate concept and allow learners to input information related to any of the six (or other) relationships. Figure 6.4 shows a heading of a Pascal program and a procedure for creating a NAIT-like text file of records for an instructional program on mammals. Each record represents a key concept and a set of elaborations. The Pascal record function is especially amenable to this sort of activity. After completing another record, the learners could then return to the main program to continue processing the information. The result of this activity would be a series of structured summaries of concepts (records) capable of providing links to each other. Research has shown that following training using this technique, learners produce more varied and complete concept definitions, integrate information better, and more consistently identify what is important in a passage (Diekhoff et al., 1982).

The NAIT method for comparing and contrasting concepts requires the use of a comparison worksheet, which is simply a sheet that presents two concepts side-by-side and requires learners to identify simultaneously the six relationships listed above for both concepts. This is intended to lead learners through a relationship-by-relationship comparison of the definitions of selected pairs of concepts. It could be integrated into courseware in the same way as the relationship-guided definition procedure presented earlier.

Hypertext.   Hypertexts are computer environments in which the text and graphics may be accessed in an order that is completely under user control. Hypertexts (Jonassen, 1986a; Nelson 1974, 1978) are nonsequential texts that are arranged in a node–link fashion which permits the viewer to explore text in a sequence which makes the most sense to the individual based on his or her existing knowledge base. The program creates multiple pathways (alternative structures or branches) so that the user may jump from any point in the text to another; she or he may ammend the text to make it more meaningful; or may initiate queries. An excellent microcomputer hypertext is Storyspace (Bolter, Joyce, & Smith, 1986). Storyspace represents a text's structure as a map or network of cells (see Fig. 6.5) which permits the reader to traverse that structure and examine text by pointing to cells she or he wants to explore (see arrow in Fig. 6.5). Storyspace provides for interactive fiction (creating a network of episodes), interactive critical reading of text, and notetaking and composition (the user can expand the structure). In Storyspace, "the reader becomes an author in the act of realizing the text as he reads" (Bolter et al., 1986).

PASCAL PROCEDURE FOR ANALYZING KEY IDEAS

```pascal
PROGRAM NAIT (INPUT, OUTPUT, Mammals);

TYPE   PhysChar = RECORD
                   Limbs, Teeth, Skull, Other:STRING [50];
                   END;
       SensChar = RECORD
                   Sight, Smell, Hearing:STRING[50];
                   END;
       BehavChar = RECORD
                   Reproductive, Feeding:STRING[50];
                   END;
       MammalRec = RECORD
                   Name:STRING[50];
                   Physical:PhysChar;
                   Senses:SensChar;
                   Behavioral:BehavChar;
                   Environment:STRING[50];
                   END;
VAR    Mammal:MammalRec;
       Mammals:Text;

(*************************************************************************)
PROCEDURE Update (VAR Mammals:Text);

BEGIN
    WITH Mammal DO
        BEGIN
            WRITELN ('Name of concept: ');
            READLN;
            WRITELN (Mammals, Name);
            WITH  Physical DO
                BEGIN
                    WRITELN ('Describe the limbs: ');
                    READLN;
                    WRITELN (Mammals, LIMBS);
                    WRITELN (Mammals, LIMBS);
                    WRITELN ('How many teeth? ');
                    READLN;
                    WRITELN (Mammals, Teeth);
                    WRITELN ('Describe the skull: ');
                    WRITELN (Mammals, Skull);
                    WRITELN ('Any other physical characteristics? ');
                    WRITELN (Mammals, Other);
                END;
                WITH Senses DO
                    BEGIN
                        WRITELN ('Describe its sense of sight: ');
                        WRITELN (Mammals, Sight);
                        WRITELN ('Describe its sense of smell: ');
                        WRITELN (Mammals, Smell);
                        WRITELN ('Describe its sense of hearing: ');
                        WRITELN (Mammals, Hearing);
                    END;
                WITH Behavioral DO
                    BEGIN
                        WRITELN ('How does it care for its young? ');
                        WRITELN (Mammals, Reproductive);
                        WRITELN (What does it feed on? ');
                        WRITELN (Mammals, Feeding);
                        END;
                    WRITELN ('What sort of environment does it live in? ');
                    WRITELN (Mammals, Environment);
                END
        END; (*Update Procedures*)
(*************************************************************************)
BEGIN (*Main Program*)
    REWRITE (Mammals, 'APPLEO:MAMMALS.TEXT');
    (*  Lesson Presentation *)
    Update (Mammals);
    (* Lesson Presentation *)
    Update (Mammals);
    (* Continued Lesson Presentation and Update of Text File *)
    CLOSE (Mammals)
END. (*Main Program*)
```

FIG. 6.4. Pascal procedure for analyzing key ideas.

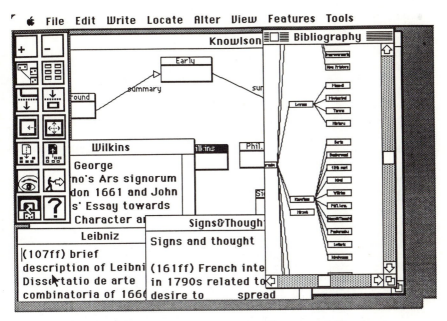

FIG. 6.5. Sample screen from hypertext, "Storyspace" (Reprinted with permission of J. Bolter).

Cross Categorization Matrix. An optional method for storing and comparing different dimensions of the interrelationships between concepts is to use a database management system (Jonassen, 1986b). Each record in the database would represent a key concept. Each field would represent one of the six (or other) relationships stated. The resulting database would represent the semantic network of concepts related to an instructional unit. Learners could search or sort on each field to group like or similar concepts. These groupings or any combinations could be printed out using the report function available in most systems.

Node–Link Classification. Another type of strategy for systematically analyzing relationships between concepts is to first identify the key concepts included in a lesson (or have the courseware identify them) and then identify and describe the possible links between the concepts. Learners would then be required to compare and contrast each pair by classifying the nature of the relationship between them (similarity, opposite, sequential, causal, supportive, part of, etc.). A list of those links could then be printed out for the learner or retained for later review. The BASIC routine shown in Fig. 6.6, included in courseware as a subroutine, first asks learners to identify the key concepts presented. These are then presented in pairs along with the algorithm for classifying the links. Learners select the best description of the relationship between each pair. A

```
100  REM  **ESTABLISH FILE**
110  D$ = CHR$ (4):R$ = CHR$ (13)
120  HOME : INPUT "WHAT IS YOUR SURNAME? ";NAME$
130  PRINT D$;"OPEN "NAME$
140  PRINT D$;"CLOSE "NAME$
1000 REM  ** DATA ENTRY **
1010 HOME :1 = 0
1020 PRINT  TAB(11)"RELATING KEY TERMS"L PRINT
1030 PRINT "YOU JUST COMPLETED A UNIT OF MATERIAL.": PRINT "IN THE INFORMA
TION YOU SAW, SOME IDEAS": PRINT "WERE KEY TO THE OVERALL MEANING OF THE"
1040 PRINT "UNIT. TRY TO REMEMBER EACH OF THOSE": PRINT "IDEAS. WHEN YOU
ARE READY, A NUMBER": PRINT "WILL APPEAR ON THE SCREEN. TYPE IN A"
1050 PRINT "TERM YOU REMEMBER AND PRESS RETURN.": PRINT "CONTINUE UNTIL
YOU CAN'T REMEMBER ANY": PRINT "MORE TERMS. WHEN FINISHED, PRESS RETURN":
PRINT "ON AN EMPTY LINE.": PRINT
1060 PRINT "    PRESS ";: INVERSE : PRINT "RETURN";: NORMAL : PRINT "WHEN
YOU'RE READY.": GET Y$
1065 PRINT : PRINT
1070 POKE 34, 18
1080 I = I + I: PRINT I;":";
1090 INPUT A$
1100 IF A$ = "" AND I  4 THEN PRINT "THERE ARE MORE KEY TERMS.":I + I - I:
GO TO 1080
1110 IF A$ = "" THEN GOTO 1200
1120 L$(I) = A$: GOTO 1080
1200 TEXT : HOME : PRINT "NOW THAT YOU HAVE RECALLED ALL OF THE": PRINT
"KEY CONCEPTS, WE NEED TO ANALYSE THE"
1210 PRINT "RELATIONSHIPS BETWEEN THEM. AT THE TOP": PRINT "OF THE SCREEN,
YOU WILL SEE 12 NUMBERED": PRINT "STATEMENTS DESCRIBING THE RELATIONSHIP"
1220 PRINT "BETWEEN TWO CONCEPTS - 'A' AND 'B'.": PRINT "UNDERNEATH THOSE,
YOU WILL SEE TWO": PRINT "TERMS WHICH YOU RECALLED, ONE 'A' AND": PRINT "THE
OTHER 'B'. DECIDE WHICH OF THE 12"
1230 PRINT "STATEMENTS BEST DESCRIBES THE": PRINT "RELATIONSHIP OF 'A; TO 'B'.
ENTER THAT": PRINT "NUMBER AND PRESS RETURN. YOU WILL THEN": PRINT "SEE A
STATEMENT WHICH REPEATS YOUR"
1240 PRINT "CHOICE FOR YOU TO CONFIRM."
1250 PRINT : PRINT "    PRESS ";: INVERSE : PRINT "RETURN";: NORMAL : PRINT "
WHEN YOU'RE READY."
1260 GET Y$
1300 HOME : PRINT "****************************************"
1310 PRINT "1. 'A' IS (ARE) THE SAME AS 'B'."
1320 PRINT "2. 'A' IS (ARE) SIMILAR TO 'B'."
1330 PRINT "3. 'A' IS (ARE) THE OPPOSITE OF 'B'."
1340 PRINT "4. 'A' DESCRIBE(S) OR IDENTIFIES 'B'."
1350 PRINT "5. 'A' IS AN EXAMPLE OF 'B'."
1360 PRINT "6. 'A' IS A PART OF THE LARGER 'B'."
1370 PRINT "7. 'A' & 'B' ARE EXAMPLES OF SAME CLASS"
1380 PRINT "8. 'A' PRECEDES 'B' IN A SEQUENCE."
1390 PRINT "9. 'A' FOLLOWS 'B' in a sequence."
1400 PRINT "10. 'A' CAUSES 'B'."
1410 PRINT "11. 'A' RESULTS FROM 'B'."
1420 PRINT "12. 'B' SUPPORTS OR DOCUMENTS 'B'."
1430 PRINT "****************************************"
1440 PRINT : PRINT
1500 POKE 34, 18:C = 0
1510 FOX X = 1 TO I - 2
1512 FOR Y = 1 TO I - X - 1
1513 C = C + 1
1515 PRINT " 'A'"," 'B'": PRINT
1520 PRINT L$(X),L$(X + Y)
1530 PRINT : PRINT "WHICH NUMBER BEST DESCRIBES THE ": PRINT "RELATION-
SHIP BETWEEN THESE";: INPUT R
1540 IF R = 1 THEN S$(C) = L$(X) + " IS THE SAME AS " + L$(X + Y)
1550 IF R = 2 THEN S$(C) = L$(X) + " IS SIMILAR TO " + L$(X + Y)
1560 IF R = 3 THEN S$(C) = L$(X) + " IS THE OPPOSITE OF " + L$(X + Y)
1570 IF R = 4 THEN S$(C) = L$(X) + " DESCRIBES OR IDENTIFIES " + L$(X + Y)
1580 IF R = 5 THEN S$(C) = L$(X) + " IS AN EXAMPLE OF " + L$(X + Y)
```

(continued)

FIG. 6.6. Example of semantic analysis subroutine in BASIC.

(Figure 6.6 continued)

```
1590  IF R = 6 THEN S$(C) = L$(X) + " IS A PART OF THE LARGER " + L$(X + Y)
1600  IF R = 7 THEN S$(C) = L$(X) + " AND " + L$(X + Y) + " ARE BOTH EXAMPLES OF
THE SAME CLASS."
1610  IF R = 8 THEN S$(C) = L$(X) + " PRECEDES " + L$(X + Y) + " IN A SEQUENCE."
1620  IF R = 9 THEN S$(C) = L$(X) + " FOLLOWS " + L$(X + Y) + " IN A SEQUENCE."
1630  IF R = 10 THEN S$(C) = L$(X) + " CAUSES " + L$(X + Y)
1640  IF R = 11 THEN S$(C) = L$(X) + " RESULTS FROM " + L$(X + Y)
1650  IF R = 12 THEN S$(C) = L$(X) + " SUPPORTS OR DOCUMENTS " + L$(X + Y)
1660  PRINT : PRINT S$(X)
1670  PRINT : INPUT "DO YOU AGREE? ";R$
1680  IF LEFT$ (R$,1) = "N" THEN  HOME : GOTO 1520
1685  NEXT Y
1690  NEXT X
3000  PRINT D$;"APPEND "NAME$
3010  PRINT D$: "WRITE "NAME$
3020  FOR X = 1 TO C: PRINT S$(X): NEXT X
3030  PRINT D$; "CLOSE "NAME$
3040  TEXT : GOTO 5000
5000  PRINT D$;"OPEN "NAME$
5010  PRINT D$;"READ "NAME$
5020  L = 0
5025  INPUT S$:L = L + 1
5030  ONERR  GOTO 5050
5040  GOTO 5025
5050  PRINT D$;"CLOSE "NAME$
5060  PRINT D$;"PR#1"
5070  FOR X = 1 TO L: PRINT S$(X): NEXT X
5080  END
```

statement expressing the pair and the relationship is then presented for confirmation. It confirmed, it is written off to disc for printing and later review. This is a simple but systematic way to require learners to think about the interrelationship of ideas, a necessary intellectual component in developing an adequate network of concepts for interpreting information. This strategy could be expanded or altered to include other functions, such as selecting pairs and creating analogies using a third term.

Cognitive Mapping.   With a more powerful microcomputer and a high level of programming and statistical skills, you could integrate into your courseware a very powerful learning strategy—cognitive mapping (Diekhoff & Diekhoff, 1982). Having identified the key concepts in your material, the procedure forms all possible pairs of concepts and requires learners to rate the strength of each relationship on a 1–9 scale, rather than classifying the relationship (as above). The procedure then forms a correlation-type matrix of values (Fig. 6.7a) which are scaled using a principal components or multidimensional scaling procedure. When plotted in two or three dimensions, it produces a map which spatially depicts the conceptual distance between all concepts included. See Fig. 6.7b for an example of principal components output for a psychology lesson (Diekhoff & Diekhoff, 1982). The programming and statistics are too complex to be considered here, but if implemented, the strategy is useful for showing the structure of relationships (i.e., structural knowledge).

	INTELLIGENCE	GENETICS	REINFORCEMENT	PREJUDICE	NEUROSIS	ATTITUDES	PUNISHMENT	INK BLOT TESTS	LANGUAGE
INTELLIGENCE	1.0	.8	.3	.5	.5	.4	.2	.1	.8
GENETICS		1.0	.5	.2	.6	.1	.1	.1	.8
REINFORCEMENT			1.0	.8	.4	.8	.9	.1	.8
PREJUDICE				1.0	.6	.9	.4	.2	.1
NEUROSIS					1.0	.7	.8	.9	.1
ATTITUDES						1.0	.7	.5	.1
PUNISHMENT							1.0	.1	.1
INK BLOT TESTS								1.0	.1
LANGUAGE									1.0

FIG. 6.7a. Intercorrelation matrix for generating cognitive map. (Diekhoff & Diekhoff, 1982, reprinted with permission of Educational Technology Publications)

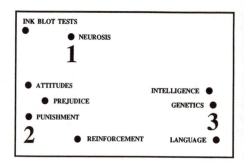

FIG. 6.7b. Cognitive map. (Diekhoff & Diekhoff, 1982, reprinted with permission of Educational Technology Publications)

Pattern Noting. Another strategy for systematically identifying and analyzing relationships among key concepts is to generate a pattern note and then classify each link identified. Pattern noting is a note taking technique (Buzan, 1974; Fields, 1982) in which learners identify the major topics in a lesson and show the linkages between them. Concepts are linked to each other by lines—sort of a spatial word association task. You start by identifying the key concept and free associating related ideas to which you associate other related ideas. The resulting map of interrelated concepts may then be semantically analyzed (Jonassen, 1984b) using a quasi-algorithm to help learners classify each link between the concepts included in the pattern note. An example of a similar concept arrangement strategy is the Concept Arrangement Scratch Pad (McAleese, 1985), a microcomputer routine which enables learners to create concept maps to depict their knowledge structures (see Fig. 6.8 for an example). A subset of a draw program could also be

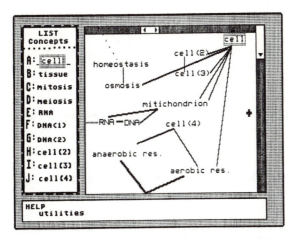

Knowledge & Information Mapping (KIM)
Concept Arrangement Scratch Pad (CASP)

FIG. 6.8.   Concept arrangement scratch pad. Reprinted with permission of R. McAleese.

used, which would use a mouse for locating the spatial position of each concept node and selecting the type of link between each concept from a selection box on the screen.

Elaboration Strategies

Elaboration strategies are those that require learners to add to the material presented, that is, elaborate or expand on it. In so doing, learners are adding personal meaning to the material, presumably because such elaborations require learners to access prior knowledge in order to interpret and expand on the information. These strategies assume a variety of forms which have implications for the electronic notebook.

Imagery.   One of the most popular elaboration strategies is mental imagery. Many learners voluntarily generate mental images of ideas, objects, or events about which they are reading. Those who naturally use imagery command a powerful retention technique. When they form an image of an event or object, they are encoding the elaborative information (the images) in a separate memory store, thereby providing additional access points for retrieving the idea. Learners can also be trained to generate mental images by periodically directing them to stop reading, close their eyes, and try to create a mental picture of what they are reading. The more elaborate the image they generate or the more they are able to manipulate or expand that image, the more retrieval cues they will have at their disposal. Recall and retention have been shown to improve substantially (Kulhavy & Swenson, 1975) as a result of generating images.

An optional strategy would allow learners to create physical images, that is, draw cartoons or maps that describe content. In courseware, this would require the use of a graphics pad or a mouse with necessary software for creating graphics. While these are expensive and not universally available (although they are becoming more widely used), courseware requiring their use would obligate users to acquire additional hardware. Another solution is to include a graphics editor subroutine, which would allow learners to draw and save images. However, these require so much mental effort to use that the purpose for using them could easily be lost. The imagery strategy, for the time, should probably remain an off-line activity.

Analogies.   A lesson could periodically present analogies using key ideas from the lesson. Analogies require learners to integrate concepts and infer from (elaborate) them. Important ideas could also be presented and learners required to draw inferences from or state implications of those ideas. The lesson could identify two key terms in analogy style with blanks to be filled in by the learner (see Fig. 6.9 as an example). Their responses could be checked easily by the program and appropriate feedback provided. Learners could also be asked to provide the concepts for which they are generating analogies. Remember, it is the nature of the information processing required by an activity that is most important.

Metalearning Strategies

Metalearning strategies focus the learner's awareness on the learning process, that is, they make learners objectively self-aware of themselves as learners. These activities promote the monitoring of the learning process—the learner's

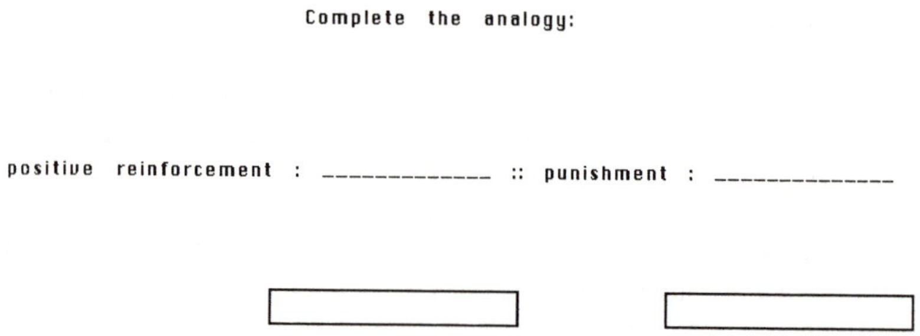

Complete the analogy:

positive reinforcement : _____ :: punishment : _____

FIG. 6.9.   Screen output for analogy strategy.

TABLE 6.2

Cognitive Operations in Learning and Retention and the
Monitoring Strategies that May Influence Them

Cognitive Operation	Monitoring Strategy
Planning	SELECT - establish learning objectives based on learning outcome PREPARE - activate relevant memory schemes GAUGE - determine "depth" of processing required ESTIMATE - predict information-processing demands of the presented material
Attending	FOCUS - direct attention to the presented material SEARCH - monitor information processing to facilitate the matching of incoming data to relevant memory schemes CONTRAST - compare incoming information to memory schemes activated by the Prepare Strategy VALIDATE - determine whether new information confirms information in the memory schemes activated by the Prepare Strategy
Encoding	ELABORATE - link new information to various other information at the same "level" in memory QUALITATIVELY RELATE - link new information to a "deeper," more meaningful level of memory organization
Reviewing	CONFIRM - use new information to demonstrate its acquisition REPEAT - recall recently established encodings REVISE - modify encodings by elaborating or qualitatively relating them further
Evaluating	TEST - determine the internal consistency and "truth" of the information JUDGE - react to the information in an affective manner

Reprinted with permission of Educational Communications and Technology Journal.

awareness of what is known and how it comes to be known. As indicated in an earlier section, Brezin (1980) has identified a set of strategies for monitoring information-processing activities. He has also developed a set of instructional manipulations to initiate these strategies (see Table 6.2). These activities can be incorporated into the instructional design of courseware in two formats. The primary format focuses the student's attention on his or her learning style and the strategies she or he is using to learn. Primary format strategies stimulate self-monitoring and self-management, that is, they prompt the learner consciously to attend to and control how they are learning. You may prompt the learner to use metalearning strategies by providing a menu of options or a Help key leading to a menu at various points in the program. The menu would list the strategy or strategies that could be used effectively at that time. The secondary format of metalearning strategies focuses more on the information-processing activities rather than self-awareness. The secondary format activities listed in Table 6.2 are like the embedded learning strategies described previously. Both primary and secondary strategies could be integrated just as easily into courseware as the previous strategies, however, space does not permit elaboration or illustration of each of these. The primary strategies would be particularly useful in prompting and supplementing the learning strategies already described. While the information processing requirements of the task are most important, it is also important that the learners realize what they are doing and why it is or is not productive. The electronic notebook provides a useful means for prompting and presenting metalearning strategies.

LIMITATIONS AND RECOMMENDATIONS

Although I believe the electronic notebook concept for integrating learning strategies into courseware is conceptually sound, some practical, conceptual, and empirical concerns should be considered.

1. The strategies that I have recommended in this paper by no means represents an exhaustive list of the strategies that might be implemented in the electronic notebook. The learning strategies literature is burgeoning. For a brief review of the kind of work being done, you are referred to O'Neil (1978), O'Neil and Spielberger (1979), and Pressley and Levin (1984).

2. These recommendations are intended primarily as short-term approaches to improving the quality of courseware. They won't revolutionize the design of courseware. As richer conceptual models of learning based on artificial intellegence work are developed and implemented in computer software (see Part IV for a discussion of these), traditional conceptions of the computer as an information presentation device, including the electronic notebook, will become obsolete.

3. The particular learning strategies that are implemented through the electronic notebook need to be carefully matched to the processing requirements of the objectives stated for the program. Learning strategies are not implicitly good or effective. They represent soft technologies that, like any other technology, can facilitate the completion of specified objectives (Jonassen, 1985). If inappropriately applied, like any other technology, they can be counterproductive.

4. Learning strategies, regardless of the instructional conditions of their presentation, are more effective if they are practiced. Merely presenting learning strategies does not guarantee their effective use. The comprehensive learning strategy systems (Dansereau et al., 1979a, 1979b; Rood & Weinstein, 1983; Weinstein, 1978) entail many hours of training time as well as follow-up use and practice. The amount of time required for practicing any strategy implemented

through the electronic notebook will vary with the complexity of the strategy, the ability and background of the learners, and the difficulty of the material with which they are being used. However, some practice with feedback will promote more effective integration and utilization of learning strategies in courseware. Courseware possesses distinct advantages for instigating the use of strategies over normal externally paced classroom instruction, in which students do not have time to pause the teacher's presentation of information to select and use a strategy. Learner control of the pace of instruction enables the learners to more effectively select and use learning strategies.

5. Without practice, and even with practice, simply giving directions to learners to engage in certain forms of generative processing will not ensure that generative processing of material, in fact, occurs (Jonassen, 1984c). Learners usually habituate a preferred set of study strategies that frequently are not generative in nature. Breaking such habits can be difficult. Practice across a range of tasks will be required to effect stable and generalizable use of strategies. If you integrate a strategy into one lesson, then learners, at best, will apply that strategy to a similar class of problems (Brown, 1978). Transfer of training is a distinct problem with both detached and embedded learning strategy instruction (Derry & Murphy, 1986). More generalized application of a strategy is likely to occur only if you integrate a strategy or set of strategies across a range of courseware. Borkowski, Levers, and Gruennenfelder (1976) recommend the following components of a strategy to produce consistent learning effects from training: (1) consistent use, (2) in a variety of materials, (3) using detailed instructions on how to use the strategy. Courseware that integrates learning strategies also needs to encourage their use through prompts and support their use with instruction.

6. By requiring learners through the electronic notebook to process information in a particular way, you may be contradicting the learner's preferred and more productive mode of studying, thereby decrementing learning. This is more probable with higher ability learners, who have been frequently shown to be deterred by compensatory instructional treatments in the aptitude-treatment interaction research (Cronbach & Snow, 1977). Three individual differences are especially important: age of the student; prior knowledge; and metacognitive proficiency (Peterson & Swing, 1983). First, older students' performances are more generalized and stable. Second, background knowledge is required for strategies to work on any content. If the learner possesses no prior knowledge to anchor new information to, learning cannot be generative. Third, the more metacognitively aware students are, the more efficiently and effectively they will apply learning strategies. For this reason, you should consider combining the metacognitive strategies (see Table 6.2) with the information-processing strategies presented in this chapter into your courseware.

7. Long-term, enduring changes in intelligence or learning ability are unlikely results from learning strategy training of any sort (Brown & Campione,

1982). Certainly, cognitive skills are trainable, but they are not sufficient for improving overall learning ability. That depends on the trainability of executive control strategies or the learner's metacognitive skills prior to training. There is good reason to believe that metalearning skills are trainable, though that issue has not been resolved.

SUMMARY

Complaints about the quality of courseware are based largely on the low levels of processing and the mathemagenic nature of responses required by most drill and tutorial microcomputer courseware. The solution proposed in this chapter is the electronic notebook—that is, the integration of learning strategies into courseware, thereby inducing more generative, deeper processing of the information presented to the learner. The implementation section described how different types of information processing strategies could be integrated into courseware. These included examples of possible BASIC and Pascal routines for implementing the strategy and some output screens from other strategy implementations. Finally, some of the limitations of learning strategies and their integration in courseware were discussed. It is probably obvious to most of you that these embedded strategies are using primarily the file creating/file handling capacities of the computer—nothing creative or original. However, it is generally recognized that information handling is what computers do best, so why not utilize it in a way more productive of learning. The consistent point of this chapter is that the nature of the information processing generated by courseware will determine what is learned and how much is comprehended by the learners. It is the information processing in which learners engage that should become the focus of courseware designs.

REFERENCES

Allen, B. S., & Merrill, M. D. (1985). System-assigned strategies and CBI. *Journal of Educational Computing Research, 1*(1), 3–21.

Bolter, J. D., Joyce, M., & Smith, J. B. (1986). *Storyspace: A computer system for reading and writing.* Chapel Hill, NC: University of North Carolina, Department of Classics.

Borkowski, J. G., Levers, S., & Gruennenfelder, T. M. (1976). Transfer of mediational strategies in children: The role of activity and awareness during strategy acquisition. *Child Development, 47,* 779–786.

Bregar W. S., & Farley, A. M. (1980). Artificial intelligence approaches to computer-based instruction. *Journal of Computer Based Instruction, 6*(4), 104–114.

Brezin, M. J. (1980). Cognitive monitoring: From learning theory to instructional applications. *Educational Communications and Technology Journal, 28,* 227–242.

Brown, A. L. (1978). Knowing when, where, and how to remember: problem of metacognition. In R. Glaser (Ed.), *Advances in instructional psychology* (Vol. 1). Hillsdale, NJ: Lawrence Erlbaum Associates.

Brown, A. L., & Campione, J. C. (1982). Modifying intelligence or modifying cognitive skills: More than a semantic quibble. In D. K. Detterman & R. J. Sternberg (Eds.), *How and how much can intelligence be increased?* Norwood, NJ: Ablex Publishers.

Brown, A., Campione,J. C., & Day, J. D. (1981). Learning to learn: On training students to learn from text. *Educational Researcher, 10*(2), 14–21.

Brunig, I. L. (1983). An information processing approach to a theory of instruction. *Educational Communications and Technology Journal, 31,* 91–101.

Buzan, T. (1974). *Use both sides of your brain.* New York: E.P. Dutton.

Clark, R. E. (1984). Research on student thought processes during computer based instruction. *Journal of Instructional Development, 7*(3), 2–5.

Cohen, V. B. (1983, April). *A learner-based evaluation of microcomputer software.* Paper presented at the annual meeting of the American Educational Research Association, Montreal, Canada.

Craik, F. I. M., Lockhart, R.S. (1972). Levels of processing: A framework for memory research. *Journal of verbal learning and verbal behavior, 11,* 671–684.

Cronbach, L. J., & Snow, R. E. (1977). *Aptitudes and instructional methods.* New York: Irvington Press.

Dansereau, D. F. (1978). The development of a learning strategies curriculum. In H.F. O'Neil (Ed.), *Learning strategies.* New York: Academic Press.

Dansereau, D. F., Collins, K. W., McDonald, B. A., Holley, C. D., Garland, J., Diekhoff, G., & Evans, S. H. (1979a). Development and evaluation of a learning strategy training program. *Journal of Educational Psychology, 71,* 64–73.

Dansereau, D. F., McDonald, B. A., Collins, K. W., Garland, J., Holley, C. D., Diekhoff, G. M., & Evans, S. H. (1979b). Evaluation of a learning strategy system. In H.F. O'Neil & C.D. Spielberger (Eds.), *Cognitive and affective learning strategies.* New York: Academic Press.

Derry, S. J., & Murphy, D. A. (1986). Designing systems that train learning ability: From theory to practice. *Review of Educational Research, 56,* 1–39.

Diekhoff, G. M., Brown, P., & Dansereau, D. F. (1982). A prose learning strategy training program based on network and depth of processing models. *Journal of Experimental Education, 50*(4), 180–184.

Diekhoff, G. M., & Diekhoff, K. K. (1982). Cognitive maps as a tool for communicating structural knowledge. *Educational Technology, 26*(4), 28–30.

Fields, A. (1982). Getting started. In D.H. Jonassen (Ed.), *The technology of text: Principles for structuring, designing, and displaying text.* Englewood Cliffs, NJ: Educational Technology Publications.

Flavell, J. H., & Wellman, H. M. (1977). Metamemory. In R.V. Kail & J.W. Hagen (Eds.), *Perspectives on the development of memory and cognition.* Hillsdale, NJ: Lawrence Erlbaum Associates.

Frase, L. T., & Schwartz, B. J. (1975). Effect of question production and answering on prose recall. *Journal of Educational Psychology, 67,* 628–635.

Hartley, J. (1983). Note-taking Research: Resetting the Scoreboard. *Bulletin of the British Psychological Society, 36,* 13–14.

Johansen, K. J., & Tennyson, R. D. (1983). Effect of adaptive advisement on perception in learner-controlled, computer-based instruction using a rule-learning task. *Educational Communications and Technology Journal, 31,* 226–236.

Jonassen, D. H. (1984a). Developing a learning strategy using pattern notes: A new technology. *Programmed Learning and Educational Technology, 21*(3), 163–175.

Jonassen, D. H. (1984b). Generative learning vs. mathemagenic control of text processing. In D. H. Jonassen (Ed.), *The technology of text: Principles for structuring, designing, and displaying text* (Vol. 2). Englewood Cliffs, NJ: Educational Technology Publications.

Jonassen, D. H. (1984c, March). *Effects of levels of generative processing of text.* Paper presented at the annual meeting of the British Psychological Society, Coventry, Warwickshire.

Jonassen, D. H. (1985). Learning strategies: A new educational technology. *Programmed Learning and Educational Technology, 22*(1), 26–34.

Jonassen, D. H. (1986a). Hypertext principles for text and courseware design. *Educational Psychologist, 21*(4), 269–292.

Jonassen, D. H. (1986b). Improving recall using database management systems: A learning strategy. *AEDS Journal, 19*(2–3), 109–123.

Jones, B. F., & Friedman, L. (1983). *Content-driven comprehension instruction and assessment: A model for army training literature,* Chicago: Chicago Public Schools.

Kulhavy, R. W., & Swenson, I. (1975). Imagery instructions and the comprehension of text. *British Journal of Educational Psychology, 45*(2), 47–51.

Lindner, R. W., & Rickards, J. P. (1985). Questions inserted in text: Issues and implications. In D. H. Jonassen (Ed.), *The technology of text: Principles for structuring, designing, and displaying text* (Vol. 2). Englewood Cliffs, NJ: Educational Technology Publications.

McAleese, R. (1985). Some problems of knowledge representation in an authoring environment: Exteriorization, anomolous state metacognition, and self-confrontation. *Programmed Learning and Educational Technology, 22*(4), 299–306.

Nelson, T. H. (1974). *Dream machine.* South Bend, IN: The Distributors.

Nelson, T. H. (1978). Electronic publishing and electronic literature. In E.C. DeLand (Ed.), *Information technology in health science education.* New York: Plenum.

Norman, D., Gentner, S., & Stevens, A. L. (1976). Comments or learning schemata and memory representation. In D. Klahr (Ed.), *Cognition and instruction.* Hillsdale, NJ: Lawrence Erlbaum Associates.

O'Neil, H. F. (1978). *Learning strategies.* New York: Academic Press.

O'Neil, H. F., & Spielberger, C. D. (1979). *Cognitive and affective learning strategies.* New York: Academic Press.

Park, O. C., & Tennyson, R. D. (1980). Adaptive strategies for selecting number and presentation order of examples in coordinate concept acquisition. *Journal of Educational Psychology, 72,* 362–370.

Peterson, P. L., & Swing, S. R. (1983). Problems in classroom implementation of cognitive strategy instruction. In M. Pressley & J. R. Levin (Eds.), *Cognitive strategy research: Educational applications.* New York: Springer-Verlag.

Pressley, M., & Levin, J. (Eds.). (1984). *Cognitive strategy research: Educational applications.* New York: Springer-Verlag.

Rigney, J. (1978). Learning strategies: A theoretical perspective. In H. F. O'Neil (Ed.), *Learning strategies.* New York: Academic Press.

Robinson, E. P. (1946). *Effective study.* New York: Harper & Row.

Rood, M.M., & Weinstein, C.E. (1983, April). *Improving higher order learning skills: Elaborative cognitive learning strategies training.* Paper presented at the annual meeting of the American Educational Research Association, Montreal, Canada.

Ross, S. M., & Rakow, E. A. (1981). Learner control versus program control as adaptive strategies for selection of instructional support on math rules. *Journal of Educational Psychology, 73,* 745–753.

Rothkopf, E. Z. (1970). The concept of mathemagenic activities. *Review of Educational Research, 40,* 325–336.

Rumelhart, D. E., & Ortony, A. (1977). The representation of knowledge in memory. In R. C. Anderson, R. J., Spiro, & W. E. Montague (Eds.), *Schooling and the acquisition of knowledge.* Hillsdale, NJ: Lawrence Erlbaum Associates.

Salomon, G. (1972). Heuristic models for the generation of aptitude-treatment interactions hypotheses. *Review of Educational Research, 42,* 327–343.

Sternberg, R. G. (1983). Criteria for intellectual skills training. *Educational Researcher, 12,* 6–12.

Tennyson, R. D. (1980). Instructional control strategies and content structure as design variables in concept acquisition using computer-based instruction. *Journal of Educational Psychology, 72,* 525–532.

Tennyson, R. D., & Buttrey, T. (1980). Advisement and management strategies as design variables in computer assisted instruction. *Educational Communications and Technology Journal, 28,* 169–176.

Tennyson, R. D., & Rothen, W. (1979). Management of computer-based instruction: Design of an adaptive control strategy. *Journal of Computer-based instruction, 5*(3), 63–71.

Weinstein, C. E. (1978). Elaboration Skills as a Learning Strategy. In H. F. O'Neil (Ed.), *Learning strategies.* New York: Academic Press.

Weinstein, C. E., & Mayer, R. E. (1985). The teaching of learning strategies. In M. C. Wittrock (Ed.), *Handbook of research on teaching* (3rd Ed.), New York: Macmillan.

Weyer, J. (1984). New bird on the branch: Artificial intelligence and computer-assisted instruction. *Programmed Learning and Educational Technology, 21*(3), 189–193.

Wittrock, M. C. (1974a). A generative model of mathematics learning. *Journal of Research in Mathematics Education, 5,* 181–197.

Wittrock, M. C. (1974b). Learning as a generative activity. *Educational Psychologist, 11,* 87–95.

Wittrock, M. C. (1978). The cognitive movement in instruction. *Educational Psychologist, 15,* 15–29.

7 Providing Meaningful Feedback in Courseware

Barry J. Schimmel
Teachers College
Columbia University

Picture a student working hard in a computerized algebra course. At one point, the student answers several examples incorrectly. How should the program respond to help the student learn? Do the errors indicate a lack of understanding, or are they merely "careless"? Should the errors be pointed out? If so, how much, or what kind of explanation should be provided about the incorrect answers? These and other questions relate to the design of feedback in courseware.

Feedback is the information given to students about the correctness of their answers (Frayer & Klausmeier, 1971). It has long been regarded as a critical component of instruction. For example, in 1960 Lumsdaine described feedback as a necessary part of programmed instruction. Feedback has also been considered a "powerful force" in learning (Glaser & Cooley, 1973), and fundamental to the rationale for computer-assisted instruction (Cronbach, 1977, p. 14). Programs in computer-assisted instruction (CAI) typically include some type of feedback to students.

Despite its wide use, however, the optimal content of feedback is still in question. Research in the past offered little guidance for determining the content of a feedback message. The purpose here is to look again at the pertinent research for generalizations that can guide the design of feedback.

The chapter is divided into three parts: (1) a selective review of research on feedback, (2) the context, or process, of learning into which feedback intervenes, and (3) prescriptions for feedback design.

RESEARCH ON FEEDBACK

Background

Students can often obtain implicit feedback on their own independently of other feedback presented (Tobias, 1982). For example, in a foreign language program a learner who can understand the foreign language instructions can be confident of having learned the earlier definitions of individual vocabulary words in the instructions. When we understand a complicated sentence in a book, we know that we have probably understood the concepts leading up to that sentence. This chapter deals with feedback whose source is external to the learner.

Feedback can have both motivational and cognitive effects. Research on the motivational effects of feedback in classrooms, for example, has found that teacher comments that sound personal and provide encouragement improve overall learner performance (Page, 1958; Schunk, 1983). Elawar & Corno (1985) found that when teacher-administered corrective feedback was combined with praise, learner achievement and attitudes toward a course improved. We focus here on the cognitive, rather than motivational, effects of feedback in computer courses, i.e., on how feedback affects our understanding of the content.

Types of Feedback

Over the years various types of feedback information have been studied. Some of this feedback was brief; other types of feedback were more lengthy. Presumably the feedback varied in the amount of information it provided to learners.

Confirmation Feedback. Confirmation feedback simply confirmed whether a learner's answer was correct or incorrect. For example, after a question was answered correctly, the program responded "right," "yes," "good job," etc. Feedback after incorrect answers included "wrong," "no," or "try again." Some programs beeped or offered verbal feedback only after correct answers or only after incorrect responses.

Correct Response Feedback. Correct response feedback presented the correct answer. The correct answer could be joined with confirmation feedback, as in "You are wrong. The capital of Iceland is Reykjavic." In other programs the confirmation feedback was not explicit. Students were given only the correct answer, and they had to infer whether their answer was correct. At times correct response feedback was given only after incorrect answers.

Explanatory Feedback. Various forms of explanatory feedback have been used. In "specific review" feedback, a step-by-step solution to an incorrectly answered problem was shown, with the exception of the final step. "General review" feedback contained summary statements of the instructional content that preceded the learner's wrong answer (M. D. Merrill, 1965; Merrill & Stolurow, 1966). For instance, in a problem-solving program in marketing, a wrong answer might indicate that the learner had failed to apply certain principles that had been taught in the program. General review feedback would present summary statements of these principles, perhaps by reminding the student of the need to analyze market demand, technology availability, and the company's product portfolio. Specific review would actually demonstrate how to perform these analyses, without presenting the overall result of the analyses. "Attribute-isolation feedback" reviewed the attributes of a concept on which the student made an error (J. Merrill, 1985). For example, the feedback would review the characteristics of a product portfolio.

Kulhavy (1977) described the various types of feedback information content as a continuum of explanatory complexity. The continuum ranged from simply confirming whether a learner's answer was correct or incorrect to explanations so lengthy that they encompassed remediation and significantly expanded the content of instruction.

Bug-related Feedback.   A "bug" is a systematic error in the learner's understanding of a procedure. For example, young students who mistakenly solve the arithmetic example shown below often do so believing that the smaller number should always be subtracted from the larger number. Since in the first column 1 is smaller

$$
\begin{array}{r}
61 \\
-\ 24 \\
\hline
43
\end{array}
$$

than 4, the 1 is subtracted from 4, and the first column's result is 3. These students may consistently solve subtraction examples with this bug in their cognitive model of the subtraction procedure.

The explanations in bug-related feedback are aimed at correcting a student's faulty mental model of a procedure. Therefore, bug-related feedback would do more than simply state the correct answer. In this example, it might explain that in subtraction the lower number is always subtracted from the upper number, and that if the upper number is smaller, the student should *borrow* from the second column.

Bug-related feedback has been used primarily in intelligent CAI, such as the system described by Anderson and Reiser (1985) which taught programming skills. The system contained a comprehensive representation of programming rules and a "catalogue" of potential bugs in learning these rules. A student's performance was continuously compared with an internal, preprogrammed model of an expert's performance on the problems presented. When a student error matched an error in the system's internal catalogue of bugs, bug-related corrective feedback was given.

A significant challenge in designing bug-related feedback is to pinpoint the specific bug causing an error. Some errors can be caused by more than one bug (Brown & Burton, 1978), or the bug causing an error may disappear without intervention. Moreover, an error may not reflect a bug at all, but merely a careless slip by a student who really knows the correct procedure (VanLehn, 1981). The bug-related feedback described by Anderson & Reiser (1985) successfully diagnosed and responded to 45–80% of the students' errors, depending on lesson complexity and prior testing to build up the catalogue of possible bugs.

Results of Feedback Research

Despite the wide acceptance of feedback in computerized instruction, empirical support for particular types of feedback information has been inconsistent or weak. Providing learners with extensive information about why their answers are correct or incorrect has proven, on the whole, no more useful than offering minimal information (Geis & Chapman, 1971; Hendrickson, 1978; Hyman & Tobias, 1981; Kulhavy, 1977). The learning outcomes of Anderson and Reiser's (1985) system were substantial, but it required a long development time and substantial computer capacity. In addition, the specific effects of feedback, apart from the rest of the program, were not described.

In sum, research provides little guidance for designing feedback. Exceptions to this general conclusion are discussed in the section on feedback design guidelines, which will be more useful if we first look at a wider context of student learning. The next section describes what learners are thought to do when they are learning, and how feedback may affect that learning process.

THE LEARNING PROCESS AND FEEDBACK

Learning is believed to consist of several cognitive processes. Optimal learning is thought to occur when these processes are engaged fully (Anderson, 1970; Craik & Lockhart, 1972). Anderson's (1970) description of the importance of intense processing is apt: "the chief problem for educational engineering is to discover how to alter the characteristics of instructional tasks so as to force students to do all of the processing required for learning" (p. 363).

Corno and Mandinach (1983) provide a useful review of these processing activities, describing five operations believed to define complex school-related learning: (1) alertness to informative stimuli, (2) selectively distinguishing relevant from irrelevant instructional stimuli, (3) connecting (searching for existing knowledge and linking it with new incoming information), (4) planning (organizing a plan of action for learning), and (5) monitoring concentration and understanding.

The learning activities of the student who corrected the error in subtracting two-digit numbers will illustrate these five operations. First, the student was alert in environments in which instruction in subtraction might occur, such as the CAI program. Second, from this stream of potential instruction the learner attended to the information that demonstrated the correct subtraction procedure. Third, the student connected the new information with already known information. For example, the student may have recalled prior classroom subtraction experiences in which learners *borrowed* a group of 10 sticks from a box containing bundles of 10 sticks, thereby increasing the number in the "ones" column. Fourth, the student planned how to improve in subtraction, perhaps deciding to do a few more examples in the CAI program. Finally, the student monitored her attention to the instruction and her understanding of when to use *borrowing* in subtraction.

At times the instructional program itself can circumvent the processing needed for learning. Carefully designed instructional programs (such as those including the "instructional events" described by Gagné (1977)) may relieve the learner's processing burden by performing processing activities for the learner. For example, the programs might set objectives for the learner, break tasks into manageable subparts, provide relevant examples, and highlight important points. Instructional supports such as graphs, summary statements, and flowcharts of events may also provide in ready-made form the potential cognitive results of learner processing such as selectivity, planning, and connecting. These supports can obviate the student's need to engage in that processing. For example, a summary may relieve students of the need to identify key content, extract its most important elements, and tie them into a coherent summary. A history program that provides a time line may relieve students of the need to organize events chronologically for themselves. The potential advantage of such assistance is that students who could not accomplish on their own the steps necessary to produce these cognitive products are thus able to learn (Salomon, 1979).

However, short-circuiting in the form of instructional supports may lead to several disadvantages. First, short-circuiting often means that learners expend less effort on their own to learn. The result is knowledge that is more superficial. Some research has shown that when students memorize surface features of information rather than labor at comprehending the material, they show more difficulty recalling the information and applying the knowledge to new situations (Doyle, 1983; Royer, 1979).

A second disadvantage of continual short-circuiting is that students lose opportunities to learn how to perform the circumvented processing (Corno & Mandinach, 1983; Salomon, 1979). For example, students who are continuously exposed to instruction that provides frequent summaries may not develop the crucial skill of summarizing. Thus, the students' future ability to learn can be weakened. Finally, students showing reduced comprehension and a more limited repertoire of learning strategies are also hypothesized to have a reduced sense of competence about learning (Corno & Mandinach, 1983). Students' feeling of competence in their ability to learn, or their self-efficacy, is influenced most strongly by actual learning achievements (Bandura, 1982; Bandura & Schunk, 1981).

In brief, instructional supports may render a program easier to learn in certain cases, but may also increase the probability that learning will be superficial in other situations (Salomon, 1979; Tobias, 1982). A steady diet of such support may prevent students from developing certain learning skills and from acquiring a sense of competence as learners (Bandura, 1982; Bandura & Schunk, 1981; Corno & Mandinach, 1983).

How does this view of the learning process apply to feedback? Like other instructional supports, feedback can either facilitate or substitute for learner processing. For example, students learning difficult new procedures in algebra or accounting may not know when they are making errors. Feedback may assist learners in monitoring their understanding, leading students to re-study or seek help on points where the feedback has identified errors. Feedback may provide helpful explanations. On the other hand, feedback might be used as a tool for obtaining quick answers and explanations that will speed one's way through the program. Feedback that reduces the need for cognitive processing has been found to reduce learning (Anderson, Kulhavy, & Andre, 1971, 1972).

It is difficult to predict when feedback will serve to support or short-circuit learning processes. From an instructional design standpoint, the use of feedback may represent a balance between assisting some learners and weakening others. Feedback would assist those students whose learning skills and familiarity with the subject matter are insufficient for understanding the content. Once students' learning skills and subject matter familiarity are adequate, feedback will begin to short-circuit learners' processing (Corno & Snow, 1986).

PRINCIPLES FOR DESIGNING FEEDBACK

Several guidelines for designing feedback are now presented. Although the empirical base for some of these guidelines is still limited, an immediate instructional design need exists to formulate at least tentative guidelines for designing feedback content.

Design Principle 1:   In verbal information tasks, provide feedback that presents the correct response.

In verbal information tasks students learn to state facts or ideas meaningfully (Gagné, 1977). Explaining the anatomy of the digestive system, the criteria for approval of a bank loan, or the advantages of a word processing program are examples of verbal information.

The large majority of feedback studies have dealt with verbal information tasks (Andrews, 1980; J. Merrill, 1985). Most reviews of these studies have concluded that feedback had inconsistent effects on learning, and in some cases was even associated with lower achievement (Anderson, Kulhavy, & Andre, 1972; Hendrickson, 1978; Hyman & Tobias, 1981; Kulhavy, 1977).

Schimmel (1983) reviewed 11 studies of two types of feedback in verbal information tasks: confirmation feedback, in which the learner's answer was confirmed as correct or incorrect, and correct response feedback, in which learners were given the correct answer after entering their own response. In the studies reviewed, groups of adult learners receiving immediate confirmation or correct response feedback were compared experimentally with groups receiving no feedback. The average student learning with feedback was found to score better than about 63% of the students in groups receiving no feedback.[1] Thus, compared with no feedback, a small positive advantage was found in using confirmation or correct response feedback in learning verbal information.

Insufficient evidence was found in that review (Schimmel, 1983) to distinguish the effects of confirmation and correct response feedback. The guideline favoring correct response feedback is based on the fact that this feedback implicitly includes confirmation. Other types of feedback in verbal information instruction have not been consistently studied. Research on feedback that provides explanation in addition to confirmation or correct response feedback has included diverse types of feedback, with conflicting results and few replications of any one type of explanation. Thus, a solid body of research on feedback with verbal information exists only with respect to the simple types of feedback. Correct response feedback, as used in the studies reviewed, provides the correct answer after both correct and incorrect responses, with no additional information. Examples of correct response feedback would include:

The capital of Norway is Oslo.

The human heart has four chambers.

The correct answer is (b): the United States Senate has 100 members.

Design Principle 2:   In intellectual skills instruction with high ability students, present a choice of feedback containing different amounts of information.

Intellectual skills are concepts and rules, or predictable relationships between types of stimuli and types of responses (Gagné, 1977). Examples include the solution of arithmetic problems in which the numbers differ from those presented during instruction; applying a set of learned banking criteria to determine

---

[1]Some of the studies used multiple experimental groups, so that 15 comparisons of feedback vs. no feedback were included in the review. An effect size (Glass, 1977) of .32 was found, with a .15 standard error.

whether or not a particular loan application should be approved; or writing a letter, which involves the use of rules of grammar.

This guideline applies to high-ability students because of their unique learning style. Higher ability students tend to seek more information and assimilate it more thoroughly to their existing knowledge than low-ability students (Brown, 1978; Gray, 1983; Mandinach, 1984). Consequently, high-ability students may be more likely than low-ability students to use feedback constructively, rather than simply reading it to replace their own thinking. High-ability learners might try hard to understand the text without feedback, monitor their need for feedback, and then incorporate the feedback information into their existing knowledge. "Self-regulated learning" is more common among high-ability students than low-ability students (Corno & Mandinach, 1983). However, many low-ability students have been found to use feedback in a pattern that may represent self-regulated learning (Schimmel, 1986).

Providing high-ability students with considerable program-controlled feedback information may also interfere with their own learning processes (Snow & Lohman, 1984). Feedback could force upon students ways of viewing the content that conflict with the learners' own mental models of the content. For example, a student trying to understand the notion of computer files may compare them to the folders in a file cabinet. Feedback that explains computer files in terms of a different analogy might require the student to reconcile the analogies, perhaps hampering the student. Learner selection of feedback information allows high-ability students to choose feedback that meets their need but does not conflict with their ongoing knowledge structure.

Snow (1980) argued that learner control may be disadvantageous for students who do not know how to make their choices productively. It is possible that with feedback containing learner-controlled alternatives for information content, students would use feedback unproductively. For instance, learners might use the feedback to find answers quickly, with little deep thinking about their responses. However, giving high-ability learners control over feedback information seems more likely to result in two learning advantages. First, students are more likely to receive the amount of information they want, thereby possibly increasing the amount of time they will persist in the program (Corno & Snow, 1986). In addition, students using a self-regulated learning style are likely to obtain the information they need, without additional information that may interfere with their own understanding.

Learner control over feedback information could be implemented in several ways. One method was used in an introductory algebra course developed by John C. Miller of the City University of New York. After each of the many practice examples in the course, students were presented with the question: "Do you want to see the correct answer?" If they answered affirmatively the answer was shown, followed by the next question: "Do you want an explanation?" The second question was presented even if students answered "no" to the first question. After the explanation (or after students answered "no" to the second question) the next content frame appeared.

This sequential menu format offered three main types of feedback: the correct answer with no follow-up explanation, (if the student answered "yes" to the first menu choice and "no" to the second choice), the correct answer with an explanation, or no feedback.[2] Using this program, Schimmel (1986) found wide individual and group differences in the use of feedback. This sequential format would be impractical with many more feedback alternatives, because the number of menu questions would become intrusively long.

Another method for implementing learner control of feedback information is to present a single feedback menu, showing all feedback alternatives, immediately after each example. The menu would be more practical for a long list of alternatives than a sequential menu. If the menu were presented before and after each presentation of feedback, learners would have the freedom to decide at multiple points whether they wanted additional feedback information. If the menu were available only once, learners would be forced to make their entire feedback choice at one time, eliminating the possibility that additional information would be requested contingent on initial feedback.

A third method for implementing learner control of feedback information is to use function keys. Different keys would call up different types of information. The function keys could be identified by a small chart, displayed either online or offline.

Design Principle 3: In intellectual skills instruction, feedback that identifies errors, provides some guidance toward correction, and offers praise for work done well may be useful.

Only one feedback method was found that both increased learning of intellectual skills and survived replication. That method consisted of identification of the error, guidance toward correction, and praise for aspects of the work done well. The intent in this feedback was to make errors salient as well as to increase motivation. Results showed that this three-part method improved both cognitive results and students' attitude toward the course. Feedback consisting of individual parts of this method did not work as well as the combination (Cardelle & Corno, 1981; Elawar & Corno, 1985).

Studies of this method took place in elementary school and college classrooms, with the feedback given by a teacher in written form. However, a feedback method that produced clearcut learning advantages even when replicated was so unusual that the method seemed useful to include here.

---

[2]Learners could also obtain a fourth possible feedback alternative: an explanation with no correct answer. In practice, this alternative was hardly selected.

Examples of this combination feedback are: "You used the correct formula to solve this problem, but the computation is incorrect." "Your description of the hand movement is accurate, but you incorrectly named three bones. Can you find them?" "You chose the correct pronoun but the form of the verb is wrong." Feedback on the incorrect subtraction example

$$\begin{array}{r} 61 \\ -\ 24 \\ \hline 43 \end{array}$$

might be "Your answer is correct for the left side of the example, but on the right side you may need help."

One cannot be sure that when this classroom feedback is translated to a computer environment the same advantages will result. In fact, implementing the combination feedback in a computer environment will present difficulties, including recognition of a wide range of possible student errors in complex learning, generation of suggestions that would provide useful guidance from among a universe of possibilities, and recognition of features of learner performance that are appropriately praiseworthy. Intelligent tutoring could handle aspects of this feedback more easily than script-based CAI. Given the extensive capabilities of intelligent CAI in comparison with CAI, the capacity for providing the combination feedback described seems more likely to come from intelligent tutoring than CAI.

Design Principle 4:   In procedural instruction, use bug-related feedback if sufficient preparatory work indicates that in the particular content area to be taught bugs can be both reliably identified and effectively corrected by feedback.

Procedural instruction is instruction for teaching procedures, such as those for solving mathematics examples. The difficulties in producing bug-related feedback have been described. Bugs can be difficult to identify, since an observed error may be caused by multiple bugs or may reflect merely a careless slip. In addition, even if the underlying bugs are pinpointed, the instruction required to correct the bug may be beyond the scope of feedback. Despite these cautions, bug-related feedback has been reported successful in several studies (e.g., Anderson & Reiser, 1985).

Bug-related feedback for the incorrect subtraction example described might be: "Your answer in the column on the right side is incorrect. The bottom number is always subtracted from the upper number. Since the 1 is smaller than the bottom number, borrow from the next column to make the 1 larger."

Responding effectively to bugs requires prior identification of the bugs. Two methods for identifying bugs that may be made by students are to have individual students explain their reasoning for their incorrect answers immediately after the answers are given (Ericsson & Simon, 1980), and to analyze large numbers of errors (Brown & Burton, 1978). Considerable formative testing will be required to confirm whether almost all the bugs causing the errors shown in the program have been identified, and whether the bug-related feedback explanations work.

Bug-related feedback has been implemented on expert systems containing catalogues of potential bugs, extensive representations of expert behavior, and programs for comparing learners' performance with that of the expert program. The computer memory capacity required is large, compared with the present capacity of most microcomputers. The usefulness of bug-related feedback in microcomputers will expand as the power of microcomputers increases. At present the use of such feedback appears limited to very small programs, which, due to their size, may also be limited in instructional capability.

SUMMARY

This chapter identifies various potential learning advantages and disadvantages of feedback. It also presents an overview of research on feedback and a set of specific principles for designing useful feedback in CAI.

Feedback was described as bringing certain potential advantages and risks to learning. Feedback may help bring difficult material within the cognitive reach of some students, enabling them to learn, or feedback may function as a replacement for thinking. Students receiving feedback may expend less effort in learning, knowing that feedback will provide quick answers or explanations. If independent thinking is systematically circumvented, students' knowledge may be superficial, they may fail to develop certain learning skills, and their confidence in their ability to learn may suffer.

Despite the wide acceptance of feedback in computerized instruction, research evidence on the information content of feedback has been inconsistent. Research has provided little guidance for designing feedback. Exceptions to this situation were presented in the following guidelines for designing feedback:

1. In verbal information tasks, provide feedback that presents the correct response.

2. In intellectual skills instruction with high-ability students, present a choice of feedback containing different amounts of information.

3. In intellectual skills instruction, feedback that identifies errors, provides some guidance toward correction, and offers praise for work done well may be useful.

4. In procedural instruction, use bug-related feedback if sufficient preparatory work indicates that in the particular content area to be taught bugs can be both reliably identified, and effectively corrected by feedback.

REFERENCES

Anderson, J. R., & Reiser, B. J. (1985). The LISP tutor. *BYTE, 10*(4), 159–175.

Anderson, R. C. (1970). Control of student mediating processes during verbal learning and instruction. *Review of Educational Research, 40,* 349–369.

Anderson, R. C., Kulhavy, R. W., & Andre, T. (1971). Feedback procedures in programmed instruction. *Journal of Educational Psychology, 62,* 148–156.

Anderson, R. C., Kulhavy, R. W., & Andre, T. (1972). Conditions under which feedback facilitates learning from programmed lessons. *Journal of Educational Psychology, 63,* 186–188.

Andrews, D. H. (1980). *The effect of three rule-related strategies of feedback on the learning of intellectual skills.* Unpublished doctoral dissertation, Florida State University.

Bandura, A. (1982). Self-efficacy in human agency. *American Psychologist, 37,* 122–147.

Bandura, A., & Schunk, D. H. (1981). Cultivating competence, self-efficacy, and intrinsic interest through proximal self-motivation. *Journal of Personality and Social Psychology, 41,* 586–598.

Brown, A. L. (1978). Knowing when, where, and how to remember: A problem in metacognition. In R. Glaser (Ed.), *Advances in instructional psychology* (Vol. 1). Hillsdale, NJ: Lawrence Erlbaum Associates.

Brown, J. S., & Burton, R. R. (1978). Diagnostic models for procedural bugs in basic mathematical skills. *Cognitive Science, 2,* 155–192.

Cardelle, M., & Corno, L. (1981). Effects on second language learning of variations in written feedback on homework assignments. *TESOL Quarterly, 15,* 251–261.

Corno, L., & Mandinach, E. B. (1983). The role of cognitive engagement in classroom learning and motivation. *Educational Psychologist, 18,* 88–108.

Corno, L., & Snow, R. E. (1986). Adapting teaching to learner individual differences. In M. C. Wittrock (Ed.), *Third handbook of research on teaching.* New York: Macmillan.

Craik, F. I. M., & Lockhart, R. S. (1972). Levels of processing. *Journal of Verbal Learning and Verbal Behavior, 11,* 671–684.

Cronbach, L. J. (1977). *Educational psychology.* New York: Harcourt Brace Jovanovich.

Doyle, W. (1983). Academic work. *Review of Educational Research, 53,* 159–199.

Elawar, M. C., & Corno, L. (1985). A factorial experiment in teacher written feedback on student homework: Changing teacher behavior a little rather than a lot. *Journal of Educational Psychology, 77,* 162–173.

Ericsson, K. A., & Simon, H. A. (1980). Verbal reports as data. *Psychological Review, 87,* 215–251.

Frayer, D. A., & Klausmeier, H. J. (1971). *Variables in concept learning: Task variables* (Theoretical Paper No. 28). Madison, WI: Wisconsin Research and Development Center for Cognitive Learning.

Gagné, R. M. (1977). *The conditions of learning* (3rd edition). New York: Holt, Rinehart and Winston.

Geis, G. L., & Chapman, R. (1971). *Knowledge of results and other possible reinforcers in self-instructional systems.* Unpublished manuscript. (ERIC Document Reproduction Service No. ED 049464).

Glaser, R., & Cooley, W. M. (1973). Instrumentation for teaching and instructional management. In R. M. W. Travers (Ed.), *Second handbook of research on teaching.* Chicago: Rand McNally.

Glass, G. V. (1977). Integrating findings: The meta-analysis of research. In L. S. Shulman (Ed.), *Review of research in education.* Itasca, IL: Peacock.

Gray, L. E. (1983). *Aptitude constructs, learning processes, and achievement.* Unpublished doctoral dissertation, Stanford University.

Hendrickson, J. M. (1978). Error correction in foreign language teaching: Recent theory, research, and practice. *The Modern Language Journal, 62,* 387–398.

Hyman, C., & Tobias, S. (1981). *Feedback and prior achievement.* Paper presented at the annual meeting of the Northeastern Educational Research Association, Ellenville, NY.

Kulhavy, R. W. (1977). Feedback in written instruction. *Review of Educational Research, 47,* 211–232.

Mandinach, E. M. (1984). *The role of strategic planning and self-regulation in learning an intellectual computer game.* Unpublished doctoral dissertation, Stanford University.

Merrill, J. (1985). *Levels of questioning and forms of feedback: Instructional factors in courseware design.* Paper presented at the annual meeting of the American Educational Research Association, Chicago.

Merrill, M. D. (1965). Correction and review on successive parts in learning a hierarchical task. *Journal of Educational Psychology, 56,* 225–234.

Merrill, M. D., & Stolurow, L. M. (1966). Hierarchical preview vs. problem oriented review in learning an imaginary science. *American Educational Research Journal, 3,* 251–261.

Page, E. B. (1958). Teacher comments and student performance: A seventy-four classroom experiment in school motivation. *Journal of Educational Psychology, 49,* 173–181.

Royer, J. M. (1979). Theories of the transfer of learning. *Educational Psychologist, 14,* 53–69.

Salomon, G. (1979). Media and symbol systems as related to cognition and learning. *Journal of Educational Psychology, 71,* 131–148.

Schimmel, B. (1983). *A meta-analysis of feedback to learners in computerized and programmed instruction.* Paper presented at the annual meeting of the American Educational Research Association, Montreal. (ERIC Document 233 708).

Schimmel, B. (1986). *Feedback use by low ability students in computer-based education.* Unpublished doctoral dissertation, Teachers College, Columbia University.

Schunk, D. H. (1983). Ability versus effort attributional feedback: Differential effects on self-efficacy and achievement. *Journal of Educational Psychology, 75,* 848–856.

Snow, R. E. (1980). Aptitude, learner control, and adaptive instruction. *Educational Psychologist, 15,* 151–158.

Snow, R. E., & Lohman, D. F. (1984). Toward a theory of cognitive aptitude for learning from instruction. *Journal of Educational Psychology, 76,* 347–376.

Tobias, S. (1982). When do instructional methods make a difference? *Educational Researcher, 11*(4), 4–9.

VanLehn, K. (1981). *Bugs are not enough: Empirical studies of bugs, impasses and repairs in procedural skills.* Palo Alto, CA: Xerox Palo Alto Research Center.

III ADAPTIVE DESIGNS FOR COURSEWARE

As I discussed in the Preface and the Introduction to Part II, interactivity in instructional technologies has less to do with the interaction than it does with adaptation. That is, an important component of interactive instruction, especially computer-based, relates to the ways the instructional system is able to adapt the style, sequence, or content of the presentation or feedback in order to meet the needs of the learner. Interactivity in instruction, then, comprises the nature of the activity performed by the technology and the learner as well as the ability of the technology to adapt the events of instruction in order to make that interaction more meaningful. Interactive instruction really means interactive, adaptive instruction. Just how can technologies adapt?

Adaptation Comes to Courseware

Computer courseware, both micro- and main-frame based, is now using more adaptive learner interactions. Early CAI, on the other hand, made virtually no attempt to adapt instruction, based as they were on the linear programmed instruction model. CAI presented information followed by questions and the user's response, which was followed by knowledge or confirmation of results. The sequence and content of instruction were invariant; only the pacing varied. But large CAI projects like PLATO and especially TICCIT have opened up new horizons to courseware designers. The fundamental design component of TICCIT are the options that it provides to the learners to control not only the rate of instruction, but also the content and sequence. TICCIT adapts to the learner, introducing the notion of learner control of instruction.

During the same period, the growth of differential psychology, manifested in aptitude treatment interaction research, increased our sensitivity to adaptive instructional designs. The mid-70s produced a great deal of interest in matching instructional treatments to learner characteristics. A number of researchers, some writing in this part of the book, began to research the capabilities of computers to adapt to learners. Figure III.1 summarizes the developments resulting from that research. Courseware now generally provides two levels of adaptation, learner control and program control. Much of the research conducted by the authors in this part of the book has focused on whether learner control of instruction in courseware is more effective than research based adaptive sequences controlled by the program. The two major components of adaptive courseware designs are selecting the optimal sequence of the instructional presentation as well as selecting the appropriate amount of practice and the nature of the feedback available to the learner (Park & Tennyson, 1984). Other models for adaptive design provide for adaptive levels of incentives and adaptation and personalization of the learning context (Ross, Rakow, & Bush, 1980). The research on these designs, much of it presented in this part of the book, has produced some of the most consistent empirical results ever evidenced in educational research. The state of the art is constantly progressing, and so is the sophistication of the designs and the theories on which they are based. The courseware design field is moving inexorably into the milieu of artificial intelligence. That trend is reflected in the Tennyson and Christensen chapter in this section and the following part of the book, which is dedicated to courseware designs based on artificial intelligence principles.

Adaptive Instructional Designs

The adaptive designs presented in Fig. III.1 reflect the developmental efforts of courseware designers but not the full range of the microcomputer's adaptive capabilities. Park and Tennyson (1984) have identified five different design models for continuously estimating and updating information about the student's ability on a given task and adapting instructional treatments to their performance and learning needs: a mathematical (all-or-none) model, regression model (see Ross & Morrison chapter), Bayesian probability model (see Tennyson & Christensen chapter), the testing and branching model (based on branching programmed instruction), and artificial intelligence systems (see Part IV of this book).

The possibilities for adapting instructional options are endless. Figure III.2 presents a variety of adaptive options for delivering alternative instructional sequences based upon a variety of learner, content, or situational characteristics (Jonassen, 1985). Figure III.2 shows two different dimensions of adaptations. In

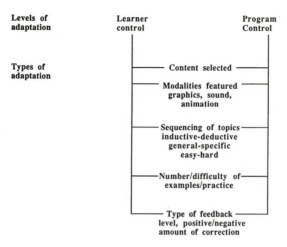

<table>
<tr><td>Levels of
adaptation</td><td>Learner
control</td><td>Program
Control</td></tr>
</table>

Types of
adaptation

— Content selected —

— Modalities featured
graphics, sound,
animation

— Sequencing of topics —
inductive-deductive
general-specific
easy-hard

—Number/difficulty of—
examples/practice

— Type of feedback —
level, positive/negative
amount of correction

FIG.III.1.   Adaptations in courseware.

the first, the instructional program may assess some characteristic of the learner's ability, or performance, or preferences or needs and then adapt the sequence, strategy, or type of instruction based on those characteristics or needs. The primary factor for prescribing instruction in current adaptive designs is on-task performance ability. Though adaptations to learners are pedagogically appealing, they are less consistent and predictable, so adaptations should perhaps be made based on the task requirements of different content (Jonassen, 1982). The second

Internal Adaptations

	Task requirements	Content sequencing	Content structure	Curriculum related
Branching on performance				
Diagnosing prior learning				
Accomodating to learner characteristics				
Learner control of instruction				
Curricular Adaptations				

FIG. III.2.   Levels of adaptations in courseware.

dimension therefore includes designs that adapt to the nature of the task or information being presented. The first dimension includes designs that adapt to external, user-supplied information assessed by the program. The second dimension includes designs in which adaptations are made based on information internal to the program. Both dimensions represent adaptations—the first to characteristics or needs of the learner and the latter to characteristics of the information being presented.

The adaptation of instruction to external information includes characteristics, capabilities, and needs of the learners. The simplest adaptive design entails branching on performance. Based on principles of branching programmed instruction, this level of courseware would provide different feedback to alternative learner responses. This level would include remedial loops and alternative sequences of instruction. Courseware may also diagnose prior learning and adapt the style, amount, or sequence of instruction accordingly. There are numerous learner characteristics, such as cognitive styles and personality preferences, which provide the basis for adaptation as well as the stronger predictor variables related to intellectual ability. For instance, knowing that some learners are better able to encode information in a particular way, we can maximize learning by allowing learners to use that method. Learner control of instruction can be implemented for any aspect of the instructional interaction. Knowledge-based designs (described in Part IV of this book), which are the logical extension of adaptive designs, make much more sophisticated assumptions about learning. They seek to model the way learners acquire information and to present corrective or facilitative instruction to fit that model. At the most abstract level, what or how a learner acquires knowledge may be controlled by curricular or processing requirements imposed by an outside agency.

Internal adaptations accommodate to the nature of the information being presented. Just as external adaptations assume that no treatment is best for all learners, internal adaptations assume that no treatment is appropriate for all content. Different information requires different processing which implies different instructional procedures. The most specific way to adapt instruction to the content would relate to the information processing requirements of the task. An information processing task analysis (Merrill, 1978) should be used to identify the type of processing required by any task. Courseware may also be adapted to meet different content requirements. You might adapt the sequence of content or, at the next level, the structure of content. The organizational structure of information depends on the content being presented. A variety of organizational structures can be used to depict different content (Reigeluth, Merrill, & Bunderson, 1978). At the broadest level of internal adaptation, different curricula are organized by different content structures. The "structure of the discipline" (Bruner, 1960) is a dated but still viable concept in course design. Internal adaptations then are those that accommodate to the nature and structure of the information being conveyed by the course.

INTRODUCTION TO PART III

The chapters in this part of the book present instructional designs for adapting instruction to both external and internal factors. The first three chapters describe *external* adaptations while the fourth describes courseware design models based on factors *internal* to the content. The majority of these chapters focus on external adaptations because of the long standing belief, pointed out earlier, that on-task performance is *the* primary determinant for prescribing instruction (Park & Tennyson, 1984). This belief has translated into more research and development on externally mediated design models. This part of the book reflects that effort.

In the first chapter, Carol Carrier and I discuss the adaptation of courseware to a broad range of individual differences. After presenting a rough taxonomy of individual differences, we show how those differences interact with instruction using an aptitude-treatment interaction context. Based on those interactions, we propose and later illustrate a generic model for adapting courseware to individual differences. This chapter is intended as an organizer for the next two chapters, which illustrate more specific approaches to adaptive courseware.

In chapter 9, Steve Ross and Gary Morrison review several different approaches or models for adapting courseware to individual learner characteristics. First, they illustrate how to adapt the level of instructional support (number of examples and/or practice items) to the learners entry level ability. They also show how to adapt incentives and to provide advice which enables the learners to make their own prescriptions. Consistent with principles of cognitive psychology, Ross and Morrison also illustrate how to adapt the learning context in order to make it more meaningful. They illustrate a database approach for adapting the content of examples or practice items based on personal characteristics of the learners. Ross' research on adaptive courseware designs has been among the most consistent findings in computer-based education research.

In chapter 10, Robert Tennyson and Dean Christensen describe the Minnesota Adaptive Instructional System (MAIS), probably the most comprehensive model of adaptive CBI available. They begin by defining intelligent learning systems and then identify those intelligent capabilities present in MAIS. They do this in a most systematic way, by deriving objectives from cognitive processes, knowledge bases from objectives, instructional variables from knowledge bases, and design enhancements from variables. Their description is theoretical but comprehensible. As a design process model, it is exemplary. The model should be studied by all instructional designers.

Finally, Wallace Hannum explores the process of adapting the structure and sequence of CBI to an important internal, instructional variable—subject matter structure. He relates domains of instruction to types of learning and then describes the structure of each domain. He concludes the argument by illustrating alternative methods for structuring presentations for each domain of instruction.

Although adapting to individual differences produces improved learning, it is a complex and inexact science. Adapting instructional treatments to subject matter differences is more feasible and potentially as (or more) effective than adapting to external adaptations. These represent content by treatment interactions (Jonassen, 1982).

The power of interactive technologies, such as microcomputer courseware, lies in their ability to adapt instruction in ways that make it more meaningful. The chapters in Part III of the book describe ongoing efforts to provide adaptive courseware designs. They lead conceptually into Part IV—intelligent CAI. Intelligent systems define more varied and sophisticated approaches to interacting with and adapting to learners.

REFERENCES

Bruner, J. (1960). *The process of education*. Cambridge, MA: Harvard University Press.

Jonassen, D. H. (1982). Aptitude- vs. content-treatment interactions: A better design model. *Journal of Instructional Development, 5*(4), 15–27.

Merrill, P. F. (1978). Hierarchical and information processing task analysis: A comparison. *Journal of Instructional Development, 1*(2), 35–40.

Park, O. K., & Tennyson, R. D. (1984). Computer-based instructional systems for adaptive education: A review. *Journal of Computer-Based Instruction*.

Reigeluth, C. M., Merrill, M. D., & Bunderson, V. (1978). The structure of subject matter content and its instructional design implications. *Instructional Science, 7*, 107–127.

Ross, S. M., Rakow, E. A., & Bush, A. J. (1980). Instructional adaptations for self-managed learning systems. *Journal of Educational Psychology, 72*, 312–320.

8 Adapting Courseware to Accommodate Individual Differences

Carol A. Carrier
University of Minnesota

David H. Jonassen
University of Colorado at Denver

INTRODUCTION

Although it has been promoted and practiced in various forms, there is little consensus regarding exactly what constitutes individualized instruction. Terms such as *individualized, personalized,* and *adaptive* instruction abound in the educational and psychological literature, suggesting that most educators agree with the premise that individuals differ in ways that affect learning. If and how educators should respond to these differences is unclear however. Perhaps as a consequence of this uncertainty, the only principle that consistently has guided attempts to individualize instruction or accommodate individual differences is that learners be allowed to work at their own pace.

Instructional designers, like other educators, profess the importance of attending to the characteristics of the learners. The Andrews and Goodson (1980) review of some forty instructional design models revealed that most advocate some form of target population analysis. For the most part, however, individual models do not present a strong rationale for assessing particular learner characteristics, nor do they prescribe how this information, once gained, might be used by designers of instructional products. Some models advocate the collection of information about general characteristics such as general ability or attitudes, while many recommend that prior knowledge be assessed. Guidance on how to incorporate knowledge about learners is typically sparse and often a statement of the obvious.

The widespread use of microcomputers and other new technologies for the delivery of instruction heightens educators' interest in the possibilities for individualized instruction. Microcomputers are a powerful delivery system for responding to differences among students for the following reasons:

1. Microcomputer environments are oriented towards individuals rather than groups. Although there are appropriate uses of computers for both large and small group instruction, their primary mode of use is with individual students. Adapting instruction and incentives to individuals produces more learning than adapting to groups or not adapting at all (Ross & Rakow, 1982).

2. Microcomputer environments provide maximum flexibility, in terms of both the quantity of instruction provided and the quality of its delivery. A single program can offer a highly elaborated and information-rich treatment of a topic or a scaled-down, leaner version depending upon the needs of the student. Such adaptations result in more learning (Ross & Rakow, 1982, and others). Similarly, courseware can provide extensive support for learning in the form of exercises, examples, feedback, and other helps, or it can minimize the use of such support elements (Carrier, Davidson, & Williams, 1985).

3. Increasingly, microcomputer environments are becoming multimodal. That is, they can present information in multiple channels, including auditory, visual, and tactile.

4. Microcomputer environments provide management systems which automate the monitoring of students' progress throughout the instructional process. They can diagnose entry skills, prescribe appropriate content and activities, and continually assess progress toward mastery. These capabilities, often using sophisticated statistical models for prescription (Tennyson, Christenson, & Park, 1984), provide productive prescriptions for learning and lighten the burden on instructors to model such processes for an entire classroom. Different students then can work on different tasks, managed by the microcomputer.

Clearly, microcomputers have much to offer in implementing individualized instruction. Technical capabilities, however, are only part of the solution. Instructional design considerations have limited our responsiveness to individual needs. In that this book is about instructional design, these needs should be addressed. The first problem is our incomplete understanding of the learner. How learner characteristics mediate the effects of both content and methods within instruction is a much needed area of knowledge for courseware designers. Second, knowing how learner characteristics interact with instructional treatments provides the basis for prescribing adaptive treatments. Third, we need to provide empirically verified prescriptions about (or a model for) how to design instructional treatments that accomodate individual differences. We consider each of these concerns in order.

INDIVIDUAL DIFFERENCES

Although the various branches of psychology can account for hundreds of individual difference variables, we are concerned here only with those that impact

TABLE 8.1
Individual Difference Variables that Impact on Learning

APTITUDE VARIABLES
    Intelligence
        Fluid
        Crystallized
        Spatial
    Achievement, academic performance
        Grade point average
        Standardized (norm-referenced) achievement tests
            SAT, GRE, LSAT
        Criterion-referenced measures

PRIOR KNOWLEDGE
    Pretests and diagnostic tests
    Word association tests
    Cognitive mapping techniques

COGNITIVE STYLES
    Field independence/dependence
    Reflectivity/impulsivity (cognitive tempo)
    Breadth of categorizing
    Scanning/focusing
    Leveling/sharpening of memories
    Visual/haptic perceptual style
    Tolerance for unrealistic experiences
    Cognitive complexity
    Serialistic/holistic style
    Cognitive style preferences
        Sensory preferences
        Temportal preferences
        Reasoning patterns

PERSONALITY VARIABLES (STYLES)
    Motivation
        Intrinsic - Achievement motive
            Achievement via independence
        Extrinsic
            Achievement via conformity (affiliation need)
    Locus on control
    Anxiety
        State/trait
        Content related
        Computer anxiety
    Introversion/extraversion
    Neuroticism
    Risk taking

the learning process. So, we consider those in roughly the order in which they affect learning (see Table 8.1 for the list of individual difference variables). That is, the learner characteristics that we discuss first are those that generally account for more of the variance in learning performance.

Aptitude

The strongest predictor of learning performance is general mental ability or aptitude—intelligence in its myriad forms. Conceptually, intelligence can be thought of as crystallized (memorial, verbal), spatial, and fluid (reasoning). In terms of component tasks, Guilford (1977) identified as many as 150 different forms of intelligence (less than that have been verified). Intelligence is definitely multifaceted and specific to the task being performed. It is usually assessed in schools through the use of nonprojective, paper-and-pencil tests. Intelligence is often fallaciously equated with IQ tests. Usually what is actually being measured is learning aptitude, that is, aptitude for performing school-related tasks. As a rule of thumb, we can predict that intelligence/aptitude generally accounts for about half the variance in learning performance. This figure varies greatly but represents a distillation of a lot of research. The fact that higher ability learners perform more accurately and facily will be readily confirmed by any teacher or any empirical verification. Although aptitude and intelligence are often vaguely understood concepts, most educators recognize and accept their presence and importance to learning.

Prior Knowledge

Perhaps the next strongest predictor of learning performance is prior knowledge, that is, how much the learner already knows about a topic or related topics prior to the beginning of instruction. Learners with greater prior knowledge possess more elaborate knowledge structures related to the instructional topic. Their knowledge structures are populated with more elaborate and better instantiated schemata which can be accessed and used to interpret the new information (see Generative Learning section in Jonassen chapter for a more extensive discussion). Being able to relate new information to these more elaborate existing knowledge structures facilitates knowledge acquisition, although not as much as aptitude. As you would expect, prior knowledge and aptitude tend to be related. Higher ability learners generally possess more knowledge to relate to new information.

Cognitive Styles

Because of differences in specific knowledge-acquisition and information-seeking aptitudes, individual learners develop unique styles for accessing and relating to new information. These differences may describe how they prefer to interrelate ideas, which modality they prefer for accessing information, how they memorize new information, or the sequence in which they prefer to gather information. Table 8.1 lists a number of cognitive styles that identify how learners interact with and acquire knowledge from their environments. Space does not permit detailed definitions of these. Examples are discussed in later sections of the chapter.

Personality Characteristics

Another set of style variables are personality differences in learners. The personality difference that most affects learning (in many instances the strongest predictor of learning after aptitude) is motivation. Motivation determines the amount of mental effort learners will invest in learning, which in turn predicts how much learning will occur (Salomon, 1983). Motivation may be internally generated (intrinsic), that is, based on internal drive states, or it may be externally stimulated through various reinforcement contingencies. Courseware can effectively accommodate to both (see the Ross and Morrison chapter and the Keller chapter for examples).

Other personality variables that have been shown to impact on learning are anxiety, locus of control (an individual's attribution of the causes of their actions), introversion/extraversion, and risk-taking. Personality variables generally have less impact on learning performance than the other variables, such as aptitude. They are also usually specific to the situation in which the learning occurs. Increased levels of anxiety are often produced by interacting with computers, for instance see Jonassen (1986b). Anxiety in high doses inhibits learning (Tobias, 1976). Their primary limitation is that personality variables are often too vague to be of much use in predicting performance on any given task. In addition, they tend to interact with each of the other types of difference variables discussed above so their effects are generally accounted for by more powerful predictors.

Knowing how learners differ is not enough to help us design better instructional courseware. We must know how learners performance differs on various tasks as a function of the kinds of instructional treatments they receive. We take up that topic in the next section.

INTERACTIONS OF LEARNER CHARACTERISTICS WITH INSTRUCTION

Efforts to individualize instruction must be guided by knowledge of learner characteristics and their affects on instructional tasks and the methods used to deliver these tasks. Gaining this knowledge has not been a simple task. New paradigms for research were needed and have been explored. Aptitude treatment interaction (ATI) research represents one of these newer paradigms. Cronbach called for this approach to research in his 1957 address before the American Psychological Association in a paper entitled "The Two Disciplines of Scientific Inquiry." He argued that what we know about the effects of individual differences on instruction is limited because previous methodologies have focused on these variables in isolation rather than in combination. Although correlational research of this nature has produced useful information describing how learners with different characteristics respond to different instructional treatments, this type of research does not permit determinations of causality. To illustrate, through correlational research we may learn that students with high amounts of anxiety tend to ask for help from teachers more frequently than low-anxiety students. What we don't gain is knowledge about types of interventions that reduce anxiety or provide the best mix of support for this student.

Traditionally, experimental educational research has focused primarily on instructional treatments. Studies in this vein allowed for causal claims to be made about the effects of different methods but typically, researchers have sought to neutralize rather than amplify the effects of individual differences. The goal was to identify optimal methods that worked well "on the average." Cronbach encouraged the combining of our knowledge from correlational research on individual differences with the search to define high quality instructional methods, such that learners falling along the continuum of a given aptitude could be accommodated.

Salomon (1972) operationalized these interactive concepts when he proposed three models that could be used to guide the design of instruction. He labeled the three *compensatory, preferential,* and *remedial.* Each model assume the diagnosis of learner states, such as level of prior knowledge, ability, or cognitive skills relative to a specific instructional task. These models for adapting instructional treatments to accommodate differences in learners' styles or aptitudes are discussed and illustrated later in this chapter.

Educational researchers actively pursued the search for ATIs in the late 60s and during the 70s. The 1977 book by Cronbach and Snow chronicled much of the work on ATIs until that time. If a general conclusion could be drawn from such a massive undertaking, it was that general ability emerged as the only individual difference variable to consistently predict learning under instructional conditions of all types. Sought-after disordinal interactions, in which regression lines for different types of learners under different instructional treatment conditions cross each other (as shown in Fig. 8.1), were infrequently found and even more infrequently replicated. A more common occurrence was the ordinal interaction (shown in Fig. 8.2), in which the regression slopes for groups of students with similar ability or aptitude, are much different for one treatment than another. The more common main effects studies seek to determine the best overall method of instruction for all students, thus seeking parallel slopes rather than interacting ones.

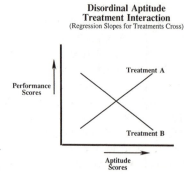

Disordinal Aptitude
Treatment Interaction
(Regression Slopes for Treatments Cross)

Performance Scores

Treatment A

Treatment B

Aptitude Scores

FIG. 8.1. Disordinal aptitude treatment interaction.

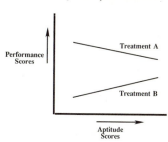

Ordinal Aptitude
Treatment Interaction
(Regression Slopes for Treatments Do Not Cross)

Performance
Scores

Treatment A

Treatment B

Aptitude
Scores

FIG. 8.2. Ordinal aptitude treatment interaction.

The following hypothetical examples illustrate the ways that aptitudes might (and in some research have) interact with alternative instructional treatments (see Fig. 8.1 or 8.2 for graphs of hypothetical interaction).

EXAMPLE 1

Aptitude: Cognitive style, Field independence/dependence - The ability to separate objects or information from its surrounding perceptual or contextual field. Field independents (analytical thinkers) are more adept.

Treatment A: Unstructured lesson where learners are required to impose their own structure or organization on the information presented.

Treatment B: Explicitly structured lesson where organization of materials is elaborately signalled (remedial match) or learner is led through the process of organizing the materials (compensatory match).

Interaction: Field independents would perform better with Treatment A, because they prefer to impose their own structure on information. Field dependents would benefit from the implicit structural support from Treatment B, whereas field independents might be deterred by the highly structured lesson.

EXAMPLE 2

Aptitude: Prior knowledge—The level of a learner's current awareness or background knowledge related to a topic. The more elaborate a learner's knowledge structure related to the lesson topic, the better she or he will be able to learn.

Treatment A: Lean treatment with few or no examples or practice items.

Treatment B: High instructional support, with more examples and/or practice items.

Interaction: Learners with greater prior knowledge need less instructional support while less informed learners need more instructional support (see Ross & Morrison chapter for detailed examples of this interaction).

EXAMPLE 3

APTITUDE: Anxiety—The momentary state or personality trait of being anxious, marked by worrying, uneasiness, fear, uncertainty, and activity.

Treatment A: No feedback about learners' performance or ability.

209

Treatment B: Positive and supportive feedback which lets the learner know how much progress she or he has made.

Interaction: Without feedback, the anxious learner becomes more anxious. Providing supportive feedback to anxious learner should aid the anxious learner more than the low-anxiety learner.

What factors accounted for the disappointing results of much of this research? A frequently quoted statement by Cronbach (1957) in which he suggested that searching for ATIs is much like entering a "hall of mirrors" summarizes a major limitation of ATI research. The potential for interactive effects in a real learning environment are staggering. Simple first order interactions may be compounded by second, third and fourth order interactions. Learners characteristics interact not only with treatments but with each other. This confounding of elements has led Snow and others to argue that what is needed are good "local" theories which prescribe instructional approaches for specified learner populations, under prescribed conditions, tasks, and content areas.

Work by Barbara McCombs and her colleagues (McCombs & McDaniel, 1981) suggests a methodology for a development of these local theories. They sought to determine whether they could develop individualized instruction through an empirical process. Air Force trainees completed a battery of aptitude and personality tests. Using stepwise multiple regression analyses, they determined which of the student characteristics assessed were the best predictors of performance in training modules where there was a wide range of performance. Based on these correlations, alternative treatments were defined for some lessons. For example if memory ability correlated highly with performance, certain memory mnemonics were built into the alternative treatment for students with poor memory ability. Once the alternative modules were developed, statistics were run to determine if the contribution of memory ability was lessened. While admittedly a slow process, the successive approximation to empirically based matches seems a step in the right direction.

Another limitation of ATI research is that the treatments studied usually have been static in nature, but the needs of learners have changed within the duration of a given instructional sequence, suggesting that it is possible to have too much of a good thing! Learners who need high levels of support at the beginning of a lesson, say in the form of inserted questions or highlighting, may require less support later on. By failing to accommodate this developmental change, the lesson may bore students and cause them to be inattentive. Research by Tennyson and his colleagues on adaptive instruction has addressed one aspect of this problem (see the Tennyson and Christenson chapter for more detail). They have made use of on-task responses to practice items to adapt the amount of instruction provided to learner throughout the lesson. They have found that the addition of on-task information enhances the predictive value of the Bayesian equation used to determine number of instances presented beyond what can be gained from assessment of prior knowledge and other student characteristics. Students in the adaptive treatments learned as much or more than those who received standard numbers of items and did so in less time. The capacity to respond immediately to on-task performance data is an important feature of computer-based instruction that can be tapped by appropriate management algorithms. Alternatives to ATI methodologies for individualizing instruction have been suggested. Gelbach (1979) proposes an "aptitude correction model." This approach calls for the progressive modification of an instructional treatment demonstrated to be effective by students of like aptitude (such as ability) to reduce the slope of its AT regression. If it can be determined that a particular treatment makes sense for practical reasons such as ease of delivery or cost of development and if it is clear that many but not all students perform well under it, there is reason to invest resources in gradually modifying it to reduce the effects of one or more individual differences. Gelbach suggests that the modifications are likely to be made to primary instructional elements such as the degree of exposure to content or the amount of practice included.

Tobias proposes a particular kind of ATI, that of achievement, rather than aptitude, treatment interactions. His work, and that of many others, has shown that a student's level of familiarity with the content to be learned is a powerful determinant of his instructional needs (more on this research is presented below).

Content treatment interactions (CTIs) are proposed by Jonassen (1982). Because the task of identifying content qualities may be more manageable than sorting out the complex array of person characteristics, CTIs may provide more stable and generalizable relationships. The limitation of this approach rests with our still limited technology to accurately assess content structures and task demands.

MODEL FOR ADAPTING COURSEWARE

We have established so far that individual differences do impact heavily on what is learned in any instructional situation. We know also that individual differences interact with the content being learned, that is, individual processing strengths will help some learners with some content but will provide no help with other content. As illustrated in the previous example, field-independent learners prefer to impose their own structure on material, so they will benefit from unstructured materials in a comprehension task. However, there is no reason to believe that field independence will help in learning a procedural task, which consists of an invariant sequence of operations. Knowing these things will help us adapt instruction to individual learner characteristics. However, two major questions remain. First, which learner characteristics do we adapt to in any given instructional situation? Second, how do we adapt to those characteristics? These are the key questions that we will attempt to answer in the following model for adapting instructional courseware. It is depicted here as a procedure; however, it represents at the very least a "complex procedure" (Hoffman & Medsker, 1983), which is a hybrid type of learning composed of two or more types of learning that has an inherent sequence.

Proposing a model for courseware design that purports to accommodate individual differences is risky, because it implies that we have definitive information about how learner characteristics interact with either the content to be presented and/or the methods that are delivered by the computer. As we have shown, many proposed "matches" are hypothetical at this point and will require validation. We suggest however that there are good leads to be followed within the four categories of learner characteristics described in Table 8.1. Attention to some of these characteristics should result in courseware that is more sensitive to the needs of different learners.

Step 1: Identify Objectives for the Courseware

Deciding on the goals and objectives for the courseware is an important first step in anticipating learner characteristics that might be influential. Different goals should alert the designer to check out particular general learner traits. Suppose, for example, that a goal for courseware for a statistics course is to illustrate the effects of different sample sizes on probability distributions. The designer might first make a mental checklist of the attributes that may influence learning. Will this topic be interesting to students? Have some had difficulty understanding the concept of random sample? How effective are students at interpreting visual information? Will their anxiety levels be high because this material will be included on the posttest? Responses to questions like these should provide an initial indication of the potential for learner characteristics that could make a difference in the courseware.

Step 2: Specify Task Characteristics

The next step, appropriately enough, is a task analysis of the instructional objective(s) for the courseware. We recommend an information processing task analysis (Merrill, 1978, 1980; Resnick, 1976; Resnick & Ford, 1982) or learning hierarchy analysis (Gagné, 1985; Gagné & Briggs, 1979). The former describes the sequence of cognitive operations required for solving a class of problems. The latter identifies and classifies the sequence of operations required to learn a skill or task. It is important to identify the information processing requirements of each task or at least the types of learning required by the objective. Knowing what types of learning or thought processes are required to complete the task is essential.

Step 3: Identify An Initial Pool of Learner Characteristics

The next step is to determine the learner characteristics which are most similar to the information processing requirements of the task or those which are known to interact with those requirements. This of course requires familiarity with a range of individual differences, such as those listed in the previous section. What type of learning is required by the objective? Which individual differences measure the ability to acquire that type of learning or process that task? For instance, if the task requires the acquisition of a defined concept (see Wager & Gagné chapter for a description of this type of task), you need to look for differences related to concept acquisition, such as breadth of categorizing (Bruner, Goodnow, & Austin, 1956), conceptual styles (Kagan, Moss, & Sigel, 1963), or associational fluency from the Kit of Factor Referenced Cognitive Tests (Ekstrom, French, & Harmon, 1976). Another approach is to access the aptitude-treatment interaction literature in hopes of finding empirical research related to the type of learning or the learner characteristics that you are analyzing. Unfortunately, although there is an extensive literature in this field, it doesn't begin to cover the range of individual differences with regard to different task characteristics. Additionally there are numerous methodological concerns with this literature base (Jonassen, 1982), which we alluded to earlier.

Step 4: Select the Most Relevant Learner Characteristics

Having identified the possible learner characteristics which may interact with the tasks required by the objective, you need to select the one or two learner characteristics on which you will base your adaptations. Narrowing the potentially large number of differences into a practical combination of one or two of the most productive differences is the key to the door out of Cronbach's "hall of mirrors." First, select those characteristic(s) that account for the most variance in the task, that is, those that best predict performance on the objective. There are at least three ways to identify predictor variables. First, peruse the research literature related either to the target task itself or to the learner characteristics of interest. An online literature search of specific terms related, for instance, to the cognitive style "cognitive tempo" should not produce a burdensome volume of literature. A term like "intelligence" will, however, so you will need to refine your search. The second option is to pretest learners with a battery of tests, similar to McCombs & McDaniel (1981, 1983) and then regress these criterion learning scores on the set of pretest scores using a stepwise procedure (see Ross & Morrison chapter for a more detailed discussion of this technique). The pretest variables that emerge first are the strongest predictors. These will be the variables on which you may wish to adapt instruction. The third method is to perform an information processing task analysis on both the task and each of the learner characteristic tests that you want to consider. The learner characteristics that most closely match the information processing requirements of the learning task are variables on which you may wish to adapt instruction. None of these options represents an exact science. All require some interpretation. The adaptation decisions require a thorough understanding of the individual difference variables you are working with.

Step 5: Analyze Learners in Target Population

If no predictions are available in the literature, you will need to conduct a preliminary investigation on some of the individual difference variables you have identified. Such a procedure would require that you test a group of learners as similar as possible to your target group. Ask them to complete each of the instruments that assess the learner characteristic identified in Step 2 as well as the instructional sequence and the criterion task. Using a stepwise regression procedure, assess which variables best predict performance. If no relevant aptitude measures are available, you will need to create your own. Salomon (1979) provides numerous excellent examples of this type of generalizable test construction.

Step 6: Select Final Differences

In making your selection, you must also consider the validity, feasibility and practicality of using various instruments to assess abilities, particularly if you plan to adapt them to computer display. Adaptation to computer display often compromises the validity and reliability of the instrument (Jacobs, Byrd, & High, 1985; Jonassen, 1986a). The characteristic(s) that you ultimately select to adapt instruction to will be those that account for the greatest differences in performance on the criterion task and which can be practically assessed, either online or in print form. If we are to consider truly adaptive courseware, we will want to move in the direction of online testing and adaptation based on those results.

Step 7: Determine How to Adapt Instruction

The most difficult decision will be how to adapt instruction once you have decided to do so. In adapting to individual differences, you are essentially considering the "matching" of instructional treatments to accommodate to differences in learner characteristics. We can accommodate to those differences in a variety of ways, using different matching models of instruction. As indicated earlier, Salomon (1972) identified three different types of matches: compensatory, capitalization, and supplantation.

Remedial. A remedial match presents instruction in which you provide supplementary instruction to learners who are deficient in a particular aptitude or characteristic. You attempt in the instruction to correct those learning deficits by explicitly teaching the skill along with the lesson. Such remediation would not be provided to learners who possess strengths in that area.

Capitalization/Preferential. A capitalization match occurs when you present instruction in a manner that is consistent with a learner's preferred mode of perceiving or reasoning. It is therefore also called a preferential match. Many

214

learner characteristics, such as field dependence/independence, are bipolar variables, which define different styles or approaches to acquiring knowledge and skills. These represent different patterns of thinking. A capitalization match presents instruction in a way that models how learners prefer to receive instruction. For instance, in providing capitalization (preferential) matching based on the prominent cognitive style, visual-haptic perceptual style, you would provide visual learners with pictorial displays while providing haptic learners with online or off-line manipulative activities that yield the same learning. Don't forget the feasibility criterion of selection. Are there indeed haptic materials available or reproducible that yield the appropriate learning and how do you interface them with the courseware?

Compensatory.   A compensatory match uses supplantation devices, which are embedded in the material and may be transparent to the learner. Supplantation devices compensate for (supplant) some processing requirements of the task for which the learner may have a deficiency. Supplantation has most often utilized media codes that help learners attend to necessary cues in learning materials. The numerous graphic and text manipulation capabilities supported by most microcomputers (e.g., graphic and sound cues or flashing or inverse text) provide rich compensatory tools for supplanting cue attendance skills. The microcomputer provides a variety of other supplantative possibilities, such as with input devices. Touch screens, mouses, or special purpose membrane keyboards will supplant literacy requirements for preliterate learners unable to use a keyboard. You need to determine what media codes or technological characteristics of the computer system for which you are developing courseware can be used to supplant skill deficiencies in learners to enable them to acquire appropriate knowledge or skills.

Challenge.   Messick (1976) identified another match, the challenge match, in which you deliberately present material in ways that call on learners to use skills in which they are deficient. A challenge match forces learners to develop new modes of processing. It stands in conflict with capitalization matches, which rely on existing skills.

Examples of Adaptive Matches.   So far, we have discussed general approaches to adaptation of instructional treatments in courseware. Table 8.2 lists some of these general approaches to adapting treatments for each type or class of individual differences listed in Table 8.1. Another level of adaptation can occur at a more micro level. These adaptations might be specific to particular presentation modes, screen displays, or feedback strategies. Table 8.2 suggests microstrategies that might be relevant to the four categories of individual differences. Several examples illustrate how these macro and micro strategies could be used to accommodate learners. The first of these is variation in feedback, specifi-

TABLE 8.2
Examples of Types of Adaptations to Learner Characteristics

	Class of Learner Characteristics			
	Aptitude	Prior Knowledge	Cognitive Styles	Personality
General approaches	*Level inst. support, *Advisement (see Ross & Morrison chapter) *Remedial/ compensatory matching	*Subject matter adaptation (see Hannum chapter) *Learner control *Knowledge-based systems *Hypertext *Personalizing context *Adaptive advisement	*Remedial match *Capitaliza-tion match *Compensatory match	*Capitali-zation match *Level instr. support *Advisement *Adaptive reward structure *Motivation strategies (Keller ARCS model)
Adaptive presentation components	*Structural/ typographic cues (see Allen, 1967) *Variable examples & practice	*Generative learning strategies (see Jonassen chapter)	*Alternative presentations based on cog-nitive styles requirements *Highlighting cuing to focus atten-tion	*Alternative feedback *Easier components *Rogerian responses *Incentives (graphic rewards) *Advice screens *Menus

cally the level of feedback provided. Figure 8.3 illustrates a feedback screen that might be used with highly anxious learners who need high levels of assurance. The screen on the left, used within the same program, is meant for less anxious students.

Another example relates to visual information. Students who are highly field dependent have difficulty disembedding relevant information in visual displays. When presenting visual information on the screen, it may be necessary to use more extensive highlighting devices for these students. Figure 8.4 illustrates two alternative representations of the visual information screen.

A third example of modifications to meet individual needs is that of the use of learner control strategies. Students differ in their ability to use learner control wisely. Hannafin (1984) uses the phrase internal control to refer to times when "individuals control the path, pace, and/or contingency of the instruction, typically by specifying choices among a range of designer embedded options" (p. 6). The research of Tennyson and his colleagues suggests that learners use learner control most effectively when given advisement about when and how much to choose. Carrier and her associates (1985, 1986) have found that among

```
Excellent job, Phil.
That problem was
tough but you
solved it!
```

```
Your response
is correct
```

FIG. 8.3. Variations on feedback screens.

children, some chose optional activities in computer-based instruction frequently, some sporadically, and some only rarely or not at all. The specific individual differences variables that may affect whether learner control should be used are not well known. However, it seems likely that those with greater prior knowledge may be able to make better decisions about what they need than those with less information.

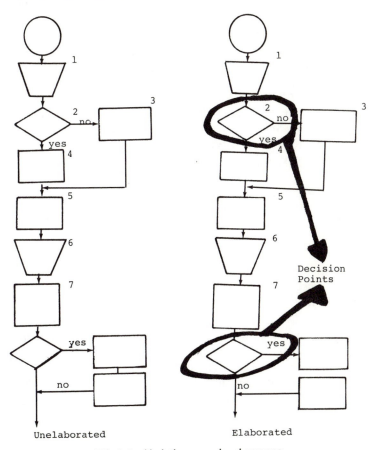

Unelaborated

Elaborated

FIG. 8.4. Variations on visual screens.

Choosing the Match.   Which of these matches to use depends on the nature and difficulty of the skills or processes you are matching, the ability of the computer to provide the appropriate matches, and the instructional situation. For instance, in an industrial training situation in which efficiency in learning is paramount, you would probably use a capitalization match if learners possessed capitalizable skills or a supplantation match if they didn't. This decision, like most of the rest, depends on a clear explication of the nature of the task and the characteristics of the learners.

Step 8: Design Alternative Treatments

Having decided upon the appropriate task, learner characteristics, and type of match, you now need to design alternative treatments which embed, call upon, or model the types of processing that you have specified. The design process requires developing treatment strategies that describe the task by characteristic by match interaction. For instance, if you are developing a remedial treatment for a task in which prior knowledge is essential, you need to ask how can that prior knowledge be remediated. If you can assess the specific knowledge deficits for each learner, perhaps you can simply provide remedial tutorial instruction. If you cannot determine specific knowledge deficits, then provide a full blown glossary with a glossary key to access it (or a pretest of vocabulary knowledge prior to each screen) and underline all of the key terms in the courseware for which entries are available. Since explicit vocabulary instruction results in comprehension gains (Jones & Friedman 1984), then be certain that learners know vocabulary prior to beginning each frame.

Steps 9 and beyond.   Design, produce, implement, and revise according to the instructional development model of your choice.

A Brief Illustration of the Use of the Adaptive Model

Background.   In this section we chronicle an account of a fictional courseware design process. Our purpose is to demonstrate how each of the steps outlined earlier might be applied to an actual courseware design and development task.

The courseware was designed for use in undergraduate education methods courses. Because it teaches general instructional design content it is appropriate for use with preservice teachers in all subject matter areas. Following the tutorial presented in the courseware the students were expected to be able to analyze the learning outcomes intended in their own lesson plans on the basis of this scheme.

Step 1.   The instructional goal for this courseware was the following:

Given a variety of instances for instructional tasks in different subject matter areas, the preservice student teacher will be able to classify each into one of the five

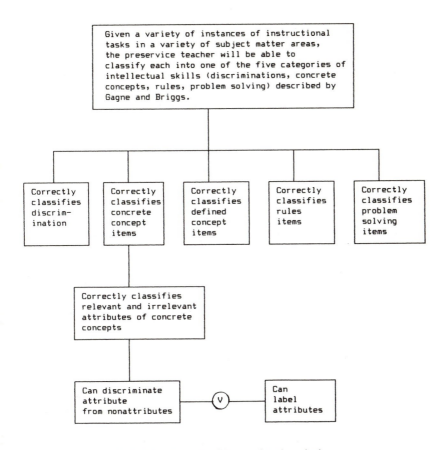

FIG. 8.5. Excerpt of instructional analysis.

categories of intellectual skills (discriminations, concrete concepts, defined concepts, rules, problem solving) described by Gagné and Briggs (1979).

Step 2. An instructional analysis of this goal revealed that the overall capability required was concept classification of coordinate concepts. Subskills included a number of discriminations and generalizations as well as learning some new labels. Figure 8.5 provides an excerpt of the instructional analysis chart created for this objective.

Step 3. Two sources of information were critical in formulating hypotheses about learner characteristics that might impact on how well this courseware would succeed in meeting the objective. The first source was the group of instructors themselves. Their perspectives, based on years of experience in teaching preservice teachers, provided a rich source of insights into the attitudes and behaviors of members of this target population. They voiced strong opinions about what would and would not "sell" with their students. The second source was the theoretical and research literature where we gleaned information about that possible link between concept acquisition processes and certain learner characteristics. Also, because the computer was a new vehicle for presenting this content, we needed to consider whether its use would require that we look at other learner dimensions, such as computer anxiety. From these initial sources, then, it seemed to us that the most potent variables were general ability, field independence, prior knowledge, and computer anxiety.

Step 4. Conversations with the instructors quickly convinced us that computer anxiety would not be a problem with these students. Most of them had worked with other CBI materials and felt comfortable using this technology as a learning tool. For this reason we decided to consider only three individual difference variables in a preliminary test of the courseware. Prior knowledge could be conveniently assessed with a short pretest that would be delivered by the computer. Items on the posttest would be similar to those in the pretest. Second we decided to obtain student scores on the undergraduate version of the Miller's Analogy Test (UMAT) as a measure of verbal ability. These scores were already in the student records and could be easily obtained. Third, we chose to administer an instrument called the Group Embedded Figures Test as a measure of field independence. Because this cognitive style has been shown to affect student's ability to discriminate between relevant and irrelevant cues in both perceptual and verbal tasks, it may affect the processing of cues in concept acquisition tasks.

The first version of the materials was meant to represent the strongest treatment that could be designed without adaptation to individual differences. A sample of students was used in a pilot of the materials and as predicted, there was a fairly broad range of scores, suggesting that the instruction worked well for some but not all of the students. Because the pretest resulted in uniformly low scores with very little range, we concluded that we should drop it as a predictor variable since it appeared that most undergraduates would do poorly.

Step 5. Available literature as well as teacher observations and the pilot results suggested that the two individual difference variables remaining, field independence and general ability, should be useful ones to guide our adaptations.

Step 6. Fortunately, the measures we planned to use were respectable in terms of traditional measurement criteria. Scores on the UMAT were available to us and the Group Embedded Figures Test was simple to administer and did not take too much time.

Step 7. Two models were drawn upon in designing the different versions of the courseware. Salomon's compensatory model guided one version. In this version, each expository and practice item included a checklist intended to help focus attention on the presence or absence of the critical attributes of the concept.

This checklist was designed to aid the field dependent learner who has difficulty recognizing cues unless they are highly salient. The alternative model, capitalization, eliminated this heavy cuing procedure and was intended to create a more efficient sequence for the more analytical field independent learner. A second adaptation that was included was the locus of control of the amount of examples presented. In the learner control version, students were given a few core examples but could choose to select or ignore additional items. In the program control version, the program presented a set sequence and no choice was allowed. The research on learner control suggests that higher ability students are more skilled at using learner control strategies and prefer to be given control. If this strategy did not reduce performance for the higher ability students, we reasoned it would be a useful adaptive technique.

Step 8. Using these variables we now created four versions of the materials: (1) Checklist, Program Control; (2) Checklist, Learner Control; (3) No Checklist, Program Control and (4) No Checklist, Learner Control.

The analysis of the effects of these different versions for learners who differed with respect to field independence and verbal ability revealed some interesting guidelines for future use of the various versions. Field dependent learners benefited from the inclusion of the checklists as a highlighting device but field independent students did not. In fact, these latter students reported some annoyance in having to complete the checklists but their performance on the posttest was not hindered by this strategy. Higher ability learners found the learner control materials more interesting than did their counterparts in the program control materials but they learned equally well under either version. Students with lower scores on the UMAT did worse under learner control than program control conditions.

Step 9. Based on our testing of the materials, we concluded that a pretest for preservice populations was likely a waste of time. Perhaps a graduate level population would reflect a distribution of scores that could be a useful predictor of treatment variations. With respect to the inclusion of the checklist, we decided that it could be mandatory for field dependent students and presented as an option for field independent students. Learner control over the amount of instances seen appeared to be disadvantageous to the learning of lower ability students in this population but appealing to higher ability students. We concluded that the benefits of learner control did not outweigh the possible disadvantages and so chose to stay with learner control over selection of the checklists only as the best approach for both field independent and higher ability learners.

STRUCTURING ADAPTIVE COURSEWARE

There are at least two ways of structuring courseware to adapt to individual learner characteristics. Since the conceptual structure for adaptive instruction is branching, the most obvious programming structure is branching. In virtually all programming languages and most authoring languages and systems, however, there are alternate forms of branching. Two forms of branching that lend themselves to adaptive courseware are tree-structured branching and case-structure branching. Tree-structures represent a sequence of decisions (see Fig. 8.6 for an example). Each junction on the tree, beginning at the top, represents a decision which would lead to an alternate action or to another decision. For instance, the first decision point might query the user about their familiarity with the courseware. If not familiar, the user would be branched to a set of directions. If familiar, the user would be branched to another decision, which would assess, for instance, their level of field independence. Having classified the user as field dependent or independent, the program might implement alternative treatments based on those styles, or it might branch to another decision which might determine which kind of match would be most productive for the particular type of learner completing the specific task. Another form of branching is the case structure, which replaces a sequence of binary decisions with a single selector which is matched to a set of options. An example of a case structure is a menu. The menu may be learner controlled or program controlled. The decision making is made all at once, perhaps using multiple criteria, and a specific treatment would be assigned.

Another approach to adaptive courseware is to use a linear approach in which a single sequence of instruction is presented to all learners. At various points in the program, variable slots would be used rather than text or graphics. Based on an instructional prescription, the program would read a set of values from a file which would be used to fill in the variables slots (see Ross and Morrison chapter for an example of this technique used for personalizing the learning context in courseware). So, alternative treatments would represent alternative files, which contain alternative versions of the program. One file, for instance, may contain compensatory examples and another capitalization examples. The point of this section is that the programming for adapting to learner characteristics in courseware is not difficult. It requires the use of very straightforward branching blocks. The instructional design is definitely more critical than the program design.

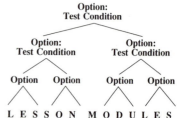

FIG. 8.6.   Tree structured branching.   L E S S O N   M O D U L E S

LIMITATIONS OF ADAPTIVE COURSEWARE

We know that learning is mediated by various learner characteristics. We also know that by altering the nature of instruction, we can improve the learning of many. Our discussion thus far has provided a rationale, model for, and illustrations of courseware which adapts the sequence, style, mode, or structure of the instructional presentation in an attempt to produce more learning from learners with different characteristics. We believe that computer courseware, because of its variety of presentation modes, instructional logic, and individualized nature, is the ideal medium for individualizing instruction by adapting aspects of the lesson to learner characteristics. Despite our belief that adaptation is desirable and the reasoning sound, there are a number of limitations to our adaptive model. We do not believe that adaptive courseware is always needed nor will it work in every situation for a variety of reasons.

The adaptive model presented in this chapter begins with the premise that dimensions of instructional treatments that interact with specific characteristics of learners can be isolated. This is an ATI perspective and for a variety of reasons, the ATI research base is suspect (Jonassen, 1982; Tobias, 1981). The ATI research base has been largely theoretical, too often driven by the post hoc empirical search for differences. Findings from this research base have been inconsistent. Few replication studies have been carried out. The results that have been produced often are not generalized to other settings. As we have pointed out before, the ATIs are subject to interactions with other variables such as the nature of the task, the locale in which the learning occurs, the incentives that might be motivating students, and so on. Fortunately, there are some individual differences, such as intelligence, that have been more systematically researched and that provide more consistent results on which to base design decisions. In our adaptation model, Steps 3 and 4 recommend that the selection of learner characteristics be based on the nature of the information processing required by the task. This will preclude some of the deficiencies of shotgun approaches to identify matches of learner characteristics with instructional variables.

Another problem with our model relates to the long standing differences between the goals of researchers and designers. Although it is axiomatic that both designers and researchers value the goal of meeting the needs of different learners, their approaches, as well as the constraints under which they operate, differ markedly. As a result, what one group learns is often viewed suspiciously by the other.

The courseware designer's starting point is a specific content area or set of skills that must be mastered by a targeted group of learners. This content or set of skills is not arbitrary; it grows out of an instructional problem that has been identified through formal or informal needs analysis. The designer's challenge is to create CBI that will solve the problem in the most efficient and cost-effective manner. Within this context, individual differences or learner idiosyncracies that

223

hinder progress toward achieving competence are viewed as a nuisance to be neutralized as much as possible. If, however, there is convincing evidence that people learn most effectively under different instructional conditions, designers become receptive, especially if (1) the target population contains sizeable subgroups of people who differ in terms of some characteristic X, and (2) delivering alternatives to these subgroups is feasible financially.

The researcher, whose primary interests are hypothesis testing and theory building, approaches adaptive instruction from a somewhat different perspective. His priority is to increase knowledge about how certain learner characteristics affect, or are affected by, various instructional manipulations. He seeks to establish reliable links between the internal conditions of learners and certain qualitative or quantitative aspects of instruction. Unlike the designer, the researcher need not be concerned with the financial or practical feasibility of actually delivering instructional alternatives. This allows the researcher greater freedom to construct instructional sequences that maintain high degrees of control over the structure and delivery of information. Consequently, designers argue that findings from research are often not applicable to practice because the instructional tasks and conditions bear little resemblance to "real" instruction.

One factor that will resolve some of these differences is the careful field testing of adaptive courseware under actual instructional conditions. How difficult is it for the teacher to administer the necessary prerequisite individual differences measures? How well do the adaptive treatments hold students' attention? Do adaptive treatments take longer to complete than nonadaptive ones and is the payoff significant in practical terms? Questions like these must become at least one focus of the researchers' work if prescriptions to courseware designers are to be well received and implemented.

Having decided how to match the instructional presentation to learner characteristics, the designer must then attempt to model various forms of information processing in the courseware. Salomon (1979) provides numerous excellent examples of how these processes can be modeled. Each microcomputer environment imposes some restrictions on the nature of the modeling capability, however. Although computer graphics and synthesized sound are developing rapidly, some very popular and widely disseminated microcomputers have very limited graphics capabilities. While these may be enhanced by hardware additions (e.g., more sophisticated graphics cards), designers cannot count on such hardware upgrades to be generally available. An important component of Steps 7 and 8 is to factor the desired designs through the limitations of the microcomputer system for which the courseware is designed.

Courseware activities play against the backdrop of rich and complex environments where serendipity and humor are as important as well defined instructional goals and valid assessment activities. Achieving any degree of predictability in our knowledge of how an individual student will respond to a particular configuration of instructional manipulations on a particular day is admirable. To introduce the additional wrinkle that students differ in terms of, for example, how they store and retrieve information, use elaborative devices, or react to different media, can add a staggering amount of complexity to the tasks of a courseware designer. It will take the cooperation of many courseware designers over a long period of time to begin to realize the potential of adaptive designs for students.

REFERENCES

Andrews, D. H., & Goodson, L. A. (1980). A comparative analysis of models of instructional design. *Journal of Instructional Development, 3*(4), 2–16.

Bruner, J. S., Goodnow, J. J., & Austin, G. A. (1956). *A study of thinking.* New York: Wiley.

Carrier, C., Davidson, G., & Williams, M. (1985). The selection of instructional options in a computer-based coordinate concept lesson. *Educational Communications & Technology Journal, 33*(3), 199–212.

Carrier, C., Davidson, G., Williams, M., & Kalweit, C. (1986). Instructional options and encouragement effects in a microcomputer-delivered concept lesson. *Journal of Educational Research, 79*(4), 222–229.

Cronbach, L. J. (1957). The two disciplines of scientific psychology. *American Psychologist, 12,* 671–84.

Ekstrom, R. B., French, J. W., & Harmon, H. H. (1976). *Manual for the kit of factor referenced cognitive tests.* Princeton, NJ: Educational Testing Service.

Gagné, R. M. (1985). *The conditions of learning* (4th ed.). New York: Holt, Rinehart & Winston.

Gagné, R. M., & Briggs, L. J. (1979). *Principles of instructional design* (2nd ed.). New York: Holt, Rinehart & Winston.

Gelbach, R. D. (1979). Individual differences: Implications for instructional theory, research, and innovation. *Educational Research, 8*(4), 8–14.

Guilford, J. P. (1977). *Way beyond the IQ guide to improving intelligence and creativity.* Buffalo, NY: Creative Education Foundation.

Hannafin, M. (1984). Guidelines for using locus of instructional control in the design of computer-assisted instruction. *Journal of Instructional Development, 7*(3), 6–10.

Hoffman, C. K., & Medsker, K. L. (1983). Instructional analysis: The missing link between task analysis and objectives. *Journal of Instructional Development, 6*(4), 17–23.

Jacobs, R. L., Byrd, D. M., & High, W. R. (1985). Computerized testing: The hidden figures test. *Journal of Educational Computing Research, 1*(2), 173–178.

Jonassen, D. H. (1982). Aptitude- versus content-treatment interactions: Implications for instructional design. *Journal of Instructional Development, 5*(4), 15–27.

Jonassen, D. H. (1986a, January). *Effects of microcomputer display on a perceptual/cognitive task.* Paper presented at the annual meeting of the Association for Educational Communications and Technology, Las Vegas.

Jonassen, D. H. (1986b, January). *State-trait anxiety and microcomputers.* Paper presented at the annual meeting of the Association for Educational Communications and Technology, Las Vegas.

Jones, B. F., & Friedman, L. (1984). Vocabulary learning strategies. In *Content-driven comprehension, instruction, and assessment: A model for army training literature.* (Tech. Report.) Alexandria, VA: Army Research Institute.

Kagan, J., Moss, H. A., & Sigel, L. E. (1963). Psychological significance of styles of conceptualization. *Monographs of the Society for Research in Child Development, 28*(2), 73–112. (Serial # 86)

McCombs, B. L., & McDaniel, M. A. (1981). On the design of adaptive treatments for individualized instructional systems. *Educational Psychologist, 16*(1), 11–22.

McCombs, B. L., & McDaniel, M. A. (1983). Individualizing through treatment matching is a necessary but not sufficient approach. *Educational Communications and Technology Journal, 31,* 213–225.

Merrill, P. F. (1978). Hierarchical and information processing task analysis: A comparison. *Journal of Instructional Development, 1*(2), 35–40.

Merrill, P. F. (1980). Analysis of a procedural task. *NSPI Journal, 19*(2), 11–15, 26.

Messick, S. (1976). Personal styles and educational options. In S. Messick & Associates (Eds.), *Individuality in learning.* San Francisco: Jossey Bass.

Resnick, L. B. (1976). Task analysis in instructional design: Some cases from mathematics. In D. Klahr (Ed.), *Cognition and instruction.* Hillsdale, NJ: Lawrence Erlbaum Associates.

Resnick, L. B., & Ford, W. W. (1982). The analysis of tasks for instruction: An information processing approach. In T. A. Brigham & A. C. Catania (Eds.), *Handbook of applied behavioral analysis: Social and instructional processes.* New York: Irvington.

Ross, S. M., & Rakow, E. A. (1982). Adaptive instructional strategies for teaching rules in mathematics. *Educational Communications and Technology Journal, 30,* 67–74.

Salomon, G. (1972). Heuristic models for the generation of aptitude treatment interaction hypoth-

Salomon, G. (1979). *The interaction of media, cognition, and learning.* San Francisco, CA: Jossey Bass.

Salomon, G. (1983). The differential investment of mental effort in learning from different sources. *Educational Psychologist, 18*(1), 42–51.

Snow, R. E. (1980). Aptitude, learner control, and adaptive instruction. *Educational Psychologist, 15,* 151–158.

Tennyson, R. D., Christensen, D. L., & Park, S. (1984). The Minnesota adaptive instructional system: An intelligent CBI system. *Journal of Computer-Based Instruction, 11,* 2–13.

Tobias, S. (1976). Anxiety-treatment interactions: A review of the research. In J. Sieber, H. F. O'Neil, & S. Tobias (Eds.), *Anxiety, learning, and instruction.* Hillsdale, NJ: Lawrence Erlbaum Associates.

Tobias, S. (1981). Adapting instruction to individual differences among students. *Educational Psychologist, 16*(2), 111–120.

9

Adapting Instruction to Learner Performance and Background Variables

Steven M. Ross
Gary R. Morrison
Memphis State University

With the availability of today's small and inexpensive microcomputers, computer-assisted instruction (CAI) has now become a reality for everyday classroom applications. For relatively little cost (e.g., $20–$30), a software disk containing one or several CAI programs in virtually any school subject can be purchased and used over time with many different classes of students. Even a fairly simple program may contain such features as graphics and animation, interactive responding, and personalized feedback, all of which serve to increase the attractiveness and versatility of the lesson relative to a textbook or programmed instruction version.

Although the above qualities provide CAI with significant "face appeal," the fundamental question is how well it actually teaches. Research findings on this topic have generally been supportive (Kulik, Bangert, & Williams, 1983; Kulik, Kulik, & Cohen, 1980; Ragosta, Holland, & Jameson, 1982), but are not (and will probably never be) sufficiently strong or consistent to proclaim CAI as "better" than traditional methods (Clark, 1983). A more reasonable interpretation is that CAI possesses different delivery capabilities than lecturers or textbooks, and thus will have advantages in some situations and disadvantages in others. From this perspective, the important goal of CAI design becomes one of discovering how to use its special attributes more productively.

Our main assumption in this chapter is that one of the computer's most powerful capabilities lies in *adapting* instruction to students. Unfortunately, the adaptive methods frequently incorporated in today's commercial software are relatively weak forms that mainly relegate decisions about pacing and sequencing of materials to the learner. This type of approach, which is commonly called "learner control" or "internal control," is adaptive only to the extent that students possess the knowledge, maturity, and motivation to exercise effective judgments about their learning needs (Hannafin, 1984; Ross, 1984). An alternative orientation is "program (or external) control" in which movement through the lesson is dictated by the lesson designer, based on how the student responds while learning. One common example, similar to programmed instruction, consists of adaptive branching to different lesson segments depending upon which multiple-choice alternative the student selects. Another is evaluation of the student's on-task performance to determine whether the lesson should end, additional practice problems should be presented, or some other action should be taken. A principal criticism of program-controlled models concerns the designer's ability to judge what type and quantity of instruction is needed at given times (Hannafin, 1984). A second criticism concerns the application of arbitrary criteria (e.g., 80% correct; "3 misses in a row") that have not been previously validated to direct branching decisions.

The purpose of the present chapter is to review several more systematic designs. The types of adaptations they provide encompass: (a) quantity of instructional support and incentives, (b) meaningfulness of problem-solving contexts, and (c) the density of narrative text used for expository teaching. The first two models have been extensively examined in our prior research and evaluation studies. The third (context density) model is still in its development stage, and thus will only be generally described here. All three models were designed specifically for teaching mathematical material, but should be applicable to most other school subjects as well. Let us now turn to their descriptions.

ADAPTATION OF SUPPORT AND INCENTIVES

Rationale

Applied individualized learning strategies, such as the Personalized System of Instruction (Keller, 1968) and Mastery Learning (Bloom, 1976) establish conditions of *high* instructional support by providing as much time and resources as the student requires to attain objectives. A limitation of typical applications, however, is reliance on subjective judgments to determine how much support is needed. A frequent result is that high-achievers select too much support and low-achievers too little. Interest in this problem led to our design of a model for systematically adapting the amount of instructional support to individuals. The model was directed to a self-instructional unit covering 10 algebraic rules taught in our introductory college statistics course. A flow diagram summarizing the steps of the model is shown in Fig. 9.1. Steps are individually examined below.

How the Model Works

As diagrammed in Fig. 9.1, the component steps of the adaptive model are as follows:

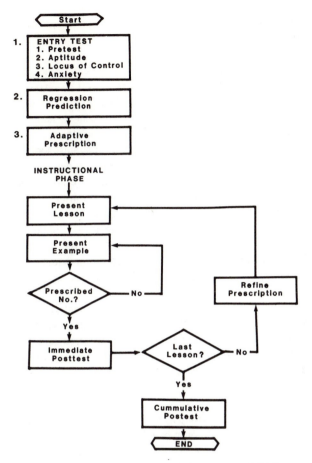

FIG. 9.1. Flow diagram of procedures used in the MSU Regression Model.

Step 1: Selecting predictor variables. The initial step involves selecting pretask (entry) variables as a basis for *predicting* student performances on the unit. This predictive process serves as the foundation for the adaptive model, with its underlying logic being "if predicted performance is low, increase instructional support; if high, decrease instructional support." For our application, the following four entry variables, when statistically combined via a multiple regression solution, yielded the most reliable predictions of overall task performances (multiple $r = .77$): achievement pretest, reading comprehension, locus of control, and anxiety. The achievement pretest, however, was by far the strongest predictor and could have been used by itself with minimal loss in predictive accuracy. Although we used a printed version of the pretest, greater automation and efficiency could be achieved by administering and scoring the test by computer. Also, using a pretest as a single predictor should suffice in most applications of the model.

Step 2: Developing predictive equations.   As indicated, the statistics unit of interest contained 10 lessons describing different rules. Our objective, therefore, was to develop a predictive equation geared to each lesson. To accomplish this, we pretested a sample of students on the entry measures, had them study the complete instructional unit, and posttested them on each lesson. Predictive equations were generated by regressing individual lesson subtest scores on the entry variables (see Hansen, Ross, & Rakow, 1977, for further details). The result was 10 separate regression equations that yielded the most reliable predicted lesson subtest scores from the student's entry scores. To illustrate, let's consider the simple case in which prediction is based on an achievement pretest only. Each equation would take the form $Y' = bX + a$, where Y' = predicted rule score, X = pretest score, b = slope of regression line, and a = the intercept. The latter two parameters (slope and intercept) are provided by the equation. Entering the student's pretext (X) score will yield his or her predicted lesson score (Y').

Step 3: Selecting prescriptions.   The next requirement is to match the predicted scores to instructional prescriptions specifying the number of examples to present for each rule. From earlier task analysis of the length and difficulty of the unit, we identified the most appropriate range of instructional support as from 2 to 10 examples, with a median of 6 examples. Briefly, this involved, as a main step, evaluating the performances and attitudes of a pilot sample that was administered differing levels of support. Performance peaked at 6 examples, with little improvement thereafter for the group as a whole. An upper level of 10 examples also seemed the most a student could handle without becoming overly fatigued and consuming too much time on that lesson. Two examples seemed a reasonable minimum level for demonstrating the rule with different values. Predicted scores, expressed as standard (z) scores, were matched to prescriptions within this range, as shown in Table 9.1. These decision rules were incorporated into

TABLE 9.1
Criteria for Matching Instructional Prescriptions to
Predicted Lesson Posttest Scores

Prescription	Predicted z Score Range
10 examples	Less than -1.38
9	-.88 to -1.38
8	-.38 to - .88
7	-.13 to - .38
6	+.13 to - .13
5	+.38 to + .13
4	+.88 to + .38
3	+1.38 to + .88
2	Greater than +1.38

the computer program, so that prescriptions would be automatically generated once predictor scores for a given student were entered. Note that this phase of the model development process requires careful content analysis of lesson materials to match appropriate prescription levels to the predicted scores.

An illustration.   To demonstrate these beginning steps, let us again consider a simplified case, this time involving an algebra unit consisting of *two* lessons. In Step 1, it is determined that an achievement pretest alone provides sufficiently reliable predictions of unit performances. Step 2 then involves relating students' pretest scores to performance on each lesson. Assume that the resultant multiple regression equations are found to be:

$$Y'_1 = .2X_1 - 1.4 \text{ (Lesson 1)}$$
$$Y'_2 = .14X_2 - 1 \text{ (Lesson 2)}$$

where Y' = the predicted lesson scores and X = the obtained lesson pretest scores. The content analysis of the unit suggests appropriate lesson prescriptions to range from 2–10 examples, with selections to be made according to the scheme shown in Table 9.1 (Step 3). The computer program, written in BASIC, would take the general form shown in Table 9.2. (Readers unfamiliar with BASIC can still follow much of the logic by reading the remarks contained in REM statements.)

The program operates by reading the student's name and pretest score (lines 20 and 2000), and the predictive equation parameters (slope and intercept) for each lesson (lines 60, 2020, and 2040). A predicted score for each lesson is calculated (line 80) using that information, and the results are displayed (line 120 and see sample output). As is reviewed below, under computer-managed instruction (CMI), the teacher could then use that information to prepare and distribute materials as prescribed. Under CAI, the prescriptions could be written to a file (see lines 140–210) and used by the main lesson program to direct the selection of content on line. The latter would operate through the following types of statements (in Applesoft BASIC):

```
3000 PRINT D$; "OPEN EXAMPLES"
3010 PRINT D $; "READ EXAMPLES"
3020 FOR V = 1 TO 2
3030 INPUT EX(V)
3040 NEXT V
3050 PRINT D$; "CLOSE EXAMPLES"
```

Lesson presentation.   Once Steps 1, 2, and 3 are completed (see Fig. 9.1), the adaptive model can be implemented. In our CMI applications (Hansen, Ross, & Rakow, 1977; Ross, 1984), the steps involved (a) prearrangement and administration of learning materials according to the individual student's prescriptions;

TABLE 9.2
Program to Generate Adaptive Prescriptions of Examples

```
]LIST

5    DIM EX(2): REM  CREATE ARRAY FOR EXAMPLES
10   REM  READ STUDENT'S NAME (NI$) AND PRETEST SCORE (PRE)
20   READ N$,PRE
30   REM     LOOP TO GENERATE PRESCRIPTION FOR TWO UNITS (V)
40   FOR V = 1 TO 2
50   REM  READ SLOPE (X) AND INTERCEPT (Y) VALUES
60   READ X,Y
70   REM  COMPUTE PREDICTED POSTTEST SCORE (PS)
80   PS = (X * PRE) + Y
90   REM  SUBROUTINE TO MATCH PS TO PRESCRIPTION (EX)
100    GOSUB 1000
110    REM  PRINT PRESCRIPTION
120    PRINT "UNIT ";V;" EXAMPLES = ";EX
130    NEXT V
140    REM  STORE PRESCRIPTIONS IN TEXT FILE
150    D$ = CHR$ (4)
160    PRINT D$;"OPEN EXAMPLES"
170    PRINT D$;"WRITE EXAMPLES"
180    FOR V = 1 TO 2
190    PRINT EX$(V)
200    NEXT V
210    PRINT D$;"CLOSE EXAMPLES"
220    END
1000   REM  PRESCRIPTION SUBROUTINE
1010   REM  ONLY PART IS SHOWN
1020   REM  SELECT NUMBER OF EXAMPLES  (EX)
1030   IF PS < - 1.38 THEN EX(V) = 10
1040   IF PS < -.88 AND PS > = -1.38 THEN EX(V) = 9
1050   REM  ADDITIONAL STATEMENTS FOR TABLE 1 ALGORITHM ARE
1055   REM  OMITTED IN THIS SAMPLE
1110   IF PS > + 1.38 THEN EX(V) =2
1120   RETURN
1130   REM
2000   DATA "ANDREW JAMES",8
2002   REM
2010   REM  SLOPE AND INTERCEPT FOR UNIT 1:
2020   DATA .2, -1.4
2030   REM  NOW UNIT 2
2040   DATA .14, -1


]RUN
UNIT 1: EXAMPLES = 5
UNIT 2: EXAMPLES = 6
```

(b) administration of a formative lesson posttest upon completion of each lesson; and (c) use of the lesson posttest score to make refinements, if indicated, in the next lesson prescription. The latter procedure simply involved adding or subtracting examples for extremely high or low posttest scores. After completing all 10 lessons, students took a cumulative test on the entire unit.   Results from several studies comparing the model to strategies offering nonadaptive or standard (fixed) amounts of support showed consistent advantages for achievement. Readers interested in more detail about that research may wish to review the articles by Hansen et al. (1977) and Ross and Rakow (1982).

Could Learner Control do the Same?

In considering alternatives to the model, it is natural to question whether a learner-control orientation, in which students self-select the prescriptions they want, would be equally effective. Our evaluation of this approach, however, produced clearly negative results, as was also Tennyson's finding in related research (e.g., Tennyson, 1980). Interestingly (but not unpredictably), high performers tended to select the maximum prescription (i.e., many more examples then they probably needed), and low performers the minimum prescription (also see Carrier, Davidson, & Williams, 1985). The implication is that many students simply do not possess the expertise and maturity to make effective decisions on their own. Low achievers, for example, might be motivated to shorten what for them is an unpleasant and difficult task. High achievers, on the other hand, may want to prolong a reinforcing experience as well as maximize their chances for success on the unit. Yet, the idea of allowing students (especially adults) freedom of choice while learning still carries considerable philosophical and pedagogical appeal. A suggested "middle ground" is an *advisement* orientation in which the adaptive model selects the prescription in the usual manner, but merely recommends it as a desirable option, leaving the final decision to the student (see e.g., Johansen & Tennyson, 1983; Tennyson & Buttrey, 1980). A sample frame illustrating advisement instructions is shown in Fig. 9.2.

Incentives as a Motivational Device

Just because students are given appropriate amounts of instructional support, provides no guarantee that they will use those materials as prescribed. This concern suggested an extension of the model using adaptive incentives to *orient* study behaviors. The general procedure involved distributing the total point value of the unit (100 points) unevenly across the 10 lessons, according to predicted lesson difficulty. Points were distributed by having the adaptive model

```
I--------------------------------I
I                                I
I            LESSON 3            I
I                                I
I      CONVERTING DECIMALS       I
I         INTO DECIMALS          I
I                                I
I--------------------------------I
```

YOU MAY SELECT FROM
2 TO 10 PRACTICE EXAMPLES

RECOMMEND PRACTICE LEVEL: 7 EXAMPLES

ENTER YOUR SELECTION <2 -10 > HERE:

FIG. 9.2. Sample computer screen for advisement strategy.

```
                    INSTRUCTIONS
           ----------PAGE-3------------------
               THIS UNIT WILL BE WORTH 100 POINTS
               DISTRIBUTED IN THE FOLLOWING MANNER:

           LESSON                                 POINTS
           --------------------------------------------
           1.  ORDER OF OPERATIONS                   0
           2.  MULT. AND DIV. OF FRACTIONS           5
           3.  FRACTIONS INTO DECIMALS              10
           4.  DECIMALS INTO FRACTIONS             15
           5.  DECIMALS INTO PERCENTAGES            5
           6.  ADD/SUB. OF EXPONENTS               15
           7.  MULTIPLICATION OF EXPONENTS         20
           8.  SUMMATION                           10
           9.  FACTORIALS                          20
           10. INEQUALITIES                         0
```

FIG. 9.3. Sample computer screen showing differential incentives for the 10 lessons.

generate predicted lesson scores in the normal fashion (see Fig. 9.1 and Table 9.2) and *rank-order* the 10 lessons by predicted score. The two "most difficult" lessons were then assigned 20 points each, the next two 15 points each, and so on, continuing with decrements of 5 points per pair, until the two "easiest" rules were reached. The rationale was that the differential incentives would motivate students to spend more time and effort on materials with which they were least familiar. Samples of what the student was shown at the beginning of the overall lesson and of an individual unit are presented in Figs. 9.3 and 9.4, respectively.

Research evaluations indicated significant learning gains for the adaptive incentives strategy relative to a standard-incentives distribution in which 10 points were assigned to each lesson (Hansen et al., 1977). The strongest results were produced, however, by combining the incentives and instructional support models. The outcome of the combined model is provision of more material to

```
       r--------------------------------7
       |                                |
       |           LESSON 2             |
       |                                |
       |   MULTIPLICATION AND DIVISION  |
       |          OF FRACTIONS          |
       L_____|


          THIS LESSON WILL BE WORTH

                  5 POINTS


          STUDY THE RULE STATEMENT AND 6 PRACTICE
          EXAMPLES THAT FOLLOW
```

FIG. 9.4. Sample introductory screen showing incentive value of individual lesson.

study when the performance incentive (and the instructional need) is high, and less material when the incentive (and need) is low.

Some "Stronger" and "Weaker" Alternatives

A more powerful alternative to the above CMI model is a CAI version that updates the predictive formula based on the student's current performances (Hansen et al., 1977). Under this system, for example, the adaptive model might begin, as usual, by predicting the student's Lesson 1 score from his or her pretest score. The Lesson 2 prediction, however, could then incorporate the student's Lesson 1 performance, thereby capitalizing on new and highly current information about student achievement. The Lesson 3 prediction could then include both the Lesson 1 and 2 performances, and so on, with each successive prediction drawing on additional recent information about the individual student. Further, immediate on-line refinements could be made based on student responses to example problems. A possible algorithm, for instance, would be "increase prescription by one example for each correct solution; decrease it by one example for each incorrect solution." These components create an "intelligent" system that varies materials as student needs change at the time of learning.

A less powerful alternative to the aforegoing models would be to orient adaptations to *class* needs. Under this type of system, lesson performance data could be manually entered on the disk by the instructor (CMI) or entered on-line as the lesson is administered to students (CAI). During each new administration, the updated group data bank would be used to distribute examples and incentives according to the "normative" projection of lesson performances for the class as a whole. For example, overall norms might indicate that Lesson 6 is associated with an average standard score of $-.50$, making it the third most difficult lesson in the unit. Using the present algorithms (Table 9.1 and Fig. 9.3), a new student would be prescribed 8 examples and offered 15 points on that lesson. As the data bank is updated with additional performance information, those prescriptions would be revised in accord with any changes in student learning. Although group-based strategies would be easier to implement (e.g., no pretesting is required), their obvious disadvantage is a loss of sensitivity to individual needs.

CONTEXT MODELS

Rationale

The models just reviewed focus on adapting *how much* is learned to individual needs. A complementary concern is making *what is learned* adaptive as well. Our instructional interest was the solving of math story problems, which has proven troublesome to students at all educational levels (National Assessment of Education Progress, 1979). The difficulty for many appears to stem less from lack of computation skills than inability to understand what the problems are asking. Specifically, story themes that are abstract (e.g., "If X is divided by Y . . . ," etc.), unrealistic (e.g., an exaggerated science fiction theme), or highly technical (e.g., centering on a physics principle such as velocity or force), may hinder learning by requiring translation of unfamiliar vocabulary and problem applications. A direct contrast is when children employ numerical concepts naturally and spontaneously to derive solutions to problems of personal interest, such as calculating percentages to determine one's intramural batting average or free-throw accuracy (see Ross, 1983).

Accordingly, our concern was developing a means of capitalizing on student interests in teaching them mathematical concepts. For this purpose, computer-based instruction offered the natural advantage of adapting and presenting materials on an individualized basis. Specific objectives of the planned adaptive model design were to: (a) personalize problem contexts so that each student would receive a unique presentation, (b) orient the adaptive contexts to diverse background and interest variables (e.g., hobbies, interactions with friends, etc.), and (c) automate the tasks of lesson preparation and administration. The actual model was prepared for use in teaching a division of fractions unit to 5th- and 6th-grade students. It operates by incorporating background information about each student within the problem contexts, thus making the individual *part* of the math application.

How the Model Works

Computer program. The computer-based lesson was written in BASIC for presentation by an Apple IIe or comparable microcomputer. The adaptive framework consists of PRINT statements containing "template" words (supporting text) and variable names. Character strings representing personal information about the student are listed in a prescribed order on DATA statements and are assigned to the variables during execution through READ statements. A simplified example is shown in the following BASIC statements:

```
10 READ BD$, FI$, FV$
20 PRINT "ON YOUR BIRTHDAY, "; BD$;",";
30 PRINT "YOUR FRIEND, "; FI$; ",";
    " Brought you "; FV$
40 PRINT "TO DIVIDE 4 WAYS."
2000 DATA "JULY 10", "BILLY", "A PIZZA"
```

Thus, by changing the three DATA values in line 2000, an unique context can be created, describing individual students' favorite foods brought by their friends on their birthdays. This format is illustrated in Fig. 9.5 in reference to an actual example from our unit. The top section shows the template into which the personalized data elements were inserted, while the lower half shows the com-

```
SAMPLE MATERIALS FROM THE PERSONALIZED CONTEXT

Template:

aStudent name had entered a contract with
teacher name to finish his/her work on
time.  He/she has earned 6 hours of
free time from teacher name to favorite activity.
He/she divides his/her free time into sessions
of 3/4 hour.  How many sessions will
student name have in all to favorite activity?

Completed Prototype:

bJoe had entered a contract with
Mrs. Warren to finish his work
on time.  He has earned 6 hours of
free time from Mrs. Warren to watch T.V.
He divides his free time into sessions
of 3/4 hour.  How many sessions will
Joe have in all to watch T.V.?

Data:

Joe, Mrs. Warren, his, he, watch T.V.

cUnderlined items represent categories that acquire
specific referents in the completed prototype.
dUnderlined items represent specific information
acquired from the student that replace general
category (variable) names. (The present data are
fictitious.)
```

FIG. 9.5. Sample materials from the personalized context.

puter display of a completed example using fictitious data. Changing the data for a different student, as illustrated in Fig. 9.6, produces the same mathematical problem, but with a new, personalized context.

Operational procedure. Step 1 involves obtaining information from students about their backgrounds and interests. In our field test, the information categories included homeroom teacher's name, parents' names, birthdate, favorite relative, most desired birthday gift, household pets, etc. Although we used a printed questionnaire, an alternative procedure would be to administer the questions by computer and store the responses in a data file on the diskette. Following appropriate editing, the data file could be accessed as needed by the CAI lesson. Our procedure involved manually entering responses from the questionnaire answer sheets into program DATA statements. DATA elements are always entered in a prescribed order; for example, Element 1 is always birthdate, Element 2 is best friend's name, and so forth. In a few instances, it may not be possible to identify a personalized referent for a category due to incomplete or inappropriate questionnaire responses. When information is missing, either a standard referent

EXAMPLE 2   FRACTIONS UNIT

```
JAMIE HAD ENTERED A CONTRACT WITH

MR. KEEGAN TO FINISH HER WORK

ON TIME. SHE HAS EARNED 6 HOURS OF

FREE TIME FROM MR. KEEGAN TO PAINT.

SHE DIVIDES HER FREE TIME INTO SESSIONS

OF 3/4 HOURS. HOW MANY SESSIONS WILL

JAMIE HAVE IN ALL TO PAINT?
```

FIG. 9.6.   The same example personalized for a different student.

can be substituted (e.g., "cake" for food), or no specific referent would be given (e.g., birthdate is left out), whichever seems more appropriate. After all data are entered, the program is saved on disk using the student's name as a label. On the average, the complete data entry process can be completed in about 5 minutes per student. When the student is ready to receive the lesson, the only requirement is to find the disk containing his or her name. From that point on, the lesson is completely self-administerable.

Results from a Field Test

To evaluate the context model, we compared its effectiveness relative to two "control" methods. In one method, the examples used "concrete" themes parallel to those of corresponding personalized examples but without any adaptation to the individual. In the second method, "abstract" contexts (using general terms such as "object," "units," and "quantities") were employed. Importantly, in all three versions the basic structure and numerical content of examples were the same. Figure 9.7 shows sample frames presenting concrete (top) and abstract (bottom) examples parallel to the personalized example just examined (in Fig. 9.6).

Comparisons between the three versions using 5th- and 6th-grade students showed advantages for the personalized contexts on measures of conventional problem solving, transfer (solving novel problems), formula recognition, and attitudes (Ross & Anand, 1986). Especially revealing were open-ended comments by students who received the personalized materials. A sample is as follows:

1. They (examples) were very easy to understand and remember. They were very good.
2. I enjoyed the problems.

```
EXAMPLE 1                    FRACTIONS UNIT

MRS. JONES TEACHES ENGLISH FOR 6
HOURS. SHE DIVIDES THAT TIME
INTO PERIODS OF 3/4 HOURS. HOW
MANY PERIODS DOES MRS. JONES
HAVE TO TEACH ENGLISH.



EXAMPLE 1                    FRACTIONS UNIT

THERE ARE 6 PERIODS OF TIME.
WE DIVIDE THAT TIME INTO
3/4 TIME PERIODS. HOW MANY
TIME PERIODS WOULD THERE BE
IN ALL?
```

FIG. 9.7. Parallel examples to the Figure 5 prototype presented in concrete (top) and abstract (bottom) contexts.

3. Surprised me with my name and everything. It was fun to do the work. They are a lot funnier than regular problems.

4. It made me understand these better with my name on it.

5. Surprised. They (examples) are more related to me and I can understand these.

These results suggest the adaptive strategy to have considerable potential as a means of making mathematical material more interesting and enjoyable to learn. An obvious drawback, however, is the effort involved in collecting the personalized information and incorporating it in the problem templates in the computer program. Another is the likelihood that the novelty of learning from personalized contexts will diminish over time. We therefore recommend orienting applications to acquisition learning of relatively difficult rules (i.e., developing ideational schemata first), and then introducing more abstract or subject-oriented (e.g., in science, business, etc.) examples as increased proficiency is gained.

CONTEXT DENSITY MODEL

The preceding models direct adaptations to the quantity and semantic content of *supporting examples* accompanying rules. Left unchanged by those variations is the "teaching component" of the lesson, specifically, the narrative text used to present and explain information. It is to this component of lesson design that our current research is directed. Our interests concern the following questions:

1. What are different students' needs regarding the density (richness or detail) of narrative text?

2. How does the density of text presentations interact with delivery mode (specifically, computer vs. book) to influence comprehension and attitudes toward the materials?

Rationale

The rationale for the model is based on two sets of assumptions. First, we reasoned that individual students require differing amounts of explanation to comprehend learning material. Our conception of the density variable encompasses such attributes as length of materials (number of words used), amount of elaboration and redundancy provided, depth of contextual support for important concepts, and the continuity of structural linkages between major idea units (e.g., an outline vs. paragraph forms). For example, Fig. 9.8a shows a narrative segment on the topic of central tendency, as it might appear in a textbook. It provides a detailed supporting context for the key information to be taught,

MEAN

The most commonly employed measure of
central tendency is the mean--symbolized
by $\overline{X}$. It is obtained by adding together all
the numerical values and dividing by N, the
number of values. You have probably used
this procedure many times in computing your
average exam score in high school and college
classess.

By definition, the mean is the number where
the deviations above it equal the deviations
below it. That is, if you subtracted $\overline{X}$ from
every number above and below $\overline{X}$ and added
the deviations together--the two sums of
deviations would be equal.

B<   press key   >N

MEAN

The mean is the most common measure of
central tendency
          Symbol--$\overline{X}$

Compute by
     Summing all numerical values
     Divide by N
          N = number of values

You may have used the mean to compute your
exam average

Definition of mean
     The number of deviations above $\overline{X}$ are equal
     to the number of deviations below the $\overline{X}$

B<   press key   >N

FIG. 9.8.   Sample screens showing parallel high density (top) and low density (bottom) segments.

namely, the symbol, computational procedure, and definition of the mean. The context consists of complete sentences in paragraph form, with elaboration (when deemed necessary) of particular points (see last sentences). In contrast, Fig. 9.8b presents only the key information, with little supporting context.

Our reasoning is that some students, as a function of possessing high learning aptitudes or prior experience with the subject matter, may learn more efficiently from and actually prefer "low density" presentations (e.g., Fig. 9.8b) that communicate important facts and concepts in the most direct, parsimonious way possible. Incorporating nonessential information such as review material or incidental explanation merely adds to their reading and time demands, without facilitating comprehension (see e.g., Ross & Anand, 1986, p. 22). Less capable or inexperienced students, on the other hand, may require extensive contextual support (i.e., high density narrative) to build sufficient knowledge structures for assimilating the new information.

The second set of assumptions concerns the issue of how to use book and computer presentations of text to their best advantage. Although there is no convincing evidence that learning from computers differs substantively from learning from other media (Clark, 1983), it is obvious that computers impose different constraints on the display of text than do print-on-paper displays (Grabinger, 1983; Lancaster & Warner, 1985). Specifically, computer text offers considerably less flexibility than books by: (a) limiting the visible display to one page at a time, (b) making backward paging for review purposes more difficult, (c) limiting size of the page layout to about 24 lines and 40–80 characters (Grabinger, 1983), and (d) offering limited cues regarding lesson length. One popular strategy for improving readability of computer text involves the use of chunking procedures that segment prose into meaningful "thought units" (Bassett, 1985; Carver, 1970; Grabinger, 1983). Unfortunately, these attempts have largely been unsuccessful with both book and computer displays, perhaps because the *content* of the presentations remains unaltered by the chunking format.

These considerations suggested that *content* rather than *format* of computer text displays may be the more critical design concern. With three or four times as many computer frames than textbook pages needed to represent equivalent content, and the necessity of reading these frames from the physically limited monitor screen, narrative segments in CAI lessons can become extremely long and cumbersome. Possible advantages therefore seem likely for briefer, more streamlined narrative designs, the type we have previously labeled "low density" contexts. In the following sections we describe our plans for building an adaptive model based on these conceptions about density effects.

How the Model Will Work

The completed adaptive model will select differing densities of text within an instructional unit and delivery mode according to predicted learner needs. For the learner needs assessment, predictive equations will be generated from a multiple regression statistical model, as employed for instructional support adaptations (Model I). Useful predictor measures are expected to include an achievement pretest and a reading comprehension test. The basic orientation of the adaptive model will be to increase density when predicted performance is low, and reduce it when predicted performance is high.

Presently, in our preliminary work, density is dichotomized into *two* variations: high (conventional text) and low (see Figs. 9.8a and 9.8b). Operationally, the low-density version is prepared by systematically transforming the conventional material as follows:

1. Reduce sentences to their main idea unit.
   a. Remove any unnecessary modifiers (or clauses).
   b. Split complex sentences into single phases.
2. Show hierarchical relation of procedures by vertical typography, i.e., using marginal indentations to show relationships between ideas, as in an outline.
3. Delete a sentence that summarizes or amplifies without presenting new information.
4. Present information in "frames" containing limited amounts of new information, as in programmed instruction.

Although these rules are not sufficiently detailed to completely objectify the conversion process, we found that we could apply them easily and confidently to produce formats having a high degree of similarity across designers (the two authors). Some subjectivity regarding what to leave, omit, or change does become necessary from time to time, given special considerations about content, format, and student characteristics. During instruction, the computer program (or learner) can select between low- and high-density versions for each lesson comprising the unit. Planned extensions of the model will involve increasing its sensitivity to permit finer gradations of density (three to five levels instead of only two) and smaller information units for density variations (e.g., separate pages instead of complete lessons). It is also planned to explore adaptive control of additional lesson properties such as inserted questions, elaboration instructions, and frame exposure time, in conjunction with density adaptations.

Present Status

Currently we are testing a preliminary (and intentionally simplified) form of the model, using learner control without advisement as the "adaptive" treatment. One variable in the evaluation is presentation mode (computer and textbook), and the other is text density selection (standard-high, standard-low, and learner-control). In the learner-control condition, the student is initially shown samples

```
PLEASE INDICATE WHICH VERSION YOU WANT TO
STUDY FOR THE NEXT UNIT:

        S     SHORT
        L     LONG


PLEASE ENTER YOUR CHOICE:
```

FIG. 9.9. Learner-control screen for text-density model.

of high- and low-density materials and asked to decide, prior to each of five lessons, which variation he or she would prefer for that lesson. A sample "decision" frame is shown in Fig. 9.9.

Our expectancy was for an interaction to occur between these variables, reflecting advantages for low-density text under the computer version and for high-density text under the textbook version. We also expected to find only modest advantages (if any) for learner control, due to some subjects' making ineffective self-selections of content. A pilot study using 48 subjects (8 per treatment) has just been completed. Results indicated significantly longer reading times in the computer mode ($M = 32.33$) than in the textbook mode ($M = 17.92$), $p < .001$. The presentation mode by strategy interaction only approached significance ($p < .10$), but indicated a tendency for longer CAI time increases in the high-density and learner-control conditions than in the low-density condition. Presentation mode by strategy ANOVAs were performed separately on achievement subtests dealing with factual knowledge, calculations, and transfer. Presentation mode main effects were significant for the knowledge ($p < .05$) and calculation ($p < .01$) subtests and approached significance for the transfer subtest ($p < .15$). In each case, subjects receiving the print materials were superior to those receiving CAI.

None of the strategy main effects or two-way interactions was significant, suggesting, as expected, that learner control was not advantageous for learning. However, the direction of the interaction means on each subtest was as predicted, showing the high-density group to score higher than the low-density group under print, with the opposite ordering under CAI. Given the small number of subjects (and absence of statistical significance), this tendency needs to be viewed cautiously. Finally, we compared the density preferences of learner-control subjects as a function of presentation mode. The result was significant ($p < .05$), with print subjects selecting the high density option only 25% of the time, and CAI subjects selecting it 73% of the time.

Our strongest impression from this preliminary evidence concerns possible limitations of the computer mode for expository-type lessons. CAI subjects generally seemed more conservative and less confident in their study behavior by selecting higher density material under learner control when given a choice, and by spending much more time than print subjects in reading displays. If this impression is valid, the program-controlled adaptive methods we have planned

243

could play an important role in promoting more effective study behaviors. As our research continues, we expect to gain much clearer insights into which types of adaptations of text are the most practical and advantageous for that purpose.

RECOMMENDATIONS

Based on our work with the three models, the following recommendations for courseware design are suggested:

1. Prior achievement is a strong predictor of current performances, and should be used, where appropriate, as information for adapting materials.

2. Learner-control often leads to inappropriate instructional decisions, and should be de-emphasized in favor of program control, especially for low achievers.

3. Students require differing levels of instructional support. Courseware should include mechanisms for adapting these levels in a *systematic* manner, for example, on the basis of pretask and on-task achievement.

4. Varying incentives can be beneficial for differentiating between the importance or difficulty of parts of a lesson. Specifically, higher points orient the student to pay greater attention to the associated lesson segments.

5. Personalization of material that goes beyond simple name recognition can increase the interest value and meaningfulness of material (see Fig. 9.5).

6. Narrative text is cumbersome to present in its original (textbook) form on monitor screens. Abbreviated or "low density" versions that convey the essential information without unnecessary elaboration should be explored as a possible design alternative for CAI.

REFERENCES

Bassett, J. H. (1985). *A comparison of the comprehension of chunked and unchunked text presented in two modes: Computer and printed page.* Unpublished doctoral dissertation, Memphis State University.

Bloom, B. S. (1976). *Human characteristics and school learning.* New York: McGraw-Hill.

Carrier, C., Davidson, G., & Williams, M. (1985). The selection of instructional options in a computer-based coordinate concept lesson. *Education Communication Technology Journal, 33,* 199–212.

Carver, R. P. (1970). Effect of a "chunked" typography on reading rate and comprehension. *Journal of Applied Psychology, 54,* 288–296.

Clark, R. C. (1983). Reconsidering research on learning from media. *Review of Educational Research, 53*(4), pp. 415–459.

Grabinger, R. W. (1983). *CRT text design: Psychological attributes underlying the evaluation of models of CRT text displays.* Unpublished doctoral dissertation, Indiana University.

Hansen, D. N., Ross, S. M., & Rakow, E. (1977). *Adaptive models for computer-based training systems* (Annual report to Naval Personnel Research and Development Center). Memphis, TN: Memphis State University.

Hannafin, M. J. (1984). Guidelines for using locus of instructional control in the design of computer-assisted instruction. *Journal of Instructional Development, 7,* 6–10.

Johansen, K. J., & Tennyson, R. D. (1983). Effect of adaptive advisement on perception in learner-controlled, computer-based instruction using a rule-learning task. *Educational Communication and Technology Journal, 31,* 226–236.

Keller, F. S. (1968). "Goodbye teacher . . ." *Journal of Applied Behavior Analysis, 1,* 79–89.

Kulik, J., Bangert, R., & Williams, G. (1983). Effects of computer-based teaching on secondary school students. *Journal of Educational Psychology, 75,* 19–26.

Kulik, D., Kulik, J., & Cohen, P. (1980). Instructional technology and college teaching. *Teaching of Psychology, 7,* 199–205.

Lancaster, F. W., & Warner, A. (1985). Electronic publication and its impact on the presentation of information. In D. H. Jonassen (Ed.), *The technology of text: Principles for structuring, designing, and displaying text* (Vol. 2). Englewood Cliffs, NJ: Educational Technology Publications.

National Assessment of Educational Progress. (1979). *Second assessment of mathematics: Mathematical applications.* (Report No. 09-MA-037). Denver, CO: Educational Commission of the States.

Ragosta, M., Holland, P. W., & Jameson, D. T. (1982). *Computer-assisted instruction and compensatory education: The ETS/LAUSD study.* Executive summary to U. S. National Institute of Education, Contract #0400-78006S. Princeton, NJ: Educational Testing Service.

Ross, S. M. (1983). Increasing the meaningfulness of quantitative material by adapting context to student background. *Journal of Educational Psychology, 75,* 519–529.

Ross, S. M. (1984). Matching the lesson to the student: Alternative adaptive designs for individualized learning systems. *Journal of Computer-Based Instruction, 11,* 42–47.

Ross, S. M., & Anand, P. (1986, April) *Using computer-assisted instruction to personalize math learning materials for elementary school children.* Paper presented at the Annual Meeting of the American Educational Research Association, San Francisco, CA.

Ross, S. M., & Rakow, E. A. (1982). Adaptive instructional strategies for teaching rules in mathematics. *Education Communication and Technology Journal, 30,* 67–74.

Tennyson, R. D. (1980). Instructional control strategies and content structure as design variables in concept acquisition using computer-based instruction. *Journal of Educational Psychology, 72,* 525–532.

Tennyson, R. D., & Buttrey, T. (1980). Advisement and management strategies as design variables in computer-assisted instruction. *Educational Communication and Technology Journal, 28,* 169–176.

10 MAIS: An Intelligent Learning System

Robert D. Tennyson
University of Minnesota

Dean L. Christensen
Control Data Corporation

This chapter presents an empirically based instructional design theory for the development of an intelligent learning system. The prescribed instructional design principles of the theory are directly related to general systems theory in which the main components are the following: (a) cognitive-based meta-learning theory; (b) learning needs and objectives; (c) knowledge base of information to be learned; (d) instructional variables and strategies, and (e) computer-based enhancements. An integral component of the intelligent learning system we are presenting is the Minnesota Adaptive Instructional System (MAIS), a computer-based management system that monitors student progress in learning according to individual differences and moment-to-moment needs.

Intelligent learning systems are characterized as holistic curricular and instructional inference-making systems that are iterative in nature such that with experience, they can continuously improve the learning of each individual learner (Tennyson & Park, 1986). This inference-making process is done by an intelligent expert tutor system which actively seeks to improve learning by (a) initially prescribing instruction that has a high probability of preventing learner error and/or misconceptions, (b) that continuously adapts the prescribed instruction according to moment-to-moment assessment and diagnosis, and (c) generatively improves its decision-making system. Figure 10.1 illustrates the various instructional variables that the MAIS expert tutor management system adapts to individual learner differences and needs during instruction. These variables, termed computer-based enhancements (see Table 10.1), are managed by the expert tutor employing both formal and informal artificially intelligent (AI) heuristic programming methods (Tikhomirov, 1983).

TABLE 10.1

MAIS Intelligent Learning System Components

Cognitive Processes (Long-Term Memory)	Learning Objective	Knowledge Base	Instructional Variables	Computer-Based Enhancements
STORAGE:	Verbal Information	Attribute Characteristics	Label and Definition	
Declarative Knowledge			Context	Worked Examples
Conceptual Knowledge		Semantic Structure	Best Example	Amount of Information
			Expository Examples	Learning Time
Procedural Knowledge	Intellectual Skills	Schematic Structure	Interrogatory Examples	Format of Information
				Advisement
			Strategy Information	Mixed Initiative
			Attribute Elaboration	Corrective Error Analysis
				Embedded Refreshment and Remediation
RETRIEVAL:				
Recall of Knowledge	Cognitive Strategies			Sequence
Creating Knowledge				

Used by permission of Tennyson & Associates, 1986.

Intelligent Learning Systems

Intelligent learning systems (ILS), in contrast to conventional computer-assisted instructional (CAI) systems that employ static frame-oriented programs, compile the instructional program at the moment the learner begins instruction and then continuously update the instruction according to accumulated assessment of individual learner progress and needs. For example, whereas most CAI programs are menu directed within a predetermined finite set of options and branching/error detection routines (i.e., a flowchart), an ILS employs a dynamic management system that prescribes the instruction based on moment-to-moment diagnoses. In other words, the expert tutor management system of an ILS exhibits those characteristics associated with the experienced teacher: that is, it knows learning theory, it is a subject matter expert, it knows learner assessment and measurement, and most important, knows how to manage an effective and efficient learning environment.

An ILS, likewise, differs from conventional intelligent CAI (ICAI) programs in a number of important ways (see also, Suppes, 1984). First, ICAI programs can be characterized as unidimensional management systems that employ only one primary instructional variable within their instructional strategy (i.e., tutor model). For example, a typical ICAI tutorial model interacts with the learner in a meaningful way only after the learner has made an error to a question. As such, most ICAI programs can be classified as reactive learning environments managed by highly defined rule systems that can assess only predetermined error patterns. For the learner in an ICAI program, knowledge acquisition within a domain of information is most often carried out through more conventional forms of instruction, with the tutorial portion of the program coming during practice sessions. In this regard, ICAIs may be most helpful when trying to rectify the difference between a student's model of knowledge and an expert knowledge model (Gable & Page, 1980). Second, most ICAIs can also be characterized as having little or no learning theory basis for the instructional strategies or rules used in the program (i.e., they are mainly software exploratory prototypes). The rule-based management strategies for ICAI tutor models are basically intuitive and without empirical evidence to support their design features (Park, Perez, & Seidel, 1987).

An ILS on the other hand takes a holistic approach to the learning process by actively monitoring student learning throughout the entire process. The teaching approach is twofold: (a) to assess the learner initially and continuously during instruction; and (b) to iteratively adapt the instruction to improve effective and efficient knowledge acquisition and to prevent errors and possible misconceptions. For example, the expert tutor in the MAIS has a whole range of instructional variables and conditions by which to adapt the learning environment to individual student differences and needs, not just a single strategy for all students (e.g., the Socratic question/answer format favored by many ICAI programs.) Also, the MAIS expert tutor uses a multivariate approach to learner assessment,

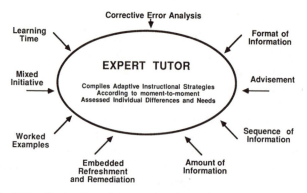

FIG. 10.1. Illustration of instructional variables monitored by the MAIS expert tutor. Courtesy of Tennyson & Associates (1986).

not just the simple assessment offered by a response to a single question. This multivariate approach allows the expert tutor to establish diagnostic scenarios to manage the instructional program and monitor learning. In fact, the ICAI approach of error detection/correction is but one of the management features of the MAIS (see Fig. 10.1).

The MAIS

The intelligent learning system presented in this chapter, the MAIS, is based on the findings of an extensive programmatic research effort investigating the direct connections among such learning environment factors as individual differences, cognitive learning theory, instructional technology, subject matter structure, and delivery systems (especially computer-assisted instruction). It is a system (see Table 10.1) that links together the five components of the instructional design system listed in the first paragraph of this chapter. From the interaction of these components, a MAIS-based CAI program can be developed with reasonable success in reference to cost-effectiveness principles of improved learning within standard production costs. That is, unlike conventional ICAI demonstration (or prototype) programs that require costly dependence on powerful hardware and software systems (e.g., a LISP machine), a MAIS-based CAI program can be developed within current microcomputer constraints of relatively limited memory.

In this chapter, our focus is on the design of an ILS using the computer as the instructional delivery system as well as the intelligent expert tutor management system. Use of the computer as a delivery system is one of many possibilities for an ILS; that is, the selection of any medium is contingent in most part on the match of the representational features of the information to be learned with the attributes of the available media (Tennyson & Breuer, 1984). Additionally, this chapter focuses on the acquisition of information associated with concepts and rules (i.e., conceptual and procedural knowledge). Our reasoning here is two-fold. First, concepts and rules, and their connecting associations, form the basic structures for most domains of information, therefore, learning of concepts and rules is of first order in most schooling and training situations. Second, as the knowledge base for thinking, they seem to be necessary for higher order cognitive processing (Klix, 1983, 1985).

MAIS Design Components

In Table 10.1, we present five components of a systems approach to the design of an intelligent learning system. In addition, associated with each of the design components is a phase of evaluation. The purpose of evaluation is to ensure that quality control of the ILS is maintained throughout the entire development process. Because the principles of evaluation as related to the instructional design system we present are discussed elsewhere (Tennyson, 1978), we do not detail the procedures here. Other sources also prescribe the procedures for various other design and development components as well; therefore, the focus of this chapter is on the actual procedures in the designing and programming of an intelligent computer-based lesson employing the MAIS.

In the past, educators have shied away from computers as instructional delivery systems because of misunderstandings in designing computer programs and their lack of adequate computer language programming skills. It is our experience, however, that even with a minimal knowledge of a computer programming language, it is possible to design and develop a highly sophisticated ILS in a relatively short period of time. The two most important variables in designing any instruction are the adequacy of the analysis of the information to be learned (i.e., knowledge base) and the selection of appropriate instructional strategies by which to present the information. Actually, production of instructional materials can be a secondary concern; and with computer technology, it can be done individually or in cooperation with a programmer. It is our design philosophy that understanding directly the effect of an instructional variable on learning will improve the design process. That is, when designing instruction, it is more important to understand "why" learning occurs in a given instructional treatment than the "how" to do development of instruction.

We propose, in this regards, that in designing any instruction, that a learning theory and model be prepared to guide the design process. Allowing, therefore, a trace from the instructional treatment back through the instructional strategy to the knowledge base to the learning objectives to the storage and retrieval of knowledge in memory. Without the confirmation of a trace from memory to instructional treatment, learning systems are nothing better than trial and error instructional systems where sometimes people learn and sometimes they do not.

In such systems, the failure to learn is most often put on the learner, not on the system.

In this chapter we present in two phases the set of principles used to design and development a MAIS-based ILS. The first phase is the design of a computer-based lesson following the system components shown in Table 10.1. Phase two consists of the means necessary to program a MAIS-based program. In the second phase we present the actual code for programming an intelligent computer-based instructional lesson.

PHASE I: DESIGNING AN ILS

Phase 1 consists of five instructional design components for the development of intelligent CAI courseware (see Table 10.1). The first component defines the learning theory model upon which the instructional process is based. Basically, the learning theory should model the learning process in two important ways: (a) the acquisition and storage of knowledge; and (b) the retrieval of knowledge. The second component, learning objectives, bridges the gap between the application of the learning theory and the instruction. Component three is analysis of the information to be learned in reference to its possible representation in memory. Thus, this knowledge base is structured for purposes of improving student knowledge storage and retrieval, not, as in expert systems, for system search efficiency. Component four provides the instructional variables by which the instructional strategy can be established. As such, the MAIS selects a meta-instructional strategy rather than the usual predefined CAI strategies (e.g., drill and practice, tutorial, Socratic, etc.). Finally, the fifth component provides the computer-based enhancements for the development of the intelligent expert tutor management system.

Component 1: Defining the Learning Theory Model

An important contribution of cognitive psychology to the field of education are the theories of cognition which explain the learning process in terms of both external experiences and internal conditions. Thus, when designing instruction, it is possible to understand how specific instructional design variables and strategies contribute to the acquisition of information. To illustrate this concept, we include in this first component an elaboration of the meta-learning theory which forms the foundation for the MAIS instructional design process. The focus here is to demonstrate the procedure of linking the learning process directly with the instructional process (Gagné & Dick, 1983).

Meta-learning theory model. The human mind is a complex system with many components; in Fig. 10.2, we illustrate the general components of what is

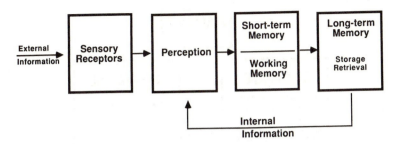

FIG. 10.2. Meta-learning model. Courtesy of Tennyson & Associates (1986).

termed an information processing model of learning. For purposes of this chapter, we present only the basic components of our meta-learning model, focusing our attention on two important concepts of learning in reference to instructional design. The first concept is that information for learning comes from sources both external and internal to the memory. That is, the sources for information to be learned come directly from within memory itself and also from the external environment. The second concept is the importance of perception as an integral component to a learning model. Given the practice of separating human phenomena into categories of content structure, perception is almost always left out of cognitive models of learning. However, for instructional purposes, perception must be included because of its direct effect on learning (Dorner, 1983).

Learning of information involves two forms of memory: short-term and long-term. Short-term memory implies only a brief remembering of information with no conscious attempt to encode it into long-term memory (e.g., remembering an unfamiliar phone number only long enough to dial the call). And, as such, short-term memory seems to have a limited storage space with information coming in and going out without much concern for acquisition. Within short-term memory is an executive control function which actively works (consciously or unconsciously) to encode information into long-term memory. This learning function is labeled "working-memory" because it processes information into memory and works to make connections with existing knowledge stored in long-term memory.

Within long-term memory are two subcomponents that form the means for storing and retrieving what is learned. In Fig. 10.3, we identify these two major subcomponents and further elaborate additional key elements within each. Basically, the storage component receives new information through its working-memory system and encodes that information and stores it in long-term memory as coded knowledge. An important coding function between working-memory and long-term memory is the connecting of new information with knowledge already stored in memory. This acquisition of connections helps with the forming of the relationships between the various concepts and rules of a domain of information. Operationally, this structure of a domain in memory is referred to as schemata.

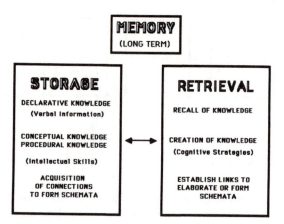

FIG. 10.3. Interaction of memory variables with learning objectives. Courtesy of Tennyson & Associates (1986).

The retrieval component both recalls knowledge by decoding it directly from storage (e.g., in the service of problem solving) and creates new knowledge internally by establishing new links between stored knowledge. This process of creating knowledge involves again the relationship of working-memory with long-term memory. Learning, then, is both acquisition of new information from external sources and creation of new knowledge from within the memory itself. The purpose of instruction is to improve both types of knowledge acquisition. From such a meta-learning theory model, it is clear that instruction requires a multiple set of variables and conditions adjusting to moment-to-moment learning situations and needs.

Within storage are three basic forms of knowledge. The differentiation of these knowledge forms provides the means to clarify the relationship between given learning processes and the specifications of appropriate instructional strategies. Declarative knowledge is an understanding of a given concept's internal semantic structure. For example, learning propositions, definitions, paired associations, and meaning of symbols. Conceptual knowledge is an understanding of the schematic structure of a domain such that the conditions of decision selection are possible. That is, the conditional knowledge of selection within a domain of information is based on appropriate rules and criteria. The third basic form, procedural knowledge, is the understanding of the inference-making possibilities of the concept or rule in the service of problem solving.

For example, if a student is to learn the coordinate concepts of central tendency (i.e., mean, median, and mode), declarative knowledge would imply an understanding of the three concepts (i.e., knowing the definitions). Conceptual knowledge would imply an understanding of the conditions for selecting the appropriate concept in a given problem situation. And, finally, procedural knowledge implies understanding the means and/or processes necessary to solve a given problem requiring application of central tendency.

To improve the acquisition of the various forms of knowledge, Gagné (1985) proposed a means for bridging the gap between given learning needs and specific instructional methods. We have extended Gagné's conditions of learning by linking them more directly with our meta-learning theory on one side and instructional variables for the MAIS on the other. Specifically, two of these conditions, verbal information and intellectual skills, are clearly associated with the acquisition of the three forms of knowledge described above (see Fig. 10.3). Therefore, instructional systems should improve the encoding and coding process for storage of external information. Gagné's third condition of learning, cognitive strategies, involves the creative use of knowledge; thus, instructional systems should likewise improve the internal creation of knowledge in the retrieval component of memory. For further discussion of this topic, see the Wager and Gagné chapter in this volume.

In our model of learning, we recognize that cognitive strategies are a retrieval condition of learning. Typically, the only condition of cognition associated with retrieval is recall of one of the three forms of knowledge stored in memory. For example, when attempting to solve a problem for a known rule, the specific rule is recalled from memory. However, for the higher order cognitive processes of problem formation, creativity, and productive thinking, new associations or links need to be made from the knowledge currently existing in memory. In this way the individual is creating new knowledge internally. Often the term "insight" is used to describe this phenomenon of creating a new form of knowledge which can then be decoded as external information.

Given modern cognitive learning theory, the first step in designing successful learning systems is the definition of a learning theory model which accounts for both *why* and *how* learning occurs. Because learning involves acquisition of information from both external and internal sources, a learning theory model should address both questions of learning. In our theoretical model, we discuss learning in reference to the two components of memory theory: storage and retrieval. On one hand we use current theories of information processing to explain acquisition of external information (i.e., through sensory registers and perception, information is encoded through working memory and transfered as coded knowledge into long-term memory where it is stored within developing schematic networks). And, on the other hand, we also use current retrieval theory to account for creation of internal information as well as the recall of knowledge in the service of problem solving. Given the scope of variations in learning theory details, individual instructional design groups should define meta-learning models reflecting the specific needs and conditions associated within the group. The important instructional design concept emphasized in Component 1 is, start the design process with an operationally defined theory of learning.

Component 2: Learning Needs and Objectives

The next design component involves an analysis of the needs and objectives of a learning problem. Tyipcally, instructional design models fail to integrate curricular design variables into the development of instruction, resulting in instructional programs that fail to identify the knowledge-based connections among the various domains of information in a curriculum. From a cognitive psychology standpoint, it should be possible to trace each learning activity back through the curricular system to the specific needs and goals of the curriculum. In this chapter we do not elaborate on the procedures of curricular needs assessment or goal clarification: However, for instructional purposes, it is important to define learning objectives as they relate to the goals of a curriculum. Learning objectives serve the design process as the bridge between the curricular plan and the instruction. They also serve as the means for clarifying the intended learning outcomes of the instruction.

In Fig. 10.3, we identify learning objectives in relation to the memory components of storage and retrieval. That is, the learning objective associated with acquisition of declarative knowledge is verbal information. For conceptual and procedural knowledge, the learning objective is intellectual skills. Both of these objectives define the need for acquiring information within a domain of information. Verbal information implies knowledge of a given domain's features and attribute characteristics. Intellectual skills, on the other hand, imply both an understanding of the domain's semantic and schematic structures and ability to employ the information in problem solving.

The highest order learning objective, cognitive strategies, is directly related to the retrieval process of creating knowledge by elaborating on existing knowledge stored in memory or establishing new knowledge. This objective refers to such desired learning outcomes as problem formation, creativity, and productive thinking. The retrieval process of remembering knowledge, even for solving problems within known domains, is embedded in the meaning of the two former learning objectives (see Figure 3, recall of knowledge). In Table 1, learning objectives bridge the gap between the information to be learned and the corresponding cognitive processes.

Component 3: Knowledge Base

An increasingly important aspect of instructional systems theories is the analysis of content within a domain of information (Reigeluth, Merrill, & Bunderson, 1978). In conventional terms, the term "content analysis" is widely used to describe this activity, which refers to the procedure of analyzing and organizing subject matter based on the relationships of content attributes. In practice, the outcome of a content analysis takes on the appearance of either: a taxonomy, which is highly structured in terms of critical attributes with superordinate and subordinate relationships or some sort of network (hierarchical) structure, which is organized around contextual cues and has no formal levels of abstraction. Memory theorists generally agree that knowledge exists in memory as part of larger, more complex conceptual networks or schematic structures (e.g., Mandler, 1979; Scandura, 1984). As individuals experience their environment and learn new information, their knowledge structures change. The cognitive processes involved in the change are necessarily complex and, as Millward (1980) has pointed out, involve at least three possibilities: (a) the codification of existing conceptual networks, (b) the sequencing and/or subsumption of conceptual networks into higher order knowledge structures, or (c) the creation of new conceptual networks.

Given that storage of knowledge from external information is an evolving and relativistic phenomenon, as opposed to a static one, it seems appropriate in structuring content for learning, that consideration be given to how the domain-specific information may be stored and retrieved from memory for procedural knowledge use as well as recall of declarative and conceptual knowledge. In complex cognitive situations, knowledge needs to be retrieved from long-term memory and manipulated in working memory in ways not originally encoded. This process of retrieving knowledge for complex usage, unlike direct recall of declarative and conceptual knowledge, implies the encoding of knowledge in reference to connections with associated schemata. Instead of only an analysis of content attributes per se, a schematic content analysis should be concerned with an analysis that identifies (a) the possible connections to necessary knowledge (i.e., prerequisite, associative, and background), (b) the connections among related or coordinate concepts and rules, and (c) the procedural and conditional skills required in using the to-be-learned concepts in problem solving situations.

In Table 10.1, we identify three forms of analysis within the process of a schematic content analysis for an instructional knowedge base. The first, attribute characteristics, refers to the identification of specific concepts or rules within a domain and the specific features of each. For example, within the domain of English grammar is the information associated with internal punctuation. An attribute characteristics analysis would identify the specific punctuation rules and their specific features. Such an identification would provide a basis for preparing the semantic structure (the second form of analysis) of the specific rules, based in part on their connections to necessary knowledge. (Note, it is assumed that the necessary knowledge is currently in the learner's memory.) The third form of analysis, schematic structure, identifies the rule connections within the given domain and among the schemata of associated domains of information (See Tennyson, 1981, for a complete review of the process of schematic analysis.) The schematic content analysis implies more than the expert system notion of the knowledge base because it allows for associations of information not controlled by limited rule structures. Expert knowledge base models are helpful in situations where experts need help in problem solving but are not helpful in learning because an expert would be able to "fill-in" missing rules which a learner would not be able to do. Also, an expert system knowledge base is composed almost entirely of higher order rules that leave out the stages of development that a learner usually goes through in acquiring new information. The purpose of the schematic analysis is to provide an initial schematic structure of the domain to which the learner will elaborate with experience.

Component 4: Instructional Design Variables

Using the meta-learning theory model described in Component 1, we have developed an instructional design theory based on an empirical set of instructional variables found to improve learning (Tennyson & Cocchiarella, 1986). This set of variables forms the basic structure of the MAIS. Table 10.1 shows the instructional variables in reference to the three conditions of learning. Within each of the three conditions of learning are instructional strategies that monitor learning through an expert tutor system composed of intelligent AI heuristics. For example, the learning of verbal information requires an expert tutor that continuously monitors the flow of new information such that the capacity of working-memory is actively receiving new information while coded information is transferred to storage (i.e., long-term memory). Repetition, in the form of drill and practice routines, have long been used in computer-assisted instruction for this condition of learning. Because Salisbury's chapter focuses on verbal information, we do not provide further elaboration here.

The focus of this chapter is on acquisition of conceptual and procedural knowledge, therefore, we will likewise not elaborate on the instructional variables for cognitive strategies beyond the brief description given in this paragraph. Our current work on instructional variables for cognitive strategies emphasize the need to develop strategies of cognitive complexity in memory (Breuer, 1984, in press). Development of such strategies requires practice in the process of establishing possible links within and among schemata (see Fig. 10.3). The use of simulations seems to enhance this learning when working in cooperation with other learners with similar levels of cognitive complexity (Breuer, 1985).

Whereas the storage of information may focus on learners working alone, learning cognitive strategies on the other hand evokes the need for cooperative learning activities. The expert tutor here monitors individual learners while they are composed in a group working on a simulation. The simulation has the task of working the learners up through increasingly more complex situations as their cognitive complexity develops. As the expert tutor senses possible failures in knowledge, it can prescribe remediation on an individual basis. The goal of cognitive strategies instruction is the development of cognitive complexity skills to improve the ability to use knowledge stored in memory for higher order cognition (i.e., problem formation, creativity, and productive thinking). In this way, the learner may be able to create in memory information associated with a domain rather than always having to receive domain specific information by external sources.

Because in this chapter we are most concerned with the improvement in the learning of external information, we focus the selection of the instructional design variables on the acquisition of conceptual and procedural knowledge (i.e., intellectual skills). Table 10.1 shows the basic instructional design variables that are directly related to specific learning processes in conceptual and procedural knowledge acquisition.

The instructional design variables of label, definition, and context are associated with the processes of making connections in memory between existing knowledge and the to-be-learned information. The instructional variables of label and definition provide the means to make the initial connections by direct reference in the definition to appropriate prerequisite information. The context variable helps establish additional connections with appropriate associative and background knowledge. The purpose of these first three instructional design variables is twofold: First, to help set up the initial schema for the information to be learned; and, second, to associate that schema within the meaning of a domain of existing knowledge. These variables are in direct contrast to the schema development constructs of advance organizers (e.g., Ausubel, 1968) and epitomies (e.g., Reigeluth, 1983) because they focus on employment of meaningful context for schema initialization rather than on conceptual abstractions.

The second set of instructional variables, best examples and expository examples, directly influence the learner's initial understanding and purpose of the information to be learned. The amount of expository instruction is basically determined by the complexity of the information. That is, the more complex a given concept or rule is in terms of its semantic and schematic structures and range of application, the more experience the learner needs in working with the complexity. Sufficient experience with expository information is needed to minimize the problems of over- and undergeneralization and learning of possible misconceptions.

The third set of variables (interrogatory examples, strategy information, and attribute elaboration) deal directly with development of production rules for retrieval purposes in the service of problem solving. Interrogatory examples provide the practice necessary to solve domain-specific problems as well as elaborating the schematic structure of the domain. Thus, interrogatory examples provide a twofold procedural skill development process: (a) selecting appropriate concept(s) or rule(s) (i.e., conditional or event knowledge); and (b) employing selected concepts or rules correctly in the solving of problems. Recall of knowledge for problem solving needs is improved if the given domain's schematic structure is well developed during the initial learning process. To further elaborate procedural knowledge development, the strategy information and attribute elaboration variables provide retrieval strategy information aimed at far transfer as well as near transfer in problem solving (Lung & Dominowski, 1985; Tennyson, Steve, & Boutwell, 1975).

Component 5: Computer-based Enhancements

Although this chapter focuses on the use of computer technology as a delivery system as well as the means for managing instruction, the selection of a medium for presentation of the information should be made in reference to a possible match between attributes of both the information to be learned and media display characteristics (Clark, 1983). In addition to the display characteristics, other characteristics of each specific medium need to be considered. That is, not all instruction should be or could be presented via computer-based instruction. For example, an important consideration in selecting the computer as an instructional delivery medium is its capabilities in the managing and/or monitoring of learning, which is a quite different selection criterion from its display capabilities (Park & Tennyson, 1980). In this regards, we consider this characteristic much more important for selecting the computer as a delivery system than its display possibilities.

For the learning of intellectual skills, we use seven basic computer-based enhancement variables to implement the instructional variables defined in Component 4 (see Fig. 10.1 and Table 10.1). (Recall that in this chapter we are not dealing directly with verbal information or cognitive strategies.) The instructional variables in component 4 are selected to form, according to the information analysis, a given meta-instructional strategy. Not all instructional strategies use all of the variables listed, the same is true for the computer-based enhancements. The computer-based enhancements are selected by the instructional designer in reference to the needs necessary to implement the instructional strategy.

Additionally, other appropriate instructional and computer-based variables may be selected for use in the MAIS program not directly mentioned here. For example, one may wish to use techniques to personalize the CAI lesson by drawing on individual indices of each learner. Ross et al. (1985) has shown that such personalizing of the lesson can improve learning of mathematics. Obviously, other attributes of the computer should be considered when known to contribute to improved learning (e.g., visuals, color, sound, graphics, text, etc.). The variables presented here are manage variables used to monitor the instruction by the expert tutor; they are not directly display variables.

The first three instructional variables, label and definition, context, and best example, may or may not be presented on the computer. In fact, it may be valuable to have these variables available to the learner in print form, even if presented on the computer. Printed expository materials are helpful during the instruction and as documents to have once the learner is away from the computer-based lesson. The purpose of these variables is twofold: (a) to provide the transitional connections between knowledge currently existing in memory and the information to be learned; and (b) to initialize the schematic structure of the domain (i.e., through the use of the context variable). Therefore, these print materials can be used for review during the instruction and as easily referenced materials for later lessons. Our research has shown that cuing declarative knowledge is very useful in retention test problem solving performance. Other research has shown that having these variables currently available during practice in problem solving improves acquisition of procedural knowledge.

Worked examples. The first of the computer-based enhancements, worked examples, focuses on the transition between declarative knowledge and conceptual knowledge. (Note. We use the term worked examples here as the computer-based application of the instructional variable, expository examples; the reason for the different labels is given below). With worked examples, the learner is able to establish an initial schema of the concept or rule, which can then be elaborated on during the acquisition of procedural knowledge. However, before a learner has a schema well established, it is more effective (and efficient) to present worked examples in which the learner has an active role in forming the complete example. Two key principles are important in the use of worked examples: First, the learner should be actively engaged in using the examples to both maintain attention and to help the learner understand the attribute characteristics and how the semantic structure is formed. That is, do not present worked examples in their totality with the learner simply as a passive viewer as is done in most expository presentations. Second, the worked (or expository) examples should demonstrate the range of the attributes associated with each given concept or rule. This is especially important to help the learner form the dimensions of the schema before attempting to develop procedural skill in problem solving.

An additional consideration in developing worked examples is the use of adjunct information. Two important features of the computer are its ability to use simultaneously both text and visuals and to construct screen displays. For example, research has shown that visual displays that are adjunct to text can improve acquisition of information; likewise, text can be used as an adjunct to visual information. In worked examples, the instructional variable of attribute elaboration can be as important as its use in interrogatory examples.

The next three computer-based enhancements are response-sensitive variables designed to improve the transition between conceptual and procedural knowledge. A major problem in machine-mediated instruction is deciding when to begin instruction for procedural knowledge acquisition once the learner has been presented instruction for declarative and conceptual knowledge acquisition. In schema theory, procedural knowledge acquisition is facilitated with problem-solving activities (i.e., interrogatory examples). However, from an instructional point of view, how can that decision be made so that the learner is not prematurely forced into problem solving before sufficient conceptual knowledge is acquired, thus avoiding mistakes and errors that may be encoded into long-term memory? An important principle of the MAIS is to improve learning through prevention of errors and mistakes. The notion of learning through mistakes is basically inappropriate, although widely used in ICAI, because of the distinct possibility that the mistakes or errors may be encoded into long-term memory and later retrieved as being correct. Also, it is much more efficient instructionally to prevent possible learning errors than trying to correct them. These three response-sensitive variables deal with the transition between conceptual and procedural knowledge acquisition by the monitoring of interrogatory examples.

Learning time.   The first response-sensitive variable is learning time. When interrogatory examples are presented, the learner must (a) try to figure out the problem question and then (b) try to formulate a solution. If a learner has insufficient conceptual knowledge to do either of these cognitive operations, they need additional expository help. How to make this decision requires intelligence on the part of the instructional system. If the system is a human tutor, a number of instructional means may be used to understand the learning need and subsequently to provide required help. However, in machine-mediated systems, the usual practice is to give unlimited time, forcing the learner to either make a solution or, if an option, admit an "I don't know," or even perhaps try to form a question to ask the program. From a learning point of view, none of these alternatives is desirable because of the possibility of an incorrect answer or an omission of failure or an inability to generate a question the program can understand. Once the learner is aware that he or she does not have to make a response or solution to keep the instruction going, the above problems are eliminated.

Basically, the MAIS expert tutor heuristic for this variable decides on the learning time interval according to two parameters: first, the difficulty of both the given problem and concept (rule); and second, the current learning level of the individual learner. The purpose of the learning time variable is to monitor the student so as to provide sufficient and reasonable time to both understand the problem and to form an answer; but, not unlimited time which can create learning errors and waste valuable time for learning. (For a complete review of this variable see Tennyson & S. Park, 1984, 1985; Tennyson, O. Park, & Christensen, 1985).

Format of examples.   The second response-sensitive variable to monitor the transition between conceptual knowledge and procedural knowledge is the format of examples enhancement. Because the number of worked examples is decided prior to instruction, the need to possibly increase this amount for learners who have not yet acquired sufficient understanding of the concept or rule is monitored in the following way (see Park & Tennyson, 1986). The expert tutor's heuristic simply states that if the learner either answers incorrectly to an interrogatory example or runs out of learning time, the next example, instead of being an interrogatory example, should be presented as an expository example. The learner then has the opportunity to once again study a worked example, and focus his or her learning attention on conceptual knowledge.

Mixed initiative. To improve access by the learner to the range of instructional variables available in the MAIS, the learner may initiate a direct connection to the tutor on a variety of options. The purpose of this response-sensitive variable is not to move the learner out of the main learning task, but rather to allow the learner the opportunity to:

a. change a given situation (e.g., decide on an interrogatory example instead of a worked example, or vice versa);

b. ask the expert tutor a question directly related to a given example or to the concept;

c. in certain situations, pose questions to the tutor concerning an aspect of an example or concept; and

d. ask the expert tutor a number of questions regarding the context of an example.

The value of this variable has long been associated with CAI systems since the late 1960s. Mixed initiative was referred to in the early literature on the topic as natural language processing.

The next set of computer-based enhancements controlled by the expert tutor deal with the monitoring of the learner in reference to amount of information, sequence, advisement, corrective error analysis, and embedded refreshment and remediation. Two of these variables, amount of information and advisement (along with the display time interval), are directly managed by the Bayesian conditional probability theory. This statistic determines continuously the number of interrogatory examples needed to learn a concept according to three parameters: the learning criterion level (i.e., the objective for mastery), the loss ratio between a false retain (i.e., learner has reached mastery) vs. a false advance (i.e., learner has not reached mastery), and accumulated on-task learning progress (Tennyson, Christensen, & Park, 1984). The values of these three parameters produce a matrix of beta values that provides the expert tutor with a moment-to-moment means of assessing whether or not a given learner has reached a given mastery criterion. The beta values in the Bayesian theory take into account an iterative updating function that provides a progressively more accurate indicator of a learner's current level of learning than either a straight percentage of correct vs. incorrect responses or a multiple regression analysis. (The Bayesian statistical function is further elaborated in Phase 2.)

Amount of information.　A major function of an expert tutor is to determine the exact amount of information needed to learn a given concept or rule. Obviously, too little information will result in incomplete knowledge acquisition, whereas too much information interferes with learning in terms of such factors as boredom, fatigue, using up valuable learning time (thus reducing total amount of learning when time is used up), and even development of the phenomena of reduced learning (see Tennyson, 1981). Using the Bayesian theory, the number of interrogatory examples is constantly adjusted according to moment-to-moment learning progress. For example, if progress is initially slow, more information is provided, but if and when learning accelerates, the amount is adjusted accordingly. The expert tutor, unlike conventional CAI does not have pre-prescribed, normative amounts of information. And, unlike conventional ICAI, it continuously updates its assessment of learner need (i.e., conventional ICAI systems react only at the moment of response to the given error (Park, in press).

Sequence.　Sequencing of information has long been a concern of adaptive instructional systems, especially through the use of response-sensitive error detection schemes. In the heuristics employed in the MAIS, the sequence of information is directly related to concept learning theory in regards to the possible errors associated with undergeneralization (i.e., failure to generalize to new problems) and overgeneralization (i.e., failure to discriminate between conditional applications) (Park, 1983; Park & Tennyson, 1980, 1986). Early in the instruction, the response-sensitive heuristic distinguishes that an error is a generalization problem (i.e., a conceptual knowledge acquisition problem), thus the focus of the instruction is on the concept or rule to which the error is associated. Later in the instruction, an error is one of overgeneralization (i.e., a conditional knowledge problem associated with procedural knowledge), thus the focus of the instruction switches to the concept or rule applied in the incorrect solution. Again, unlike conventional CAI with predetermined sequence routines (or branches), the expert tutor selects the needed instruction, and in this case the sequence, at that given moment of learning need.

Advisement.　A recurring problem in machine-mediated learning systems is learner control of important decision-making options. Two important learning decisions are amount of information and what kind of example (e.g., easy or difficult, or expository or interrogatory). Initially, CAI was viewed as an instructional system in which control of learning could be managed solely by the learner. However, research and evaluation studies have shown that learners do not make appropriate decisions in regards to their learning needs, especially in learning new and/or complex information (Gay, 1986). Conventional ICAI programs have responded to this situation by eliminating learner control in the quest for controlling the match between the student model and the expert (knowledge) model.

Accepting the value of learner responsibility in instructional decision making, we use the concept of advisement to inform the learners of their learning progress continuously during the instruction. When learner control is used within the MAIS expert tutor management system, instead of the tutor controlling the instruction, the learner is advised both of his or her progress in learning and of the necessary instruction to continue progress towards mastery. This form of advisement uses the concept of preventive instruction. In contrast to the moment-to-moment advisement offered in the MAIS, advisement in both conventional CAI (e.g., the TICCIT system, Bunderson, 1981) and ICAI (e.g., coaching routines as in SPADE, Miller, 1982) programs is *ex post facto*: that is, in the TICCIT system, after the learner has failed a lesson, remediation information on instructional options is provided the next time through the lesson; or, as in the coaching programs, only immediately after a failure (in conventional ICAI, learner management is not a variable of concern). (A complete review of the advisement concept is reported in Johansen & Tennyson, 1984; Tennyson, 1981; and Tennyson & Buttrey, 1984).

One of the most important attributes of ICAI programs is the error detection and correction process. The purpose of error detection is to identify how the learner's knowledge (i.e., student model) differs from the expert tutor's knowledge base. Most often this is done through a question/answer format in which it is assumed that the learner has actually learned the information elsewhere, and the system is now trying to make sure that misconceptions and/or incomplete knowledge is corrected. As such, many ICAI programs are basically reactive learning environments. In contrast to this reactive format of instruction, the MAIS expert tutor system approaches error correction during the initial learning process as an integral component of the intelligent learning system. We use two forms of error analysis. The first is concerned with detecting an error as only an initial knowledge acquisition problem; whereas the second focuses on detecting possible prerequisite knowledge problems. The first form we term *corrective error analysis* and the second *embedded refreshment and remediation*.

Corrective error analysis. The corrective error analysis follows conventional ICAI error detection methods. Unfortunately, these schemes are for the most part directly related to the specific content to be learned, therefore, the specific detection methods are program dependent rather than generic as with our other enhancements. For example, in Tennyson and Lau (1979) we used a method of algorithmic error detection in which we reduced the search of the error down to the learner's understanding of the concept's critical attributes. This type of error analysis focused on conceptual knowledge formation. In another study (Tennyson, Steve, & Boutwell, 1975), our concern was with the detecting of possible procedural knowledge development learning needs. Here we used the strategy information variable (see Table 10.1) to detect and correct the learner's conditional knowledge of how to select the appropriate rule to solve both a given problem and a case of problems in a specific domain of information.

Embedded refreshment and remediation. The final computer-based enhancement variable for the expert tutor system deals with how to help the learner establish connections in memory both within the new information to be learned and with existing knowledge. The importance of this learning process for schema development is witnessed by the number of instructional variables attempting to improve this process. One such instructional method is the principle of reviewing prerequisite information prior to the introduction of the information to be learned; the assumption being the immediate retrieval (or cuing) of knowledge from long-term memory to make it available in working memory. Another method is the theory of advance organizers where a framework schema is presented prior to the instruction to give the learner hooks on which to hang the new information. However, when learning complex information, the very complexity of the schematic associations may create instructional problems where the learner, in the former method, is not aware when specific associations between the new information and prerequisite knowledge are necessary, or, in the latter method, can not retain with sufficient elaboration the advance organizer during instruction.

To account for these problems, we have employed the tutorial variable of embedded refreshment when only the connection to a specific association is needed or embedded remediation when the expert tutor senses the need for extended refreshment on specific prerequisite information only. In the former situation, when a learner either fails to respond to an interrogatory example or is incorrect, the instructional correction is to present the necessary prerequisite information that is directly associated with the example. For example, if a lesson is on internal punctuation, and a learner is having trouble with a comma rule associated with dependent clauses, the learner is at that moment presented information on dependent clauses. However, if the learner is additionally having trouble with dependent clauses, embedded remediation on dependent clauses is provided. In this case then, the MAIS expert tutor is actively monitoring the learner much like in a coaching situation. Several ICAI programs use the concept of the coaching environment (e.g., SPADE, Miller, 1982; ALBEGRA, Lantz, Bregar, & Farley, 1983), but only do so within the context of the given lesson, without direct connection with information outside that lesson.

The nine computer-based enhancements for the instructional variables presented in component 4 (see Table 10.1), form the basic structure of the expert tutor in our ILS. Because these enhancements are primarily management variables, other possible enhancements for nonmanagement variables should be considered when designing an ILS. For example, the use of dynamic graphics for information that has motion as a critical feature, or the use of sound as an attention getting device, or the use of attribute elaboration techniques in screen displays, or the balancing of text and visual materials on screen displays. These other enhancements make-up what is considered the ''art'' of courseware design, and they certainly should not be neglected when developing courseware. However, they are beyond the scope of this chapter.

PHASE 2: PROGRAMMING

The purpose of this section is to present the BASIC programming code for the computer-based enhancements. We have tried to make the following code as generic as possible so that anyone with at least a working knowledge of BASIC or some other language could easily design and program an ILS. Remember that each of the enhancements is independent of the others, thus the selection of the individual enhancements is up to the designer, based on the conditions of the other four components of design. The only major dependent function needed to operate the MAIS expert tutor is the Bayesian conditional probability statistic. The Bayesian function sets both the parameters of the learning objectives and the mastery learning quality control; that is, the decision on whether to advance or retain the learner.

The statistical parameters in the Bayesian method allow the designer to determine the difficulty of the mastery learning decision. In our research we have established a standard format for the three parameters of the Bayesian statistic. Within this chapter we present only this standard format because it uses a heuristic that is very simple to program for use on a microcomputer. Advanced users may want to deal directly with the formula that calculates individual beta value tables. This information is in Tennyson, Christensen, and S. Park (1984).

The computer-based enhancements of the expert tutor are presented below as subroutines. Copies of an operating disk with a sample lesson are available by writing directly to the authors.

Beta Value Computation

The Bayesian subroutine returns a two digit beta value for calculations that are needed in computing amount of information, advisement, and display time interval. The calculations in this standardized subroutine are an approximation of the incomplete beta function. The values from the incomplete beta function with a loss ratio of .3 (this figure is a statistical value in the Bayesian formula and ranges between values of .275 and .325, with the higher values resulting in increasingly conservative control over a false advance vs. a false retain), a mastery criterion level of .75 (recall that this figure must include learning error, thus it may seem lower than usual levels for posttest mastery learning objectives), and the number of interrogatory examples at 14 (this number could be increased, but should not really be decreased to maintain power of the statistic) is sent to a nonlinear regression program that fits the best polynomial. The reason for the polynomial fit is to eliminate the need for calculating the beta value continuously throughout the program (this is certainly possible however on larger mini- and main frame computers).

INPUT: The only input required is the number of examples correct and the number of examples presented.

OUTPUT: Two place beta value.

Variable List and explanation:

CORRECT   Number of examples that were correct.
PRESENT   Number of examples that were presented.
              (Note. The code PRESENT $\char94 2$, means to the second power.)
BETA   Beta value.
C0, C1, C2   Variables used in polynomial.
Code:

100 C0 = $-.385747$ + .0507146 * PRESENT $-$ .00328486 * PRESENT $\char94 2$
    + .0000935574 * PRESENT $\char94 3$
200 C1 = 1.37385 $-$ .2958510 * PRESENT + .02450580 * PRESENT $\char94 2$
    $-$ .0007305730 * PRESENT $\char94 3$
300 C2 = $-.273399$ + .0767955 * PRESENT $-$ .00725163 * PRESENT $\char94 2$
    + .00023077470 * PRESENT $\char94 3$
400 BETA = C0 + C1 * CORRECT + C2 * CORRECT $\char94 2$
500 BETA = INT(ABS(BETA * 100 + .5)) / 100

Mastery Check and Advisement

This subroutine uses the computed beta value to determine whether a given learner has mastered a given concept or rule. The mastery decision is used by the expert tutor to make a decision on when to terminate instruction. For learner control situations, the expert tutor advises the learner of his or her progress and recommends an appropriate decision, but allows the learner to decide when to terminate. This subroutine reports to the learner, after each example, his or her current level of mastery regardless of learner control or program control. Note that multiple concepts and rules (coordinate) can also be used in this subroutine. In the following example code, the lesson has four concepts.

INPUT   Beta value.
              Number of examples presented for each concept.
OUTPUT   Booleen statement—mastered or not mastered concept(s).
              BETA value PRINTED to advise learner of progress.
Variable List and explanation:

BETA(Beta values from subroutine in array format
MASTERED(Array to determine concept mastered (1) or not (0)
PRESENT(Array for number of examples presented in each concept
CONCEPT   Number of concept
MAST   Accumulate mastery of all concepts
EX   Accumulate exhausted pool for concepts
Code:

XX10 REM Reset EX and MAST to 0
XX20 EX = 0: MAST = 0
XX30 REM Mastery check
XX40 FOR CONCEPT = 1 TO 4
XX50 IF BETA(1) > 75 THEN MASTERED(I) = 1: DONE = MAST = MAST
     + 1

XX60 IF PRESENT(CONCEPT) > 13 THEN EXHAUST = EX = EX + 1
XX70 NEXT CONCEPT
XX80 REM Determine if all concepts mastered or example pools exhausted
XX90 IF EX + MAST = 4 THEN (EXIT TO END OF PROGRAM)
X100 REM Print advisement
X110 FOR CONCEPT = 1 TO 4
X120 REM Format screen for your desired presentation
X130 PRINT BETA(CONCEPT)
X140 NEXT CONCEPT
X150 RETURN

Learning Time Interval

This subroutine monitors and updates the learning time of the interrogatory examples by increasing the amount of time for correct solutions. Recall that this MAIS enhancement monitors learning time for two purposes: (a) to provide immediate instructional help if the learner has not yet developed sufficient conceptual knowledge; and (b) to prevent the learner from being forced into making an incorrect response. Monitoring the learning time is not only a means to improve effectiveness of the instruction, but also to maintain efficiency of the learning environment. That is, time available for learning is a finite variable controlled by both external factors (e.g., school time periods, time of the day, excess to appropriate facilities, etc.) and internal factors e.g., fatigue, attention, effort, etc.).

Because the parameters of this subroutine include statistical values concerning (a) difficulty of the concept, (b) difficulty of each example, and (c) update in learning progress, it is necessary to establish these values before using the learning time subroutine. In practice, we initially estimate these values and then collect actual times to precisely set the values. A detailed discussion of these parameters is given in Tennyson, O. Park, and Christensen (1985).

INPUT	Beta Value
	Example to be presented next
	Example Difficulty Index (EDI) (mean time for experts to answer problem correctly)
	Concept Standard (statistical mean time of EDIs)
	Concept Difficulty Index (CDI) (statistical variance of EDIs)
	Lapsed time on example
OUTPUT	Learning time
	Concept Difficulty Index (value added to increase learning time)

Variable List and explanation:

LAPSE	Total elapsed time
LOCAL	Local current example's learning time
CDI(	Array for concept difficulty index
BETA	Beta value

EDI(Array for concept difficulty index
RESPONSE   Last response 0 = Incorrect; 1 = Correct; 2 = Time elapsed
CONCEPT   Current concept being presented
STANDARD(Array of concept standard
EXAMPLE(The specific example to be presented next
Code:
XX10 REM Check learning time against elapsed time
XX20 IF LAPSE > LOCAL THEN RESPONSE = 2
XX30 REM Concept difficulty index subroutine
XX40 CDI(CONCEPT) = CDI(CONCEPT) + BETA * STANDARD
    (CONCEPT)
XX50 REM Learning time subroutine
XX60 LOCAL = EDI(EXAMPLE) + CDI(CONCEPT)
For example, if the total set of examples for a given concept has a mean value of
17 sec. (STANDARD), and a variance of 2.5 sec. (CDI), and a current beta value
of .55, the calculation for the concept difficulty index would be the following:
    CDI(Concept) = 2.5 + .55 * 17
    CDI(Concept) = 11.85
For the next example (if current example correctly answered and an EDI value of
15 sec.), the learning time value would be increased as follows:
    LOCAL = 15 + 11.85
    LOCAL = 26.85

This heuristic allows for an iterative learning time increase with each succeeding
correct response.

Format of Examples and Sequence

This subroutine selects the format of the next example according to the response
given to the current example, as follows: if correct or if time elapses, the next
example will be in an interrogatory format; if incorrect, it will be presented as an
expository example. Also, this subroutine selects the sequence of the next example according to, first, the generalization rule (usually for the first four interrogatory examples) and, second, the discrimination rule (usually starting with the fifth
example). This subroutine also determines that no example is presented more than
once and that no example is presented if the example pool is exhausted.

INPUT   Last response
           Concept presented and selected
           Number of examples for each concept presented
OUTPUT   Sequence of next concept and format of example
Variable List and explanation:
RESPONSE   Last response, 0 = Incorrect; 1 = Correct; 2 = Time elapsed
ANSWER   Last concept selected
EXAMPLE   Number of example selected
SEQUENCE   0 = Generalization; 1 = Discrimination

MASTERED(Array to determine concept mastered (1) or not (0)
PRESENT(Array for number of examples presented in each concept
CONCEPT   Number of concept
XX10 REM Select example number from pool
XX20 EXAMPLE = INT(RND(1) * 14 + 1
XX30 REM First four examples presented in each concept are generalization
XX40 IF SEQUENCE = 1 AND PRESENT(CONCEPT) < 5 THEN SEQUENCE = 0
XX50 IF SEQUENCE = 1 AND PRESENT(CONCEPT) > 4 THEN SEQUENCE = 1
XX60 REM When response is incorrect or time elapsed and generalization is in effect then concept to be selected remains the same
XX70 IF RESPONSE = 0 OR (RESPONSE = 2 AND SEQUENCE = 0) THEN GOTO X120
XX80 REM If response is incorrect and discrimination then next concept to be selected is the learner's incorrect response
XX90 IF RESPONSE = 0 THEN CONCEPT = ANSWER: GOTO X120
X100 CONCEPT = INT(RND(1) * 4 + 1)
X110 REM Determine example pool exhausted / If exhausted then response must be changed to correct so random select of concept occurs
X120 IF PRESENT(CONCEPT) > 13 THEN RESPONSE = 1: GOTO XX10
X130 REM If response is correct and concept not mastered then start over
X140 IF RESPONSE = 1 AND MASTERED(CONCEPT) = 0 THEN GOTO XX10
X150 REM If example was used before start over
X160 IF SELECTED(CONCEPT,EXAMPLE) = 1 THEN GOTO XX10
X170 SELECTED(CONCEPT,EXAMPLE) = 1
X180 RETURN

The variables of corrective error analysis and embedded refreshment and remediation are task-specific enhancements that are designed at the point of individual lesson development. The important concept for the former variable is to consider the type of analysis as a function of the instructional strategy to be employed. For the latter variable, the design decision comes from the structure of the information component of the ILS (see Table 10.1). Both of these variables need attention so as to provide adequate instructional help, but not to the point of reducing efficiency of the learner. For example, too much intereference from adjunct instruction can distract the learner and consequently use up valuable learning time.

SUMMARY

Our purpose in this chapter was to, first, present an authoring system for designing computer-based learning programs, and, second, to clearly show the relationships between learning, design, and instruction. The intelligent learning system presented here, the MAIS, is supported by both learning theory and instructional theory. Also, the instructional variables and the computer-based enhancements of the MAIS are supported by empirical verification; tested in a well-defined program of research, and evaluated by disciplined peer review. The value of a theory-based instructional design system supported by direct research findings is that it can be generalized to specific learning needs and conditions. And, for implementation purposes, the MAIS is readily transferable to most currently available hardware and software. And, as computer technology itself improves, it will be possible to both enhance the present variables and variables yet to be discovered. Some of these new variables will come from research in such diverse areas as individual differences, human-machine interface design, neuropsychology, psychometrics, computer software, perception, and the continuing significant research and theory development in the field of instructional technology, curricular management as well as hardware and software developments.

REFERENCES

Ausubel, D. P. (1968). *Educational psychology: A cognitive view.* New York: Holt, Rinehart, & Winston.

Breuer, K. (1984). Zur Lehr-lerntheoretischen Grundlegung der Computerunteruetzten Unterricht. *Log In, 2*(2), 11–14.

Breuer, K. (1985). Computer simulations and cognitive development. In K. A. Duncan & D. Harris (Eds.), *The proceedings of the world conference on computers in education 1985 WCCE/85.* Amsterdam, The Netherlands: North Holland.

Breuer, K. (in press). Simulations and artificial intelligence. *Educational Technology.*

Bunderson, C. V. (1981). Courseware. In H. F. O'Neil Jr. (Ed.), *Computer-based instruction: A state-of-the art assessment.* New York: Academic Press.

Clark, R. E. (1983). Reconsidering research on learning from media. *Review of Educational Research, 53,* 445–459.

Dörner, D. (1983). Heuristics and cognition in complex systems. In R. Groner, M. Groner, & W. F. Bischof (Eds.), *Methods of heuristics.* Hillsdale, NJ: Lawrence Erlbaum Associates.

Gagné, R. M. (1985). *Conditions of learning (4th ed.).* New York: Holt, Rinehart, & Winston.

Gagné, R. M., & Dick, W. (1983). Instructional psychology. *Annual Review of Psychology, 34,* 261–295.

Gable, A., & Page, C. V. (1980). The use of artificial intelligence techniques in computer-assisted instruction: An overview. *International Journal of Man-Machine Studies, 12,* 259–282.

Gay, G. (1986). Interaction of learner control and prior understanding in computer-assisted video instruction. *Journal of Educational Psychology, 78,* 225–227.

Johansen, K. J., & Tennyson, R. D. (1984). Effect of adaptive advisement on perception in learner controlled, computer-based instruction using a rule-learning task. *Educational Communication and Technology Journal, 31,* 226–236.

Klix, F. (1983). An evolutionary approach to cognitive processes and creativity in human beings. In R. Groner, M. Groner, & W. F. Bischof (Eds.), *Methods of heuristics.* Hillsdale, NJ: Lawrence Erlbaum Associates.

Klix, F. (1985). On microanalysis of cognitive performance: Correspondance with psychological and psychophysiological parameters. In F. Klix, R. Naataner, & K. Zimmer (Eds.), *Psycho-*

physiological approaches to human information processing (pp. 3–30). Amsterdam, The Netherlands: Elsevier.

Lantz, B. S., Bregar, W. S., & Farley, A. M. (1983). An intelligent CAI system for teaching equation solving. *Journal of Computer-Based Instruction, 10*, 35–42.

Lung, C., & Dominowski, R. L. (1985). Effects of strategy instructions and practice on nine-dot problem solving. *Journal of Experimental Psychology: Learning, Memory, and Cognition, 11*, 804–811.

Mandler, J. M. (1979). Categorical and schematic organization in memory. In C. R. Puff (Ed.), *Memory organization and structure*. New York: Academic Press.

Miller, M. L. (1982). A structural planning and debugging environment for elementary programming. In D. Sleeman & J. S. Brown (Eds.), *Intelligent tutoring systems*. New York: Academic Press.

Millward, R. B. (1980). Models of concept formation. In R. R. Snow, P. Federico, & W. F. Montagne (Eds.), *Attitude, learning and instruction* (Vol. 2, pp. 134–162). Hillsdale, NJ: Lawrence Erlbaum Associates.

Park, O. (in press). A comparison of the advantages and disadvantages of CAI and ICAI. *Educational Technology*.

Park, O., Perez, R. S., & Seidel, R. J. (1987). Intelligent CAI: Old wine in new bottles or a new vintage? In G. P. Kearsley (Ed.), *Artificial intelligence and instruction. Applications and methods*. Boston: Addison-Wesley.

Park, O., & Tennyson, R. D. (1980). Adaptive design strategies for selecting number and presentation order of examples in coordinate concept acquisition. *Journal of Educational Psychology, 72*, 499–505.

Park, O., & Tennyson, R. D. (1984). Computer-based instructional systems for adaptive education: A review. *Review of Contemporary Education, 2*, 121–135.

Park, O., & Tennyson, R. D. (1986). Response-sensitive design strategies for sequence order of concepts and presentation form of examples using computer-based instruction. *Journal of Educational Psychology, 78*,

Reigeluth, C. M. (1983). *Instructional-design theories and models: An overview of their current status*. Hillsdale, NJ: Lawrence Erlbaum Associates.

Reigeluth, C. M., Merrill, M. D., & Bunderson, C. V. (1978). The structure of subject-matter content and its instructional design implications. *Instructional Science, 1*(2), 11–16.

Ross, S. M., McCormick, D., Krisak, N., & Anand, P. (1985). Personalizing context in teaching mathematical concepts: Teacher-managed and computer-assisted models. *Educational Communications and Technology Journal, 33*, 169–178.

Scandura, J. (1984). Structural learning theory and cognition. *Journal of Computer Based Instruction, 11*, 43–61.

Tennyson, R. D. (1978). Evaluation technology in instructional development. *Journal of Instructional Development, 2*(1), 19–26.

Tennyson, R. D. (1981). Use of adaptive information for advisement in learning concepts and rules using computer-assisted instruction. *American Educational Research Journal, 73*, 326–334.

Tennyson, R. D., & Breuer, K. (1984). Cognitive-based design guidelines for using video and computer technology in course development. In O. Zuber-Skerritt (Ed.), *Video in higher education*. London: Kogan.

Tennyson, R. D., & Buttrey, T. (1984). Advisement and management strategies as design variables in computer-assisted instruction. In D. F. Walker & R. D. Hess (Eds.), *Instructional Software*. Belmont, CA: Wadsworth.

Tennyson, R. D., Christensen, D. L., & Park, S. I. (1984). The Minnesota adaptive instructional system: An intelligent CBI system. *Journal of Computer-Based Instruction, 11*, 2–13.

Tennyson, R. D., & Cocchiarella, M. (1986). An empirically based instructional design theory for teaching concepts. *Review of Education, 56*, 40–71.

Tennyson, R. D., & Lau, C. C. (1979, April). *Error correction as an adaptive instructional strategy for computer-based instruction*. Paper presented at the meeting of the American Educational Research Association, San Francisco.

Tennyson, R. D., & Park, O. (1986). Artificial intelligence and computer-assisted learning. In R. Gagné (Ed.), *Instructional technology: Foundations*. Hillsdale, NJ: Lawrence Erlbaum Associates.

Tennyson, R. D., Park, O., & Christensen, D. L. (1985). Adaptive control of learning time and content sequence in concept-learning using computer-based instruction. *Journal of Educational Psychology, 77,* 481–491.

Tennyson, R. D., & Park, S. I. (1984). Process learning time as an adaptive design variable in concept learning using computer-based instruction. *Journal of Educational Psychology, 76,* 452–465.

Tennyson, R. D., & Park, S. I. (1985). Interactive effect of process learning time and ability level on concept learning using computer-based instruction. *Journal of Structural Learning, 8,* 241–260.

Tennyson, R. D., Steve, M. W., & Boutwell, R. C. (1975). Instance sequence and analysis of instance attribute representation in concept acquisition. *Journal of Educational Psychology, 67,* 821–827.

Tikhomirov, O. K. (1983). Informal heuristic principles of motivation and emotion in human problem solving. In R. Groner, M. Groner, & W. F. Bischof (Eds.), *Methods of heuristics*. Hillsdale, NJ: Lawrence Erlbaum Associates.

11

Designing Courseware to Fit Subject Matter Structure

Wallace Hannum
University of North Carolina

Among the factors that might affect the design of courseware is the structure of the subject matter itself. Just as courseware might be adapted to differences among individual learners, it can also be adapted to differences in subject matter structures. The intent of this chapter is to describe structures of subject matter knowledge and indicate how courseware might adapt to these structures.

Knowledge is not a collection of unorganized facts existing in relative isolation one from the other (West, Fensham, & Garrard, 1985). Rather there are certain orderly structures inherent within subject matter knowledge (Reigeluth, Merrill, & Bunderson, 1978; Wilson, 1985). These structures reflect the interconnections or interrelationships among the facts, concepts, and principles that make up subject matter knowledge (Anderson, 1983). When students learn subject matter knowledge, they learn both the specific content (the facts, concepts, and principles) and the structure that interrelates this content (Champagne, Gunstone, & Klopfer, 1985; Champagne, Klopfer, Desena, & Squires, 1981; Geeslin & Shavelson, 1975; Naveh-Benjamin, McKeachie, Lin, & Tucker, 1986; West & Pines, 1985). Because there is an orderliness or structure within subject matter knowledge, courseware developers can design lessons that "fit" or adapt to the underlying structure. Knowledge of the subject matter structure can be used by courseware developers to assist in organizing and sequencing CAI lessons and this knowledge can be communicated to students in order to assist them in structuring the information to be learned.

There are two primary sections to this chapter: (a) the organization and structure of subject matter knowledge, and (b) the design of courseware that adapts to the organization and structure of subject matter knowledge. Our logical starting point is a description of the different domains of learning into which subject matter knowledge can be classified. This forms the backdrop for a discussion of the structure of subject matter knowledge. The next step is to examine the types of structures of subject matter knowledge found within the different domains. Once the various structures have been examined, specific procedures for analyzing subject matter content are presented. That is, once the underlying structures within each domain are described, procedures for analyzing subject matter content to derive these structures will be presented. Finally, procedures are presented for using information about the content structures in designing CAI lessons that adapt to these structures.

DOMAINS OF LEARNING

Gagné (1985) has indicated that learning outcomes can be placed into one of five domains of learning (discussed in greater detail in the Wager and Gagné chapter). These domains are: (1) information, (2) intellectual skills, (3) motor skills, (4) attitudes, and (5) cognitive strategies. The instructional content within each domain differs from content in other domains in several fundamental ways: different instructional conditions are required to bring about the acquisition of the content within the different domains, different assessment procedures are required in different domains, and the organization and structure of the subject matter content differs for each domain. It is this last point about the organization and structure of the subject matter content within different domains of learning that forms the basis for this chapter.

You may recall that each domain is defined according to certain characteristics that learning outcomes in each domain possess. The five domains of learning identified by Gagné (1985) are:

Domain of information.   The learning outcomes in the domain of information all involve the restating or retelling of facts, names, labels, or larger bodies of knowledge such as theories. The performance of the learner in each case is a repeating or retelling of the information.

Domain of intellectual skills.   The domain of intellectual skills includes learning outcomes that require active mental processes involving the manipulation of symbols by the learner. Rather than just repeating some fact or knowledge, in the domain of intellectual skills the learner must solve a problem, apply a rule, or use a concept. Although Gagné identified eight different intellectual skills, the instructional outcomes in most of education and training seem to include only the four most complex skills. These are, from simple to complex: (1) discrimination, (2) concept learning, (3) rule learning, and (4) problem solving.

Domain of motor skills.   The domain of motor skills includes those learning outcomes that primarily require the movement of the muscles of the body. There is, of course, some mental aspect to each of these; motor skills do require thought. However, when the principle learning outcome is some movement or motion, the domain of that outcome is a motor skill.

Domain of attitudes.   The attitude domain includes those beliefs, values, and opinions that influence our actions. They are particularly obvious in a choice situation, when a learner can choose from among two or more options.

Domain of cognitive strategies.   The last domain of learning outcomes is called cognitive strategies. Cognitive strategies are those self-governing skills that determine how we approach a learning situation. Cognitive strategies differ from the other domains because there are no specific, observable instructional outcomes in cognitive strategies. Rather cognitive strategies are involved in whatever we are learning.

STRUCTURE OF SUBJECT MATTER CONTENT

Since the underlying structures of the instructional content differ by domain, the way a CAI lesson designed to teach intellectual skills should be structured different from the way a CAI lesson teaching information or motor skills should be structured. Determining the domain of the learning outcomes gives the CAI developer an initial idea about organizing and sequencing the instructional content for teaching those outcomes. Thus, the starting point in organizing instructional content for courseware development is to identify the domain of the instructional outcome. Then based on this knowledge of the domain, further exploration of the structure of the content is possible.

Before addressing specific approaches to analyzing instructional content, let's examine the types of content structures found in different domains of learning. What are the logical organizations that might be inherent in subject matter content in different domains of learning?

Structure of the domain of information

Content within the domain of information seems to be organized into semantic networks that include the specific items of content as nodes and the relationships among other content as lines connecting these nodes (Lachman, Lachman, & Butterfield, 1979; West et al., 1985). The semantic networks are represented primarily by two types of structures: a web, or network, structure and a hierarchical, or tree, structure (Collins & Loftus, 1975; Collins & Quillian, 1969;

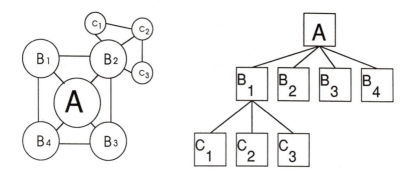

WEB STRUCTURE   HIERARCHICAL STRUCTURE

FIG. 11.1.   Representation of a semantic network.

Mayer, 1981; McNamara, 1986). An illustration of such networks is shown in Fig. 11.1.

Information exists within such conceptual or semantic networks, not in isolation. Facts or propositions are interrelated and it is these interrelationships that give meaning to the facts or propositions (Ausubel, 1963, 1968). Representations of information and the interrelationships among information can be called *knowledge structures.* Reigeluth and Stein (1983) described several different types of knowledge structures that exist in subject matter. Two of the knowledge structures they identified seem appropriate for the domain of information. These are conceptual structures and theoretical structures.

A conceptual structure shows the structure among ideas, or information, in terms of superordinate, coordinate, and subordinate relationships. There are three different types of conceptual structures: a parts structure, a kinds structure, and a classification matrix.

Parts structure.   A parts structure depicts the component parts of some object or idea. Such a structure would be appropriate when describing a microcomputer to a novice. A microcomputer consists of a microprocessor, memory, input device, and output device. These are the *parts* that comprise a microcomputer. The nature of the relationship in a parts knowledge structure is that the lower level, or subordinate, nodes (microprocessor, memory, input device, and output device) represent the parts of the ordinate node (microcomputer). An example of a parts knowledge structure for a bicycle is shown in Fig. 11.2. An example of a parts knowledge structure for an automobile is shown in Fig. 11.3. Note that each division further specifies the parts of the higher level. In each of these figures you will notice that the highest level entry, e.g., bicycle, is broken down

278

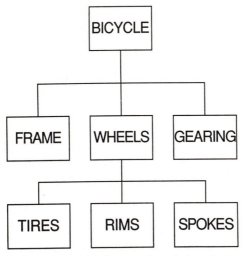

FIG. 11.2. Example of a parts knowledge structure.

into its component parts. Of course each part can often be further divided. A wheel which is a part of a bicycle can be divided into its parts: tires, rims and spokes. In a parts knowledge structure, you have a network of such relationships of objects.

Kinds structure. A kinds structure shows various kinds or types of a concept. For example, there might be a kinds structure for computer printers. Printers might be divided into letter quality, dot matrix, ink jet, and laser printers. A kinds knowledge structure for musical instruments is shown in Fig. 11.4. A kinds knowledge structure for transportation vehicles is shown in Fig.

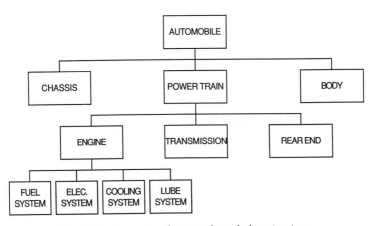

FIG. 11.3. Example of a parts knowledge structure.

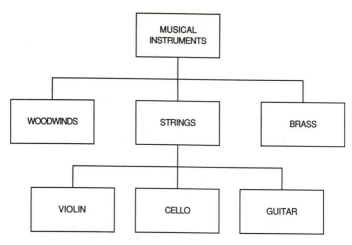

FIG. 11.4. Example of a kinds knowledge structure.

11.5. The entries in these kinds structures don't refer to the component parts of musical instruments or transportation vehicles but rather to different kinds of instruments and vehicles. The essential distinction between a *parts* knowledge structure and a *kinds* knowledge structure is the nature of the relationship. Does the lower level node reflect a part of the higher level node or a kind of the higher level node?

Classification matrix structure. A classification matrix structure includes two dimensions: objects to be classified and a set of attributes, or dimensions, on which the objects are to be classified. See Fig. 11.6. Of course it is possible to classify not only concrete objects but also abstract ideas. A classification matrix structure could be constructed for types of governments or for types of religions. In any case, the central feature of a classification matrix structure remains the same—it is a chart that compares the various attributes of related objects or ideas along similar dimensions.

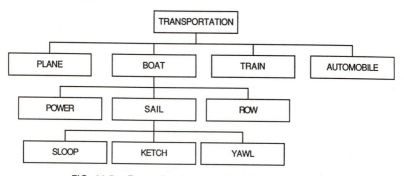

FIG. 11.5. Example of a kinds knowledge structure.

	Gypsum	Flourite	Feldspar	Garnet	Quartz
Symbol	$CaSO_4 \cdot 2H_2O$	CaF_2	$KAlSi_3O_8$	$Mg_3Al_2Si_3O_{12}$	SiO_2
Color	White, gray, brown	White, green, yellow, purple, red, blue	White to gray, red, green (rare)	Deep yellow-red	Colorless through various colors
Streak	White	Colorless	Colorless	Colorless	Colorless
Hardness	2	4	6	7.5	7
Specific gravity	2.3	3-3.3	2.5	3.5	2.65
Shape	Monoclinic, massive	Cubic, octahedral	Monoclinic, massive	Cubic	Hexagonal, massive
Breakage pattern	Basal cleavage, fibrous fracture	Octahedral cleavage, conchoidal fracture	Two cleavage planes meet at 90^0 angles	Uneven to conchoidal fracture, no cleavage	Conchoidal fracture

FIG. 11.6.   Example of a classification matrix. From Bishop, Lewis, & Sutherland (1976).

These three knowledge structures (parts, kinds, and classification matrix) are conceptual knowledge structures. In addition to these, Reigeluth and Stein (1983) described theoretical knowledge structures. A theoretical knowledge structure shows the relationships among certain events. The relationships in a theoretical knowledge structure may be either *descriptive* of some natural phenomena or *prescriptive* of some recommended ordering or sequence. The relationships among pressure, volume, and temperature can be described in a theoretical knowledge structure. Examples of theoretical structures are shown in Figs. 11.7 and 11.8.

These different knowledge structures seem to capture much of the structure and organization that exists in the domain of information. Perhaps the most important point for persons interested in developing courseware to teach information is that information is not discrete, isolated bits of knowledge but rather information exists with an organized structure (Eylon & Reif, 1984). If courseware is to effectively teach information, then that information must be presented within its structure.

Structure of the domain of motor skills

A different type of knowledge structure exists for content in the domain of motor skills. The relationship among motor skills content usually consists of a procedural structure or sequence. A procedural structure shows the various parts of a motor skill (the steps in performing the skill) and the sequence in which these

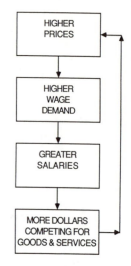

FIG. 11.7. Example of a theoretical knowledge structure.

parts are executed to form a coordinated motion. Thus, a procedural structure consists of both the discrete, or part, skills and the sequence in which these part skills are executed. Examples of procedural structures are shown in Figs. 11.9 and 11.10.

Structure of the domain of intellectual skills

Content in the intellectual skill domain is structured in yet another fashion. This domain is composed of problem solving, rule using, and concept learning. The

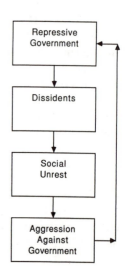

FIG. 11.8. Example of a theoretical knowledge structure.

282

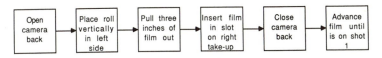

FIG. 11.9.   Example of a procedural knowledge structure.

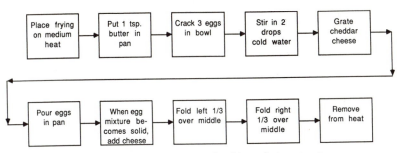

FIG. 11.10.   Example of a procedural knowledge structure.

relationships among these seems to be one of prerequisites in which certain concepts are prerequisite knowledge to certain rules which, in turn, are prerequisites to problem solving (Gagné, 1985). This learning prerequisite structure represents the knowledge that must be learned before the higher order knowledge can be mastered. For example, one must first learn the concepts of side, angle, and equality before learning to apply the rules that states that two triangles are congruent if two adjacent sides and the adjoining angle are equal. Likewise, before one can learn to determine the amount of liquid necessary to fill a cylindrical container, he or she must know the concepts of side, radius, and base. Examples of learning prerequisite structures, or learning hierarchies, are shown in Figs. 11.11 and 11.12. These learning prerequisite structures are found only in the domain of intellectual skills.

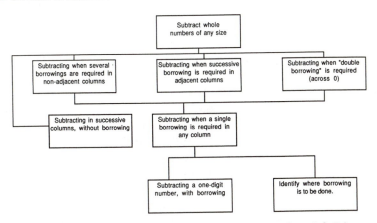

FIG. 11.11.   Example of a learning hierarchy. From Gagné & Briggs (1979).

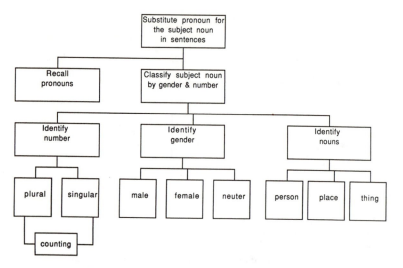

FIG. 11.12.   Example of a learning hierarchy.

Structure of the domain of attitudes

The organization of content within the domain of attitudes is somewhat different from the other domains. When we think of certain attitudes, we don't think of specific content but rather we think about some internal predisposition to respond or act in a certain rather consistent fashion. When we think about a backhand in tennis or about the causes of inflation, we usually have some tangible content or ideas in mind. But what about appreciation for good work? That is an attitude that usually doesn't bring such specific content to mind. The reason, of course, is the nature of an attitude as an internal entity rather than as some body of content external to a person. Because of this, it is difficult to describe specific knowledge structures in the domain of attitudes or to pictorially represent such structures.

ANALYSIS OF INSTRUCTIONAL CONTENT

The analysis of instructional content is a procedure that can take much of the "guess work" out of defining, organizing, and sequencing the instructional content for courseware development. If the courseware is to be judged successful then it must focus on teaching the essential content to support the learners' attainment of instructional goals. Thus, rather than rushing in and trying to write the student-courseware interactions, a CAI developer should first spend time in determining exactly *what* the learner must acquire in order to reach the goal. This is where the analysis of the instructional content will help in developing courseware. By analyzing the instructional content to identify the underlying structure,

284

the courseware developers have more guidance as they prepare lessons and develop courseware that adapts to the structure of the subject matter content.

Procedures for the analysis of content

Because there are differences in subject matter structures for learning outcomes in different domains of learning, the first step in the analysis of the instructional content (or *instructional analysis*) is to identify the domain of learning implied by the instructional goal. The analysis of learning outcomes in different domains of learning requires different analytical techniques (Hannum, 1980). Once the particular domain is identified then the appropriate analysis technique for that domain can be applied. This section describes four different instructional analysis techniques that can be used for analyzing the learning outcomes within different domains of learning.

Elaboration analysis. An elaboration analysis is the technique recommended for analyzing instructional content in the domain of information. In this approach the key idea or real essence of the information is first identified. Regardless of how complex the information may at first seem, there is some key aspect or central idea to it. This has been called the epitome by Reigeluth & Stein (1983). In analyzing information you must first identify this epitome. For example, in a lesson on American government the epitome may be that our government is a representative form of government composed of three branches. Once this core has been identified then you proceed to identify the next level of information, the information that *elaborates* on the epitome. This depends on the type of structure that exists. The next level might reflect a kinds structure or a parts structure depending on the nature of the relationship. In turn you would develop *further elaborations* of this information, including more detail each time. The steps involved in an elaboration analysis, including the action taken and an example of each step, are shown in Fig. 11.13. In this elaboration approach you first identify the main ideas or the big picture then go back and successively identify the secondary or supporting ideas. First the forest, then the trees. This approach is recommended to: (1) make sure that all the important information is included in the lesson, (2) make sure that no unrelated information is included, and (3) help provide the much needed structure of the information for learners. When we can order or structure information, we tend to learn it better and retain it longer.

Hierarchical analysis. The development of a learning hierarchy is the approach recommended for the analysis of instructional content in the domain of intellectual skills. Because the learning of any intellectual skill depends on the prior mastery of prerequisite skills, these prerequisite skills must be identified. The approach suggested by Gagné (1985) is to begin with the instructional goal

Step	Action	Example
1	Identify main idea/ central concept	Types of musical instruments
2	Determine the type of knowledge structure (parts/kinds/classification matrix/theoretical)	Since you will identify different kinds of musical instruments, it is a Kinds Knowledge structure
3	Identify first level breakdown	String instruments, wind instruments, brass instruments, etc.
4	For each level breakdown, identify second level breakdown	
5	Repeat this division into more specific ideas or concepts as in Step 4	

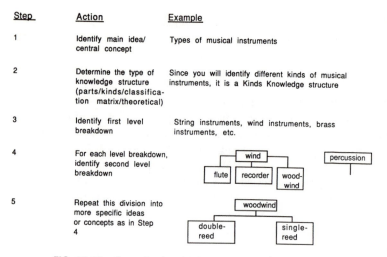

FIG. 11.13. Steps in developing an elaboration analysis.

and ask "What must the learner be able to do in order to reach this goal?" The goal is broken down in successive stages to identify the prerequisite skills. For example, suppose we wanted to develop a lesson to teach the rule for finding the size of the hypotenuse of a right triangle when given the size of the two legs. Before a learner could do this she would have to be able to sum the squares of the legs. Before she could do this she would have to identify the legs of a triangle and be able to square numbers. Before she could do this she would have to be able to multiply two numbers, etc. The steps in doing a hierarchical analysis, including the specific action and an example of the results of each step, are shown in Fig. 11.14. In such a manner, we have worked backwards from the

Step	Action	Example		
1	Identify the final outcome or instructional goal/task	goal:	substitute pronoun for noun	
2	For this task, identify the specific prerequisite skill by asking "What must the learner be able to do in order to accomplish this?"	first level breakdown:	recall pronouns	match pronoun with noun in terms of gender/number
3	For the task identifed in Step 2, repeat the question	second level breakdown:	identify gender	identify number
4	Continue to identify the prerequisite skills for each task	third level breakdown:	singular	plural
5		fourth level breakdown:	determine if person, place or thing	

FIG. 11.14. Steps in developing a learning hierarchy.

instructional goal and identified the prerequisite skills necessary for accomplishing that goal. These prerequisite skills then are the basis for our instructional content. In our lesson we would include instruction on each of the prerequisite skills and *not* include instruction on other nonessential topics.

Procedural analysis.   A procedural analysis is the recommended technique for analyzing instructional goals in the domain of motor skills. In a procedural analysis, motor skills are broken down into a series of specific steps which when executed comprise the motor skill. The motor skill of starting a car can be broken down into several steps that must be executed in a sequence. For example, placing the key in the ignition, making sure the parking brake is set, placing the transmission in neutral, depressing the gas peddle slightly, turning the key clockwise, and then releasing the key upon starting. The specific steps for developing a procedural sequence and an example of each step are shown in Fig. 11.15. If the instructional goals of the lesson are motor skills, then the CAI developer must carefully identify the sequence of steps that must be performed to accomplish this motor skill.

Goal analysis.   Goal analysis is the recommended technique for analyzing instruction in the domain of attitudes. Since attitudes can not be directly observed but must be inferred from behaviors, the analysis of attitudes involves the identification of these behaviors. In doing a goal analysis of an attitude you ask ''What is the behavior that would mean that a person possessed this attitude?'' (Mager, 1970). If we were developing a lesson to teach a positive attitude towards safety

Step	Action	Example
1	Identify end point of the motor skills	New air filter cartride installed on carbuerator of car
2	Identify starting point	Person fixing car has new filter cartridge and pliers
3	Identify the first movement or step after the starting point	Locate hood release
4	In turn, identify each succeeding movement or step until the end point is reached	Squeeze and hold hood release
5		Raise hood until it stops
6		Locate air filter on top of carbuerator
7		Remove nut securing top of air filter
8		Remove top of air filter
9		Remove old filter cartridge
10		Place new filter cartridge in air filter and seat
11		Replace top of air filter
12		Secure nut on top of air filter

FIG. 11.15.   Steps in developing a procedural sequence.

Step	Action	Example
1	Write down a statement of the attitude	Good sportsmanship in playing tennis
2	Construct a list of behaviors that would indicate someone had this attitude	Follows rules, doesn't make close calls, plays a let if opponent is distracted, doesn't rush game, etc.
3	Edit the list to combine or remove duplication	Combine water break with not rushing the game
4	Verify the list by asking "If a person routinely engaged in behavior X, behavior Y and behavior Z, would you consider him/her to have attitude A?"	When imagining a person doing all these specific things, we are willing to say he/she is a good sport
5	If the list verifies, then stop; if not, repeat steps 2-4	Since we were satisfied in step 4, we stop

FIG. 11.16.   Steps in developing a goal analysis.

in the workplace then what behavior would we accept as evidence that a person had the desired attitude? Alternatively, we could think of an employee that had a good attitude towards safety and one who didn't. We could then think of what it was that they did differently to make us think one had the desired attitude and the other did not. In any case the intent is the same, to describe the behavior that indicates or represents the attitude. In this example, if an employee could verbally state all safety regulations, used safety precautions in his work, could describe how to handle potentially dangerous situations, or could respond in simulated emergency situations, then we may say he had a positive attitude towards safety. It is these specific behaviors that correspond to the attitude that would be the basis for the instruction. The steps in goal analysis, along with an example of each step, are shown in Fig. 11.16.

Summary.   Thus, there are four different analytical techniques that can be applied to learning outcomes, or instructional goals, in the different domains of learning. Applying a technique that is appropriate for one domain, such as a hierarchical analysis of an intellectual skill, to another domain, such as a hierarchical analysis of information, is not recommended. There are different subject matter structures in the domains of intellectual skills and information; these different structures require different analytical techniques.

USING KNOWLEDGE STRUCTURES IN COURSEWARE

Information about knowledge structures can be used by courseware developers in two ways: (a) to organize and sequence lesson content, and (b) to communicate

288

the subject matter structure to learners (Wilson, 1985). The first case is a matter of fitting or adapting the CAI lesson to the structure of the subject matter content. The latter case involves helping learners adapt their internal representations of the knowledge, or schemata, to the knowledge structures.

When organizing lesson content, the CAI developer must determine what specific content to include in support of the instructional goals. While these decisions may require a blend of art and science, a carefully completed instructional analysis will assist CAI developers in identifying the essential content and its organization. When representations of the structure of subject matter knowledge have been identified through instructional analysis, they can serve to guide the selection and organization of courseware (Gardner, 1985; Wilson, 1985). For example, if the instructional outcome is an intellectual skill, the instructional analysis would identify the necessary prerequisite skills whose mastery leads to the acquisition of the intellectual skill. The courseware, then, can focus on teaching those prerequisite skills. This prevents unnecessary content from *creeping* into the courseware. The resulting lesson is much more likely to be effective (it will include instruction on all necessary prerequisite skills) and efficient (it will not include superfluous materials). For example, if we were developing courseware for teaching learners how to substitute a pronoun for a subject noun, we could refer to the learning hierarchy for this instructional outcome. The learning hierarchy would indicate the specific content that must be mastered for this outcome to be attained. As shown in Fig. 11.12, the learners must be able to identify number, gender, and nouns prior to learning how to substitute a pronoun for a noun. Thus, our courseware must include instruction on these prerequisite skills unless we had determined that the learners had previously acquired these skills.

Similar situations exist in the other domains of learning outcomes. The analysis of a motor skill will identify the essential steps, or part-skills, that must be mastered. The courseware, then, would include instruction on these part-skills but not on unrelated skills. For example, if the courseware was designed to teach someone how to load film in a camera, reference to the procedural knowledge structure shown in Fig. 11.9 would indicate what specific steps must be taught. These steps, then, form the basis for the content for that courseware.

The analysis of information will identify the specific information to be mastered and the context, or structure, in which it exists. These elaborations form the basis for the design of the courseware. For example, if we were developing courseware to teach someone about kinds of musical instruments, we could use the kinds knowledge structure for musical instruments shown in Fig. 11.4 to guide our lesson development. The courseware would include instruction for all the musical instruments identified in the instructional analysis. The courseware would show the instruments in each part of the knowledge structure and how these relate. Information that is not part of the knowledge structure would not be included in the lesson.

The analysis of attitudes identifies the specific behaviors that indicate presence of the attitude. Once an instructional analysis of attitudes has been completed, the courseware developer can focus the lesson content on these specific behaviors. The resulting lesson will likely involve vicarious learning in which a person is depicted engaging in these behaviors and receiving positive reinforcement for his behavior. The analysis of the attitude to be taught can guide the courseware development by identifying the behaviors that indicate the presence of the attitude and the context surrounding these behaviors. For example, if we were developing courseware to teach good sportsmanship in playing tennis, then we could use the goal analysis partially shown in Fig. 11.16 to identify the content for our lesson. The courseware would show a player following the rules, playing a let when her opponent was distracted, taking a water break, and the like. In short, the courseware would be based on those behaviors that indicate presence of the attitude. Again, the instructional analysis would guide the courseware development.

Although courseware developers have much freedom in how they present the specific instruction, they should adapt the lesson content to the structure of the subject matter. There is no reason that using information about the structure of the subject matter content should result in a dull uniformness to courseware. Rather, different CAI developers may use quite different approaches in presenting a lesson on the same content. This is to be applauded. However, if the courseware is to be as effective as it should be, then each developer must include instruction on the essential content. Thus, knowing the structure of the subject matter content guides CAI developers but does not limit their creativity as they prepare courseware.

Information about the structure of the subject matter knowledge also assists CAI developers in making decisions about sequencing the courseware (Wilson, 1985). We know that mastery of higher level intellectual skills depends on prior mastery of the prerequisite skills (Gagné, 1985). Thus, courseware in the domain of intellectual skills should be sequenced according to learning hierarchies. The lower level skills in any specific learning hierarchy would be presented prior to the higher level skills. In the example of substituting pronouns for nouns shown in Fig. 11.12, the concepts of male and female are prerequisite to being able to identify gender, thus the courseware should present instruction on male and female prior to instruction on gender. Likewise, since being able to identify gender and number are prerequisites to being able to classify subject nouns by gender and number, the courseware should include instruction on gender and number before presenting instruction on classifying subject nouns.

The sequencing of instruction for the domain of motor skills usually follows the same progression as the specific steps in the motor skill. That is, the learner usually follows the same sequence in learning a motor skill as he would follow in executing the motor skill. Thus the procedural knowledge structure for a motor skill provides information about the instructional sequence. Motor skills are typically taught in the sequence in which they are performed. Thus in the example of teaching someone how to load film into a camera shown in Fig. 11.9, the courseware would begin by providing instruction on how to open the camera back, how to place the film roll into the camera, etc. The sequence followed in the courseware would parallel the sequence in the procedural analysis.

The preferred sequence in the domain of information seems to be from general to specific or whole to part (Reigeluth & Stein, 1983). The courseware would first present the main idea, or epitome, of the lesson, then successively add detail. The sequence may be a kind of back and forth progression, showing the main idea, then more detail, then back to the main idea, and so on. If the courseware dealt with types of transportation as shown in Fig. 11.5, the lesson might begin by describing transportation and indicating that there are various forms of transportation. The lesson would then show the first level elaboration which divides transportation into planes, boats, trains, and automobiles. The lesson might then put these four major kinds of transportation back together stressing that they all represent ways to transport people and things. The lesson would progress by describing kinds of planes, kinds of boats, etc. Such a sequence stresses the organization of the knowledge by clearly showing the interrelatedness of the subject matter content.

In the domain of attitudes, unfortunately, there do not appear to be such clearcut guidelines for sequencing courseware. The instructional analysis will be helpful in identifying the behaviors that indicate the presence of the attitude but will reveal little about how to sequence the lessons.

This discussion of sequencing CAI lessons implies that the sequencing decisions are made by the CAI developer and remain fixed for all learners. That is, that each learner is forced to follow that same sequence through the courseware. However, CAI lessons do not have to have a fixed linear sequence as most films or textbooks appear to have. The decision about sequencing the lesson content might be relegated to the learner. In some learner controlled courseware each learner can determine his or her own sequence through the lesson by selecting the specific topic to study. Often this learner control is achieved by having a topic menu in each lesson. The learner, then, selects the specific topic to study next thus determining his sequence through the lesson. In other courseware, the menu may include an indication of a preferred or optimal sequence to the topics within a lesson. The learner retains control over the sequencing but does have this advice to help them make sequencing decisions.

Perhaps one of the very best uses of information about the structure of subject matter knowledge is to communicate this structure to the learners. In addition to the specific subject matter knowledge, students must have learned the structure or organization of that knowledge if they are to be successful (Gardner, 1985; Resnick, 1981). Cognitive psychologists have suggested that if students learn the structure, their learning is more meaningful and more resistant to forgetting. The learners also should be able to better transfer their new learning to different

Computers

I. Input
   A. Keyboard
   B. Touch screen
   C. Mouse

II. Storage
   A. Primary
      1. RAM
      2. ROM
      3. PROM
   B. Secondary
      1. Disk
      2. Tape wheel

III. Central processor
   A. Control unit
   B. Arithmetic and logic unit

IV. Output
   A. CRT
   B. Printer
      1. Impact
         a. Daisy wheel
         b. Dot matrix
      2. Non-impact
         a. Laser
         b. Ink jet
   C. Plotter

FIG. 11.17.   Example of a topic outline.

situations. Thus, it seems desirable to communicate the structure to the learners so that they may use it to organize and guide their learning (Eylon & Reif, 1984).

There are several ways that this might be accomplished within courseware. Prior to the lesson you could present the lesson structure to the learner in the form of: (a) a topic outline as shown in Fig. 11.17, (b) an advance organizer, or (c) an appropriate graphic representation (web structure, tree structure, sequence of steps) as shown in Fig. 11.18. The structure could be presented within the courseware during the lesson by: (a) allowing the learner to refer to a topic

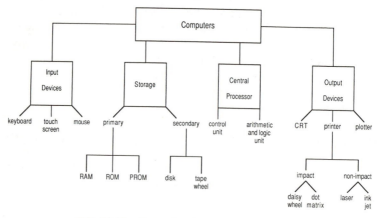

FIG. 11.18.   Example of a graphic organizer.

292

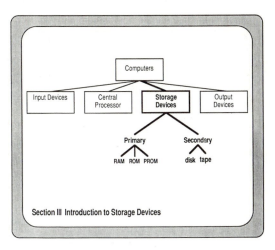

FIG. 11.19. Example of a graphic organizer displayed at the beginning of each new segment.

outline or graphic representation of the structure any time he chooses, (b) displaying the structure as an outline or graphic each time the learner begins instruction on a new segment within the lesson as shown in Fig. 11.19, (c) displaying a part of the structure at the top of each screen to show the learner where she is as shown in Fig. 11.20, (d) having a pop-up or pull-down window under the learner's control so that she can ask to see that overall structure at any time and will have that superimposed over a portion of the screen as shown in Fig. 11.21, (e) using analogies to familiar content that has a structure similar to the new

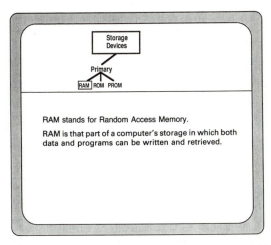

FIG. 11.20. Example of continuous display of a partial graphic organizer.

293

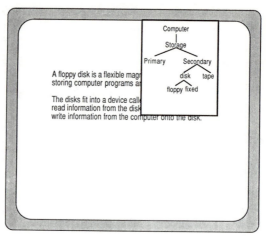

FIG. 11.21.   Example of a graphic organizer in a pull down window.

content, and (f) using a form of hypertext in which the learner can "leave" the lesson and refer to (or create) his own notes about the structure. The structure could be presented following the lesson by: (a) having a verbal summary that highlights the structure, (b) displaying a graphic that shows the structure as previously shown in Fig. 11.18, and (c) having the learners generate the structure when given a part of it as a prompt as shown in Fig. 11.22. There are many ways to communicate the subject matter structure to learners either before, during, or after a lesson. CAI developers can select from these approaches, shown in Fig. 11.23, to communicate the structure to learners as a way to enhance the courseware.

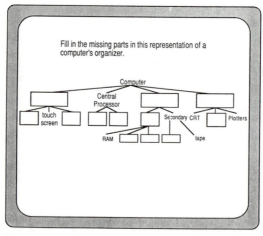

FIG. 11.22.   Example of a prompt for a learner generated structure.

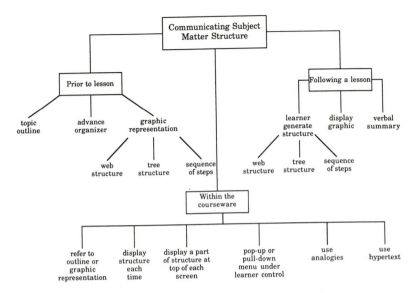

FIG. 11.23. Communicating subject matter structure.

SUMMARY

In summary, courseware can be designed to adapt to the different structures of subject matter knowledge. When CAI lessons are adapted to the subject matter structure, their effectiveness and efficiency can be enhanced. These structures seem to be different for content within different domains of learning outcomes. Because of this, different techniques must be used to analyze subject matter in different domains to identify the underlying structures. If the instructional goal is in the domain of information an elaboration approach is used. If the goal is in the domain of intellectual skills a learning hierarchy is developed to identify the necessary prerequisite skills. If the goal is in the domain of motor skills a procedural analysis is used to identify each step in the motor skill and the sequence of these steps. Finally, if the goal is in the attitude domain goal analysis is used to identify the behavior that is indicative of the attitude. Regardless of which procedure is used the purpose is the same—to identify the necessary content that, when learned, will lead to reaching the instructional goals. The structure of the subject matter content also has implications for organizing and sequencing individual lessons. Finally, the structure can be communicated to learners to assist them in the learning process.

REFERENCES

Anderson, J. R. (1983). *The architecture of cognition.* Cambridge, MA: Harvard University Press.
Ausubel, D. P. (1963). *The psychology of meaningful verbal learning.* New York: Grune & Stratton.

Ausubel, D. P. (1968). *Educational psychology: A cognitive view*. New York: Holt, Rinehart & Winston.

Bishop, M. S., Lewis, P. G., & Sutherland, B. (1976). *Focus on earth science* (3rd ed.). Columbus, OH: Charles Merrill.

Champagne, A. B., Gunstone, R. F., & Klopfer, L. E. (1985). Effecting changes in cognitive structures among physics students. In L. H. T. West & A. L. Pines (Eds.), *Cognitive structure and conceptual change* (pp. 163–187). Orlando, FL: Academic Press.

Champagne, A. B., Klopfer, L. E., Desena, A. T., & Squires, D. A. (1981). Structural representations of students' knowledge before and after science instruction. *Journal of Research in Science Technology, 18,* 97–111.

Collins, A. M., & Loftus, E. R. (1975). A spreading-activation theory of semantic processing. *Psychological Review, 82,* 407–428.

Collins, A. M., & Quillian, M. R. (1969). Retrieval time from semantic memory. *Journal of Verbal Learning and Verbal Behavior, 8,* 240–247.

Eylon, B., & Reif, F. (1984). Effects of knowledge organization on task performance. *Cognition and instruction, 1*(1), 5–44.

Gagné, R. M. (1985). *The conditions of learning* (4th ed.). New York: Holt, Rinehart & Winston.

Gagné, R. M., & Briggs, L. J. (1979). *Principles of instructional design* (2nd ed.). New York: Holt, Rinehart & Winston.

Gardner, M. K. (1985). Cognitive psychological approaches to instructional task analysis. In E. W. Gordan (Ed.), *Review of research in education* (pp. 157–195). Washington: American Educational Research Association.

Geeslin, W. E., & Shavelson, R. J. (1975). Comparison of content structure in high school students' learning of probability. *Journal for Research in Mathematics Education, 6,* 109–120.

Hannum, W. H. (1980). Task analysis procedures. *NSPI Journal, 19*(3), 6–14.

Lachman, R., Lachman, J. L., & Butterfield, E. C. (1979). *Cognitive psychology and information processing: An introduction*. Hillsdale, NJ: Lawrence Erlbaum Associates.

Mager, R. F. (1970). *Goal analysis*. Palo Alto, CA: Fearon.

Mayer, R. E. (1981). *The promise of cognitive psychology*. San Francisco: W. H. Freeman.

McNamara, T. P. (1986). Mental representations of spatial relations. *Cognitive Psychologist, 18,* 87–121.

Naveh-Benjamin, M., McKeachie, W. J., Lin, Y. G., & Tucker, D. G. (1986). Inferring students cognitive structures & their development using the "ordered tree technique". *Journal of Educational Psychology, 78*(2), 130–140.

Reigeluth, C. M., Merrill, M. D., & Bunderson, C. V. (1978). The structure of subject matter content and its instructional design implications. *Instructional Science, 7,* 107–126.

Reigeluth, C. M., & Stein, F. S. (1983). The elaboration theory of instruction. In C. M. Reigeluth (Ed.), *Instructional-design theories and models: An overview of their current status* (pp. 335–381). Hillsdale, NJ: Lawrence Erlbaum Associates.

Resnick, L. B. (1981). Instructional psychology. *Annual Review of Psychology, 32,* 660–704.

West, L. H. T., Fensham, P. J., & Gerrard, J. E. (1985). Describing the cognitive structures of learners following instruction in chemistry. In L. H. T. West & A. L. Pines (Eds.), *Cognitive structure and conceptual change* (pp. 29–49). Orlando, FL: Academic Press.

West, L. H. T., & Pines, A. L. (Eds.). (1985). *Cognitive structure and conceptual change*. Orlando, FL: Academic Press.

Wilson, B. G. (1985). Using content structure in course design. *Journal of Educational Technology Systems, 14*(2), 137–147.

IV TOWARD INTELLIGENT CAI ON MICROCOMPUTERS

Most of the low-quality, behaviorally oriented CAI that critics have been inveighing against for years is what Carbonell (1970) referred to as ad-hoc, frame-oriented CAI. Ad hoc refers to the decision making which drives the branching options in the instruction—ad hoc. That is, each and every branching decision is made on an ad hoc basis and separately programmed based on the contingencies unique to the frame. Frame-oriented means that the structural basis of instruction is the individual information frame (individual screen), having derived from programmed instruction frames. The archetypal ad hoc, frame-oriented program presents text, asks a question, provides confirmation of the response, and perhaps branches on an ad hoc basis to alternative frames based on the user's response and a simple if–then algorithm. An ad hoc, frame-oriented CAI author must anticipate every possible learner response and then predetermine branches to appropriate remedial material based on his or her idea about what underlying misconceptions resulted in the incorrect response (Barr, 1982). In this type of courseware, decision making and initiative resides in the computer program. The student has no control over what, how, or when she or he learns, except through their correct or incorrect responses. This programmed-instruction-based design still dominates a great deal of microcomputer courseware. Although it is a useful design, it does not reflect current cognitive learning theory. There is an inexorable revolution in courseware, both micro- and main frame based, toward more intelligent designs—designs that are capable of engaging the learner in a dialog, designs that themselves possess logic and knowledge structures that emulate human intelligence. These intelligent designs are evolving from research and development in artificial intelligence. They are the subject of this fourth part of this book.

Artificial intelligence is the science of getting machines to emulate human intelligence. The goal of artificial intelligence researchers is to model the way humans represent knowledge and then to ''approximate the contextual, often para-logical or quasi-logical behavior of human beings'' through the use of the Boolean logic endemic to computers (Wyer, 1984). So, research in artificial intelligence is concerned above all with the ways in which humans represent knowledge in memory and during cognitive processing. Knowledge representation is not enough however, as researchers also focus on the language-based communication processes. The study of the syntax and semantics of natural language is prominent in AI research, since the semantic aspects are integrally involved in knowledge representation. Additionally, AI programs are normally designed to interact with the user in a natural language dialog, so being able to parse user input to the computer in order to assign meaning to it is an essential albeit incredibly complex process. Finally, AI research is concerned with the cognitive activities which comprise intelligence. In order to emulate human intelligence, AI programs must not only know how to decode human communications and assign meaning to it and store it in memory, but also they need to be able to engage in complex cognitive activities such as making inferences, reasoning, generalizing, and so on. The key to artificial intelligence is the software, which translates representational symbols, which are manipulated, and output to humans who recode it into memory (Wyer, 1984). Because of the assumptions made by such software and the processing required to fulfill those assumptions, AI software is much more complex than the ad hoc, frame-oriented CAI with which we are more familiar.

Just as artificial intelligence represents a complex process, it also represents a complex concept. It is a term that is used to describe a wide range of development activities. Most of those activities remain very much developmental and conjectural. Researchers are faced with technical limitations of existing computers as well as theoretical limitations related to our incomplete understanding of human information processing. Because of the developmental nature of the AI science, it remains more of a pure science than an applied science. Since educational application of technology is an applied science, few implications of AI have been exploited in education. However, that is changing as rapidly as the science of AI evolves. Figure IV.1 presents a graphic outline of the applications of AI techniques to education. Many of these are implementable in a microcomputer environment. So, since the field of courseware design is moving inexorably into the milieu of artificial intelligence, this part of the book looks at some of those efforts. I discuss each of these applications briefly but concentrate only on those that affect courseware development.

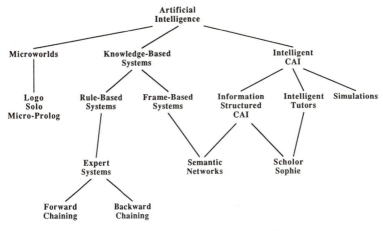

FIG. IV.1. Applications of AI to education.

Microworlds

The process of using computer environments to explore how individuals think is the basis for developing educational microworlds. Papert (1980) observed that the process of building natural language computer programs provided an excellent instructional environment for getting children to think about thinking. Computers, he observed, are carriers of powerful ideas, and they are the seeds of cultural change. Since programming a computer means nothing more than communicating with it in terms that both the programmer and computer can understand, he used the AI language LISP as a base to develop the language, Logo. Logo enables children to direct the actions of a robotic turtle through a computer to draw pictures and to process lists of characters (text) just like LISP. The language is a simplified, mediating language which is premised on our ability to design computers to provide a natural language interface. In learning to program the computer, children use the computer model, which is invested with powerful ideas such as state and state variables, subproblems and subgoals, local-global connections, recursion, and debugging, to enhance their own thinking abilities. Rather than getting a problem right or wrong, children learn that through an iterative process of feedback-correction they can always get it right. Computer environments, such as Logo, have not fulfilled the promises of their progenitors, but they have not been sufficiently integrated into the instructional process to yet make a difference. Other Logo subsets, such as Solo (see the Denenberg chapter, this volume) have been created to fulfill the same purpose. Kay (1977) created the SMALLTALK language and operating system to make the computer as a device even more transparent. All of these efforts have been aimed at making the computer a tool that becomes a true "extension of man," so flexible and powerful that one cannot help but learn from using it. Such microworlds make different assumptions about how computers should be used than does most courseware. However, as courseware becomes more intelligent, it too should provide an epistemological mirror that can reflect the user's thought processes to him or her.

Knowledge Based Systems

Knowledge based software systems are information systems built around a knowledge base—a network of related facts, rules, or problems. All knowledge base systems (KBS) possess at least three features: knowledge representation (a semantic network of information), a formal grammar for interacting with users, and a production system of rules for accessing the information in the knowledge base (Bregar & Farley, 1980). The semantic network consists of objects, properties, or concepts which possess a name, values for each object, and tags to make them accessible. The grammar for interacting with users defines the natural language interface. The interface is a system of rules for parsing the user's input in order to interpret its meaning. The production system, otherwise known as an inference engine, represents the reasoning ability of the knowledge-based system. The inference engine retrieves rules, checks to see if the rule is usable, and then applies it to retrieve information from the knowledge base or retrieve another rule to evaluate. The goals and applications of KBSs differ substantially. There are two fairly distinct types of KBSs—rule-based systems (expert systems) and frame-based systems.

Expert Systems.   Expert systems are specific kinds of applications of KBSs that are designed to capture and make accessible the operational knowledge of an expert. They are used for solving finite classes of problems, such as troubleshooting, diagnosis and correction (especially in medicine), and analysis of situations. Most expert systems are also able to explain how they solved the problem. Expert systems are able to make decisions as well as experts in various fields, because their structures reflect the manner in which human experts arrange and make inferences from their knowledge (Michaelson, Mickie, & Boulanger, 1985). Most expert systems are rule-based, that is, they consist of hierarchical networks of if–then rules. Each rule consists of one or more premises (if) and a conclusion (then). For example, IF distance to subject > 30 feet AND depth of field = shallow, THEN focal length > 200 mm. The system chooses a rule to evaluate, evaluates it (true, false, or unknown quantity) and then applies the rule. Rules may be chosen by searching through the conclusions (THEN) in order to solve goals (backward chaining or consequent-driven) or by searching the premises in order and finding all rules that contain certain premises (forward chaining or antecedent-driven). When the search conditions are satisfied, the rule is applied. The application may entail accessing another rule, asking the user for more information, or taking some action. So, expert systems consist of a set of rules for making decisions to solve specific problems. The rules are derived by emulating the decision making of human experts. Expert systems have enjoyed the most success as problem solvers in industrial and medical environments. They are gaining popularity in education, but their implications for courseware are not well understood or established and so have not been exploited. So none of the chapters in this section explore the implications of expert systems for courseware design. They probably have implications for simulation design, which are beyond the scope of this book. When combined with databases, expert systems resemble other forms of knowledge based tutors. In problem-solving instruction, they are capable of emulating decision making and information processing in many different subject areas, so there is a potential modeling effect. All of these applications auger a significant future for expert systems in education. However, the courseware implications are still largely conjectural.

Frame-Based Systems

Frame-based KBSs (see Fig. IV.1) are less rule oriented and more knowledge-based than expert systems. Frame-based systems are structured by a knowledge base, which consists of frames and nodes to represent knowledge schemata. Each frame or node represents an object or concept, which is composed of properties and which is associatively linked to other frames. The properties are arranged hierarchically, with super-ordinate properties subsuming sub-ordinate attributes. In combination, the associative concepts form a semantic network. Frame-based systems may also be referred to as information-structured CAI (see Fig. IV.1). The common classification reflects the overlap and interdependency of many efforts in artificial intelligence.

Probably the best known frame-based system or information structured tutor is SCHOLAR (Carbonell, 1970), which tutored students about geographic facts of South America. SCHOLAR possessed several strategies for assessing the learner's queries and using information in the response to access the knowledge base through the associative network. SCHOLAR represented a quantum advance in courseware design, because it was mixed initiative. That is, the learner could initiate a question to the system as well as being drilled by it.

Knowledge-based courseware must provide a model for structuring the knowledge in it. The problem of knowledge representation in courseware authoring is being increasingly explored. For instance, McAleese (1985) has developed a microcomputer system for exteriorizing the learner's knowledge, so that the learner may become aware of knowledge gaps and engage in meaningful searches of a knowledge base. This obviously requires that the system manifest the structure of the knowledge base, that is, exteriorize the author's knowledge structure. That necessarily entails constructing a frame-based knowledge base (semantic network) in the courseware. The future of courseware is very dependent upon being able to organize and represent knowledge in a system as well as provide a means to access that knowledge that is predicated on what the learner already knows. Frame-based KBSs represent an important developmental step in that direction. Intelligent CAI goes a step further by modeling the learner's knowledge structure.

Intelligent Computer-Assisted Instruction

Intelligent computer-assisted instruction (ICAI) represents a collection of efforts by many researchers to apply principles of artificial intelligence to CAI, hence intelligent CAI. ICAI systems vary substantially in their conception of intelligent behavior and approach to instruction. I have discussed briefly information structured (frame-based) approaches. The other general category of ICAI (see Fig. VI.1) is known as intelligent tutoring systems.

Intelligent Tutoring Systems

In defining properties of an intelligent tutor, Gable and Page (1980) began by identifying the properties of a good human tutor, such as

- adopting a student's strategy, if superior
- providing examples, problems, and help
- adjusting to the background of the student
- working examples generated by the student
- suggesting better solutions to the student and others.

As indicated in Fig. IV.1, intelligent tutors overlap knowledge-based systems. The overlap consists of their knowledge-based framework, that is, they both structure their information by developing semantic networks. These networks organize and provide access points to the information contained in the course. Intelligent tutors, though, add a significant capability not found in plain frame-based systems.

Intelligent tutoring systems vary extensively (see Sleeman & Brown, 1982), however. The most significant dimension of intelligent tutors is their ability to build a model of the student's knowledge through their interaction with the student. By modeling the student's knowledge, the program is better able to map the subject matter more directly onto the student's knowledge structure. Intelligent tutors assess the learner's logic or background through rules governing their interactions.

Most intelligent tutors are either problem-solving tutors or simulations. One of the best known intelligent tutors is SOPHIE (Sophisticated Instructional Environment) (Brown, Burton, & Bell, 1975). It is a problem-solving environment in which the learner can "try out" solutions to problems in electronics posed by the program. It uses a model of its problem-solving ability in the form of rules to generate alternatives for the student, answer their questions, as well as showing how to solve the problem. Problem-solving tutors constitute the bulk of intelligent tutors. Another form of intelligent tutoring may be found in simulations. Computer-based simulations model a process and an environment, allowing the learner to work in that environment, usually in order to solve problems. The accuracy and realism of interactive, computer-based simulations that are afforded by larger, higher speed microcomputers and related technologies such as videodisc, are phenomenal. The realism in modeling the learning environment is one of the important distinctions between simulations and problem-solving tutors. Simulations vary greatly in design, though their purpose remains similar—to engage the learner in relevant, meaningful processing associated with a particular learning or working environment. Simulation design is a very complex process. Since simulations represent a distinct design technology, they are not discussed further in this book on courseware.

INTRODUCTION TO PART IV

Courseware designers want to know where they should begin in the milieu of artificial intelligence. Since knowledge representation is such a fundamental component of all AI work, learning how to represent knowledge in courseware would be appropriate. An excellent beginning is Stewart Denenberg's chapter, "Semantic Network Designs for Courseware." After describing and illustrating semantic networks and the relationships which may exist between nodes in networks, he discusses how they could be used to structure a knowledge based system. Denenberg then provides an example of such a system for academic advising. He shows how semantic networks can be used in educational curricula through creating microworlds using the Logo subset, SOLO. The experiences that he describes are among the most useful for communicating principles of cognitive psychology that are available, since semantic networks are so fundamental to the discipline.

So, if knowledge is structured in semantic networks, the information in the courseware should be organized in ways that reflect the content (knowledge) structure. In the next chapter, Wendy Mackay presents a process for developing a pseudo-intelligent tutor based on an information database, which represents the knowledge structure being communicated. The information database contains facts, inferences, and procedures in the form of text, graphics, and even video ("objects" which can be accessed from the database). The type of instructional sequence that is accessed (documentation, computer based drill, simulation, or tutoring) depends on the student's knowledge state. This "object-oriented relational database" is capable of integrating all of the above instructional styles into the learning experience. Perhaps the most interesting part of the chapter is Mackay's description of the interative design process they use for building prototype tutors. Rather than building an arbitrary model of the learner, the designer interacts with the learner during development and builds an empirical model based on the interaction. The illustrations of both the information database and the tutor are fascinating.

For many instructional designers interested in developing intelligent tutoring systems, the problem is how to get started. Joseph and Alice Scandura explicate that process using his Structural Learning Theory (SLT), rather than the mathematical model used for many tutors. After an introduction, they show how to represent rules in a tutoring system, both in logic trees and FLOWforms (block diagrams). A particular advantage of the FLOWform method of representing tutorial processes is that they map conceptual knowledge in a form that reflects programming structures, which facilitates coding of components of the tutor. They then expand the rule discussion into instructional strategies based on SLT. The Scanduras then describe both verbally and in FLOWforms the conceptual process underlying an intelligent tutor. A major advantage of the tutoring system that they are developing is the PRODOC operating system, which automates most of the processes of tutor construction, enabling designers to concentrate on the content while constructing the tutor. This system is one of the most highly developed instructional design-based systems available for creating intelligent courseware.

The final chapter in this section, by Greg Kearsley, defines the components of an ICAI authoring system. After identifying the limitations of existing authoring tools, Kearsley describes and illustrates the basic characteristics of ICAI programs. From that description, he evolves a generalized authoring system, which includes a discourse editor, database editor, lesson assembler, and course interpreter. Kearsley then illustrates how such a system will work. The system that he describes represents a potentially important mediational link between instructional design and artificial intelligence. Such a system will help designers exploit the power of artificial intelligence in creating courseware. This chapter is an excellent conclusion to this section, since the authoring tools he describes are truly a cutting edge technology.

REFERENCES

Barr, A. (1982). Applications-oriented AI research: Education. In A. Barr & E. A. Feingenbaum (Eds.), *The handbook of artificial intelligence*. Stanford, CA: Heuristech Press.

Bregar, W. S., & Farley, A. M. 1980). Artificial intelligence approaches to computer-based instruction. *Journal of Computer Based Instruction, 6*(4), 104–114.

Brown, J. S., Burton, R. R., & Bell, A. G. (1975). SOPHIE: A step towards creating a reactive learning environment. *International Journal of Man-Machine Studies, 12*, 259–282.

Carbonell, J. R. (1970). AI in CAI: An artificial intelligence approach to computer-assisted instruction. *IEEE Transactions on Man-Machine Systems, 11, 4*, 190–202.

Gable, A., & Page, C. V. (1980). The use of AI techniques in computer-assisted instruction: An overview. *International Journal of Man-Machine Studies, 12*, 259–282.

Kay, A. C. (1977). Microelectronics and the personal computer. *Scientific American, 237*(3), 239–244.

McAleese, R. (1985). Some problems of knowledge representation in an authoring environment: Exteriorisation, anaomolous state metacognition, and self-confrontation. *Programmed Learning and Educational Technology, 22*(4), 299–306.

Michaelson, R. A., Mickie, D., & Boulanger, A. (1985). The technology of expert systems. *Byte, 10*(4), 303–312.

Papert, S. (1980). *Mindstorms: Children, computers and powerful ideas.* New York: Basic.

Sleeman, D., & Brown, J. S. (1982). *Intelligent tutoring systems.* New York: Academic Press.

Wyer, J. (1984). New bird on the branch: Artificial intelligence and computer-assisted instruction. *Programmed Learning and Educational Technology, 21*(3), 187–193.

12 Semantic Network Designs for Courseware

Stewart A. Denenberg
Dept. of Computer Science
SUNY, Plattsburgh

INTRODUCTION

A semantic network can be used to allow the learner and the author in an instructional software system much greater control and flexibility than is usual within the normal modes of Computer Assisted Instruction. In this chapter we illustrate how a semantic network can facilitate an active-learner pedagogy, and how a semantic network can be used to structure the curriculum in three areas: Psychology, Literature, and Computer Science/Business.

Semantic networks evolved as attempts to model the associative way knowledge is perhaps stored and retrieved in the human mind. They have been described by Quillian (1966) and applied by Carbonell (1970) in a computer assisted instruction system called Scholar which, using a semantic network to represent knowledge, can answer as well as ask questions about a particular knowledge space—geography in this instance. Wexler (1970) and Koffman and Blount (1973) have also designed and implemented similar systems based on semantic networks that are able to interact with student users.

Semantic networks are a declarative representation of knowledge consisting of a set of relationships between a set of topics. A convenient symbolism for a semantic network is a graph where the topics are nodes and the relations between the topics are arcs. A semantic network can be understood as a graph representation of topics with relationships between these topics.

A simple illustration to clarify how a semantic network actually represents knowledge may be useful. Consider the following miniature world consisting of a family of four—a father named Bob, a mother named Mary, and two children, a boy, Billy and a girl, Suzy. A semantic network representation of this knowl-

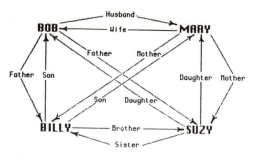

FIG. 12.1. Semantic network representation of familial knowledge.

edge is shown in Fig. 12.1 and has four nodes (BOB, MARY, BILLY, and SUZY) and twelve relationships (only eight of which are unique) that make associations between the nodes. We "read" the semantic network by choosing a node and following the relation arc from it to another node; for example, on the right side of Fig. 12.1 we can read, "Suzy is the Daughter of Mary" or "Mary is the Mother of Suzy." Together, the nodes and the relationships form a semantic network which is a representation of knowledge about this family.

A simpler semantic network to represent the same miniworld is shown in Fig. 12.2. Here we have the same four nodes in the network but only three relations; two of the three are symmetric or reversible relations, i.e., Spouse and Sibling. The third is the inverse relation-pair "Parent-Child" which is simply denoted as Parent; that is, if Node A is a parent of Node B then it is implied that Node B is a child of Node A. Either version of the semantic network can be used to represent the knowledge inherent in the miniworld; one is more detailed than the other, and the choice of which to use depends on how much knowledge we wish to draw from the representation: if Billy's name were Claire (a male or female first name) instead, we would need the more detailed representation of Fig. 12.1 to establish who was brother and who was sister to whom because the "Sibling" relation does not provide this information. The important point is that there is more than one way to represent knowledge using a semantic network and the choices made are influenced by practical considerations such as computer memory space (in-

FIG. 12.2. A simpler semantic network.

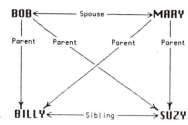

deed if space were not at a premium we could combine Figs. 12.1 and 12.2 storing the four nodes and fifteen relationships in a redundant but rich representation of the family) as well as how we intend to use network.

Now that we have some idea of the structure of a semantic network, let us examine its use in the design of pedagogy and curriculum for the learner.

USING A SEMANTIC NETWORK TO FACILITATE AN ACTIVE-LEARNER PEDAGOGY

If we define pedagogy rather broadly as learning/instructional strategies then we can facilitate an active-learner pedagogy by letting the learners actively select their own learning strategies via a semantic network. The learner can use a semantic network as a *map* of the content knowledge in a curriculum and use this map to explore topics that are of interest to him or her *at the time the interest is present*. Thus, the semantic network is a very powerful search tool for knowledge because it allows the learner a high degree of motivated control and flexibility. Let us examine an example of this use of a semantic network which is described in more detail by Denenberg (1980) using computer literacy as the curriculum we wish to apply the active-learner pedagogy to.

A Pedagogy For Computer Literacy Development

A semantic network of computer literacy topics and relationships was developed for the ACCOLADE System and implemented on the Control Data Corporation PLATO IV System. The topics are listed in detail in the author's dissertation (Denenberg, 1977) and the relations are of seven types:

1. *General-Specific* is an inverse relation-pair where 'general' implies a more abstract categorization and 'specific' implies a more concrete one. If topic A is the general case for topic B, then topic B is a specific topic instance of topic A.

Example:

$$\begin{array}{ccc} B & & A \\ \text{Astronomy} & \text{------- General} \longrightarrow & \text{Natural Sciences} \end{array}$$

$$\begin{array}{ccc} A & & B \\ \text{Natural Sciences} & \text{------Specific} \longrightarrow & \text{Astronomy} \end{array}$$

2. *Technique-Application* is an inverse relation-pair where "technique" refers to a body of knowledge or set of technical skills and methods that are utilized for a particular purpose or "application." If topic A is a technique used in the application of topic B, then topic B is an application of topic A.

Example:

B   A
Astronomy ——————— Technique ——→ Numerical Analysis

A   B
Numerical Analysis —— Application ——→ Astronomy

3. *Prerequisite-Sequel* is an inverse relation-pair where "prerequisite" suggests that certain knowledge or skills should be mastered before the "sequel" topic is attempted by the learner. If topic A is a prerequisite for topic B, then topic B is a sequel to topic A.

Example:

B   A
Artificial Intelligence——————— Prerequisite ——→ Programming Knowledge

A   B
Programming Knowledge —— Sequel ——————→ Artificial Intelligence

4. *System-Component* is an inverse relation-pair where "system" is a set of interdependent "components" such that each component exerts an influence on the operation or definition of every other component and the components taken as a whole comprise the system. If topic A is a system containing topic B, then topic B is a component of topic A.

Example:

B   A
Optics ——————— System ——→Astronomy

A   B
Astronomy—— Component ——→ Optics

To distinguish this relation pair from "general-specific" note that the "general" for Optics is Physics:

Example:

B   A
Optics —————— General —————→ Physics

5. *Synonym* is a symmetric relation which implies equality or equivalence between two topics. If topic A is a synonym for topic B, then topic B is a synonym for topic A.

Example:

$$A \qquad\qquad B$$

Meteorology ◄──── Synonym ────► Weather

6. *Different* is a symmetric relation which supplies information by counterexample and implies that two topics are different enough to be considered antonyms for each other. If topic A is different from topic B, then topic B is different from topic A.

Example:

$$A \qquad\qquad B$$

Hardware ◄──── Different ────►Software

7. *Related* is a symmetric relation used when it is clear that there is some sort of relation between two topics but that one cannot yet specify it. At a later time, the relation may be identified and would replace the last resort "related" relation. If topic A is related to topic B, then topic B is related to topic A.

Example:

$$A \qquad\qquad B$$

Problem Solving ◄──── Related ────► Programming Knowledge

Because a semantic network with N nodes and R relations can have NR (N − 1) possible associations, it is necessary to devise a method to show the inherent structure without overwhelming the user with too much information. Therefore, instead of displaying the whole Network or even two levels of relations as Eland (1975) does in his Guide system, the ACCOLADE semantic network shows only the structure around one node or computer literacy topic at a time. For example, if the learner wishes to see the topics one relationship away from "Artificial Intelligence" in the computer literacy knowledge space, he is shown a display similar to Fig. 12.3.

Next the learner may request to see the structure around one of the noncentral topics such as "Problem Solving" and that would place Problem Solving in the center as shown in Fig. 12.4.

In this manner, the learner may see all of the topics in the computer literacy knowledge space and all of the relationships between them. The viewing mechanism is similar to a spotlight—the entire semantic network resides in the darkness inside the computer, but the learner may shine the spotlight on any one topic and see the topics in the immediate neighborhood (one relationship away). Topics n-relations away could be seen by augmenting the ACCOLADE implementation and increasing the size of the spotlight.

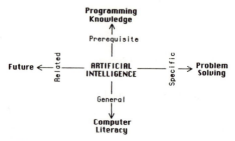

FIG. 12.3. ACCOLADE semantic network focused on "artificial intelligence."

The search or inquiry functions provided for a semantic network can be extended well beyond the "spotlight" capability; for example, a "scatterlight" capability would take a relation as input and produce all pairs of nodes connected by this relation as output (e.g., I want to see all pairs of nodes connected by the "Synonym" relation). Table 12.1 shows a menu of possible Inquiry Functions that could be provided to learners to allow them to explore a curriculum in a curiosity-driven mode. The author of the semantic network facilitates this type of active learning pedagogy by providing the user with a "smart menu" (or "intelligent index") through which the learner can browse or peruse as the intellectual need arises.

In practice such a searching system would also be provided with an update system, invisible to the learner, but indispensable to the author so that the Network could be updated when necessary. The update function provides the ability to add, delete or change nodes and relations.

Implementation of the ACCOLADE System

Because ACCOLADE was designed expressly for execution on the Control Data Corporation PLATO IV System in 1976, the particular hardware and software tools provided by that system were used extensively. The TUTOR programming

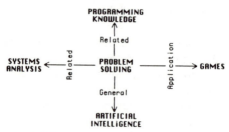

FIG. 12.4. ACCOLADE semantic network focused on "problem solving."

TABLE 12.1
Inquiry Functions

Input (s)	Output (s)
One Node	All outpointer Relations and the Nodes they point to (Spotlight)
One Node	All inpointer Relations and the Nodes they are outpointers from
One Node	All paths that terminate at the Node
One Node	All paths that emanate from the Node
One Relation	All pairs of Nodes connected by the Input Relation (Scatterlight)
One Relation	All paths in the semantic network that use that Relation
Two Nodes	All Relations between the two Nodes
Two Nodes	All paths between the two Nodes
Two Nodes, One Relation	All paths between the two Nodes that use only the given Relation
Two Nodes, R Relations	All paths between the two Nodes that use only the given R Relations

language and the specialized plasma PLATO Terminal were used in the design and development of the Semantic Network component of ACCOLADE. The PLATO Terminal allowed high resolution graphics (512 × 512 pixels) and animation as well as providing five function keys labeled HELP, NEXT, BACK, LAB and DATA which, in conjunction with the SHIFT key, allowed the user 10 functions that could be recognized by a TUTOR program.

A TUTOR program was a collection of Units that executed conditionally on learner response. In general, a Unit contained instructions that accepted input information, evaluated it, displayed information on the screen, and branched to another Unit usually based on either the input information or the function key pressed by the learner. For example, the user could press the BACK key to return immediately to the previous Unit because the PLATO system automatically supplied the stacks necessary to preserve path traversal information. Thus, the PLATO system implementation allowed each node in the Semantic Network to be represented as a Unit that could be executed under learner control by appropriate choice of the function keys.

This same approach can be used to implement a Semantic Network in the more common environment of a personal or microcomputer. Each node can be represented as a procedure and a global software stack can be used to hold the names of the nodes (procedures) visited. Most microcomputer languages have constructs that trap the key last pressed so the conventional keyboard could be used to search or traverse the Network in a learner-directed mode. Additionally each node could contain pointers to resources for acquiring more information on the Node-Topic being visited. The ACCOLADE System had seven types of Resources:

1. Printed Material (books, magazines, journals, etc.)
2. University and College courses
3. CAI Lessons
4. People
5. Movies
6. Videotapes
7. Audiotapes

For example, Fig. 12.3 could be presented on a microcomputer text screen as follows:

Artificial Intelligence

Sometimes referred to as "machine intelligence" is man's attempt to create intelligence in the computer (or some say in any form). What is your definition of intelligence? Have computers influenced that definition? for more information see Resources 1–2 pp. 128–140, 1–8 pp. 219–220, and 3–4.

1. Prerequisite is PROGRAMMING KNOWLEDGE
2. Specific is PROBLEM SOLVING
3. General is COMPUTER LITERARY
4. Related is FUTURE

Type a Number (1–4) to see that Topic or press the letter B to go Back to the previous Topic.

The disadvantage to this procedural type of implementation of a Semantic Network is that in most programming languages the procedures cannot be treated as data and therefore updating the Network cannot be automated. This means that the update operations (such as adding a new procedure-Node) would have to be performed manually by the author using whatever program editor was available on the system. The advantage to this approach is, of course, conceptual simplicity—when a new Node is to be added a new procedure is simply written and, of course, existing procedures linked to that Node are modified accordingly.

On the other hand, if the Semantic Network is to be represented as a data structure which *can* be modified by update procedures, it is most easily implemented in a high level functional language such as LISP or LOGO that provides List data structures. It is then a fairly straight-forward exercise to represent each node in the Network as a List of Inpointers (Relations pointing into the Node) and Outpointers (Relations pointing out of the Node). For example, if Node A has Inpointers from Node D under Relation R_1 and Node C under Relation R_2 and Node B under Relation R_2 and Node A has Outpointers to Node B under Relation R_1 and Node D under Relation R_3 then Node A would be stored as a variable named "A whose value was [[[D R_1] [C R_2] [B R_2]] [[B R_1] [D R_3]]] where by convention the first sublist describes the Inpointers to A and the second the Outpointers. Then all that needs to be done is to write the procedures that update these lists when nodes or relations are added, deleted or changed (no small task, but a good project for upperclass computer science majors). If efficiency is desired, Property Lists should be used as they are primitives in both LOGO and LISP and will consequently execute the update operations faster (see Davidson [1892] or Abelson [1982] for more details). In the next section we describe a much simpler List representation for Semantic Networks using LOGO.

A Pedagogy For Advisement

Another example of using a semantic network as an intelligent index to facilitate an active learner Pedagogy is in the area of course selection at advisement time in college. The college catalog of courses would supply the nodes and the relations could include "prerequisite," "co-requisite," "sequel." The advisor and the student using the Inquiry Functions of Table 12.1 could put together a schedule flexibly and efficiently.

An extension of this idea is even more interesting. Some colleges provide (even require) *integrative* learning experiences whereby the student takes several courses usually in different disciplines but which are connected by a common theme such as war, marriage, power, love, etc. These themes serve to integrate for the student the knowledge and experience gained from the courses. In this example, the nodes are again the courses but the relations would be the integrative themes such as those just mentioned. A semantic network that allowed the student and advisor to assemble packages of courses that attempted to integrate knowledge in this way would provide a formal method to facilitate a stimulating and exciting intellectual experience for the student that usually only happens haphazardly.

USING A SEMANTIC NETWORK IN THE CURRICULUM

We have already shown how a semantic network can be used to explore the curriculum of Computer Literacy within the discussion of the previous section. In this section we continue to provide examples of how a semantic network can be used to represent knowledge in the curricular areas of: Psychology, Business/Computer Science, and Literature.

FIG. 12.5a. SOLO semantic network: Graph representation.

Curricular Area: Psychology

We shall develop the example in this area in detail in order to show the power of a semantic network when fully integrated into a curriculum.

One topic usually studied in a Cognitive Psychology course is human memory. SOLO is a computer language (designed and developed by Marc Eisenstadt of the Open University in Milton Keynes, England) based on semantic networks which can be used by Cognitive Psychology students to investigate the human memory function (Eisenstadt, 1983b). We have described a project which allows a class of Computer Science students to write a set of procedures in the LOGO computer language which emulate the primitive commands of SOLO (Denenberg, 1985). The discussion which follows is drawn largely from the cited references describing that project. We assume the reader understands LOGO (if not see Abelson, 1982 or Ross, 1983) but not SOLO.

We begin by describing the SOLO language using examples drawn from the semantic network representations shown as Figs. 12.5a and 12.5b.

Figure 12.5a is another example of a semantic network in graph form; the nodes of the graph are nouns such as HARRY, DOG, and MAMMAL and the edges of the graph are the relationships between the nodes such as Member, Likes, and Has. The function of the semantic network is to provide a "memory" structure for holding information—in our simple example shown as Fig. 12.5a, we are representing the facts that HARRY is a Member of the DOG class, that JIM Likes all Members of the DOG class, etc.

In order to be a useful data structure for a computer, we must map or transform the graph representation into a more suitable structure such as an Array or a List as shown in Fig. 12.5b. Here we have a List of three-element Lists called Triples. Each Triple consists of a Node followed by a Relation followed by a second Node that the first Node is associated with via the Relation. For example, the Triple [MAMMAL Has HAIR] in the List of Fig. 12.5b represents the rightmost part of the graph shown in Fig. 12.5a.

The SOLO language also provides the user with a small but powerful set of operators for manipulating the Nodes, Relations and Triples of the semantic

```
[ [HARRY Likes HARRY] [HARRY Likes JIM]
  [HARRY Member DOG] [DOG Member MAMMAL]
  [JIM Likes DOG] [JIM Member MAMMAL]
  [MAMMAL Has HAIR] ]
```

FIG. 12.5b. SOLO semantic network: List representation.

network. Each of the SOLO primitives will be discussed in terms of its LOGO syntax; some modifications have been made to the original design of the language which is described in detail by Eisenstadt (1983b).

1. NOTE is a SOLO primitive whose argument is a Triple and whose function is to add that Triple to the semantic network.

> *Example:* If the semantic network looks like this:
>   [[HARRY Member DOG]]
> Then after the invocation:
>   NOTE [HARRY Likes HARRY]
> The semantic network will look like this:
>   [[HARRY Member DOG] [HARRY Likes HARRY]]

2. FORGET deletes Triples from the semantic network; it is the inverse function of NOTE.

> *Example:* FORGET [HARRY Likes HARRY]
> restores the semantic network in the example above to its state before NOTE [HARRY Likes HARRY] was applied.

3. CHECK tests to see if a Triple or part of Triple is in the semantic network.

> *Example:* If the semantic network is as shown in Figure 5b, then
>   CHECK [HARRY Likes HARRY] returns "TRUE
>   (because that Triple exists in the semantic network)
>   CHECK [JIM Likes HARRY] returns "FALSE
>   (because that Triple does not exist in the semantic network)
>   CHECK [HARRY Member ?] returns [DOG]
>   CHECK [HARRY Likes ?] returns [HARRY]
>   (only the first occurrence is found)
>   CHECK [HAIR MEMBER ?] returns [ ]
>   (the null or empty list)

4. FOREACH is an extension of CHECK which returns a List of Nodes with common Relation names emanating from a given Node; a ? wildcard symbol is always in the third position of the argument Triple and the List which is returned contains the Nodes which satisfy the wildcard.

> *Example:* If the semantic network is as shown in Figure 5b, then
>   FOREACH [HARRY Likes ?] returns [HARRY JIM]
>   (compare to the fourth example of CHECK above)
>   FOREACH [JIM Likes ?] returns [DOG]
>   FOREACH [DOG Likes ?] returns [ ]

5. DESCRIBE is the inverse of FOREACH in that the ? wildcard is in the first position of the Triple.

> *Example:* If the semantic network is as shown in Figure 5b, then
> DESCRIBE [? Member MAMMAL] returns [DOG JIM]
> DESCRIBE [? Likes DOG] returns [JIM]
> DESCRIBE [? Likes MAMMAL] returns [ ]

It may have occurred to the reader that FOREACH and DESCRIBE can be generalized into a function that would allow the ? wildcard symbol to be in any combination of the three possible positions in a Triple and would return a List of Triples satisfying the wildcards. Although that function is not in the original SOLO specification, we have included it here as the MATCH function.

> *Example:* If the semantic network is as shown in Figure 5b, then
> MATCH [JIM Likes ?] returns [[JIM Likes DOG]]
> MATCH [? Likes ?] returns [[HARRY Likes HARRY]
>   [HARRY Likes JIM] [JIM Likes DOG]]

6. PRINT is used to print messages and values for the Nodes and Relations of the Triples in the semantic network.

> *Example:* PRINT SENTENCE [THE FIRST NODE IS:]
>   FIRST [HARRY Member DOG]
> will print the message:
> THE FIRST NODE IS: HARRY

7. TO allows us to create procedures.

8. EDIT allows us to modify already created procedures.

9. LIST allows us to list procedures that have been created or modified.

· Now that we have the nine primitives of SOLO embedded within the LOGO language (which has a complete complement of List processing primitives itself) (Davidson, 1982) we can show example programs that would be assigned and written by Cognitive Psychology students in the course of using SOLO/LOGO to model human memory. The following three examples are also described by Eisenstadt (1983a).

The Assess Procedure

The ASSESS procedure adds knowledge to a semantic network based on some simple judgmental criterion such as political persuasion. It uses the CHECK and NOTE primitives of SOLO and the IF, SENTENCE and PRINT primitives of LOGO to achieve its function: if the individual named (:NAME in the value of the input to ASSESS) votes independent ([:NAME VOTES INDEPENDENT] exists as a Triple in the semantic network) then the PRAISE procedure is invoked, otherwise the CONDEMN procedure is invoked.

The function of PRAISE is to add the Triple [:NAME IS MARVELOUS] to the semantic network and to print out the message ":NAME IS REALLY GREAT!"

The function of CONDEMN, on the other hand is to add the Triple [:NAME IS EVIL] to the semantic network and to print out the message

" :NAME THINKS FUNNY."
The SOLO/LOGO versions of these procedures are:

TO ASSESS :NAME
    IF CHECK SENTENCE :NAME "VOTES "INDEPENDENT
    [PRAISE :NAME] [CONDEMN :NAME]
    END

TO PRAISE :NAME
    NOTE SENTENCE :NAME "IS "MARVELOUS
    PRINT SENTENCE :NAME [IS REALLY GREAT!]
    END

TO CONDEMN :NAME
    NOTE SENTENCE :NAME "IS "EVIL
    PRINT SENTENCE :NAME [THINKS FUNNY . . .]
    END

The ASSESS, PRAISE, and CONDEMN procedures explicate only low level features of human memory; the next two, INFECT and CONFIRM can be used to model aspects of simple inferential reasoning.

The Infect Procedure

If the semantic network looks like Fig. 12.6a, then the invocation:

INFECT "LIZ

should modify the semantic network to look like Fig. 12.6b.

That is, the function of the INFECT procedure is to propagate the following inference through the semantic network:

"If Node A is associated with Node B via the 'Kisses' Relation then if Node A is Infected both Nodes A and B get the FLU."

LIZ——Kisses ➤ JIM—— Kisses ➤ JRNE—— Kisses ➤ BOB

FIG. 12.6a.   Eisenstadt network before infection.

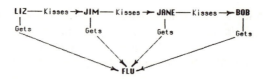

FIG. 12.6b. Eisenstadt network after infection.

The SOLO/LOGO definition of INFECT is:

```
TO INFECT :N1
    IF EMPTYP :N1 [STOP]
    IF LISTP :N1 [(INFECT FIRST :N1) (INFECT BF :N1) STOP]
    IF NOT MEMBERP (SE :N1 "GETS "FLU) :SN
                    [NOTE (SE :N1 "GETS "FLU)]
                    [STOP]
    INFECT FOREACH (SE :N1 "KISSES "?)
END
```

In LOGO the primitives EMPTYP, LISTP, and MEMBERP are predicates that return "TRUE or "FALSE depending on the value of their argument(s). MEMBERP as used in the INFECT procedure will return "TRUE only if the given sentence exists as a Triple in the semantic network (represented here by the global variable :SN).

We make the NOTE conditional on the Triple [:N1 Gets FLU] not being already present in the semantic network to prevent cases where a node gets kissed more than once and contracting flue more than once. NOTE also implicitly marks visited nodes so the search cannot recurse indefinitely.

The Confirm Procedure

CONFIRM is a procedure that makes simple inferences from the information stored in the semantic network based on the the law of inherited traits, i.e., any trait the superset has is inherited by its members: Given any node N1 that has the Member relation to a node N2 such that N2 has the relation R with N3, we can infer that N1 also has relation R with N3 as shown in the Venn-like diagram of Fig. 12.7a. For example, within our semantic network of Figure 12.5a we see that DOG is a Member of MAMMAL and that MAMMAL Has HAIR; thus we can infer that DOG Has HAIR as shown in Fig. 12.7b. Of course the nesting (and corresponding inferencing) can go to any depth. As an example of what we would like our CONFIRM procedure to do, let us examine the operation of the particular invocation:

CONFIRM [HARRY Has HAIR]

FIG. 12.7a. General inference diagram.

Given the semantic network shown in Figure 5a, we want CONFIRM to infer and then return the value "TRUE.

We can infer that DOG Has HAIR because DOG is a Member of MAMMAL and MAMMAL Has HAIR is present in the semantic network; therefore HARRY Has HAIR because HARRY is a Member of DOG.

CONFIRM should check to see if [HARRY Has HAIR] is a triple in :SN and if it is not, using FOREACH, find all nodes for which HARRY is a Member and then check to see if any of them has HAIR and if none of them do then check to see which nodes they in turn are Members of—and so on until one of the generated nodes has HAIR; if nothing can be found then we want CONFIRM to return to "FALSE. For our particular example of Fig. 12.5a:

1. [HARRY Has HAIR] is not in :SN and HARRY is a Member of DOG so we check to see if [DOG Has HAIR].

2. [DOG Has HAIR] is not in :SN but DOG is a Member of MAMMAL so we check to see if MAMMAL Has HAIR.

3. We confirm that [MAMMAL Has HAIR] is in fact in :SN and thus CONFIRM returns "TRUE.

The CONFIRM procedure looks as follows:

```
TO CONFIRM :L
IF EMPTYP FIRST :L [OP "FALSE]
IF LISTP FIRST :L
    [OP OR CONFIRM (SE FIRST FIRST :L FIRST BF :L LAST :L)
         CONFIRM (LIST BF FIRST :L FIRST BF :L LAST :L)]
IF MEMBERP :L :SN [OP "TRUE]
OP CONFIRM FPUT FOREACH (SE FIRST :L "MEMBER "?)
                LIST FIRST BF :L LAST :L
END
```

This version of CONFIRM only inferences from left to right within a Triple i.e., although it is able to confirm that HARRY Has HAIR, it is not able to

FIG. 12.7b. Specific inference diagram.

321

confirm that JIM Likes HARRY (which he should because JIM likes all DOGs and HARRY is a Member of the DOG class). This deficiency is corrected as an assignment for the Computer Science students on the project.

Summary

The preceding example procedures show the power of using a semantic network to model a content area such as human memory. Not only is knowledge represented succinctly, the idea of procedures which manipulate that representation is reinforced—a notion that holds great appeal for many cognitive psychologists.

Some important criticisms can, however, be made regarding the underlying model itself: namely representing the human memory function as a semantic network which is manipulated algorithmically. For example, Eisenstadt (1983a) points out that the model takes too long to return "False to the statement CONFIRM [DOG Has PLANET] (i.e., [DOG Has PLANET] is a Triple which does not exist in the semantic network). Our experience indicates that human memory does not work this way—we know almost instantly that [DOG Has PLANET] is nonsense, and so the model is deficient or at least naive in this instance. Despite the model's flaws, however, it also has many appealing features:

• It represents the memory function as a symbol structure plus the procedures which manipulate that structure—an appealing idea to many cognitive psychologists.

• It is iconographic: A semantic network resembles the network of synapses, neurons, axions, and ganglia in the brain.

• It represents the associative feature of memory where one idea spurs another much like a fishnet where a node cannot be picked up without perturbing all of the others.

• It allows hands-on learning: Because it is a computer model hypotheses can be formulated, tested, and reformulated easily because the response is essentially immediate.

• It is easily extensible: It would be very easy to model a simple form of learning by extending the CONFIRM procedure to *add* Triples to the semantic network that it had inferred as "TRUE thus simulating the process of learning by raising a question, inferring the answer from already known information and, finally, storing or incorporating the new fact into memory.

Finally, note that we have allowed the learners to write their own inquiry and update procedures for examining and changing the knowledge in the semantic network, as opposed to the "smart menu" approach represented as Table 12.1.

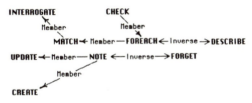

FIG. 12.8.   Semantic network representation of SOLO.

The advantage to this approach is that it encourages a very high degree of ac!iveness by giving the learners almost ultimate control over the computer—they are writing their own procedures to interrogate, update, create, and generally manage the information stored in the semantic network. As a capstone to this project, we can use the semantic network to extend our understanding of the total process by applying it to the SOLO/LOGO system itself as shown in Fig. 12.8.

As Landa (1976) points out, "The difference between 'knowing' and 'thinking' is now clear. Knowing is having concepts and ideas of objects, phenomena, and the relations among them. Thinking is being able to operate with these conceptions and ideas. We note in this regard that knowledge may not be only about objects and phenomena but also about operations themselves" (p. 62).

All things considered, the semantic network model of human memory seems a good one. It captures Feynman's definition of the most natural of sciences: He defines Physics as an attempt to understand the behavior of nature. This particular model is an attempt to understand the behavior of human memory, and it is an elegant attempt.

Curricular Area: Literature

Any story with a large cast of characters and a complex set of human relations can be better understood using a semantic network to organize and represent the characters and relations. For example, the reading of any Tolstoy novel would be enhanced by a semantic network representation where the nodes were names of the characters and their nicknames, and the relations included "synonym" (to link name and nickname), *friend, enemy, colleague* as well as an extended set of familial relations including *cousin, uncle, step-brother,* etc.

Another interesting application in this area would be to create the semantic network for the historical characters in du Maurier's, *House on the Strand* from the family tree in the front of the book; then when that is realized to extend the network and link the historical characters to the characters in the present that carry the rest of this very clever story.

In both cases, we would then use the Inquiry Functions described in Table 12.1 to interrogate the knowledge stored in the semantic network representation of the piece of literature.

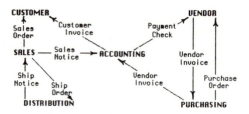

FIG. 12.9. Semantic network representation of document flow in a business.

Curricular Area: Business/Computer Science

The curricular area of Systems Analysis is one that spans Business and Computer Science. One important tool of Systems Analysis is the Information Flowchart which represents the flow of documents through the various departments within a business system. For example, in Fig. 12.9 we show a *partial* semantic network representation of the document flow between the several departments of a hypothetical business.

A complete semantic network would include all departments and all document types.

This semantic network representation is interesting because the nodes and relations can be interchanged with such ease; that is, we could as easily have viewed the documents as nodes and the departments as the relations between the nodes and had as valid a semantic network. For any content area, it is always a useful exercise to ask the question: Can the nodes and relations be interchanged with no loss of information or incurrence of awkwardness?

Again, we would use the Inquiry Functions shown in Table 12.1 to explore the knowledge represented in the semantic network.

CONCLUSION

In this chapter we have attempted to show how a semantic network can be used to enhance both the curriculum and the pedagogy within an instructional software system.

A semantic network is an extremely useful and powerful way to represent knowledge; when represented as a graph, it comes very close to being a picture of the reality it attempts to represent. A useful feature of the semantic network is that it can be used as a map of a knowledge space—not only does it reveal the structure of the space via the relationships, it can also be used as a search tool to find topics that are of interest to the learner. Depending on the educational intent of the teacher, the learners can write their own search or inquiry procedures or they can be provided by an "intelligent index" or "smart menu" as shown in Table 12.1.

Finally, the use of a semantic network in itself can be an educational experience for the learner. Because every topic in a semantic network is connected by certain relationships to various other topics in the network, the user can begin to see that the meaning of any topic is not absolute but relative to its relationships with other topics. As a matter of fact, the meaning of any topic can be defined as the rest of the semantic network as seen through that topic (Quillian, 1966). Indeed if a node is itself a semantic network, then this recursive representation approaches a sort of hologram with infinite resolution where every piece is a representation of the whole. This insight is similar to the one described in Buddhist literature as the Vajracchedika Sutra (Humphreys, 1962) or "Diamond" Sutra where each manifestation of reality is represented as a many-faceted diamond reflecting all other diamond-manifestations. Not one single aspect of reality stands alone; everything is interdependent. As an educational experience, this insight alone makes the use of a semantic network worthwhile.

ACKNOWLEDGMENTS

I would like to thank Miss Robin Wing for the careful and timely typing of the manuscript, Mrs. Judy Duken, Director of the North Country Teacher Resource Center for her kind loan of a Macintosh to create the figures and Dr. Lonnie Fairchild for her useful comments, suggestions, and perspective on programming languages.

REFERENCES

Abelson, H. (1982). *LOGO for the Apple II*, Byte Publications.
Carbonell, J. (1970). AI in CAI: An AI approach to CAI. *IEEE Transactions on Man-Machine Systems, 11*, 190–202.
Davidson, L. J. (1982). *Apple LOGO Reference Manual*, LOGO Computer Systems (Available as a document when Apple LOGO is purchased).
Denenberg, S. A. (1977). *An alternative curriculum for computer literacy development.* Doctoral dissertation, University of Massachusetts, Amherst.
Denenberg, S. A. (1980). Using a semantic information network to develop computer literacy. *Journal of Computer-Based Instruction*, November, *7*, 33–40.
Denenberg, S. A. (1985). A Service Project for an Introductory Artificial Intelligence Course: Implementing SOLO in LOGO. *SIGCSE Bulletin, 17*, 8–20.
Eisenstadt, M. (1983a). A user-friendly software environment for the novice programmer. *Communications of the ACM, 26*, 1058–1064.
Eisenstadt, M. (1983b). *Cognitive psychology artificial intelligence project: The SOLO primer.* The Open University Press, Walton Hall, Milton Keynes, England, 2nd edition.
Eland, D. R. (1975). An information and advising system for an automated introductory computer science course. *University of Illinois Computer Science Document UIUCDCS-R-75-788.*

Humphreys, C. (1962). *Buddhism*. Baltimore, MD: Penguin.

Koffman, E. B., & Blount, S. E. (1973). Artificial intelligence and automatic programming in CAI. *Proceedings of Third Joint International Conference on AI*, 86–94.

Landa, L. N. (1976). *Instructional regulation and control*, Educational Technology Publications, Englewood Cliffs, NJ, 62.

Quillian, M. R. (1966). Semantic memory. In M. Minsky (Ed.), *Semantic information processing*, Cambridge, MA: MIT Press.

Ross, P. (1983). *Introducing LOGO*. Reading, MA: Addison-Wesley.

Wexler, J. D. (1970). Information networks in generative computer-assisted instruction. *IEEE Transactions of Man-Machine Systems, 11*, 181–189.

13 Tutoring, Information Databases, and Iterative Design

Wendy E. Mackay
Digital Equipment Corporation

INTRODUCTION

Computers are capable of delivering many kinds of instruction, as evidenced by the wide variety of educational software available today. Unfortunately, such software is often disappointingly rigid or limited in scope. In an effort to better adapt instruction to student needs, Digital's Educational Services Research and Development group has been investigating new, more flexible approaches to building environments for learning (Mackay, 1986a).

We began with two fundamental changes in our thinking. First, we redefined what we mean by instruction. Instead of trying to model each educational software program after a particular style of paper-based instruction, such as programmed instruction or documentation, we found that we could easily simulate the major instructional styles by varying the means of access to a database of information (Mackay, 1985). This allowed us to concentrate on the more general problem of providing the right information to the right person at the right time.

Second, we re-examined our development process. Instead of using a top-down design process, with the goal of finding some optimal structure for a body of information, we adopted an iterative design process which enabled us to rapidly simulate and test a variety of interaction styles. We borrowed a number of concepts and techniques from artificial intelligence to make our software as responsive as possible to each individual student.

This chapter introduces the concept of an *information database* and describes how it can effectively handle the major instructional styles of educational software. Within this framework, we discuss the particular problems of tutoring, our approach to designing on-line tutors, some examples of our work, and brief descriptions of several implementation strategies.

MAJOR INSTRUCTIONAL STYLES

Educational software tends to fall into one of several categories: drill-and-practice, on-line help, computer-based instruction, simulations, and tutoring. These categories are not mutually exclusive and distinctions exist within categories, but they represent the major instructional styles. After briefly describing each style, we show how each can be reimplemented as a different method of obtaining information from an information database.

One of the simplest kinds of educational software is *drill-and-practice*. Students who need to improve specific skills, such as multiplication or spelling, can practice answering problems until they get them right. Another simple kind of educational software is on-line *help* or a *glossary* which lets students find the definitions of words or commands. Students type in a word and see a prepackaged definition of the term.

Some forms of computer-based instruction (CBI) are derived from B. F. Skinner's (1968) work in programmed instruction. An instructional designer begins with a "task analysis" to identify a set of tasks or behaviors that students should be able to perform. These "behavioral objectives" form the basis for the final examination. The designer then gathers and organizes the information to be presented and divides it in small segments, each followed by one or more questions. Students read the information, answer the questions and are "branched" to the next information segment. If the course is properly programmed, and if students begin with the appropriate prerequisite behavior, all students should be able to complete the final exam successfully.

In contrast to most kinds of computer-based instruction, which emphasize testing and the structure of the information, *simulations, games,* and *microworlds* stress the benefits of "learning-by-doing," creating environments in which the student can explore and try out new ideas. Papert (1980) describes how children can discover powerful ideas in mathematics and science by using the Logo language to program the movements of a "turtle" on the computer screen. Burton and Brown (1979) describe how children can learn problem-solving skills in a more structured environment, with a program called "How the West Was Won."

The last form of educational software, *tutoring,* is based on a dialog between a student and a teacher. The teacher observes what the student is doing and interrupts with a suggestion or a question, depending on the particular tutoring style. Intelligent tutoring, described by Sleeman and Brown (1982) is a relatively new area for educational software, and relies on artificial intelligence techniques. Intelligent tutoring systems usually include a model of the student, a model of the optimal methods for solving the problem, and rules for when the tutor should interrupt the student. The tutor "observes" the students as they work and provides advice whenever a particular pattern of behavior is recognized. Tutoring provides something of a middle ground between CBI and "learning-by-doing" in which students can explore and at the same time be guided toward optimal performance.

PROBLEMS WITH AUTHORING TOOLS

While educators debate the merits of instructional styles at length, that is not our purpose here. We are concerned with the effect this controversy has had on authoring tools. Because most authoring languages strongly reflect one educational philosophy over another, it is difficult for an author to combine styles or try new ones. Authoring languages such as Control Data's Tutor and Digital's Producer encourage hierarchically organized, menu-driven CBI courses. Languages such as Logo encourage the development of simulations and microworlds. Some specialized tools have been developed that require no programming skills and produce very limited drill-and-practice or on-line help applications. A quick glance at the screen is often sufficient to determine which authoring language was used to create which course.

Such consistency among courses is not necessarily bad, particularly if that consistency makes it easier for students to learn the material. Problems arise when authors want to create educational experiences for which the tools were not designed. Authors must either choose a particular language and inherit the corresponding instructional style or spend inordinate amounts of time developing their own tools. Most limit their instruction to the style dictated by the software tool and do not try to implement combinations of other approaches. Even those who attempt to build their own tools usually find that it takes far more time than anticipated and rarely produces the desired results.

We decided to avoid the debate about the efficacy of particular instructional styles, since all have been shown to be useful in different contexts. Instead, our goal was to identify the situations in which students need information and specify the best methods for delivering it to them. We wanted to identify a simple framework that successfully handles all these styles, so that we could build extremely flexible software tools that encouraged more creative uses of the computer.

RE-EXAMINING STYLES OF INSTRUCTION

The major instructional styles share several key characteristics. All begin with a body of information out of which small segments are presented. All require someone to initiate a request for a specific segment of information, and all specify rules for when to present that segment. The specific requirements differ, as illustrated in Table 13.1. Two questions serve to distinguish the four major instructional approaches:

TABLE 13.1

	Student initiates information request	Expert initiates information request
Presentation predetermined by an expert	Documentation	Computer-Based Instruction
Presentation determined by student behavior	Stimulations	Tutoring

1. Is the student able to ask for the required information or must an expert do it?
2. Is the presentation dependent on the student's behavior or can it be prepackaged?

If we reexamine the major instructional styles, documentation is the best solution when students can successfully ask for information and the presentation can be prepackaged by an expert. In order to ask for information, students must not only know what information they need, but they must also be able to clearly indicate to the teacher or computer system (verbally or graphically) what they want. Providing more sophisticated methods of asking questions, such as natural language, speech input, or graphical input, will not change the fact that this form of access is limited by the student's ability to ask the question in the first place. Students who are unaware of their own misconceptions, are unable to articulate what's wrong or are simply unfamiliar with the mechanics of asking for help, will all need outside assistance.

For example, a student working on a data analysis problem may be unsure of the definition of standard deviation. The student will refer to the most convenient reference source; perhaps a textbook with an index or glossary, perhaps a fellow student who already knows the material, or perhaps an on-line help system. Note that the answer may take multiple forms, including text, formulae, graphs, or perhaps a visual example that the student can manipulate on-line. For on-line documentation to work, the student must be able to ask the question directly and be satisfied with a prepackaged answer.

Prepared instruction, including lectures, textbooks, programmed instruction, and CBI are most appropriate when students can't yet ask specific questions, and the material lends itself to logical presentation. The student follows a path prepared by an expert which provides an efficient means of learning critical concepts, clarifying difficult points, and identifying what is important. Students may learn the basics this way or be exposed to advanced concepts they would be unlikely to discover themselves.

If the student in our previous example realized that she was confused about how to formulate a t-test, she would probably ask someone to explain the procedure and the related concepts. A classroom teacher, a book or a CBI course would all organize the information in a logical order, including all the necessary items and omitting extraneous information.

Simulations, games, and microworlds are most appropriate when students want to initiate their own explorations of the material. Students can ask *questions* by manipulating the system in various ways and watching what happens. The resulting presentation of information depends entirely on the student's behavior.

If the student in our statistics example was working in a statistics microworld, she might decide to investigate the t-test. By applying the t-test to a set of data, observing what happens and comparing it to other tests, she will develop an intuitive feel for how a t-test works. She may decide that she wants to understand how changes in the standard deviation affect the results of the t-test. She can make systematic changes in the data, and watch how the corresponding changes in the standard deviation affect the results of the t-test. The various forms of the information about standard deviations continue to be available, but their order of presentation is now based entirely on her behavior within the simulation.

Finally, tutoring is most effective for students when they, in the context of exploring the system, have fundamental misunderstandings but do not realize it. A fellow student, teacher, or on-line tutor may observe what the student is doing, see that it is the result of a misunderstanding, and interrupt the student with information, suggestions or further questions designed to help the student recognize the misunderstanding.

If the student in our statistics example does not fully understand the difference between standard deviations and variances, the on-line tutor may observe a consistent pattern in which she uses standard deviations when variances are called for. The tutor has a number of options about how and when to interrupt the student. It might ask if she would like to learn more about standard deviations and variances. It might suggest that she go through some instruction that clarifies the differences. Or it might ask her to demonstrate when each measure should be used, and point out errors as they occur.

In all four cases presented in Table 13.1, the information presented is the same. The student experiences differences based on who initiates the specific requests for information, and whether or not the presentation is based on the individual student's behavior.

In summary, on-line help and documentation systems work well for students who know what they need to know and can ask easily anticipated questions. Prestructured CBI lessons are useful when students want to learn well-understood topics but have limited time, don't know where to start, or are unable to discover concepts on their own. Simulations and microworlds provide an open-ended medium for exploration, particularly when students are trying to discover things for themselves or want an in-depth, conceptual understanding. Finally, an intelligent tutor that reacts to the student's behavior can help students who are unaware of their own misconceptions and provide immediate feedback when the student has learned something correctly.

We are not claiming that this is an exhaustive list of effective instructional approaches nor do we advocate one approach over another. On the contrary, we claim that many of the distinctions among these approaches are arbitrary. Tools for developing educational software should not be devoted to one approach or another but should instead enhance the ability of the software designer to deliver a body of information in different ways to serve different student needs.

INFORMATION DATABASES

If the actual information presented to the student is the same for each instructional approach, can we take advantage of this redundancy? Can we create a single program that delivers information according to students' needs without relying on a single instructional style? Our solution was to create an information database, loosely modeled after the knowledge bases found in expert systems (Barr & Feigenbaum, 1982).

Unlike an ordinary database, which contains a large quantity of uniform data, a knowledge base contains a collection of facts, inferences, and procedures that correspond to the kinds of things people actually know. We use the concept of an information database to cover a range of actual implementations, from very simple to very complex. An information database may contain text, graphics, moving video, and sound. In some cases, the information database will share many of the properties of a knowledge base, including an internal representation of the meaning of each piece of information and how they relate to each other. Yet the "intelligence" inside the database is not the critical feature; later we show how a very simple version of an information database can be used to generate a full range of instructional styles.

What is most important is the means of access to the information. Students, teachers, authors, and other programs must be able to get to items directly, through visual examination, verbal commands, or via structures such as menus. In addition, information must be interconnected to other related information, often represented in different formats. A single topic may include several textual descriptions, video sequences, and graphic or symbolic representations.

The second important concept is that of an "object," borrowed from the Smalltalk language and its descendents (Goldberg & Robson, 1983). Each object has some private memory and a set of operations which define how it may act. Objects can answer inquiries about themselves and can send messages to other objects to ask them to do things. In an "object-oriented database," an object can display text, computer-generated graphics, sound, and still and moving video images, as well as identify other objects that are related to it in various ways.

Objects provide tremendous flexibility and are especially useful when we apply the concept of information databases to tutoring.

To summarize, information databases can be very simple or very complex, depending on the requirements of the problem. Because of their flexibility, they can easily be modified to handle new information or new means of access to information. Each of the four instructional styles described in Table 13.1 can be simulated separately or integrated to be optimally responsive to each student. Issues such as who controls what students learn are now policy rather than technical issues.

NAVIGATION: AN EXAMPLE OF A COMPLEX INFORMATION DATABASE

Once we have developed an information database, how can we create different instructional experiences for students (and experts)? The following example is drawn from a 3-year research effort at Digital (Hodges, 1986) called the Navigation Videodisc project. The goal was to develop an object-oriented information database with fully integrated text, graphics, and video. We chose coastal navigation for its conceptual complexity and its requirements for high-quality real images. We wanted to thoroughly test and understand the concepts described in this chapter as well as provide a testbed for experimenting with instructional strategies, exploring new development processes, and addressing the myriad technical problems associated with building an object-oriented relational database that handles multiple representations of text, graphics, real images, and sound.

The heart of the navigation information database is a videodisc containing over twenty discrete bodies of information, including nautical charts, aerial views, tide tables, navigation instruments, graphs, and other reference materials. In addition, the videodisc contains over 10,000 still photographs taken systematically from a boat in Penobscot Bay, enabling us to simulate movement in any direction on the water.

We wanted to simulate and compare divergent teaching strategies, from highly structured U.S. Power Squadron courses to highly experiential Outward Bound courses, and reduce the control problems usually associated with such experiments. We wanted to develop an intelligent tutor that understands what students see and touch on the screen and relate it to the other visual, textual, and quantitative information in the rest of the information database.

The following example provides a sense of how this object-oriented information database can integrate the major instructional styles into a single educational experience. We will follow a particular student as he learns to sail with our on-line version of Outward Bound. (Outward Bound places a group of nonsailors on a boat with an experienced sailor and sends them off for a week. Students are immediately faced with the problems of determining where they are and where they are going. The experienced sailor is trained to act as a resource, not a teacher, and does not try to prevent students from making mistakes (unless the boat is about to crash).)

The student gets on the boat at Green's Island and decides to set sail for North Haven Island, a short distance away. He decides to take a look around and see if he can spot North Haven Island from the boat. He turns in a complete circle so that he can look out in all directions. (The videodisc presents a sequence of eight real images on his screen, all shot from that location on the water, turning a full 360°.)

He sees two islands, either of which might be North Haven, and decides that he needs a chart. He uses the information database as a reference system and makes a direct request for information about charts. The "chart object" appears and provides him with several options, including a brief verbal description of how charts are used and the option of looking at the chart of Penobscot Bay. He examines the chart, and, after a bit of searching, finds Green's Island. He zooms in on his current position and sees North Haven Island nearby.

His next problem is to figure out how to translate the information he sees on the chart to what he sees from the boat. How will he choose between the two islands? He does not know how to ask a direct question, so he treats the information database as an instructional system and asks to learn about basic navigation. The database contains many objects that relate to different aspects of navigation. A specially created object provides an introduction to navigation by presenting information from these other objects. This "introduction to navigation" object appears and asks the student a few questions to determine what he already knows. It then asks particular information objects to present themselves in a specified sequence and describe the basic tools and concepts of navigation.

As the student progresses through the sequence of instruction, he comes across a description of a hand-bearing compass. He decides that this is exactly what he needs, tells the instruction object that he's done, and immediately begins to try the hand-bearing compass. The information database acts like a microworld, providing information based on his actions. He discovers that he can touch any object on the screen, say an island or a buoy, and the "hand-bearing compass object" will display the compass direction in degrees. He figures that he can determine what the compass bearings should be for each island by looking at the chart. Based on this strategy, he decides that the island on the left is North Haven, plots his course on the chart and sets sail.

Over the next few minutes, he watches the island get closer and takes several more bearings to check his position. Feeling pretty confident, he relaxes and experiments with various navigation instruments to see how they work. Suddenly, the sailing tutor appears on the screen and asks him if he is sure he is going in the right direction. The information database is now actingly like a tutor, because one of the objects has detected a pattern in his behavior that indicates something is wrong and has sent the appropriate message to the tutor object. The student checks his procedure one more time. The tutor calls another object which compares the bearings he's taken with the course plotted on the chart and reports that they do not match. The tutor informs the student and asks if he would like to watch the tutor plot a course from those bearings. The student agrees and suddenly realizes that he has been looking at the chart up-side-down. He discovers that he's actually traveling in the opposite direction from North Haven Island.

We have shown that, in a few minutes, this student required all the major instructional styles. The information database was able to provide the complete range of experiences, without forcing the student to call different programs or even differentiate among the styles. From the student's perspective, the system simply provides the kind of information he needs when he needs it.

We can change the student's environment (for example, changing the weather conditions), add new objects, create new paths of instruction, and experiment with different tutoring strategies, without affecting the generality of the software. Because each object contains information about itself as well as information about how to act, there is never a lag between adding features to the system and adding information about those features.

The Navigation project was designed to test the limits of this approach. We have also explored simpler versions of the information database, to ensure that the concept is still useful in the micro computer environment. For example, in some applications, tutoring can be effective without relying on artificial intelligence. Instead of requiring *intelligence* within each object, it may be more practical to provide a separate program that observes patterns of the student's behavior and communicates with the information database directly. We have established that an information database can produce a range of educational experiences for the student. Yet use of an information database is no guarantee of quality. The system is very flexible. It will deliver both excellent and aggravating tutoring, useful or frustrating documentation and informative or confusing instruction. The only way to ensure that students can obtain the information they need is to include users in the development process. The remainder of the chapter describes the iterative design process and how it can be used to develop effective tutoring with an information database.

INTELLIGENT TUTORING SYSTEMS

Tutoring is growing in popularity because it helps solve some of the problems of microworlds and CBI; it gives students the freedom to explore while providing guidance as it is needed. Information databases provide a flexible way to implement and test tutors, without losing the benefits of microworlds or CBIs.

Intelligent tutoring, also known as intelligent computer-assisted instruction, is a growing subfield within Artificial Intelligence. Sleeman and Brown (1982) provide an excellent introduction to the field and present a series of articles that cover the significant research areas. These tutoring systems share some important characteristics. Students work in an environment that permits open-ended problem solving in an area such as mathematics or programming.

The on-line tutors must not only be able to solve the problems but also identify misconceptions on the part of students and provide appropriate advice. Advice must be provided at the right levels of detail and specificity in order to be effective. The development of appropriate models of an individual student's understanding remains one of the most difficult tasks in developing these systems.

Burton and Brown (1979) describe an intelligent coach for a game to teach children arithmetic skills called "How the West Was Won." Anderson, Boyle, and Reiser (1985) describe an intelligent tutor that teaches undergraduates how to write programs in the LISP language. Both rely on a large amount of knowledge about the subject domain. Burton and Brown's coach is a better player than the students. Anderson's LISP tutor "knows" LISP and the best ways of solving a predetermined set of LISP problems. Both require computer resources and programming skills far beyond those of most developers of educational software for microcomputers.

Building full-scale expert tutors on microcomputers is impractical, not only because of the size and speed limitations, but also because the design problems are very complex. Fortunately, not all tutoring applications require artificial intelligence. The emphasis on building a tutor should be on its effectiveness as a teaching strategy, not its sophistication as an intelligent system. We should look for applications that do not require sophisticated software in order to be beneficial and develop methods for determining when and how to tutor. The information database will then allow us to implement a tutor with only as much intelligence as deemed necessary.

DECIDING ON A TUTORING STRATEGY

The literature does not provide much help in deciding on a tutoring strategy. In fact, researchers sometimes advocate opposite tutoring strategies. Burton and Brown emphasized "efficient and appropriate tutoring . . . with as few interruptions as possible." Anderson emphasized immediate feedback, provided every time a student deviates from the optimal performance. The data do not clearly identify which strategy is more effective.

Nonetheless, the tutoring strategy must be considered carefully. Mistakes can be costly. Inaccurate advice may cause students to distrust the tutor. Too many interruptions may distract students from learning the material or cause them to focus on unimportant points. Students may come to resent or ignore the tutor or feel as if Big Brother is watching.

One possible source of ideas is to observe when a human tutor gives advice. Just as designers of expert systems ("knowledge engineers") interview experts to discover the expert's decision rules, the designer of an on-line tutor should spend time observing successful interactions between a human tutor and students before attempting to build an on-line tutor. The goal is to generate a set of rules for when it is appropriate to interrupt and what information to provide after the interruptions.

Unfortunately, these rules may not be sufficient. Human tutors have access to certain kinds of information about students that the computer will never have. They can respond to eye contact and interpret body language; they have access to information about students' behavior outside of the computer system; they possess a different kind of understanding of the subject matter than the computer, and they may be able to understand certain behavior patterns in terms of their own or other students' behavior. We must therefore draw our rules from human tutors who have been placed under the same constraints as those of the on-line tutor.

Subject areas differ in how amenable they are to tutoring, making it difficult or impossible to predict in advance the best tutoring strategies. In order to design the software, we need a way to test each strategy, iteratively improving it until it performs effectively. This is called an iterative design process, shown in Fig. 13.1.

The typical iterative design process begins when a designer gathers preliminary information about the subject area and the ultimate users of the system. The next step is to design and build a prototype as quickly as possible and test it on users. After each iteration, the prototype should be modified and tested again until it works properly. The problem with this particular iterative design process is that building the prototype may take as long as building the final product.

We needed a faster prototyping method that would enable us to simulate rather than build the software. We developed an extension of a technique called

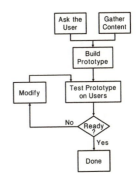

FIG. 13.1.   Basic implementation strategy.

the "Wizard of Oz" to create the illusion of an intelligent tutor, prior to actually building one.

THE WIZARD OF OZ TECHNIQUE

Chapanis (1982) and Kelley (1983) first use the term "The Wizard of Oz" to describe their iterative development of a natural language interface to a checkbook and calendar management program. Good, Whiteside, Wixon, and Jones (1983) used Oz to develop a natural language interface to an electronic mail system that was defined entirely by novice users. The name is derived from a scene in the movie "The Wizard of Oz" in which an old man, the Wizard, hides behind a curtain and operates a simulated Wizard for his audience.

The basic Oz setup consists of two terminals connected to a computer running the Oz program and whatever parts of the test software have been developed, as shown in Fig. 13.2. A student sits at one terminal, and the software designer sits hidden at a second terminal. The designer watches everything the student types and periodically sends the student information. Students see only the text, graphics, and video sent by the human tutor and may be completely unaware that tutoring is provided by a person rather than a computer. Because the goal is to test tutoring interactions that will ultimately be performed by the computer, it is important that the human tutor prepare in advance rules for interrupting and choosing what to say, rather than deciding during the session.

The designer (or human tutor) can also send messages directly to the computer and intercept messages between the student and the computer. The designer can thus prevent students from making major errors and give them the opportunity to go back and try something again. Every action by the designer, the student and the software is automatically logged for later analysis. We have found that videotapes of the screen can be useful as well. The text and video logs make it possible to systematically evaluate these interactions after each session and modify the test software (or rules used by the researcher) accordingly. Because the human tutor can simulate partially written or nonexistent software, designers

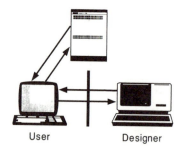

FIG. 13.2.   Wizard of Oz.   User   Designer

obtain information about how to structure interactions between the computer and the student before actually writing any code.

The most common use of the Wizard of Oz technique has been to study natural language interfaces. We were interested in extending it to handle educational design questions. We developed a generalized Oz program (Mackay, Parkes, Fineblum, & Berger, 1986) that allowed us to intercept text and graphics from almost any program running under the VAX/VMS operating system. We used it as a research tool to help develop an automatic natural language generator, (Van Praag, 1985) and to investigate effective tutoring strategies, described below. We also used it as a design tool to explore alternative approaches to interactive video and computer-based instruction (Mackay, 1986b). Oz can also be used for real-time consulting or as an aid in "computer classrooms." The instructor can observe the student's work, make comments, or even fix problems directly, without rewriting the original software. Oz has proven useful for developing all kinds of information-intensive software.

THE EDITOR TUTOR EXPERIMENT

We decided to build a tutor for a text editor (Mackay, 1986c) and used Oz to help answer questions about effective tutoring strategies. We chose text editing because it is possible to successfully edit documents with a minimal set of commands. We reasoned that if we prevented access to documentation and on-line help, we could determine which tutoring strategies were most effective in teaching students new editing commands.

We wanted to simulate exactly how the editor tutor would appear to students, so we prepared a set of messages to be sent only if the human tutor observed predefined patterns of behavior. Thus the human tutor relied on the same information that would ultimately be available to the on-line tutor and students received messages in the same format as would be sent by the on-line tutor.

The first experiment was designed to discover whether it was necessary to base tutoring interventions on the students' behavior. If we could establish that randomly delivered tutoring messages were as effective as rule-based tutoring, we could save ourselves a great deal of time and money by simply building the random tutor.

Six subjects participated in both random and rule-based tutoring conditions, as well as conditions with no tutoring at all. Subjects were taught six basic editing commands (delete a character, insert a character, movement with the four arrow keys) and asked to edit a very large document for 1 hour each day for 4 successive days. We divided the remaining editing commands into three groups and applied a different tutoring strategy (random, rule-based, control) to each. Groups of commands were chosen so that learning a command from one group would not provide information about commands from the other group.

The human tutor watched each subject's screen and, based on a set of rules, decided when to interrupt with information about a new editing command. Although the individual data were highly variable, some trends did emerge. First, tutoring was clearly effective. All six subjects learned a significant number of new commands as a result of both random and rule-based tutoring.

However, subjective ratings of the two strategies were very different. Subjects reported that they enjoyed the rule-based tutor but greatly disliked the random tutor. So we faced a dilemma. Should we use the random tutor, which is inexpensive but unpopular, or the rule-based tutor, which is expensive but popular? Further studies will be necessary to determine whether we can make random tutoring acceptable to students, or whether the more complex rule-based version is really required.

In summary, while it may be possible to begin with general principles for when to tutor, the specifics for a particular tutor must still be determined empirically. It is not always necessary to base decisions about when to tutor on an in-depth knowledge of the subject matter or on a model of the student. Sometimes, it may be possible to respond to simple patterns of behavior or even interrupt randomly.

BUILDING A TUTOR ON A MICROCOMPUTER

Digital produces several hundred CBI courses that run on 8-bit and 16-bit personal computers. We felt that a simplified information database, developed with an iterative design process, would improve the effectiveness of these courses. The rest of this section describes our experiences with the Interactive Trouble-Shooting Simulator, (Kuhlman & Hale, 1985), which successfully blends CBI, simulation, and on-line tutoring on a personal computer.

The Interactive Trouble-Shooting Simulator grew out of an evaluation of an existing IVIS (Interactive Videodisc Information System) course designed to teach field service technicians how to repair computer equipment. Most of the course followed a traditional CBI approach, but one section presented a series of trouble-shooting exercises. These proved popular with students because they simulated the actual repair process in the field.

Each trouble-shooting exercise presented video segments of a field service technician diagnosing and repairing an equipment problem. The program would periodically stop and ask the student to choose the next step from a menu of alternatives. The exercises had several drawbacks. First, they were very expensive to create and update, and students did not feel that there were enough of them. Second, the exercises did not expose students to real field conditions. Recognizing the correct choice from a menu is quite different from recalling it without help during an actual repair. Also, the exercises did not help students learn when a repair was finished, a skill many students lacked. Finally, the CBI sections of the course were separate from the trouble-shooting exercises, so updates to one required additional work to update the other.

THE DESIGN OF THE INTERACTIVE TROUBLE-SHOOTING SIMULATOR

The Interactive Trouble-Shooting Simulator was designed to address these issues by creating a problem-solving environment for the student. We felt that it was important to simulate actual field conditions as closely as possible. Field service technicians perform a wide range of diagnostic and repair procedures in any sequence; they must respond to a variety of possible failures and symptoms and must decide when the equipment is actually repaired. A technician can replace every component in the system in any order.

We decided to simulate 38 equipment failures based on their actual probability of occurrence in the field. Students could specify any repair action in any sequence and compare their repair times to the average repair times reported in the field. We began by specifying all of the possible replacement and repair sequences and finding appropriate text, graphics and video for each. The original course kept this kind of information in a randomly accessible library, separate from the code that controlled the program. We simply used this information in a different way.

For each repair action, such as "replace," we identified one or more corresponding objects, such as "power supply." We then created a table of these action/object pairs and added a pointer to the appropriate text, graphics, and video. When the simulator received a message, such as "replace the power supply," it would look in the library and present a video sequence that illustrated how to replace a power supply.

Together, the library and table form a simple information database that can be accessed by the simulator, the student, and the tutor. Repair problems are coded as a set of action/object pairs from the table, plus additional information from the library, such as the problem statement and the average repair time. When a student specifies an action, the simulator looks in the table for the appropriate information from the library and presents it on the screen. This arrangement made it easy to later add a tutor, which compares the student's actions with the correct repair procedures and provides advice accordingly.

The simulator begins by presenting a paragraph describing a problem reported by a customer. "My computer is broken" may be all the information available. The student can then run diagnostic tests, perform and observe the results of repair procedures, and ask for information, such as a list of the actions already performed, the hot-line recommendations, or the contents of the spares kit.

The simulator responds to natural language requests, such as "Run the diagnostics" or "Turn on the machine." A simple key-word parser, similar to the famous Eliza parser developed by Weizenbaum (1976), identifies the salient actions and objects, refers to the table of action/object pairs and presents the appropriate closeup shots of the repair or diagnostic procedures. Since many field service technicians dislike typing, abbreviations are accepted for the major actions. Thus "Please run the diagnostic tests" and "run diag" are equivalent.

The use of a keyword parser is an example of a strategy that is responsive to students but not really intelligent. When students understood the rules and limitations of the parser, they limited their vocabulary automatically and did not expect it to understand complex phrases. These students, all of whom were adults, rarely tried to break the parser. They were too busy trying to solve the problems and beat the average repair time.

When the student states that the repair is done, the simulator provides a list of the student's actions, the student's estimated repair time, the average repair time in the field, and suggestions for improvement. A typical evaluation might report:

> You solved this problem in 25 minutes, 5 minutes faster than average. However, you should have tried to reseat the video controller before replacing it.

Because we developed the simulator iteratively, we were able to fine-tune the parser to accept most of the students' commands. For example, we found that field service technicians often used "swap" instead of "replace." During the session, the designer could override the student's command and type "replace" instead. The simulator would then act appropriately and the student would never know there was a problem. Later, the designer could look at the logs provided by the Oz software and see if the term "swap" was commonly used. If so, the new term would be added to the table of action/object pairs.

THE TROUBLE-SHOOTING TUTOR

"On-the-job" training usually consists of several types of tutoring or coaching. Initially, when the novice technician knows very little, an experienced technician demonstrates how things are done. As the novice gains experience, he or she begins taking a more active role, suggesting actions and listening to explanations. Eventually, the novice is the one in control of the repair, and the experienced technician only provides advice when asked or when the novice is about to make a dangerous mistake. Finally, the novice is able to go out alone and relies on the hot line or reference materials if there is a problem.

Based on our redefinition of instruction, it is easy to see how tutoring, as well as reference and instruction could be added to the interactive trouble-shooting simulator. Because the program already "knew" an optimal way to solve each problem, it was easy to add a guide who could show the best way of solving a particular problem. It was also easy to introduce a tutor or coach who could compare the student's actions to the optimal actions and provide appropriate advice. The tutor in the simulator acted as a mentor for the student. The student could control the interaction with the tutor, from leading, to interrupting occasionally, to operating alone. The tutor could be programmed to show short or long explanations of repair sequences, to prevent mistakes or provide tips on things to remember.

We found that setting the students' expectations about the tutor was important. Since we cannot build on-line tutors that are identical to top-notch human tutors, we need to use students as allies in determining when to tutor. If students are aware that the tutor is simply responding to a limited set of rules and have some control over those rules, they will work within the tutor's limitations. (Our experience has been with adults who are interested in learning the subject matter. Students in other situations may try to fool the tutor.)

The iterative design of the simulator allowed us to experiment with a variety of ways to make the tutor more acceptable to students. We first tried pop-up menus in different colors to differentiate between the tutor's comments and other forms of information. We then introduced an animated character, named Dwayne, as the tutor. Dwayne is a small clay figure, created by Betsy Connors. He was photographed sitting on the equipment, demonstrating repair sequences and "talking" in a window in one corner of the screen. We gave Dwayne a voice with Digital's synthetic speech device, DECtalk. Field service technicians tended to like Dwayne as the personification of the tutor when he gave them quick advice, but objected to listening to him talk at any length.

In summary, even though the interactive trouble-shooting simulator was based on a limited version of the information database, it was very effective and successfully presented the full range of instructional styles. Variations were easy to add and we gave the students freedom to choose among them. The iterative design process allowed us to be responsive to students without developing elaborate student models and showed how tutoring need not be intelligent to be effective. We were able to adapt the design of the simulator to a number of other courses, which were an unqualified success with students.

CONCLUSIONS

We wanted to build educational software development tools that kept simple things simple while providing flexibility and power to try new instructional strategies. The navigation project and the interactive trouble-shooting simulator demonstrate how an information database and an iterative design process meet these goals. The information database made it easy to implement traditional forms of instruction as well as experiment with new instructional strategies. Iterative design reduced development costs and ensured that the instructional strategies were effective.

We have demonstrated that authoring languages need not be restricted to particular instructional styles. Even when authors prefer a particular style, it is often easier to implement that style with an information database than with an authoring language restricted to that style. Subsequent expansion of the program or updates based on changes in the subject matter can be handled easily.

Although most people agree that early testing with students is important, it is usually neglected because of the additional time and cost. Iterative design techniques, such as Oz, actually help with the design, reducing time and costs while providing feedback early in the development cycle. This is particularly important with the development of on-line tutors, because we do not yet know enough to build them without developmental testing.

The computer is a new medium for delivering information; we should move beyond imitations of paper-based instruction and explore the computer's unique capabilities. It is our hope that these concepts will help to reduce the debates about the ''correct'' instructional approach and focus attention how best to use the computer to meet the information needs of students.

REFERENCES

Anderson, J. R., Boyle, C. F., & Reiser, B. J. (1985). Intelligent tutoring systems. *Science, 228,* pp. 456–462.

Barr, A., & Feigenbaum, E. (1982). *The handbook of artificial intelligence, Vol. 2.* Stanford, CA: HeurisTech Press.

Burton, R. R., & Brown, J. S. (1979). An investigation of computer coaching for informal learning activities. *International Journal of Man-Machine Studies, 11,* 5–24.

Chapanis, A. (1982). Man/computer research at Johns Hopkins. In *Information Technology and Psychology: Prospects for the Future,* R. A. Kasschau, R. Lachman, & K. R. Laughery (Eds.), Proceedings of 3rd Houston Symposium. New York: Praeger Publishers.

Goldberg, A., & Robson, D. (1983). *Smalltalk-80: The language and its implementation.* Reading, MA: Addison-Wesley.

Good, M., Whiteside, J. A., Wixon, D., & Jones, S. J. (1983). Building a user-derived interface. *Communications of the ACM.*

Hodges, M. (1986, May). *The visual database project—Navigation.* Internal Technical Report, Educational Services, Digital Equipment Corporation.

Kelley, J. F. (1983). An empirical methodology for writing user-friendly natural language computer applications. In *Proceedings of CHI '83 Conference on Human Factors in Computing Systems.* Boston, MA.

Kuhlman, B., & Hale, J. (1985). An interactive trouble-shooting simulator using simple natural language. In *Proceedings of the Society for Applied Learning Technology: Conference on Interactive Video Learning Systems.* Orlando, FL.

Mackay, W. E. (1985). Interactive videodiscs: Database-driven courseware. In *Proceedings of the Conference for International Federation for Computer-Based Education in Banking,* North Holland: Amsterdam.

Mackay, W. E. (1986a). Integrated learning environments. EURIT 86. *Proceedings of the European Conference on Information Technology in Education.* Enschede, The Netherlands, 20–23 May, 1986. Pergamon Press: Oxford, England.

Mackay, W. E. (1986b). Managing CBI Projects. EURIT 86. *Proceedings of the European Con-*

ference on Information Technology in Education. Enschede, The Netherlands, 20–23 May, 1986. Pergamon Press: Oxford, England.

Mackay, W. E. (1987). *A Semi-Intelligent Tutor for a Text Editor.* In Preparation

Mackay, W. E., Parkes, C. H., Fineblum, M., & Berger, I. (1986). *Beyond the Wizard of Oz.* Presented at the CHI '86 Conference on Human Factors in Computing Systems. Boston, MA.

Papert, S. (1980). *Mindstorms: children, computers and powerful ideas.* New York: Basic Books.

Skinner, B. F. (1968). *The Technology of Teaching.* New York: Appleton.

Sleeman, D. & Brown, J. S. (Eds.). (1982). *Intelligent tutoring systems.* London: Academic Press.

Van Praag, J. (1985). *A New Approach to English Language Learning by Computer by Means of Template Extraction from Wizard of Oz Transactions.* Digital Technical Report #413, Software Human Engineering. October, 1985.

Weizenbaum, J. (1976). *Computer Power and Human Reason.* San Francisco: Freeman.

14

A Structured Approach to Intelligent Tutoring

Joseph M. Scandura
University of Pennsylvania

Alice B. Scandura
Intelligent Micro Systems, Inc.

INTRODUCTION

Most contemporary computer-based instruction (CBI) authoring systems are of the "fixed content" variety; that is, they require authors to input explicitly the instruction and questions to be presented as well as possible answers and feedback that might be given. In addition, the CBI author must specify for each intended application the exact conditions governing the selection and sequencing of information used in diagnosis and instruction.

This chapter is concerned with the application of recent advances in the cognitive sciences, instructional systems, and microcomputer technology that make it possible to develop Intelligent CBI (ICBI) authoring systems which are generative in nature. Unlike instructional systems created with "fixed content" authoring systems, generative authoring systems create instructional systems in which content is generated dynamically as testing and/or instruction proceeds. Generative authoring systems which are intelligent also determine automatically what test items and/or instructions are to be given and when (they are to be given).

At the present time, the latter problem is being investigated from several perspectives. The predominant approach derives from programming techniques associated with artificial intelligence.

This approach is typically characterized by use of the programming languages LISP and, to a growing but lesser extent, Prolog. These languages are especially good for rapid prototyping. More uniquely, their very nature lends them to logical deduction and open ended programming tasks—that is, tasks where it is infeasible for the programmer to fully anticipate all possibilities during program construction. Unanticipated possibilities may be inferred from relatively small sets of basic assumptions. In this context *giving reasons* for an assertion is equivalent to being able to derive the assertion (from mutually agreed assumptions). Consequently, some who are working in this tradition actually equate the word *intelligent* with the ability to give reasons.

Educational applications have tended to parallel this approach. So called "microworlds", for example, generally provide an open ended environment within which the learner may explore the possibilities inherent in some domain of knowledge. The programming language Logo (which is based on LISP) is a well-known example. Microworlds may be viewed as generative systems in which the learner has full control over the goals to be achieved and how to achieve them. Intelligent tutoring systems in this tradition provide *advice* but tend to stress the idiosyncratic. In large part, this is because *learning* within the AI tradition is often equated with fixing *bugs* (rather than the acquisition of new knowledge). More generally, it is because languages like LISP presuppose a certain ordering on the world, one which has little directly to do with cognition or instruction.

The goals these investigators have set for themselves have a certain attractiveness. One can hardly question the desirability of generating problems and solutions dynamically as needed, allowing learners to investigate subjects from alternative perspectives, dealing with individual idiosyncracies and reasoning logically on the basis of available knowledge. Nonetheless, judging from the sparsity of concrete results after so many years of generous funding, one can seriously question whether traditional AI provides the best or even a good way of producing practical (much less commercially viable) products.

There are two basic issues here. One has to do with the ICBI systems themselves (or "intelligent tutors" as they are sometimes called); the other has to do with development strategy. Granting that ICBI systems ideally should include (but not be limited to) the above characteristics, we personally believe there are more efficient means of achieving these goals. Clearly, just developing large numbers and varieties of ICBI systems will not do it. Questions pertaining to quality aside, cost alone would have made development prohibitive without generous federal support. Although experience can reduce such costs to a degree, order of magnitude improvements are needed if we are to produce (and properly maintain) the needed systems. Equally important, it is essential that content and pedagogical experts be able to participate directly in such development.

In this chapter we describe a microcomputer-based ICBI authoring system that will allow instructional designers and content experts who are not skilled programmers to create ICBI systems in their areas of expertise. Toward this end a highly structured, cumulative approach to ICBI development is described. Central to this approach is a sharp conceptual distinction between content and the tutorial aspects of ICBI systems. Making such a distinction is increasingly recognized as crucial in making ICBI development more efficient.

To date, no one has succeeded in developing such an ICBI system, much less an easy-to-use authoring system for developing such systems. However, there are conceptual, pragmatic, methodological, and technological reasons for believing that such systems can be developed: (a) a well-researched theory (Structural Learning Theory) in which content/tutorial distinctions are central, (b) the commercial availability of an ICBI type system (the MicroTutor II intelligent arithmetic tutor) which approaches (but does not fully achieve) complete modularity, (c) a carefully phased, disciplined and cumulative approach to system development (as opposed to the more idiosyncratic, less cognitively and/or instructionally based approaches characteristic of AI-based development), and (d) the current availability of a software development system, called PRODOC, which makes it possible to represent content in precisely the form needed for use by any of the planned modular ICBI tutorial systems.

The system being developed by Intelligent Micro Systems, Inc. (IMS) is represented schematically as shown in Fig. 14.1. ICBI systems are depicted as having two parts: an intelligent RuleTutor system (including the learner & tutor models) and a set of rules representing the content to be taught. Although not represented explicitly, one can envision intelligent RuleTutor systems ordered according to complexity of the content (e.g., the numbers and types of rules) they can handle. In particular, we shall detail requirements for an intelligent RuleTutor designed to provide optimal diagnosis and remediation with respect to cognitive procedural tasks (i.e., single rules). In addition, we show how this RuleTutor might be extended in principle to accommodate any type of content.

Figure 14.1 also shows that IMS has developed PRODOC (solid line) and intends to develop intelligent RuleTutors based on the Structural Learning Theory (dashes). PRODOC in turn can be used by subject matter and pedagogical experts (e.g., instructional designers) to represent the rules to be learned. In contrast to traditional AI-based approaches to ICBI development, the IMS ap-

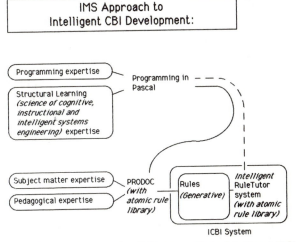

FIG. 14.1. Schematic depicting IMS approach to intelligent ICBI (tutor) development and high level structure of proposed ICBI system.

proach is highly structured. As we shall see in the following sections, it provides a systematically structured approach to the unbounded and/or unanticipated.

Given its centrality in both PRODOC and the planned intelligent RuleTutors, we begin with a discussion of rules and related constructs. Following this are sections on: (a) Introduction to the Structural Learning Theory (as it pertains to simple ICBI systems and authoring), (b) MicroTutor II Arithmetic Tutor, (c) Intelligent Tutoring Systems, a description of the intelligent RuleTutor systems IMS has under development and/or planned in the context of the structural learning methodology, (d) Sample Arithmetic and Library Rules (in a form that can be used by the intelligent RuleTutors), and (e) PRODOC (with emphasis on those aspects to be used in ICBI authoring to create rules for use by the intelligent RuleTutors). The final sections deal with relationships to other research followed by a summary of major points.

RULES AND RELATED CONSTRUCTS

The problem and rule constructs serve as the key underlying cognitive constructs in all structural learning theories (Scandura, 1970, 1971, 1973a, 1977a, 1981a) . . .

In order to accommodate the top-down nature of the proposed RuleTutor authoring system, the ORDERED SET was chosen as our basic building block. The reasoning underlying this choice is detailed in Scandura and Scandura (in press). It is sufficient to note here that structures consisting of ordered sets, whose elements in turn may be ordered sets, are partial orderings (a generalization of the ''tree'' concept which is widely used in computer science). This choice has the added advantage of uniformity: procedures, structures, problems, domains, ranges, etc., can be represented as ordered sets . . . the uniform use of ordered sets also will facilitate future implementations involving higher-order rules. In particular, since all components (domain, range, and procedure) of rules must be represented as ordered sets, rules can easily be included as components of other (higher-order) rules (e.g., Scandura, 1971, 1974).

Consider the long division problem, 4278 divided by 316, for which there are two components in the answer, the (integer) quotient and the remainder. It would have the following tree representation:

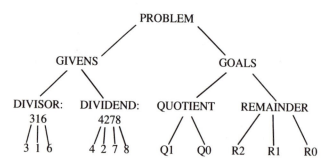

As described by Scandura (e.g., 1977, Scandura & Scandura. in press), domains and ranges of rules are structures in which some of the specific values or relations are replaced with variables (e.g., 8 by D1). Thus, we can easily derive a domain representation from the GIVENS portion of the above tree and a range representation from the GOALS portion of the tree.

In these trees, the terminal nodes are variables which designate elements from the set of decimal digits (with appropriate place values). The actual domain and range representations for long division would be somewhat more general because the number of digits in the various elements can vary. Higher-level variation of this type is accommodated naturally by allowing variable numbers of elements (terminal nodes) in the higher level (e.g., divisor) nodes.

We represent rule procedures in terms of Scandura FLOWforms (see Scandura, 1987). In FLOWforms, a sequence of operations is represented by a vertical sequence of adjacent rectangles (e.g., the sequence B, C, D in the following diagram). The alternatives in a selection construct (e.g., A and (B, C, D)) and the body of a WHILE or UNTIL loop (e.g., If X, then A, else (B, C, D)) are rectangles inset within the rectangle representing the structure of which they are a part.

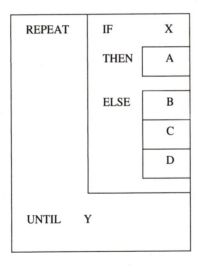

The tree representation of this procedure is as follows:

In the above picture, X and Y are conditions and the operations A, B, C and D are atomic rules. The same structure may be represented in terms of ordered sets as shown below.

REPEAT < SELECTION < X,
                    A,
                    SEQUENCE < B,
                               C,
                               D
                             >
                  >,
          Y
        >

Given the central role of problems and rules in both IMSs' PRODOC developmental system and the proposed RuleTutor, computer implementation of trees or ordered sets in the latter (RuleTutor) will directly parallel that used in PRODOC.

INTRODUCTION TO STRUCTURAL LEARNING THEORY

In the Structural Learning Theory (SLT) a sharp distinction is made between general diagnostic testing and instructional functions, on the one hand, and the content being taught on the other (e.g., Scandura, 1971, 1977a, 1980, 1981a). As described by Scandura (e.g., 1980, 1981a, 1981b, 1984a, 1984b; Scandura & Durnin, 1977, Scandura et al., 1971), all content in this theory is represented in terms of rules. In turn, all diagnosis (testing) and instruction is based on such rules—rules which are identified via prior structural analysis of some body of subject matter content.

Once an analysis has been completed, designing an effective instructional strategy follows directly from the theory (e.g., see Scandura, 1981b). Specifically, once an analysis has been completed, one knows: (a) what kinds of things the student is to be able to do after learning, and (b) what the student must learn in order to be able to do that. . . . (See Scandura & Scandura, 1987 in press, for directly related discussion. Further details may be found in the literature on the SLT approach to instruction (e.g., Scandura, 1977b), the role of determinism in the SLT (e.g., Scandura, 1971, 1977a, 1977c, 1978), the role of higher order rules in learning and creative behavior (e.g., Scandura, 1973b, 1974; Wulfeck & Scandura, 1977) and the SLT generally (e.g., Scandura, 1971, 1973a, 1977a, 1980, 1985).)

MICROTUTOR II ARITHMETIC TUTOR

Between 1980 and 1982, Intelligent Micro Systems, Inc., implemented a reasonably intelligent diagnostic and instructional system, called the MicroTutor II

Arithmetic tutor, on the Apple II computer (e.g., see Scandura, Stone, & Scandura, 1986). This system has been available commercially to schools since 1982 with the latest version released in 1984. The MicroTutor II Arithmetic tutor is based generally on the Structural Learning Theory and, consequently, incorporates a considerable amount of intelligence concerning both diagnostic testing and instruction. First, diagnostic testing is completed in a conditional and highly efficient manner. Then, instruction is provided on those paths of the rule that the student has not yet mastered.

More specifically, the Apple-based Arithmetic tutor can determine in a highly efficient manner exactly what a learner does and does not know about the task in question. It also infers what is needed to overcome inadequacies and presents that information to the learner in an optimal sequence. As currently implemented, the Arithmetic tutor deals not only with procedural skills per se, but with underlying meaning, "metacognition" (or verbal awareness of what one knows) and short-cuts commonly achieved by experts.

Despite these generalized diagnostic and tutorial capabilities, the system needs content for its completion. This content takes the form of software for generating problems (tasks) and for solving whole number arithmetic problems. The Arithmetic tutor then utilizes these capabilities in deciding which problems to present during testing and which instruction to provide during training.

Among the major conceptual limitations of the MicroTutor II Arithmetic tutor are the following: First, rule diagnosis and rule instruction in the current RuleTutor are totally independent activities. Thus, all diagnostic testing is completed (albeit in a conditional and highly efficient manner) before any instruction is provided. In fact, however, testing and teaching are highly interrelated both in practice and in principle. Thus, partial information from testing may provide a sufficient basis for (some) instruction. Conversely, instruction on a portion of a rule may influence test performance on other items and, hence, reduce the amount of instruction that otherwise might be prescribed.

Second, design limitations of the Arithmetic tutor fundamentally restricted instruction to individual rules (i.e., cognitive procedures). Consequently, the design used could not be extended to deal with sets of lower- and higher-order rules, even in principle.

Third, the basic design of the system reflected the Structural Learning Theory in only general terms. Consequently, many features of the Arithmetic tutor were fortuitous and opportunistic. In effect, the ability to deal with such things as rule meaning and verbal awareness was bought at the price of significant loss of extensibility.

Fourth, even though modularity and structured programming were at the forefront of the MicroTutor II development effort, the use of BASIC (because of its broad availability on microcomputers) and memory limitations of the Apple II computer resulted in unavoidable compromises along these lines. Thus, for example, it was not always possible to maintain modularity between rule content, on the one hand, and the diagnostic and remedial components, on the other.

Adding new content, even in whole number arithmetic, typically required (minor but often subtle and hard to identify) changes in basic diagnostic and instructional aspects of the system.

In summary, design limitations imposed restrictions on efficiency as well as on both immediate generality (limiting the variety of different content rules that could be accommodated) and future generalizability to more complex content (involving sets of rules including higher-order rules).

INTELLIGENT TUTORING SYSTEMS: DESIGNS AND METHODOLOGY

In this section we describe an approach to ICBI development, which not only improves on the MicroTutor II design but is more general, more transportable, and in future work more extensible. Specifically:

1. The design specifications not only optimize testing and instruction independently with respect to individual rules but optimize testing and instruction collectively.

2. These specifications can naturally be extended in future work to encompass arbitrary curricular content involving any number of higher- as well as lower-order rules. This includes the possibility of alternative perspectives, along with "error" (i.e., idiosyncratic or "buggy") rules (see the section on related research.)

3. The designs ensure that the current implementation will accurately and, to the extent practicable, fully reflect the underlying theory. In the arithmetic tutor, for example, basic constructs such as that of *rule* and *problem,* were formulated in terms designed more to facilitate implementation in BASIC than to reflect underlying theory. Even where a concept or construct is not proposed for current implementation, every attempt was made to allow for its addition at a later time.

4. All specifications were made as modular as humanly possible. Every effort was made to define all major ideas rigorously in a form independent of any computer language. Adherence to structured techniques, of course, necessarily biased our designs toward computer languages such as Pascal, Modula 2 and Ada, which readily lend themselves to structured programming. This difference, as much as any other, differentiates our work from traditional AI-based systems.

All structural learning theories (SLT) (e.g., Scandura, 1971, 1977a, 1980) include two major components: (1) a problem domain or domain of discourse (e.g., what is to be learned), and a set of (cognitive) rules derived by the process of Structural Analysis, and (2) the individuals (e.g., a teacher and/or learner) participating in the discourse.

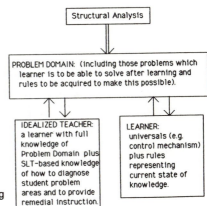

FIG. 14.2. Overview of structural learning theory.

In their simplest form, SLT's involve one individual interacting with its environment. In this case an observer (e.g., psychologist) attempts to explain, predict and/or control the individual's behavior with respect (relative) to some proscribed domain of discourse (characterized in terms of problems in the problem domain and the rules, including higher-order rules, associated with them).

The teaching-learning process involves a variation of the above in which one of the participants is an *idealized* teacher and the other, a learner. This relationship is represented schematically in Fig. 14.2.

Various aspects of this characterization of the teaching-learning process have been discussed in detail in previous publications. The process of structural analysis (SA), for example, has evolved over a period of many years (e.g., Scandura, Durnin, & Wulfeck, 1974; Scandura, 1977a; 1984a, 1984b). Today, SA has reached the point in its evolution where critical aspects of the process might reasonably be automated.

The current ICBI research is concerned primarily with those portions of the teaching-learning process pertaining to the "idealized" teacher and a learner. Notice, in particular, that in this model the idealized teacher knows (i.e., has direct access to) all of the prototype rules (representing what is to be learned), and can recognize and/or generate arbitrary problems in the Problem Domain. In addition, this idealized teacher assumedly has built into it all of the theoretically optimal machinery for diagnosing learner difficulties and for providing optimally efficient remediation. This may or may not include idealized inferencing capabilities of the sort used in expert systems.

The learner, in turn, is characterized in terms of some subset of the idealized knowledge plus universals. See the FLOWform for more details. Far more extensive discussion of the learner model may be found in a variety of publications (e.g., Scandura, 1971, 1973a, 1977a (esp. Chapter 2), 1980).

This idealized teacher is characterized at a very high level in the FLOWform in Fig. 14.3. Notice that no constraints are placed on the content to be taught;

```
learner (with all rules in rule_derivation_hierarchy mastered) :=
        CURRICULUM_TUTOR (rule_derivation_hierarchy, learner)

(CURRICULUM_TUTOR = provides optimal diagnosis and instruction needed to
                    produce learner mastery on all rules in rule hierarchy.
 learner = characterized by an universal control mechanism and processsing
         capacity, and a rule set (list of mastered rules plus current rules
         may be sufficient but, in general, complete characterization of rule
         derivation hierarchy, path hierarchy or problem types hierarchy and
         path components for all rules in rule_derivation_hierarchy might be
         needed).}
```

```
REPEAT  learner (with all paths of teachable target_rule mastered) :=
           GENERALIZED_RULE_TUTOR (rule_derivation_hierarchy, learner)

        (GENERALIZED_RULE_TUTOR = determines initial target_rule, tests
                          to update undetermined (target and
                          prerequisite) rules, reassigns
                          target_rule if necessary, and provides
                          instruction on teachable
                          target_rules.)

UNTIL MATCH (learner, rule_derivation_hierarchy)

        (MATCH = determines whether or not learner mastered rules are
                 equivalent to those in rule_derivation_hierarchy.)
```

FIG. 14.3.   Curriculum tutor.

hence the term "Curriculum_Tutor." Provision is made in the FLOWform for arbitrary problem domains, involving sets of higher- and lower-order rules, albeit at a rather high level. If fully implemented, such a system might be used to provide instruction on learning strategies, including logical inference (higher-order rules), lower-order rules (cognitive procedural tasks) and interactions among them. It also provides for alternative perspectives (including error rules) and perturbations on prototypes.

The Curriculum_Tutor takes a formal characterization of the learner as input and provides optimal diagnosis and instruction needed to produce learner mastery on all rules in the rule derivation hierarchy. The learner, formally speaking, is characterized by a universal control mechanism, a processing capacity and a set of rules (possibly including higher-order rules) representing that portion of available knowledge that is relevant to the problem domain (i.e., curriculum). At the beginning of instruction, the Curriculum_Tutor does not know which parts of which rules the learner knows. Its task is both to determine that information and to assure mastery in a theoretically optimal manner (cf. Wulfeck & Scandura, 1977).

Refinement of the CURRICULUM_TUTOR into components involves a RE-PEAT...UNTIL loop: a GENERALIZED_RULETUTOR, which would work with arbitrary rule_derivation_hierarchies, constitutes the body of the loop and MATCH constitutes the terminating condition.

In our research, the body of the main loop has undergone further refinement. The basic gist of this design (refinement) is to determine tasks which maximally

356

```
target_rule (with all paths mastered) := RULETUTOR (target_rule, learner,
                                                    P1, P2, P3)

(RULETUTOR = provides optimal diagnosis and instruction on target_rule
             until mastery of all paths is achieved.
 stop criteria: P1 = success %.
                P2 = failure %.
                P3 = maximum_number_of_test_items.)
┌─────────┬──────────────────────────────────────────────────────────────┐
│ REPEAT  │ learner (with teachable problem_type mastered) :=             │
│         │                         DIAGNOSTIC_PATH_TUTOR (learner, target_rule)│
│         │                                                              │
│         │ (DIAGNOSTIC_PATH_TUTOR = provides optimal testing and instruction on│
│         │                          problem_type.                        │
│         │   problem_type = equivalence class of problems defined by     │
│         │                  a path of the target_rule.)                  │
├─────────┴──────────────────────────────────────────────────────────────┤
│ UNTIL MATCH := (learner, target_rule)                                   │
│                                                                         │
│        (MATCH = determines whether all problem types for target_rule    │
│                are mastered.)                                           │
└─────────────────────────────────────────────────────────────────────────┘
```

FIG. 14.4.   Rule tutor.

stretch, but still lie within, the learner's capabilities (at each point of time). Normally, this will require the learner to mobilize a variety of higher- and lower-order rules, and may involve attacking the problem from any of the perspectives considered during structural analysis of the content.

After testing on each such task, the learner's status is updated. This essentially involves keeping current the list of known and unknown rules. The basic process (loop body) is repeated whenever the learner is successful (until the learner's status matches the rule_derivation_hierarchy). Before looping on failure, the Intelligent Curriculum_Tutor determines an unmastered rule nearest the bottom of the hierarchy and provides instruction on that rule.

The fact that the RULETUTOR is an essential component of the CUR-RICULUM_TUTOR is especially important given our stated interest in future generalizability. At a high level, notice that the RuleTutor (see Fig. 14.4) has the same general form as the CURRICULUM_TUTOR. Thus, the latter repeats the GENERALIZED_RULE_TUTOR until the rule_derivation_hierarchy characterizing the entire curriculum has been mastered. Analogously, the RuleTutor repeats the PATH_TUTOR until the targeted rule (cognitive procedural task) has been mastered (see Fig. 14.5).

Although reduced in scope, the RuleTutor also is designed to provide highly efficient testing and teaching. In general terms, an expanded version of the RuleTutor tests the learner to determine which parts of the to-be-learned target_rule have been mastered and which have not. At appropriate points in the testing process (e.g., when all prerequisites to a failed problem type are known to have been mastered), instruction is provided on missing information. This process is continued until the entire rule has been mastered. Specifically, the high-level REPEAT construct in the FLOWform indicates that the testing/teaching

357

```
[RULETUTR.RUL]:RuleTutor                          Copyright 1987  Scandura

learner {with rule mastered} := RULETUTOR (target_rule, learner {with rule
                                                    status undetermined}, P1, P2, P3)
{RULETUTOR = initializes learner status on target_rule, then provides optimal
             diagnosis and instruction on target_rule until mastery of all
             paths is achieved.
   stop criteria: P1 = success %.
                  P2 = failure %.
                  P3 = maximum_number_of_test_items.}
┌─────────────────────────────────────────────────────────────────────────────┐
│ learner {with knowledge of target_rule initialized}                         │
│        := INITIALIZE_LEARNER (target_rule, learner)                         │
│                                                                              │
│ {INITIALIZE_LEARNER = makes a copy of target_rule under learner's knowledge  │
│                       with status of all paths undetermined.}               │
├──────┬──────────────────────────────────────────────────────────────────────┤
│REPEAT│ path_level := SET_LEVEL (learner)                                    │
│      │                                                                       │
│      │ {SET_LEVEL = Reset test level so as to minimize                      │
│      │             expected number of levels that need                      │
│      │             to be tested -- e.g., determines                         │
│      │             highest and lowest level paths whose                     │
│      │             status is still undetermined, then                       │
│      │             computes the average,                                    │
│      │             [(highest - lowest) / 2] + 1    .}                       │
│      ├──────────────────────────────────────────────────────────────────────┤
│      │ problem_type := GET_PROBLEM_TYPE_AT_LEVEL (path_level)               │
│      │                                                                       │
│      │ {GET_PROBLEM_TYPE_AT_LEVEL = Find next undetermined problem_type     │
│      │              at level unless learner has specified                   │
│      │              problem_type or a specific problem,                     │
│      │              k := zero (k = problem_counter).}                       │
│      ├──────────────────────────────────────────────────────────────────────┤
│      │ k := "0"                                                             │
│      │                                                                       │
│      │ {NOTE:  Set number of test problems to 0.}                          │
│      ├──────┬───────────────────────────────────────────────────────────────┤
│      │REPEAT│ test_problem := PROBLEM_GENERATOR (problem_type)             │
│      │      │                                                               │
│      │      │ {PROBLEM_GENERATOR = generates a test problem.               │
│      │      │  test_ problem = test item for specified problem_type.}      │
│      │      ├───────────────────────────────────────────────────────────────┤
│      │      │ k := add (k, "1")                                            │
│      │      ├───────────────────────────────────────────────────────────────┤
│      │      │ problem_solution := GET_SOLUTION (test_problem, k)           │
│      │      │                                                               │
│      │      │ {GET_SOLUTION = presents problem to learner as prompt        │
│      │      │                 and inputs learner's response.               │
│      │      │  problem_solution = learner's sequence of responses to       │
│      │      │                 current problem.}                            │
│      │      ├───────────────────────────────────────────────────────────────┤
│      │      │ P(k) := GRADE_SOLUTION (problem_solution, learner,           │
│      │      │                         test_problem, k)                     │
│      │      │                                                               │
│      │      │ {GRADE_SOLUTION = compares problem_solution with             │
│      │      │                   solution to test_problem                   │
│      │      │                   generated by target_rule                   │
│      │      │                   (idealized learner) and                    │
│      │      │                   computes new probability of                │
│      │      │                   mastery, P(k);                             │
│      │      │                   this computation may be based              │
│      │      │                   on answers to steps in                     │
│      │      │                   problem_solution and/or may                │
│      │      │                   include partial credit for a               │
│      │      │                   partially correct answer.}                 │
│      │UNTIL GREATER_THAN (P(k),P1) OR                                      │
│      │      LESS_THAN (P(k),P2)    OR                                       │
│      │      GREATER_THAN (k, P3)                                            │
│      │                                                                       │
│      │      {P(k) > P1 (e.g., 80%) or                                      │
│      │       P(k) < P2 (e.g., 20%) or                                      │
│      │       k > P3 (e.g., 4); i.e., problem_type success or failure is    │
│      │       known with measured certainty or a pre-specified number of    │
│      │       problems have been tested.}                                   │
│      ├──────────────────────────────────────────────────────────────────────┤
│      │ learner {with status updated} :=                                    │
│      │          UPDATE_LEARNER_STATUS (P(k), learner, P1)                  │
│      │                                                                       │
│      │ {UPDATE_LEARNER_STATUS = evaluates proposed solution and            │
│      │                  updates learner's status: If                       │
│      │                  probability of mastery, P(k),                      │
│      │                  is greater than given minimum,                     │
│      │                  P1, then mark problem_type and                     │
│      │                  all of its descendants/                            │
│      │                  prerequisites mastered,                            │
│      │                  else mark problem_type and its                     │
│      │                  ancestors failed.}                                 │
│      ├──────────────────────────────────────────────────────────────────────┤
│      │ problem_type := GET_MINIMAL_PROBLEM_TYPE (learner)                  │
│      │                                                                       │
│      │ {GET_MINIMAL_PROBLEM_TYPE = selects lowest level                    │
│      │                    problem_type/path                                │
│      │                    failed by learner.}                              │
│      ├──────────────────────────────────────────────────────────────────────┤
│      │ IF PREREQUISITES_PASSED (problem_type, learner)                     │
│      │                                                                       │
│      │    {PREREQUISITES_PASSED = determines whether all paths             │
│      │                    prerequisite to problem_type                     │
│      │                    have been mastered.}                             │
│      │    ┌─────────────────────────────────────────────────────────────────┤
│      │THEN│ {*****}                                                        │
│      │    │ learner {with path mastered}                                  │
│      │    │      := PATH_COMPONENT_TUTOR (learner, target_rule,           │
│      │    │                               problem_type)                   │
│      │    │                                                                │
│      │    │ {PATH_COMPONENT_TUTOR = provides instruction on missing       │
│      │    │              components of solution path (if all              │
│      │    │              prerequisites are mastered).}                    │
├──────┴────┴─────────────────────────────────────────────────────────────────┤
│UNTIL RULE_MASTERED (learner)                                                 │
│                                                                              │
│      {RULE_MASTERED = determines whether learner has mastered all problem    │
│                       types for target_rule.}                               │
└──────────────────────────────────────────────────────────────────────────────┘
```

FIG. 14.5.   An expanded version of the Rule tutor.

process is repeated until problem types associated with ALL paths of the given rule are mastered by the student. An expanded version of the RuleTutor is given in Fig. 14.5. More details on the Curriculum_ and Rule_ tutors can be found in Scandura & Scandura (in press).

SAMPLE ARITHMETIC AND LIBRARY RULES

As already emphasized, the RuleTutor works in conjunction with (individual) rules. Consequently, to construct a working ICBI Ruletutor system, one must first create rule specifications for the content (i.e., some cognitive procedural task).

Our work with potential ICBI authors (e.g., Scandura, 1984a, 1984b) shows that by applying the method of structural analysis systematically, they typically are quite able to construct FLOWforms representing procedures for solving tasks in their areas of expertise—so long as they can express the components of those procedures in terms with which they are familiar. In a similar manner, they also are able to identify (and hence represent) critical features of the tasks themselves.

Note: These abilities have been demonstrated empirically using a recent formulation of the method of structural analysis (e.g., Scandura, 1984a, 1984b). Given content and pedagogical competence, and guidance in the use of structural analysis, potential ICBI authors were able to create rule representations functionally equivalent to those constructed by expert analysts.

The FLOWform in Fig. 14.6 is illustrative. This FLOWform can be used to

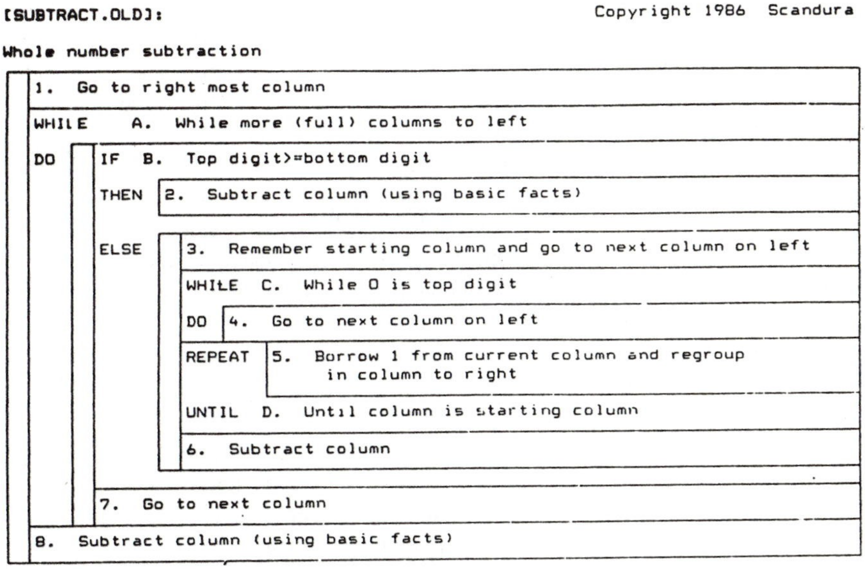

[SUBTRACT.OLD]:   Copyright 1986   Scandura

Whole number subtraction

```
1.  Go to right most column

WHILE     A.  While more (full) columns to left

DO    IF  B.  Top digit>=bottom digit

      THEN 2.  Subtract column (using basic facts)

      ELSE 3.  Remember starting column and go to next column on left

           WHILE  C.  While 0 is top digit

           DO  4.  Go to next column on left

           REPEAT 5.  Borrow 1 from current column and regroup
                      in column to right

           UNTIL  D.  Until column is starting column

           6.  Subtract column

7.  Go to next column

8.  Subtract column (using basic facts)
```

FIG. 14.6.   Subtraction: Old flowform.

solve any given column subtraction problem. By carrying out successive steps of the FLOWform, one effectively simulates the process of column subtraction. (In a similar manner, one can simulate essentially any process.)

Although authors can be taught how to perform a structural analysis, they do not normally do so—nor for that matter is it absolutely essential in identifying rules in their areas of expertise. Potential authors with some programming experience will often prefer to construct FLOWforms directly without following any particular systematic method of analysis. (Indeed, as powerful as it is, we believe that structural analysis will come into widespread use only when users have access to computer based systems which perform the many time consuming but necessary steps automatically.)

The availability of PRODOC greatly facilitates the task of specifying rules in this manner (i.e., directly). Instead of having to draft rule specifications (usually on paper) and converting these to increasingly precise designs, all of this can be done using PRODOC (Scandura, 1987) in an integrated, graphically supported top down structured development environment.

In structural analysis, users are required first to represent data (problem) structures and rule procedures at a very high level by describing what they do in very general terms. Then, these high level descriptions are refined step-by-step until each component step (of the procedure) is atomic (elementary)—in the sense that it is either already available to the members of the targeted school population, or is so simple that it would be impossible to teach only part of the step (to members of the population) without their mastering the entire step (i.e., the step is all-or-none as defined by Scandura, 1971, 1973a).

PRODOC makes this possible by allowing the user to view, create, modify, and revise graphical representations of rules directly on the IBM PC AT (XT) screen. The clarity of FLOWforms makes it easier to detect errors, if not avoid them altogether. In addition to being easy to read, FLOWforms make excellent use of available screen space, and allow the simultaneous representation of as many (or as few) levels of refinement as may be desired.

Not just any FLOWform will do, however. In order for a rule/FLOWform to be usable by the RuleTutor the terminal (atomic) operations and conditions of the rule must be interpretable. Analogous to the above requirements for human atomicity, these atomic operations and conditions must correspond to subroutines in the atomic rule library available to the ICBI RuleTutor.

In the case of arithmetic, for example, we would need an atomic rule library which provides an adequate basis for constructing rules associated with cognitive procedural tasks in arithmetic—tasks such as column subtraction, addition of fractions, etc.

Fortunately, the atomic library rules currently available to PRODOC provide an adequate foundation for this purpose. One can use these library rules to create a FLOWform (rule) representing essentially ANY cognitive procedural task. For example, the subtraction FLOWform below is constructed entirely from atomic rules in a current PRODOC library (see Fig. 14.7).

Whole_number_subtraction (minuend, subtrahend)

```
I.    ┌─────────────────────────────────────────────────────────────────────┐
      │ Go to right-most column.                                           │ │
      ├─────────────────────────────────────────────────────────────────────┤
      │ share_component_after (next_component (top_row), current_top_digit)   │
      ├─────────────────────────────────────────────────────────────────────┤
      │ share_component_after (next_component (bottom_row), current_bottom_digit) │
      ├─────────────────────────────────────────────────────────────────────┤
      │ share_component_after (next_component (answer_row), current_answer_digit) │
      └─────────────────────────────────────────────────────────────────────┘

A.    WHILE not (match (next_component (top_row,
                                        current_top_digit),
                         NILL))

B.    DO    IF greater_than_or_equal (current_top_digit,
                                      current_bottom_digit)

2.          THEN   (***) current_answer_digit := subtract (current_top_digit,
                                                           current_bottom_digit)

            ELSE   ┌────────────────────────────────────────────────────────┐
3.                 │ Remember starting column and go to next column on left. │ │
                   ├────────────────────────────────────────────────────────┤
                   │ share_component_after                                   │
                   │        (current_top_digit,                             │
                   │         last_nonzero_top_digit)                        │
                   ├────────────────────────────────────────────────────────┤
                   │ share_component_after                                   │
                   │        (next_component (top_row,                       │
                   │                        current_top_digit),             │
                   │         current_top_digit,                             │
                   │         current_top_digit)                             │
                   ├────────────────────────────────────────────────────────┤
                   │ delete_component                                       │
                   │   (current_top_digit, next_component (current_top_digit)) │
                   └────────────────────────────────────────────────────────┘

C.          WHILE match (current_top_digit, '0')

4.          DO   ┌──────────────────────────────────────────────────────────┐
                 │ Go to next column on left.                             │ │
                 ├──────────────────────────────────────────────────────────┤
                 │ share_component_after                                   │
                 │        (next_component (top_row,                       │
                 │                        current_top_digit),             │
                 │         current_top_digit,                             │
                 │         current_top_digit)                             │
                 ├──────────────────────────────────────────────────────────┤
                 │ delete_component                                       │
                 │   (current_top_digit,                                  │
                 │    next_component (current_top_digit))                │
                 └──────────────────────────────────────────────────────────┘

5.          REPEAT  ┌────────────────────────────────────────────────────────┐
                    │ . Borrow 1 from current column and regroup in        . │
                    │ │ column to right.                                   │ │
                    ├────────────────────────────────────────────────────────┤
                    │ current_top_digit :=                                  │
                    │         subtract (current_top_digit, '1')            │
                    ├────────────────────────────────────────────────────────┤
                    │ share_component_after                                │
                    │        (prev_component (top_row,                     │
                    │                        current_top_digit),          │
                    │         current_top_digit,                          │
                    │         current_top_digit)                          │
                    ├────────────────────────────────────────────────────────┤
                    │ delete_component                                    │
                    │   (current_top_digit,                               │
                    │    next_component (current_top_digit))             │
                    ├────────────────────────────────────────────────────────┤
                    │ current_top_digit :=                                │
                    │         add (current_top_digit, '10')              │
                    └────────────────────────────────────────────────────────┘
```

FIG. 14.7. Library: Subtraction.

FIG. 14.7. continued

The numbers to the left of the various structures (higher level steps) of the FLOWform correspond to the numbered conditions and operations in the previously discussed SUBTRACT.OLD FLOWform. The detailed (terminal) steps in the LIBRSUBT FLOWform use the current names of library rules and are not necessarily optimal for use by educators.

In addition, PRODOC can be used to create all of the needed data structures, such as current_top_digit, current_bottom_digit, current_answer_digit, and last_nonzero_column (used to determine how far to go back in borrowing across zeros).

To maximize ease-of-use, at the minimum, certain rules in the existing library would have to be modified so that they perform many of the auxiliary operations automatically (and transparently from the perspective of the user). For example, the *display* rule might be enhanced to operate on location parameters which are more directly meaningful. Thus, the position on the screen where an answer _digit is to be displayed might be represented at a level higher than the top and left margins associated with the normal text screen (which contains 25 × 80 characters). Thus, *location* might be defined more naturally in terms of rows and columns in the subtraction problem. In this case a sample display rule might take the form

display (answer_digit, location (answer_row, column))

Notice that the above *display* operation has a parameter *location* which is itself an operation with two parameters: "answer_row" and "column."

This *slight of hand,* of course, would require that the display rule have considerably more *intelligence* than it currently has. Given the row and column specifying where something is to be displayed, the (new) display rule would have to calculate the corresponding position on the screen.

Ideally, one might go beyond this minimum, and make the required display operations totally transparent to the user. That is, once a bottom digit has been subtracted from a top digit, the *subtract* rule might not only subtract the digits but also display the difference on the screen in the proper location. The basic question, in effect, is how easy it will be to construct a given rule from an available library.

Making rule construction as easy as possible for potential ICBI authors will involve the availability both of atomic rules that are especially well suited for constructing rules associated with particular content domains; the availability of appropriate data structures also will be highly desirable.

The overall goal, of course, is to come up with a set of atomic library rules which are adequate, not only for constructing rules associated with whole number arithmetic, but others as well. Hence, we included in our sample analysis a variety of tasks associated with fractions and decimals.

In algorithms for adding and subtracting mixed number fractions, for example, certain components correspond to the whole number algorithms. In effect, what are high level rules in one (the whole number) context are atomic ingredients in other (e.g., fraction) contexts.

Higher *level* (not higher *order*) rules of this type can be accommodated using the PRODOC system without requiring the user to specify details of these higher level component rules. This can be accomplished as follows: Once a new rule (or set of new rules) has been constructed using atomic rules in a given library, that rule (or rules) can be added to the library using the PRODOC1g (library generation) capability. The result in this case would be a new PRODOC prototyping environment with an extended library.

In the fullest sense, of course, teaching arithmetic may involve the meaning of the operations, and potentially even verbal descriptions of arithmetic problems and solution procedures as in verbal problem solving.

Characterization of arithmetic in terms of rules in this broader sense is beyond the scope of the current RuleTutor since it clearly involves sets of lower and higher order rules (e.g., Scandura, 1971, 1973a, 1973b). The general nature of these relationships may be summarized as shown below. See Scandura, 1971, 1973a, ch. 5) for a more general discussion of the relationships between syntactic and semantic knowledge in mathematics.

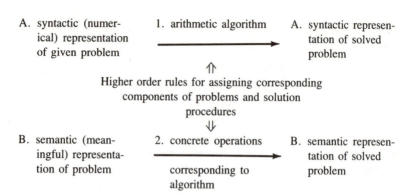

A. syntactic (numer-
ical) representation
of given problem

1. arithmetic algorithm

A. syntactic represen-
tation of solved
problem

Higher order rules for assigning corresponding
components of problems and solution
procedures

B. semantic (mean-
ingful) representa-
tion of problem

2. concrete operations

corresponding to
algorithm

B. semantic represen-
tation of solved
problem

In this case, problems of type A would include column subtraction, multiplication of fractions, etc. Those of type B might include Dienes blocks, packets of dowels grouped by powers of ten, pie charts (for fractions), etc. Similarly, procedures of type 1 would include the subtraction algorithm, the algorithm for multiplying fractions, etc. and procedures of type 2, concrete manipulations on Dienes blocks, pie charts, etc. The double arrow represents two higher-order rules, one of which can generate concrete rules (e.g., concrete manipulations on Dienes blocks) from the corresponding syntactic rules (e.g., whole number algorithms). The other higher-order rule does the reverse.

Clearly, the proposed RuleTutor would not (simultaneously) accommodate the sets of lower- and higher-order rules implied by such a broad conception of arithmetic. What it could do, however, is provide diagnostic learning and instruction with respect to any individual (lower order) rule associated with arithmetic.

In the case of subtraction, for example, the meaning of subtraction as taking away and the place value concept in representing numbers are crucial. More particularly, the meaning of a rule (e.g., for subtraction) can be represented in terms of manipulations on concrete objects represented in a standard place value format. Thus, for example, consider the pair of numbers, 132 and 27. represented concretely as

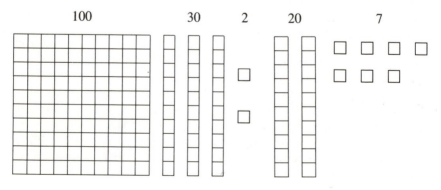

In this case, the student might be shown how to take away the amount represented by the smaller quantity from the larger by taking away from the larger quantity as many groups of each size as there are in the smaller quantity. Where the number of groups of a particular size (e.g., ones) in the larger quantity is smaller than that in the smaller quantity, the student learns to first convert the next larger grouping (e.g., tens) in the larger quantity into a smaller grouping. For example, one ten's group would be converted into ten ones so that the seven ones in the smaller quantity might be taken away. Implicitly, the student also learns to begin work with the smaller place values (groupings) and to work toward larger ones.

Normally, students are not taught general rules (procedures) for performing arithmetic operations on concrete objects in a systematic way. Rather, students gradually acquire an informal awareness of such rules by solving a variety of specific concrete problems, with concrete objects and/or pictorial representations of such objects. Dienes blocks (e.g., Dienes, 1960) are commonly used for this purpose. Nonetheless, manipulative rules can be taught explicitly.

Allowing a prospective author to specify manipulation rules (in a form the RuleTutor can use) could require extending the above library by adding (to it) atomic rules corresponding to the above components (e.g., regroup, etc.).

It is important to emphasize in this regard that new atomic rules identified as a result of analyzing the arithmetic domain can be used to supplement the general purpose library that is currently available. In turn, still additional atomic rules may be added as new domains are analyzed. The only limitations in this regard are computer memory and/or addressing capacity of the operating system.

IMS'S PRODOC SYSTEM

In its most basic sense software development involves describing the tasks to be solved—including the given objects and the operations to be performed on those objects. Moreover, such descriptions must be precise in order for a computer (or human) to perform as desired. Unfortunately, the way people describe objects and operations typically bears little resemblance to source code in most contemporary computer languages.

There are two potential ways around this problem. One is to allow users to describe what they want the computer to do in everyday, typically imprecise English (or to choose from a necessarily limited menu of choices). This approach has some obvious advantages and a considerable amount of research is underway in the area. The approach, however, also has some very significant limitations: (a) it currently is impossible to deal with unrestricted English, and this situation is unlikely to change in the foreseeable future, and (b) even if the foregoing limitation is eventually overcome, the approach would still require the addition of complex, memory intensive ``front ends.'' These front ends interact with the user's typically imprecise English statements and effectively ``try to figure out''

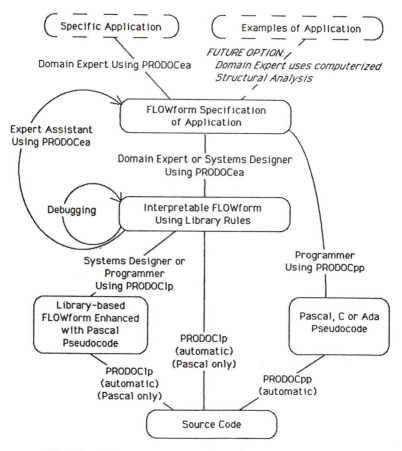

FIG. 14.8. IMS's PRODOC—Software development environment.

what the user intends. The result invariably is a system that is both sluggish in performance and limited in applicability.

PRODOC is based on a second, possibly more flexible approach. The terminology used in PRODOC may be customized so as to match the way human experts in any given application area naturally describe the relevant data and operations. This customized terminology is all based on a uniform, very simple syntax that might easily be learned by an intelligent human (in a few minutes time). The approach taken with PRODOC is absolutely general, as well as far more efficient and easy to use.

The PRODOC system, shown in Fig. 14.8, supports the entire software development process, including requirements definition, system design, testing, prototyping, code generation, and system maintenance. It consists of four distinct but complimentary and fully compatible environments running in 640K of memory under MS–DOS. Each of these environments makes use of Scandura FLOWforms.

1. Applications Prototyping Environment (with interpreter and expert assistant generator) (PRODOCea)—is suitable for use by nonprogrammers as well as programmers for designing, documenting, implementing, and maintaining software systems in an integrated, graphically supported, top-down structured environment. In addition to supporting simulation in English text, the availability of high level library rules makes PRODOCea ideal for rapid prototyping. The availability of graphical support for input and output data structures also makes it possible to directly reflect arbitrary semantic properties.

A recent version of PRODOCea employs a general purpose but relatively low level set of library rules (see Table 14.1).

In conjunction with PRODOC's Library Generation facilities (see (4) below), custom versions of PRODOCea (and PRODOClp) can quickly be created to accommodate library rules having arbitrary semantic properties, and thereby to facilitate rapid prototyping in desired application areas.

An unique feature of PRODOCea is its ability to immediately execute not only interpretable library rules but to simulate execution statements using library syntax and/or written in ordinary English. Among other things, this adds discipline to the traditionally unsystematic task of programming. It also makes the difficult and expensive process of developing performance aids or expert assistants almost trivial. Once an (nonprogrammer) expert knows exactly what a human/computer assistant is to do, for example, it is a simple task to develop a computerized performance aid to assist less qualified personnel in performing the required tasks.

2. Applications Prototyping Environment (for use with a Pascal compiler) (PRODOClp)—is identical to PRODOCea in so far as prototype design and the use of library rules in rapid prototyping is concerned. Instead of an interpreter, however, PRODOClp includes a code generator which makes it possible to arbitrarily mix Pascal code with library rules, thereby gaining the prototyping advantages of any number of customized, arbitrarily high-level languages, along with the flexibility of Pascal. This feature makes it possible, for example, for a programmer to speed up or otherwise add finishing touches to a working prototype created by a nonprogrammer.

3. Programming Productivity Environment (PRODOCpp)—has all of the design, etc. features of PRODOCea. PRODOCpp comes in standard form which supports text and source code in any programming language.

In addition, full pseudo code support currently is available as an option for Pascal, C, and Ada. These options combine the clarity and ease of use of high-level fourth generation languages with the flexibility of third generation languages, and include full syntax checking, consistency checking, automatic declarations generation, and full source code generation. Pseudocode support is totally data driven so similar support for other third and fourth generation languages may be added without modifying PRODOC itself.

TABLE 14.1
Rule Library Catalog

Input/Output	Standard Rule Name	Application-Specific Rule Name
DISPSTAT.BRL	display_state (ROOT_ELEMENT)	display_state
DISPELT.BRL	display_element (ELEMENT,DISPLAY_PARAMETERS)	display
LOAD.BRL	load (ROOT_ELEMENT,DOS_NAME,DRIVE,FILE_TYPE)	load
SAVE.BRL	save (ROOT_ELEMENT,DOS_NAME,DRIVE,FILE_TYPE)	save
GETINPUT.BRL	get_input (ELEMENT,DISPLAY_PARAMETERS)	get_input
LOADPIC.BRL	load_picture (NUMBER)	load_picture
CLRVIDEO.BRL	clear_video	clear_video

Operations

INSRTCPT.BRL	insert_component_after (VALUE,SET,PREVIOUS_COMPONENT)	insert_component-after
DELETCPT.BRL	delete_component (SET,COMPONENT)	delete_component
SHRCPTAF.BRL	share_component_after (COMPONENT,SET,PREVIOUS_COMPONENT)	share_component_after
DELAY.BRL	delay (SECONDS)	delay

Parameter Functions (Arithmetic)

ADD.BRL	add (ADDEND1,ADDEND2)	add
SUBTRACT.BRL	subtract (TOP,BOTTOM)	subtract
MULTIPLY.BRL	multiply (FACTOR1,FACTOR2)	multiply
DIVIDE.BRL	divide (DIVIDENT,DIVISOR)	divide
POWER.BRL	power (BASE,EXPONENT)	power
GRTSTINT.BRL	greatest_integer (X)	greatest_integer
MODULO.BRL	modulo (X,BASE)	modulo
ABSVALUE.BRL	absolute_value (X)	absolute_value
ROUND.BRL	round (X,PRECISION)	round

Parameter Functions (Relationships)

FIND.BRL	find (VALUE,SET)	find_component_with_valu
NEXTCPT.BRL	next_component (SET,PREVIOUS_COMPONENT)	next_component
COMNCPT.BRL	common_component (SET1,SET2,NTH ONE)	common_component

Conditions

LEQUAL.BRL	lequal (STRING1,STRING2)	match
NUMEQUAL.BRL.	numerically_equal (X,Y)	equal
NUMUNEQL.BRL	numerically_unequal (X,Y)	unequal

(continued...)

(Table 14.1 continued...)

LESSTHAN.BRL	less_than (X,Y)	less_than
LESOREQL.BRL	less_than_or_equal (X,Y)	less_than_or_equal
GRTRTHAN.BRL	greater_than (X,Y)	greater_than
GTROREQL.BRL	greater_than_or_equal (X.Y)	greater_than_or_equal
HASCPTAF.BRL	has_component_after SET,PREVIOUS_COMPONENT)	has_component_after

Logical Connectives

LOGCLAND.BRL	logical_and (EXPRESSION1,EXPRESSION2)	and
LOGCLOR.BRL	logical_or (EXPRESSION1,EXPRESSION2)	or
LOGCLNOT.BRL	logical_not · (EXPRESSION)	not

Assignment

ASSIGN.BRL	assign_value (VALUE,ELEMENT)	assign or ELEMENT := VALUE

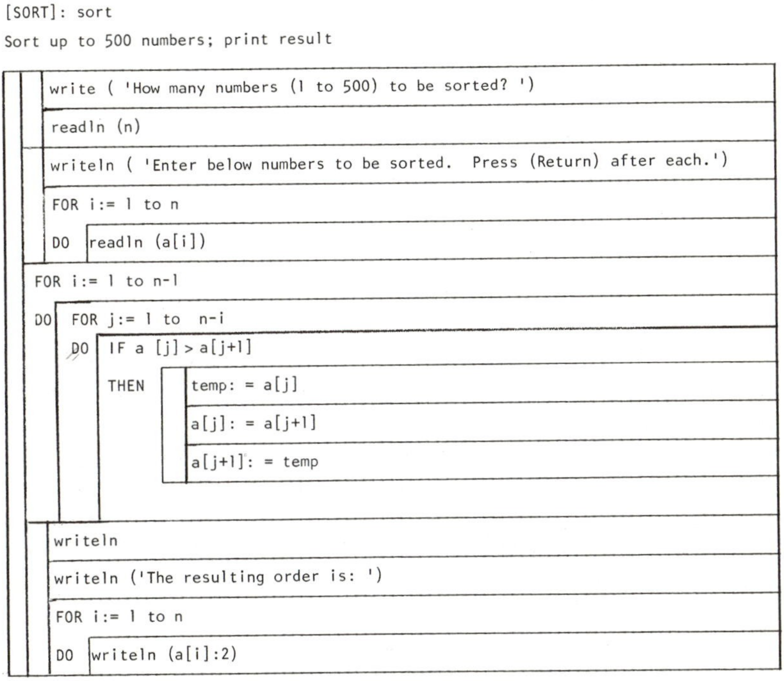

[SORT]: sort
Sort up to 500 numbers; print result

```
write ( 'How many numbers (1 to 500) to be sorted? ')

readln (n)

writeln ( 'Enter below numbers to be sorted.  Press (Return) after each.')

FOR i:= 1 to n

DO   readln (a[i])

FOR i:= 1 to n-1

DO   FOR j:= 1 to  n-i

     DO   IF a [j] > a[j+1]

          THEN    temp: = a[j]

                  a[j]: = a[j+1]

                  a[j+1]: = temp

writeln

writeln ('The resulting order is: ')

FOR i:= 1 to n

DO   writeln (a[i]:2)
```

FIG. 14.9a.   Sort Flowform.

```
PROGRAM sort;

VAR n : INTEGER;
    i : INTEGER;
    a : ARRAY[1..500] OF INTEGER;
    temp : INTEGER;

BEGIN
  (Sort up to 500 numbers;print result)
  Begin
    write ('How many numbers (1 to 500) to be sorted? ');
    readln (n);
    (Prompt user, then get numbers.)
    BEGIN
      writeln ('Enter below numbers to be sorted. Press (Return) after each.');
      ( Get the numbers from the user. )
      FOR i:=1 to n DO
        readln (a[i])
    END;
    ( Sort them. )
    FOR i:= 1 to n-1 DO
      ( Scan thru items and swap if necessary. )
      FOR j:= 1 to n -i DO
        ( Compare and swap if necessary. )
        BEGIN
        IF a[j]> a[j+1] THEN
          ( Swap )
          BEGIN
            temp:= a[j];
            a[j]:= a[j+1];
            a[j+1]:= temp
          END
        END;
    ( Identify and then print the resulting ordered set. )
    BEGIN
      writeln;
      writeln ('The resulting order is:');
      ( Print the result. )
      FOR i:= 1 to n DO
        writeln (a[i]:2)
    END
  END
END.
```

FIG. 14.9b. Sort source code.

The relationship between Pascal pseudo code in the SORT FLOWform (Fig. 14.9a) and the corresponding full source code (Fig. 14.9b) is shown above.

Note: This illustration shows only terminal elements of the FLOWform. All design levels of the sort routine are displayed in the second FLOWform (see Fig. 14.9c).

4. Library Generation (PRODOClg) (see Fig. 14.10)—makes it possible to integrate available rule libraries and new library rules into either PRODOC prototyping environment, thereby creating customized versions of PRODOC for particular uses. Since this requires access to PRODOC source code, customized versions of PRODOC will normally involve collaboration between users and IMS.

The PRODOC series has been implemented in Pascal and currently runs under MS-DOS. It may be ported to other operating systems as need dictates.

[SORT]:sort

Sort up to 500 numbers;print result

```
.........................................................................................................
. Specify the number of numbers to be sorted.

  write ('How many numbers (1 to 500) to be sorted?   ')

  readln (n)

.........................................................................................................
. Prompt user, then get the numbers.

  writeln ('Enter below numbers to be sorted. Press ⟨Return⟩ after each.')

.........................................................................................................
. Get the numbers.

  FOR i: = 1 to n

  DO │ readln (a[i])

.........................................................................................................
. Sort them.

FOR i: = 1 to n − 1

DO │ .........................................................................................................
   │ . Scan thru items and swap if necessary.
   │
   │ FOR j: = 1 to n − i
   │
   │ DO │ .........................................................................................................
   │    │ . Compare and swap if necessary.
   │    │
   │    │ IF a[j] > a[j + 1]
   │    │
   │    │ THEN │ .........................................................................................................
   │    │      │ . Swap
   │    │      │
   │    │      │ temp: = a[j]
   │    │      │
   │    │      │ a[j]: = a[j + 1]
   │    │      │
   │    │      │ a[j + 1]: = temp

.........................................................................................................
. Display description, then print the ordered set.

  writeln

  writeln ('The resulting order is:')

.........................................................................................................
. Print the ordered set.

  FOR i: = 1 to n

  DO │ writeln (a[i]:2)
```

FIG. 14.9c. · Full sort design.

371

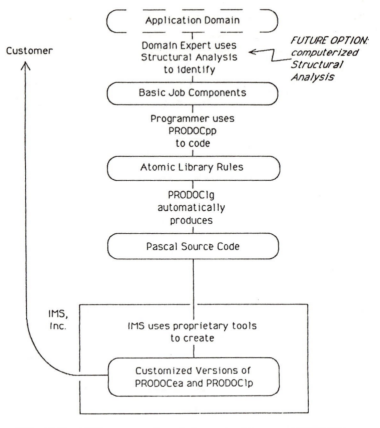

FIG. 14.10. IMS's structural analysis methodology and PRODOC1g library generator.

RELATIONSHIPS TO OTHER RESEARCH

Much of the most directly related research and development work has been cited and/or referenced in the body of this proposal. By way of summary, Prof. Joseph M. Scandura and his group at the University of Pennsylvania have been primarily responsible for:

a. the Structural learning Theory generally, and particularly the theory of diagnostic testing and instruction on which the intelligent RuleTutor is based (e.g., Scandura, 1971, 1977a, 1980).

b. the concept of a rule, including both structural and procedural aspects, which provides the basic theoretical construct on which this work is based (e.g., Scandura, 1970, 1971. 1973a, 1973b, 1980).

c. the method of Structural Analysis (e.g., Scandura, 1982, 1984a, 1984b; Scandura & Durnin, 1977; Scandura, Durnin, & Wulfeck, 1974).

d. the conceptualization and design of IMS's PRODOC programming environment (Scandura, 1987).

While independently derived, these conceptual formalisms share certain features with other work in artificial intelligence and the cognitive sciences. The essential equivalence of structural and procedural representations of knowledge, for example, is well recognized (e.g., Anderson, 1976). Rule domains (or structure schemas) are similar to "frames" (Minsky, 1975), "schema" theory (Ausubel, 1963), etc., although as far as can be determined the particular characteristics of rule domains, range and procedures are original.

The structural-learning-based instructional theory parallels Pask's (1975) Conversation Theory at a general system level. The instructional theory also shares certain elements in common with other algorithmic formulations, such as that by Landa (1978). It does, however, provide a more rigorous base for computer implementation.

Also, as mentioned previously, the method of structural analysis (e.g., Scandura, 1982, 1984a, 1984b) is potentially compatible with other methods of task analysis (cognitive and otherwise) and automatic programming. Thus, task analysis (proposed by R. B. Miller during the 1950s & Gagné in 1962) can be viewed as a more restricted case of structural analysis where the emphasis is on task requirements rather than cognitive processes. Work by Paul Merrill and that by Lauren Resnick (1984) on cognitive task analysis also shares some features in common with structural analysis. What distinguishes structural analysis is its degree of systematization and rigor, and the fact that it makes provision for higher- as well as lower-order rules, thereby accommodating arbitrarily complex content.

More specifically in artificial intelligence, the ICBI RuleTutor is an intelligent tutorial system that has various features in common with J. S. Brown's (e.g., Brown & Burton, 1978) systems for identifying procedural "bugs" (i.e., rules which generate incorrect outputs). Some confusion exists in the literature concerning the question of diagnosis based on the structural learning theory (e.g., Scandura, 1971, 1977a) and its relationship to "error patterns" based on the "bug" concept in programming (e.g., Brown & Burton, 1978). In the former case, emphasis has been given to identifying which parts (subrules or subskills) of a to-be-learned rule have and have not been mastered. In the latter case, the emphasis is on the kinds of bugs (e.g., misconceptions) students may have—even bugs "which have no vestiges in the correct skill" (Burton, 1982, p. 177).

In terms of structural learning theories, "bugs" correspond to what Scandura (e.g., 1977a, pp. 75–77) has called "error" rules—rules which generate incorrect responses but which nonetheless are prototypic of the way certain classes of students behave. Such "bugs" may be characterized either as "pertubations" on some standard (e.g., correct rule) or as distinct rules. In the former case, the concept of a prototype "rule procedure" must be generalized to allow nondeterminism (e.g., see Scandura, 1973a, Ch. 8). Individual steps in the prototype may allow for more than one possible response; deterministic procedures will be assigned to individuals (e.g., students) based on diagnosis. This approach parallels that proposed by Brown et al. (1982) and has the apparent advantage of simplicity. However, as one of us (Scandura, 1973a, Ch. 8) has shown, resorting to nondeterminism "camouflages" the issue of rule selection.

In the latter case, recall that a given structural learning theory may involve any (finite) number of alternative prototypes or perspectives (rules or sets of rules) (e.g., Scandura, 1977a, pp. 68–72). As demonstrated by Durnin and Scandura (1973a), the behavior of an individual student will be more or less compatible with any given prototype—in this case, the behavior of most American 4th graders was shown to be more compatible with borrowing in column subtraction than with equal additions. That is, they tended to be either consistently successful or unsuccessful on problems associated with various kinds of borrowing. This was NOT true for those students in the case of equal additions.

To be sure, the behavior of some (particularly European) students is more compatible with equal additions, just as others may be more consistent with error, or "buggy" rules. See Scandura (1977a, Ch. 10) for a discussion of considerations involved in determining which of two or more rule prototypes provides the best account of overall performance.

Irrespective of the additional information that may be provided when a variety of prototypic rules (including "error" or "buggy" rules) is used in knowledge assessment, explicit verbal attention to such defects may NOT be desirable from an instructional point of view. In particular, as confirmed in recent research, calling attention to incorrect skills can lead to later confusion. According to the Structural Learning Theory (e.g., Scandura, 1971, pp. 41–44; 1973a, Ch. 8) this is because students must choose between or among the two or more rules which may be used in the situation—the error rule originally learned and the correct one. This ambiguity must be resolved via higher-order selection rules and is a frequent source of difficulty for students. In effect, it is almost always better to learn new skills correctly the first time. The proposed ICBI RuleTutor deals with this problem by combining testing with teaching at the lowest meaningful levels. As soon as a problem is established, remedial instruction is provided immediately, thereby avoiding debilitating misconceptions which otherwise would inevitably surface.

Our research is also paralleled in many ways by the recent work of John Anderson and his associates (unpublished research proposal) on intelligent tutors. Both approaches start with a model of the learner (albeit quite different ones). In Anderson's case, the learner is modeled by his ACT theory (Anderson, 1976). Originally inspired by S–R association principles, this theory currently is based on productions (condition-action pairs). Even today, however, it retains such S–R constructs as "strength," "spreading activation," and "probability."

In the Structural Learning Theory (SLT) the learner is characterized exclusively in terms of lower and higher-order rules, plus universals such as processing capacity and speed and a common control mechanism. Equally fundamental, knowledge in the SLT is treated deterministically (e.g., Hilke, Kempf, & Scandura, 1977c; Scandura, 1971, 1973a, 1977a). Rather than talking about "productions" being available with some probability, as Anderson does, "rules" in SLT's are either in an "undetermined" state, or available or unavailable.

In the more explicitly instructional aspects of their research, Anderson et al. have adopted the structural learning concept of idealized (or prototypic) knowledge (cf. Scandura, 1971, 1973a, 1977a, 1977b). As in our research, prototypes are used to characterize what is to be learned. According to Anderson et al., however, they have not been able to completely modularize tutorial and content portions of the system.

Inference based instructional systems such as those developed by A. Collins and his colleagues (e.g., Collins et al., 1975) also deserve mention because of their relevance to the proposed Curriculum-Tutor. Inference in structural-learning-based tutors can involve higher order rules (to be learned by students) as well as "idealized" inferencing on the part of the computer tutor.

In short, like other intelligent tutors (and some CAI systems), the ICBI RuleTutor provides for the automatic generation of content. It also allows for future extensions including provision for "bugs," alternative perspectives, and logical inference.

Unlike other intelligent tutors, however, there is a sharp distinction in the RuleTutor between the diagnostic/tutorial system, on the one hand, and content (e.g., arithmetic) on the other. The desirability of this type of modularity has never been fully achieved but also has been recognized by others (e.g., Clancey, 1982; Brown, Burton, & de Kleer, 1982, p. 280). Like our original RuleTutor, for example, GUIDON (Clancey, 1982) is a multiple-domain tutorial program. However, in neither case is the conceptual distinction between content and instruction fully reflected in modular code. Some, indeed, have voiced the opinion that it may not be possible.

What makes modularity feasible and is unique about the proposed RuleTutor and Curriculum_Tutor systems is an explicit theoretical foundation which has been demonstrated empirically to have the desired modularity and universality (e.g., Scandura 1971, 1973a, 1977a, 1980). In combination with PRODOC (used as an authoring system) this modularity will facilitate future development. Instead of taking 250 hours or so to produce an hours worth of intelligent tutoring (e.g., Anderson, unpublished talk), it should take barely more time than it takes to specify the rules to be learned—by the most conservative estimate a five-fold improvement. Equally important, it may be feasible for the first time for instructional designers (who are not skilled programmers) to develop their own intelligent tutoring systems. Only content will have to be dealt with directly since all of the necessary diagnostic and tutorial intelligence will already have been built in.

SUMMARY

In this chapter we have focused on how to utilize current understanding of cognitive and instructional processes as a basis for creating intelligent tutoring systems. Among other things we have determined the feasibility of implementing a new class of ICBI authoring/development systems having two distinct but complementary parts: First is a general-purpose, intelligent (ICBI) RuleTutor (or Curriculum_Tutor) which is able to perform both diagnostic testing and instruction—but which does not contain content specific knowledge, either of the problem/tasks to be generated or the cognitive procedures (rules) to be taught. The second part would consist of IMS's PRODOC software development system. To facilitate its use by educators, PRODOC may be supplemented with a rule library specifically designed to simplify authoring of the desired content. Such a system would provide an easy-to-use medium for creating arbitrary cognitive procedures (rules) in the intended content area. Each such rule, in turn, would be interpreted by the ICBI RuleTutor, resulting in a fully operational ICBI RuleTutor system for the given cognitive procedure.

More specifically, we have outlined a general-purpose ICBI RuleTutor which can be used in conjunction with ANY cognitive procedure formulated as a rule (i.e., as defined in the Structural Learning Theory—e.g., Scandura 1970, 1977a, 1984a). (See Scandura & Scandura, in press, for more detailed specifications.) We also have described the kinds of rule components (atomic rules) needed in a rule library optimized for use in arithmetic. The atomic rules in such a library provide a natural basis for formulating arbitrary rules (corresponding to to-be-learned cognitive procedures) in arithmetic.

Taken together, the RuleTutor and PRODOC should provide a sound basis for developing intelligent tutorial systems for any cognitive procedural task. Moreover, when coupled with an optimized library (e.g., in arithmetic) such an authoring system would make it possible for subject matter and/or curriculum experts to automatically generate ICBI systems in arithmetic with little actual programming.

Of perhaps even greater importance, such an authoring system could easily be customized to accommodate ANY new content domain. Since PRODOC already includes a general purpose library of relatively low-level rules it can, in principle, be used with any content. Nonetheless, customization for various particular domains could be desirable to make it even easier to use by subject matter experts who are not skilled programmers.

The diagnostic/tutorial (RuleTutor) system currently under development is best suited for cognitive procedural tasks. Nonetheless, this system is based on an extensible design, and thereby opens up the possibility of eventually extending the system to include more general curricular content involving higher-order rules (e.g., problem solving—Scandura, 1977a, heuristics—Scandura, Durnin & Wulfeck, 1974, inference—Scandura, 1973a, learning—Scandura, 1974) and alternative perspectives on that content (e.g., Durnin & Scandura, 1973; Scandura, 1977a, Ch. 10). Also on our long-term agenda are plans to automate the method of structural analysis (Scandura, 1984a). Combined with the proposed ICBI authoring system, authors would not even have to use PRODOC (to create rule FLOWforms). Automated structural analysis would do this inductively, given only samples of solved problems.

AUTHOR NOTE

This project is being funded in part with Federal Funds from the Department of Education under contract numbers 400-85-1020 and 400-86-0060. The contents of this publication do not necessarily reflect the views or policies of the Department nor does mention of trade names, commercial products or organizations imply endorsement by the U.S. Government. A more detailed account of many of the issues raised in this chapter is given in Scandura, J. M. and Scandura, A. B. The intelligent RuleTutor: a structured approach to intelligent tutoring— phase II. *Journal of Structural Learning*, 1987, 9.

REFERENCES

Ausubel, D. P. (1963). *The psychology of meaningful verbal learning: an introduction to school learning.* New York: Grune & Stratton.

Anderson, J. R. (1978). *Language, memory and thought.* Hillsdale, NJ: Erlbaum Associates.

Anderson, J. R., et al. (1984). *Development of intelligent computer-based tutors for high school mathematics.* Unpublished NSF proposal.

Brown, J. S., & Burton, R. R. (1978). Diagnostic models for procedural bugs in basic mathematical skills. *Cognitive Science, 2*(2) 155–192.

Brown, J. S., Burton, R. R., & de Kleer, J. (1982). Pedagogical, natural language and knowledge engineering techniques in SOPHI I, II, and III. In D. Sleeman & J. S. Brown (Eds.), *Intelligent tutoring systems.* New York: Academic Press.

Burton, R. R. (1982). Diagnosing bugs. In D. Sleeman & J. S. Brown (Eds.), *Intelligent tutoring systems.* New York: Academic Press.

Clancey, W. J. (1982). Tutoring rules for guiding a case method dialogue. In D. Sleeman & J. S. Brown (Eds.), *Intelligent tutoring systems.* New York: Academic Press.

Collins, A., et al. (1975). Reasoning from incomplete knowledge. In D. G. Bobrow & A. Collins (Eds.), *Representation and understanding: Studies in cognitive science* (pp. 383–414). New York: Academic Press.

Dienes, Z. P. (1960). *Building up mathematics*. London: Hutchinson.

Durnin, J. H., & Scandura, J. M. (1973). An algorithmic approach to assessing behavior potential: Comparison with item forms and hierarchical analysis. *Journal of Educational Psychology, 65,* 262–273.

Hilke, R., Kempf, W. F., & Scandura. J. M. (1977). Deterministic and probabilistic theorizing in structural learning. In H. Spada & W. F. Kemp (Eds.), *Structural models of thinking and learning*. Bern: Huber.

Landa, L. N. (1978). Some problems in algo-heuristic theory of thinking, learning and instruction. In J. Scandura & C. Brainerd (Eds.), *Structural/Process models of complex human behavior*. Alphen aan den Rijn, The Netherlands: Sijthoff & Noordhoff.

Minsky, M. A. (1975). Framework for representing knowledge. In P. Winston (Ed.), *The psychology of computer vision*. New York: McGraw-Hill.

Pask, G. (1975). *Conversation, cognition and learning*. Amsterdam: Elsevier.

Resnick, L. B. (1984). *Intelligent tutors for elementary school mathematics*. Unpublished NSF proposal.

Scandura, J. M. (1970). The role of rules in behavior: Toward an operational definition of what (rule) is learned. *Psychological Review, 77,* 516–533.

Scandura, J. M. (1971). Deterministic theorizing in structural learning. *Journal of Structural Learning, 3,* 21–53.

Scandura, J. M. (1973a). *Structural learning I: Theory and research*. London: Gordon & Breach.

Scandura, J. M. (1973b). On higher-order rules. *Educational Psychologist, 10,* 159–160.

Scandura, J. M. (1974). The role of higher-order rules in problem solving. *Journal of Experimental Psychology, 120,* 984–991.

Scandura, J. M. (1977a). (with collaboration). *Problem solving: A structural/process approach with instructional implications*. New York: Academic Press.

Scandura, J. M. (1977b). Structural approach to instructional problems. *American Psychologist, 32,* 33–53.

Scandura, J. M. (1977c). A deterministic approach to research in instructional science. *Educational Psychologist, 12,* 118–127.

Scandura, J. M. (1980). Theoretical foundations of instruction: A systems alternative to cognitive psychology. *Journal of Structural Learning, 6,* 347–394.

Scandura, J. M. (1981a). Problem solving in schools and beyond: Transitions from the naive to the neophyte to the master. *Educational Psychologist, 16,* 139–150.

Scandura, J. M. (1981b). Microcomputer-based system for authoring, diagnosis and instruction in algorithmic content. *Educational Technology,* 13–19.

Scandura, J. M. (1982). Structural (cognitive task) analysis: A method for analyzing content; Part I: Background and empirical research. *Journal of Structural Learning, 7,* 101–114.

Scandura, J. M. (1984a). Structural (cognitive task) analysis: A method for analyzing content; Part II: Toward precision, objectivity and systematization. *Journal of Structural Learning, 8,* 1–28.

Scandura, J. M. (1984b). Structural (cognitive task) analysis: A method for analyzing content; Part III: Validity and reliability. *Journal of Structural Learning, 8,* 173–193.

Scandura, J. M. (1985). System issues in problem solving research. *Journal of Structural Learning, 9,* 49–62.

Scandura, J. M. (1987). A cognitive approach to software development: the PRODOC system and associated methodology. *Journal of Pascal, Ada and Modula 2, 6,* 10–25.

Scandura, J. M. (1978). Discussion of selected issues in structural learning. In J. M. Scandura & C. J. Brainerd (Eds.), *Structural/process models of complex human behavior*. Alphen ann den Ryn. The Netherlands: Sijthoff & Noordhoff.

Scandura, J. M., & Durnin, J. H. (1977). Algorithmic analysis of algebraic proofs. In J. M. Scandura, *Problem solving: A structural/process approach with instructional implications.* New York: Academic Press.

Scandura, J. M., Durnin, J. H., et al. (1971). *An algorithmic approach to mathematics: Concrete behavioral foundations.* New York: Harper & Row.

Scandura, J. M., Durnin, J. H., & Wulfeck, W. H. II. (1974). Higher-order rule characterization of heuristics for compass and straight-edge construction in geometry. *Artificial Intelligence, 5,* 149–183.

Scandura, J. M., & Durnin J. H. (1977). Algorithmic analysis of algebraic proofs. In J. M. Scandura, *Problem solving: A structural process approach with instructional implications.* New York: Academic Press.

Scandura, J. M., Stone, D., & Scandura, A. B. (1986). An intelligent RuleTutor for diagnostic testing and instruction. *Journal of Structural Learning, 9,* 15–61.

Scandura, J. M., & Scandura, A. B. (1987). The intelligent RuleTutor: a structural approach to intelligent tutoring—phase II. *Journal of Structural Learning, 9,* 195–259.

Wulfeck, W. H., & Scandura, J. M. (1977). Theory of adaptive instruction with application to sequencing in teaching problem solving. In J. M. Scandura, *Problem solving: A structural/process approach with instructional implications.* New York: Academic Press.

15 Authoring Systems for Intelligent Tutoring Systems On Personal Computers

Greg Kearsley
*Courseware, Inc.**

INTRODUCTION

A major obstacle to the wider use of ICAI programs is the significant amount of time required for their development as well as the scarceness of ICAI development expertise. At the current time, ICAI programs are written in AI languages such as LISP or PROLOG. To construct an ICAI program, a great deal of knowledge about AI methodology and programming techniques is needed.

To increase the availability of ICAI programs, it is necessary to substantially reduce the development time involved and the heavy reliance on AI knowledge. This can be achieved through the development of an Intelligent Authoring System (IAS), i.e., a program generator for ICAI programs. A wide range of authoring tools exist for conventional CAI (see Kearsley, 1982, 1984) ranging from authoring languages such as Pilot, Tutor or Tencore to authoring systems such as PCD (Control Data PLATO), IAS (McGraw-Hill), SAM (LearnCom) or WISE (Wicat). There is no reason why analogous authoring tools should not be developed for ICAI. The development of a prototype IAS for a personal computer is the goal of our research.

A large number of program generators now exist for expert systems (e.g., M1, TIMM, Rulemaster, EXSYS, etc.). These program generators provide inference engines capable of producing inferences (via backward or forward chaining) based on the rules provided by the author. The author specifies the knowledge network in terms of facts and their relationships. All information required is prompted and entered in specified fields. Harmon and King (1985) provide a

---

*Author's current address: Park Row Software, 1135-C Garnet Ave., San Diego, CA 92109.

good overview of the features and capabilities of current expert system generators.

The first question that arises is whether these expert system generators could be used as an IAS. While these expert system programs contain components that are needed for an IAS (e.g., rule formation and inferencing capabilities), they lack many of the essential ingredients of an IAS including the ability to construct a student model, design screens, create graphics, organize lessons, and provide learner control options. Furthermore, the purpose of the resulting programs are different. An expert system program is designed to ask questions and provide advice based on the answers given. An ICAI program is intended to teach something and uses diagnostic and tutoring rules. Most importantly, the student should be able to *ask* questions about the subject domain, which is not a current capability of expert systems (other than how or why questions about the inferences made).

A major issue in developing an IAS is the question of whether a single authoring framework would be suitable for the development of different types of ICAI programs. For example, are the authoring processes involved in developing a game like WEST (Burton & Brown, 1979) similar to those involved in the development of a procedural simulation such as SOPHIE (Brown, Burton, & de Kleer, 1982) or STEAMER (Hollan, Hutchins, & Weitzman, 1984), or in casual reasoning programs such as WHY (Stevens & Collins, 1980)? It is difficult to use a conventional authoring system designed primarily for drills or concepts for the development of procedural simulations or games; hence, the generality of an IAS across different authoring approaches is a critical question to this project.

A related issue has to do with the generality of the knowledge representations, tutoring rules, and diagnostic (debugging) strategies that have been described and used by ICAI workers. It is not clear that such structures apply across different kinds of instructional settings (even at the meta-levels). In fact, it is not even obvious for programs that tackle the same task domains. For example, in the domain of programming tutors, BIP (Barr, Beard, Atkinson, 1976) provided the student with a set of control options to gauge their own learning progress, FLOW (Gentner, 1979) tried to understand what the student was learning and PROUST (Johnson & Soloway, 1985) is a goal-driven bug analyzer. Although each of these programs deals with programming, they all work quite differently.

Another way of stating this issue is whether it is better to adopt a top-down (generalizable) vs. bottom up (data driven) approach to the development of an IAS. In the top-down strategy, the same IAS would be used to generate any ICAI program. With a bottom-up strategy, an IAS would generate a specific kind of ICAI program (e.g., a coach, diagnostic tutor, etc.). Current work on expert systems generators and past work on conventional authoring systems suggests that the top-down strategy will work. However, the diversity of ICAI programs argues for a bottom-up approach. We have explored both strategies and discuss the respective merits of each in this paper.

Ideally, the design of an IAS would be based on research and theory about the development of ICAI programs. However, this kind of information is very scarce. ICAI workers tend to focus on the cognitive science or AI programming techniques associated with their programs and not on the development process itself. Clancey (1981) compares the process of developing MYCIN (an expert system program) versus GUIDON (a tutor for MYCIN). He states:

> At a certain level, MYCIN is aphasic—able to perform, but unable to talk about what it knows. Teaching and explanation, we came to realize, place different demands on an expert than simply solving problems. A teacher can provide analogies, multiple views, and levels of explanation which are unknown to MYCIN. (p. 12)

Anderson, Boyle, and Reiser (1985) argue that the ACT theory of cognition provides a basis for developing ICAI programs and illustrate this argument with descriptions of a geometry and LISP tutor. The major component of the ACT theory that forms the basis for ICAI programs is production rule methodology, specifically forward and backward inferencing. Other aspects of ACT which are relevant to the design of ICAI programs are goal structures, working memory limitations, and "knowledge compilation" (acquisition of new production rules through experience).

Woolf and McDonald (1984) discuss the design of a Meno-tutor, a generic tutor. A critical component of their tutor is a discourse management network that operates at three hierarchial levels: pedagogy, strategy and tactics. The pedagogical level includes very general states such as introduce, tutor, or complete. Strategic states are more specific such as explore a competency, describe the domain or repair a misconception. Tactical states are very detailed operations, e.g., generate an exploratory question, propose an analogy or suggest a new topic. Corresponding to each state are rules and meta-rules which attempt to satisfy the condition. The control structure of Meno-Tutor is suggestive of the mechanism that might be required for an IAS.

One point worth emphasizing is that even though ICAI programs represent a fundamentally different type of learning environment than provided by conventional CAI programs, quite a lot of the features of conventional authoring systems apply to the design of ICAI. This includes screen design, error handling, user control, using student response data, and graphics (Kearsley, 1986). Thus, attention should be paid to incorporating those capabilities in the design of an IAS.

BASIC COMPONENTS OF ICAI PROGRAMS

As mentioned in the Introduction, each ICAI program created to date has been unique. However, a set of basic components can be identified that are present in

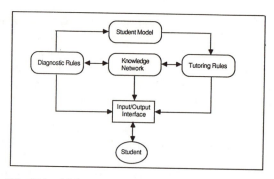

FIG. 15.1. Major components of an ICAI program.

most, if not all, ICAI programs. These components are depicted in Fig. 15.1: a knowledge network, a student model, error diagnostic rules, tutoring rules,and an input/output interface. The knowledge network represents the content to be taught in terms of concepts, rules, examples and their interrelationships. The student model is the representation of what the student has learned and currently knows. Error diagnostic rules are used to identify student misunderstandings and update the student model. Tutoring (coaching) rules determine what should be taught to the student given the current state of the student model. The input/output interface handles all input analysis and display functions.

The basic operation of an ICAI program is as follows: The student model is continuously compared to the knowledge network to determine what the student knows and does not know. This comparison generates discrepancies which are analyzed by the teaching rules. The teaching rules identify what components of the knowledge network should be presented next. The error rules identify misconceptions and mistakes in the responses or questions produced by the student, provide appropriate feedback, and update the student model accordingly. The teaching process continues until there is no identifiable discrepancy between the student model and the knowledge network.

At the heart of an ICAI program is a set of inferencing mechanisms. All input to the program must be parsed (i.e., decoded) regardless of what format it takes (e.g., keywords, menu selections, mathematical expressions, natural language, etc.). This input must be translated into some canonical form such as a list/tree structure. Once the input has been parsed, it is operated upon by one or more pattern matchers. Pattern matchers compare a response against expressions in the knowledge network, error/tutoring rules, or student model components. Whenever a match is found, the appropriate action is taken or output is generated.

Inferencing occurs between each component of an ICAI program as indicated in Fig. 15.1. For example, inferencing may be needed to decode or disambiguate input (particularly if natural language is used). Inferencing may be needed to determine what is wrong with a student response (i.e., apply diagnostic rules).

384

Inferencing may also be needed to determine what the specific discrepancy is between the student model and knowledge network and what tutoring rule to apply. All of these inferencing steps require sophisticated pattern-matching and searching techniques.

It is important to realize that some ICAI programs do not contain all of these components but focus on one or two of them. For example, a diagnostic tutor may only identify students mistakes and not provide any corrective feedback. In addition, past ICAI programs have implemented the four major components in different ways. The challenge in constructing an IAS is to establish a generic form of the four basic components and inferencing mechanisms that can be used across different instructional applications and problems.

How does the basic structure of an ICAI program just described compare with conventional CAI programs? All of the components of an ICAI program exist in conventional CAI programs in a rudimentary form. However, these components are not explicit and distinct in conventional CAI programs. The knowledge network is implemented as text display instructions (facts) or equations (procedures). The student model is some sort of counter or buffer that accumulates student performance data. Teaching and error rules are embedded in the branching instructions used to control the sequence of presentations or generate feedback messages.

While all conventional programming/authoring languages provide capabilities to parse input, match strings, and generate output, only a crude level of inferencing is available (e.g., downshifting, spelling tolerances, variable substitutions). Because it is primarily the inferencing mechanisms that provide the intelligence in ICAI programs, it is no surprise that this aspect would largely be absent from conventional CAI programs.

The implications of these differences for authoring systems are as follows. Traditional authoring tools have allowed people to create courseware in which the content and logic is intermixed. Flow of control is determined by prespecified branching. Teaching and error rules are embedded in these branching instructions and cannot be made explicit. There is also no facility for building an explicit student model other than in terms of counters and buffers. Because of these limitations, it is not possible to develop programs that are capable of understanding what they teach and what the student has or has not learned.

Compared to authoring systems for conventional CAI, an IAS requires the same specifications of content, instructional strategies, and response feedback. However, this information is provided in a much different form. Content is stored as a knowledge network, instructional strategies are implemented as tutoring rules, and response feedback is provided via diagnostic rules. In addition, an IAS does a considerable amount of "housekeeping" in the process of creating an ICAI lesson (e.g., generation of inference rules, modification of property lists, student model creation, etc.).

An intelligent authoring system must allow the author to:

- Create and modify a knowledge network consisting of either facts/concepts or procedures/functions.
- Specify and modify error and teaching rules linked to the information in the knowledge network.
- Specify and modify the format of user input, program output, and screen displays.
- Link together different lessons based upon specific states of the student model.
- Identify inconsistencies and incompleteness in the knowledge network, error rules, and teaching rules.

The ICAI program created must be able to:

- Create a student model and continuously modify the student model based on actions of the error and teaching rules.
- Compare the student model and knowledge network and identify differences.
- Apply the error/teaching rules to the differences between the student model and knowledge network to generate output (in the form of error diagnostics or tutoring/coaching).
- Parse and match all input.
- Derive inferences for the four basic components.

In the following sections, we discuss the design of two versions of an IAS: A generalized authoring environment for creating mixed initiative tutors and a specific authoring environment for a search space diagnostic tutor.

A GENERALIZED AUTHORING SYSTEM

This section describes attempts to design a generalized authoring system for a mixed initiative tutor. A prototype system was implemented on a Cemcorp ICON system. The prototype was implemented in C and generated Prolog programs.

The distinctive characteristic of a mixed initiative tutor (e.g., SCHOLAR, SOPHIE) is that it can carry on a conversational dialog with the student. The tutor attempts to guide the student to discover the major concepts or principles of the subject matter. The student always has the capability to ask questions and hence can direct the course of instruction.

The pedagogical unit in a mixed initiative tutor is a dialog. The author constructs the framework for a series of dialogs about different topics. The IAS must allow the author to create these dialogs and assemble them together into a conversation. The role of diagnostic and tutoring rules is to direct the course of the dialog and determine when a shift from one dialog to another is appropriate. In conventional CAI, dialogs correspond to lessons and a conversation corresponds to a curriculum.

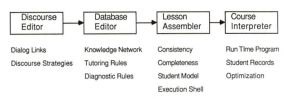

FIG. 15.2.   IAS structure.

Figure 15.2 provides an overview of the four major components of the IAS. The discourse editor allows the author to organize the dialogs (lessons) into a conversation (curriculum) and specify different discourse strategies. The database editor is used to create the knowledge network, diagnostic rules, and tutoring rules. The lesson assembler performs consistency/completeness checking and generates the run-time ICAI program. The course interpreter assembles a conversation out of separate dialogs. Associated with each of these major functional components are data and help files. Each of these major functions is described in more detail below.

Discourse Editor

The discourse editor allows the author to graphically define and modify (add, delete, copy, describe) the dialogs in a conversation and to select different dialog strategies for a dialog. It also allows the author to specify the rules that dictate when a conversation should shift from one dialog to another (i.e., sequencing of dialogs). This is done by specifying the state of the student model that will result in leaving one dialog and starting a new one.

The discourse editor consists of a single screen as shown in Fig. 15.3. When the edit function is selected, the author can define dialogs and specify the kind of discourse strategy associated with each (e.g., generalize from examples, use analogies, derive examples from rules, etc.). By means of a link function, the author can connect dialogs together and specify when the link occurs (e.g., a certain state of the student model, total number of types of errors, presence or absence of knowledge objects).

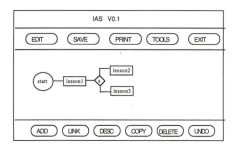

FIG. 15.3.   Discourse editor.

Database Editor

The database editor allows the author to specify eleven types of knowledge objects. These objects are: knowledge, answer, text, picture, window, dictionary, state, precision, entry and exit. Knowledge objects are used to represent the concepts or procedures to be taught. Knowledge objects define the knowledge network and are also used to answer questions asked by the student. Answer objects present error diagnostic rules and are used to analyze or acknowledge student responses and modify the student model. Text objects contain text statements to be displayed. Picture objectives are used to display graphics objects. Window objects are used to define when/where text and picture objects are displayed. Texts, picture, and window objects correspond to teaching rules and are referred to by knowledge and answer objects.

Dictionary objects are used to define the words used in knowledge and state objects. State objects provide a mechanism to simulate systems in the subject domain and are needed to evaluate/generate answers to student questions. Precision objects are used to define when the student's understanding of a knowledge object is complete and allow the author to set the precision of the student model. Note that the student model itself is automatically generated by the system according to the characteristics of the dialog as specified by the author in the discourse editor. Entry and exit objects are used to set the student model to default values and to specify when to exit a dialog. Entry and exit objects are defined by the author in the discourse editor.

The database editor screen provides a set of fields corresponding to these eleven objects (as well as a message window). The author can enter objects in any order desired. The editor checks the syntax of all objects entered and identifies errors.

Lesson Assembler

The lesson assembler controls the translation and linking of the database files into an executable form. It consists of two major functions: the translator and a checker. The translator converts database files into an executable program and links to a run-time shell. The lesson checker checks the consistency and completeness of the database files, particularly the interaction of the knowledge, display and answer objects. The run-time shell contains a number of critical input/output functions including natural language and display management capabilities.

The lesson assembler screen with the translate function invoked is shown in Fig. 15.4. The database name field specifies the name of the IAS database file that the user wants to translate. The target name field identifies the name of the file to which the resulting output should be written. When the translate pop-up window appears the initial value of the database name field is the lesson the user last worked on, either in the IAS database editor, or in the lesson assembler.

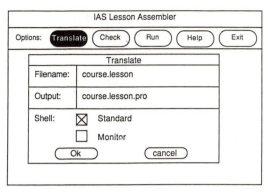

FIG. 15.4.   IAS lesson assembler.

The lesson checker takes an IAS database file created by the database editor and checks for contradictory and conflicting rules. Since the order of the rules is used during execution to resolve all conflicts (the first rule wins), the checker is a useful tool to identify possible authoring errors to the user. Inconsistency may occur between any two knowledge objects, state objects, answer objects, or presentation objects. All pairs of objects within these groups are checked.

The execution shell provides the "glue code" that guides the interaction of the lesson objects. This code is appended to a translated IAS database file by the translator. There are two execution shells. The standard execution shell is the one normally chosen. The monitor shell is chosen when the user wishes to include debugging tools in the linked output. While this shell is slower, it allows the user three additional run-time commands that can be used to debug the flow of the ICAI program. These commands are:

Student Model.—This command causes the ICAI program to print out each value of the student model and its associated knowledge objects. If unexpected program flow is occurring, this can be used to monitor the student model between each prompt.

Explain n. (where n is a positive integer)—This command displays the last n rules (knowledge, state, presentation, and answer) that fired with resulting responses. This allows the user to determine how the present state was reached.

Completeness n. (where n is a positive integer)—This command generates the entire execution tree from the current state to a depth of n and identifies any sequences of rules that would cause the ICAI program to reach a state from which it can't proceed. This happens when no presentation objects can be presented to evoke a response about the student's understanding of any knowledge object.

Course Interpreter

The course interpreter initiates the execution of dialogs that make up the course. The order of the dialogs and the entry/exit conditions are specified by the author using the discourse editor. The course interpreter takes different actions depending upon the student's course status. If the student is just starting the course, a student record file must be initiated. If the student has previously been through the course, the interpreter must determine how to restart the student.

The course interpreter includes functions to register students and allow the author to specify what response records are to be stored. It also includes functions to optimize the run-time program. This includes program compression and identification of inefficient program execution. An additional function of the course interpreter could be copy protection.

A DATA-DRIVEN AUTHORING SYSTEM FOR A SEARCH SPACE DIAGNOSTIC TUTOR

This section describes work on SEARCH, a search space diagnostic tutor. This system was originally implemented on an IBM PC (512K) with Golden Hill Common LISP as the run-time language and subsequently converted to Pascal. The system is described in more detail in Sleeman (1987).

In contrast to the generalized mixed initiative tutor just discussed, the authoring capabilities for SEARCH are specific to the needs of a particular learning environment. SEARCH resembles a number of ICAI programs that have been developed such as the geometry tutor of Anderson (Anderson et al., 1985) and ANNOLAND (Brown, 1983).

The Tutor

SEARCH is intended to help students with derivations and proofs within a specified domain of mathematics or science (e.g., Algebra, Trigonometry, Predicate Calculus, Mechanics, etc.). The system presents a problem for the student to solve. The problem is either an identity or other expression that the student is required to manipulate. The problem is generated by the system, or retrieved from a list of problems that are supplied by the author. In either case, the selection of the problem is based on issues specified by the author and the state of the student model. An issue is meant to be a method of transforming equations, whether a single transformation, or the interaction of several transformations and represents the skills to be acquired by the student.

The transformation is applied to the current expression and results in a new current expression. A tree is built from the current expressions. The student is allowed to backtrack through the tree and pick other branches. The system automatically re-displays the updated tree after each student action.

The system analyzes the student's transformation choice. If the choice matches the system's preferred choice, positive feedback is given to the student and the student model is modified to show that the student understands the use of that transformation and possibly derivation issues that include the use of that transformation. If the student's choice does not match the system's preferred choice, further analysis is required.

The system applies the student's transformation and attempts to solve the problem from the new point. If the problem is solvable in equal or less steps than before, then the student is assumed to be taking an alternate but equally good solution path. However, the student model is modified to reflect that the student may have chosen the alternate path because he or she doesn't understand the transformation or issues involved in selecting the preferred path.

If the student's choice results in a worse (or at least no better) position for solving the problem, the system suggests that the student might backtrack and try something else. However, as long as the system can solve the problem from a given point, the student is allowed to continue. If the solution path exceeds the specified maximum depth, the student is required to backtrack. The student model is modified to reflect the student's lack of understanding of the issues involved in picking a better path.

Eventually, the student solves the problem (the student is not allowed to fail). The system then shows the student what it would have picked at each step that doesn't match the student's choice. If the student's perceived understanding of the lesson is determined to be incomplete (according to the tutoring rules), the system presents the next problem. After the student demonstrates the level of understanding specified by the author or completes all of the problems provided for a lesson, a diagnostic summary of the student's performance across all problems is generated focusing on the issues learned and not learned.

The main display screen for SEARCH is shown in Fig. 15.5. It consists of the following components: lesson title, problem status window, display window, the control options, and the prompt/response window. The problem status window displays the goal expression to be derived and the current form of the expression to be transformed. The display window is used to give the initial directions, list

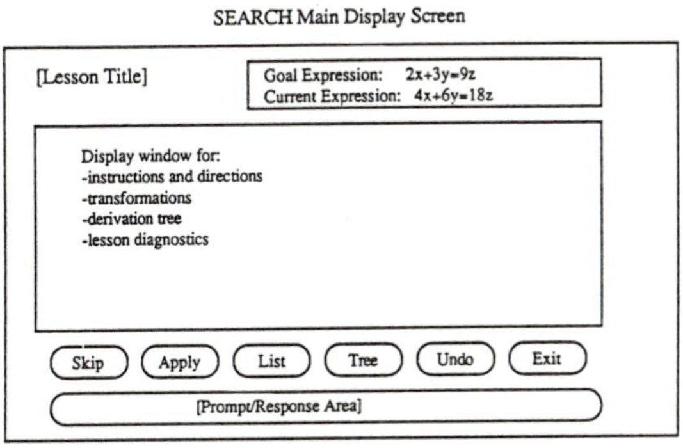

SEARCH Main Display Screen

| [Lesson Title] | Goal Expression: 2x+3y=9z |
| | Current Expression: 4x+6y=18z |

Display window for:
-instructions and directions
-transformations
-derivation tree
-lesson diagnostics

(Skip) (Apply) (List) (Tree) (Undo) (Exit)

[Prompt/Response Area]

FIG. 15.5.   SEARCH main display screen.

the transformations, show the derivation tree, and provide diagnostic analysis after the student has finished the problem.

Authoring Capabilities for SEARCH

The author specifies the content, logic, and other major parameters of SEARCH. This includes:

- the lesson name
- a problem description (optional)
- the initial and goal expressions
- the transformations
- the issues
- tutoring rules associated with specific issues or transformations
- the search depth
- selection rules for problems

In addition, the author has standard editing functions (e.g., add, delete, copy).

Authoring in SEARCH takes place at two levels: course and lesson. Course level authoring involves the specification and modification of the lessons that make up a course. The author can add, delete or copy lessons and specify branching rules between lessons, i.e., if certain lessons are to be skipped based upon the state of the student model in a previous lesson.

Figure 15.6 shows the SEARCH authoring display for the lesson level. The author completes the fields for each problem in the lesson. The most important part of the specification is the Tutoring rules (T-rules) which specify actions to be taken within a lesson if a certain state of the student model is present. This allows the author to adapt the presentation of problems to the performance of the student. In the absence of a T-rule specifying otherwise, problems are displayed to a student in the original order defined.

Note that this authoring capability will work for any problem domain that

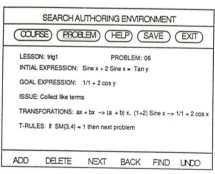

FIG. 15.6.   Lesson level authoring display.

involves derivations or proofs. Thus, it represents a fairly general authoring interface within the given confines of a certain type of problem domain.

LANGUAGE CONSIDERATIONS

A major consideration in the design and implementation of an IAS is the choice of programming languages. Note that the criteria for selecting the language for development of the authoring system may be different than the criteria for the generated ICAI programs. While some symbolic and recursive processing is required of the authoring system, most of the processing involves guiding the author through the courseware development process. This process includes extensive use of graphics and screen layouts and involves close interaction with the file management component of the operating system. As a result, we chose C as the development language for our prototype authoring systems.

For the ICAI programs, however, Wallach and Izdebski (1985) found that ICAI programs took ten times longer to develop in C as compared to LISP. This difference is due to the noninteractive nature of the C development environment and the difficulty of keeping track of the symbolic structures in C. Yet once the program was developed in LISP it was relatively easy to convert to C or PAS-CAL. This conversion is highly desirable from a performance viewpoint because the C program ran 20 times as fast as the LISP program and was considerably more memory efficient.

LISP was unavailable on the system used to develop our ICAI prototypes so we used PROLOG instead. Each authoring system generated PROLOG code that was linked to a PROLOG execution shell. If performance (either response time or memory) had been a problem, the ICAI program would have been converted to C.

There are a number of theoretical and practical factors that need to be taken into account in the selection of an implementation language for ICAI including data representation structures, memory management, performance, transportability, costs, and licensing. On the basis of our work, we feel that it is best to use an AI based language for design and development work and then to translate to a conventional language such as C or PASCAL for run-time programs. This strategy takes advantage of the power and flexibility of AI languages for design, and the performance, efficiency and portability of general purpose languages for delivery. Further discussion of ICAI programming issues can be found in Wallach (1987).

CONCLUSIONS

The primary rationale for developing an IAS is to reduce the development time of ICAI programs and reduce the dependence on specialized programming exper-

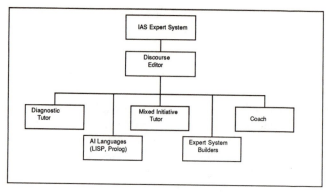

FIG. 15.7. Authoring environment for ICAI development.

tise. Based on our experience designing and implementing IAS prototypes, we believe that authoring systems can achieve both of the objectives. We also believe that construction of an operational IAS on a personal computer is both feasible and highly desirable. However, we think that an ICAI authoring environment is an important consideration in the cost-effective development of ICAI programs. Figure 15.7 illustrates our conception of what tools should be available in such an environment. The key concept is a variety of different tools to meet different development needs.

One major conclusion about the use of an IAS relative to a conventional CAI authoring tool is that the effectiveness of the resulting ICAI lesson is much more dependent upon the completeness of the teaching model as represented in the knowledge network, teaching rule, and error rule components. In particular, if the knowledge network is not sufficiently detailed, then the student model generated will not allow much precision in terms of representing student understanding. Also, if the teaching rules are not very elaborate or detailed, the resulting instruction is very simple minded. In a conventional CAI program, only the fragments of a teaching model needed for specific branches is revealed; in an ICAI program, the entire model is required.

A major stumbling block in the design of an IAS is the user interface. In both our generalized and specific IAS prototypes, the author needed to know how to structure the knowledge network and tutoring rules, i.e., had to already be knowledgeable about the design of ICAI programs. There is no guidance provided to help the author identify what concepts/procedures to teach, what diagnostic or tutoring rules to formulate, etc. Thus, as a prerequisite to the use of an IAS, the author must understand the design principles of ICAI programs, (or these principles should be built into the user interface).

As a pragmatic strategy for IAS development, we suggest that more IAS prototypes be built and used to develop different types of ICAI programs, revising the IAS as inadequacies are discovered. We further suggest that these IAS prototypes be used by experienced ICAI developers rather than novice developers. We believe that this strategy will lead to the fastest evolution of authoring systems for ICAI.

On the basis of our comparison of the generalized and data driven approaches to developing an IAS, we feel that a range of different authoring tools will be needed to create different types of ICAI programs. We suggest that intelligent authoring environments consisting of a collection of IAS and AI authoring tools will be needed (Fig. 15.7). As Fig. 15.7 shows, we anticipate that a discourse editor would be the common link or interface across different tools. In addition, an expert system that gives advice and guidance on how to design ICAI programs would also be desirable.

There are many important aspects of IAS design that have not been touched upon in this article. We have not discussed graphics or videodisc which are important elements of conventional CAI programs and will undoubtedly be significant factors in future ICAI programs. We have also not discussed hardware considerations such as memory or processing requirements. Most fundamentally, we have not addressed the research implications of IAS design for cognitive science or the practical implications of IAS availability for classroom use. Those issues constitute an agenda for further research in this area.

ACKNOWLEDGMENT

This work was done in conjunction with Bret Wallach of AP Labs and Iain Begg of Burroughs Canada who contributed many of the ideas presented in this article. The development of SEARCH was done in collaboration with Derek Sleeman of Stanford.

REFERENCES

Anderson, J. R., Boyle, C. F., & Reiser, B. J. (1985, April 26). Intelligent tutoring systems. *Science*, p. 456–462.

Barr, A., Beard, M., & Atkinson, R. C. (1976). The computer as a tutorial laboratory: The Stanford BIP project. *International Journal of Man Machine Studies, 8*, 567–596.

Brown, J. S. (1983). Idea amplifiers—New kinds of electronic learning environments. *Educational Horizons, 11*, 108–112.

Burton, R. R., & Brown, J. S. (1979). An investigation of computer coaching for informal learning activities. *International Journal of Man-Machine Studies, 11*, 5–24.

Brown, J. S., Burton, R. R., & de Kleer, J. (1982). Pedagogical, natural language, and knowledge engineering techniques in SOPHIE I, II, and III. In D. Sleeman & J. S. Brown (Eds.), *Intelligent tutoring systems*. New York: Academic Press.

Clancey, W. J. (1981, October). *Methodology for Building An Intelligent Tutoring System*. Depart. Computer Science Report STAN-CS-81-894, Stanford University.

Gentner, D. R. (1979). Toward an intelligent computer tutor. In H. O'Neil (Ed.), *Procedures for ISD*. New York: Academic Press.

Hollan, J. D., Hutchins, E. L., & Weitzman, L. (1984, Summer). STEAMER: An interactive inspectable simulation-based training system. *The AI Magazine*, pp. 15–25.

Johnson, W. L., & Soloway, E. (1985, April). PROUST. *Byte*. pp. 179–190.

Kearsley, G. (1982). Authoring systems in computer-based education. *Communications of the ACM, 25*(7), 429–437.

Kearsley, G. (1984). Authoring tools: An introduction. *Journal of Computer-Based Instruction, 11*(3), 67.

Kearsley, G. (1986). *Authoring*. Reading, MA: Addison-Wesley.

Sleeman, D. (1987). Micro-SEARCH: A "shell" for building systems to help students solve non-deterministic tasks. In G. Kearsley (Ed.), *Artificial intelligence and instruction*. Reading, MA: Addison-Wesley.

Stevens, A. L., & Collins, A. (1980). Multiple conceptual models of a complex system. In R. E. Snow, P. Federico, & W. E. Montague (Eds.), *Aptitude, learning and instruction* (Vol. 2). Hillsdale, NJ: Lawrence Erlbaum Associates.

Wallach, B. (1987). Development strategies for ICAI using small computers. In G. Kearsley (Ed.), *Artificial intelligence and instruction*. Reading, MA: Addison-Wesley.

Wallach, B., & Izdebski, L. (1985). Language tradeoffs in developing artificial intelligence programs for small computers. In G. Kearsley & I. Begg (Eds.), *Moving Intelligent CAI Into the Real World* (Burroughs Canada Technical Report PPD MTL-85-3).

Woolf, B., & McDonald, D. (1984, September). Building a computer tutor: Design issues. *IEEE Computer*, 61–73.

V DESIGNING MOTIVATING COURSEWARE

The exponential growth of microcomputers for both personal and educational use has resulted largely from the popularity of video games. Video games are not limited to the video arcades, into which adolescents and adults were pouring more than $5 billion worth of quarters per year a few years ago. While the personal computer has numerous functions in the home, by far their major home use has been for playing video games. In fact, some home computers were developed primarily to support games, only later adding the utility and applications software necessary for marketing a full product line. Although video games have fallen off in popularity and proportion of the computer market, they still are very prevalent. Why have they been so popular?

The video game phenomenon bears scrutiny by courseware developers for two reasons. First, we should know why video games are so compelling. Second, and related, gaming has become an increasingly prevalent technique in educational computing programs. In a study conducted by EPIE (Dunne, 1984), gaming techniques appeared in 48% of the educational software evaluated. So, knowing why gaming is so popular and how it best can be designed, designers can infer when and how to best apply gaming techniques to courseware.

The answer to the first question (why games are so compelling) is simple. Gaming increases student interest and motivation, so the motivational appeal of games is high (Dunne, 1984). Why are games so motivating? This question has produced many answers.

Loftus and Loftus (1983) point out three conceptual ingredients: sound and fury, death and destruction, and control of the computer. We all agree that these are probably unacceptable building blocks for instructional courseware. The most recurrent answer that is normally provided is competition—competition with ones' self, competition among peers, or competition against the machine. Competition with oneself and among others has been found to consistently motivate students to attend and perform (Neuman, 1985). However, I think that we would all agree that competition alone is also insufficient for designing instructional courseware with its learning orientation. We need a stronger, more psychologically based set of guidelines.

Based on his dissertation, Malone (1981a, 1981b) has provided the most comprehensive analysis of the characteristics that make instructional environments motivating. Those characteristics fit into three categories—challenge, fantasy, and curiosity. To make an instructional environment challenging, it should have a clear goal whose outcome is uncertain (variable difficulty level or multiple goal levels) yet is personally meaningful to the learner. Uncertainty, according to Malone, can be provided through such techniques as hidden information or randomness in the presentation, scorekeeping, and timed responses. Games must provide an increasing amount of challenge to the user in order to maintain their attention. Second, good instructional games provide fantasy goals in their environment. The computer environment should assume aspects of the environment in which the learner is playing, e.g., a space trip, a football game, or a train robbery. The instruction can be interwoven into the fabric of the fantasy in a variety of ways. The third characteristic of good instructional games is that they elicit and then satisfy curiosity. Most simply, gaming environments should be novel and surprising. These can be achieved by graphics, animation, or music. Malone (1981b) points out that they also maintain curiosity by increasing the level of difficulty and complexity that challenges the learner, and, he has provided one of the most useful sets of guidelines for developing instructional games that we have.

The compelling effects of video games result from some well-established psychological effects. For instance, the most compelling games provide only partial reinforcement (variable interval and/or ratio reinforcement schedule, to be more precise), which produces performance that is most resistant to extinction, so users keep plugging the quarters in (Loftus & Loftus, 1983). Other reinforcement techniques also function to enhance the schedule effects. For instance, large magnitude and/or multiple reinforcement and immediate reinforcement are often used by game designers. This combination of reinforcement effects provides the basis for the intrinsic motivation (competition with oneself or against the machine). Loftus and Loftus also mention the extrinsic effects implicit in the admiration of peers for being a game champion. But these reinforcement techniques all have focused on positive reinforcement. They also mention a form of negative reinforcement which also compels the investment of an additional quarter—the reduction or elimination of regret. Over time, a player's skill improves as she or he comes closer to winning or completing the game. The mistake that prevents it is more frustrating the closer the player comes. So, with the investment of another quarter, the player can reduce the regret associated with the mistake and in doing so, come closer to the ideal performance. So she or he plays again.

The characteristics of good instructional games provided by Malone's work, and the other psychological effects noted provide designers with some useful guidelines for designing instructional courseware . . . probably the best available to date. Courseware designers may have difficulty with them for two related reasons. First, they are not comprehensive, and second, they aren't presented in the context of a development model with which they are likely to be familiar. They do not emerge from the instructional development field and are not associated with any well-known courseware or instructional development process. This final section of the book seeks to provide just that orientation.

INTRODUCTION TO PART V

John Keller has been one of the few (if not only) instructional designers who has tried to systematically and comprehensively incorporate motivation theory into the instructional design process. Instructional design models and instructional development processes most often focus on the cognitive behavior and its performance characteristics, ignoring the need to motivate that performance. Too frequently, they make the implicit assumption that learners are intrinsically motivated. In his chapter, Keller begins by reviewing his ARCS model of instructional design. The model claims that there are four critical factors in the motivation of performance—attention, relevance, confidence, and satisfaction. The learner must attend to material in order to learn. The material must be relevant to the learner if learning is to occur. If the learning is to transfer, the learner must acquire confidence in his or her ability. Finally, learning must be reinforcing or satisfying. Keller applies the ARCS model to instructional development by identifying motivating strategies for each of the four factors. He then applies them to courseware design, providing some useful examples of the results. Courseware designers need to incorporate the principles presented in this chapter into their product, because they are truly relevant and will result in more satisfying courseware. That should be satisfying to the designer as well as the learner.

REFERENCES

Dunne, J. J. (1984). *Gaming approaches in educational software: An analysis of their use and effectiveness.* (ERIC Document ED 253 207).

Loftus, G. R., & Loftus, E. F. (1983). *Mind at play: The psychology of video games.* New York: Basic Books.

Malone, T. W. (1981a). Toward a theory of intrinsically motivating instruction. *Cognitive Science, 4,* 333–369.

Malone, T. W. (1981b). What makes computer games fun? *Byte, 6*(12), 258–277.

Neuman, D. (1985, April). *Learning disabilities and microcomputer courseware: A qualitative study of students' and teachers' interactions with instructional dimensions.* Paper presented at the annual meeting of the American Educational Research Association, Chicago.

16 Use of the ARCS Motivation Model in Courseware Design

John M. Keller
Katsuaki Suzuki
Florida State University

Motivation is a frequently used word in the literature of computers and education. The literature is filled with testimonials from educators who portray the excitement they have felt in working with students on computers. Yet there are frequent criticisms of courseware, and the overall number of students who can or even want to use computers is still surprisingly small (Pulos, Fisher, & Spage, 1985).

Several explanations of these discrepancies are possible. One is the distinction between the computer as a tool and a teacher. When used as a tool, as in the Logo programs (Papert, 1980), the computer is being used to help solve problems in the same way that a hammer, scalpel, or microwave oven does in the appropriate setting. The student identifies a goal, constructs a solution, then programs it on the computer to test it. Motivation is derived primarily from the person's interest in the task, and motivation for the tool will remain high as long as it helps accomplish the goal.

When used as a teacher, or tutor, in the instruction of regular subject matter such as math or language, a similar situation exists, but there are some important differences. The computer is still a means to an end; its function is to deliver the instruction. However the task to be accomplished tends to reside within the machine, and the form and structure of the task are governed in many ways by the machine. For example, access to information is controlled by the machine. Even when the learner is given control over access to different parts of the program, the machine has been programmed to control sequence, feedback, and other aspects of the information flow.

This external control has both positive and negative effects. In contrast to a book which allows easy access to any of its parts, and which is easy to scan to overview its style, structure, and content, a student gets an overview of course-ware gradually by means of menus, branching, and scrolling. This can be confin-ing and irritating, but it can also be stimulating. The ability to withhold access to information until the student has qualified for it allows the designer to build inquiry and mystery into the lesson.

Another reason for the discrepancy in the enthusiasm of some users and the lack of utilization by most is due to the way in which the computer's features are used in instructional design. Initially, in working on computer based instruction, there are features that are novel and appealing to many people. Instructional programs often contain animated graphics, sound effects, interactive commu-nication, automatic feedback, games, and freedom to make mistakes without fear of censure.

However, the novelty effect of these features extinguishes, and the learner becomes more responsive to the same features that influence motivation and performance in other learning settings. If the instruction is not well designed, or lacks motivational appeal beyond the novelty level, then learner involvement wanes, and the computer is abandoned. Pulos et al. (1985) document the low level of computer utilization in a typical middle school with a well-equipped computer facility.

Consequently, a central question in software design is how to make it appeal-ing at a level beyond the novelty effect in addition to making it efficient and instructionally effective. The purpose of this chapter is to describe a systematic approach to designing the motivational aspects of courseware. An overview of the approach, called the ARCS Model (Keller, 1984), is followed by a discussion of some general issues in regard to motivation and courseware design. This provides the basis for the remaining parts of the chapter. The first of these is a description of specific categories of strategies within the ARCS Model, and the second is a description of the motivational strategies that would typically be associated with the various parts of a characteristic piece of instructional soft-ware. The chapter concludes with a summary of strategies presented in a tabular format.

ARCS MODEL

Keller (1979, 1983) has developed a four factor macro-level theory to explain individual motivation. The theory was derived from a synthesis of the many areas of research that pertain to human motivation, and its purpose is to help answer questions about how to design motivational strategies into instruction that will stimulate or sustain students' motivation to learn. Although this theory has properties of both descriptive and prescriptive theories, it would best be classi-fied as a heuristic theory at this point of its development process. The elements of human motivation, even when narrowed to a concern for the motivation to learn

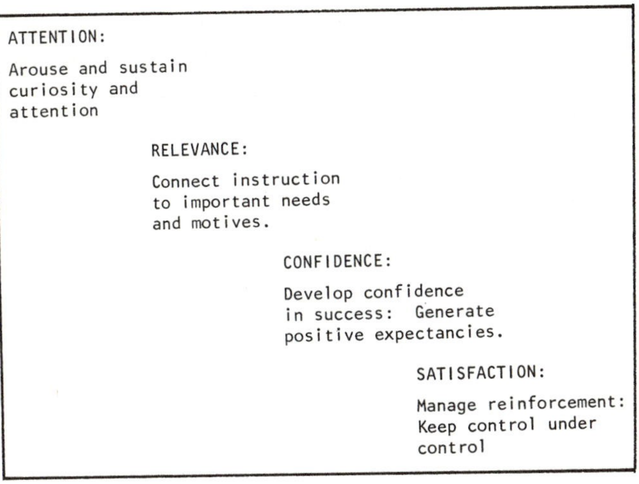

```
ATTENTION:

Arouse and sustain
curiosity and
attention

            RELEVANCE:

            Connect instruction
            to important needs
            and motives.

                        CONFIDENCE:

                        Develop confidence
                        in success:  Generate
                        positive expectancies.

                                    SATISFACTION:

                                    Manage reinforcement:
                                    Keep control under
                                    control
```

FIG. 16.1.   Four factors of the ARCS Model.

(Brophy, 1983; Brophy & Kher, in press), are complex and interactive which makes it difficult to create useful prescriptions. Instead, a problem-solving approach, using the ARCS Model for suggestions and guidance, will help insure improved motivational properties of courseware.

The ARCS model (Keller, 1984) postulates that there are four factors in the motivation to learn (Fig. 16.1). The first is attention (A), the second relevance (R), the third confidence (C), and the fourth satisfaction (S). In addition to defining the four factors, the model includes subcategories of motivational characteristics, and examples of strategies that stimulate or sustain each motivational element (Keller, 1984; Keller & Kopp, 1987). The model is used in conjunction with a systematic instructional design process to identify the motivational profile of the audience, establish motivational objectives, design motivational strategies, and field test and evaluate them.

Attention

The first element in student motivation to learn is attention. To be motivated, a learner's attention has to be aroused and sustained (Fig. 16.1). Information processing models, which are concerned with learning and performance rather than motivation, also begin with attention, but the emphasis is different. Their concern is with *directing* attention to the salient elements of the learning task or performance conditions. The motivational concern is with *getting* and *sustaining* attention.

In the ARCS model, the category called Attention includes those things that relate to curiosity (Berlyne, 1965; Maw & Maw, 1968), sensation seeking (Zuckerman, 1971), and other factors that help explain how attention is obtained.

In some respects, this is the easiest step in the motivational process. Our attention is aroused by things that are novel, surprising, incongruous, or uncertain (Berlyne, 1965; Kopp, 1982). To stimulate and sustain attention, the educator can introduce startling or unexpected events which arouse a perceptual level of curiosity, or engage the learners in inquiry oriented behavior that stimulates a deeper level of interest, which Berlyne (1965) calls epistemic curiosity.

Relevance

The second element in the ARCS model (Fig. 16.1) is Relevance. After the student's attention has been obtained, the student is likely to wonder why he or she should study the given material. "How," the student might ask, "does this relate to my interests or goals?" A positive answer to this question contributes to having a motivationally engaged student.

There is both an ends and a process aspect to relevance. The ends aspect is largely utilitarian. If the content of the instruction is perceived to be helpful in accomplishing important goals in the student's future, then the student is more likely to be motivated (Raynor, 1974). This is a traditional rationale offered by teachers for much of the material they teach. They will claim that the material might not have much immediate utility, but it will be important in the student's future. This works for students who have a future orientation, whose parents and culture provide modeling that supports the long-term benefits of presently useless knowledge, and who are simply more accepting of authority. It doesn't work for students who tend to live more totally in the present.

Ends oriented relevance does not always have to be aimed at the future. People like to enhance their current view of themselves and their feelings of being important and accepted human beings. Whenever the content of instruction can be related to the current interests and past experiences of students, then relevance will be increased.

Process influences on relevance are related primarily to methods of teaching in relation to need satisfaction in the students. For example, people who are high in the need for affiliation will be attracted by noncompetitive group situations (Alschuler, 1973). People high on the need for achievement enjoy situations that allow them to set goals and standards, and to have a high degree of personal responsibility for accomplishing the goal. A writing style that communicates a sense of enthusiasm for the topic and its importance can help generate similar feelings in the student.

Confidence

In addition to being interested and perceiving the relevance of the instruction, students have to believe that there is an acceptable probability of success before they will be highly motivated. In other words, they have to have confidence (Fig.

16.1). This does not mean that success has to be guaranteed. People often enjoy a challenge. But, the challenge has to be within acceptable boundaries.

There are several dimensions to confidence. Three of the most important are perceived competence, perceived control, and expectancy for success.

People have a desire to feel competent (White, 1959), and they are more motivated to engage in a task when they believe they have the competencies necessary to succeed. Yet, in learning situations, people are often faced with the requirement to master new skills and knowledge in areas that they don't feel competent. The conditions that are appropriate for optimizing motivation during the learning process are different from those which optimize motivation to perform a task after mastering it. In the first case, they need freedom to make mistakes without embarrassment, and in the second case they need a degree of challenge or risk to bring out their best.

Perceived control (Bandura, 1977; deCharms, 1976; Rotter, 1966) also contributes to confidence. When people believe that the choices they make and the degree of effort they expend have a direct influence on the consequences of their behavior, then they tend to be more confident about their behavior. In contrast, attitudes or feelings of helplessness (Keller, 1975; Seligman, 1975), or belief that luck and uncontrollable external forces are the primary influences on one's life (Weiner, 1980) tend to result in depression and lack of persistence. Features in the instruction that promote feelings of personal control over outcomes will help develop confidence and persistence.

A third component of confidence is expectancy for success which is similar to the self-fulfilling prophecy (Jones, 1977). When people believe that they can succeed at a task, they tend to exert greater effort which in turn leads to a higher rate of actual success. This would be a trivial observation if it weren't for the fact that people's expectations often differ from the objective probabilities of success. Consequently, a person may hold a belief which is untrue in an objective sense, but the belief itself leads to behaviors that make it come true.

Satisfaction

The fourth category of the ARCS Model is satisfaction (Fig. 16.1). If the outcomes of learners' efforts are consistent with their expectations, and if they feel good about the outcomes, then they are likely to remain motivated. Hence, the primary effect of Satisfaction is on continuing motivation as defined initially by Maehr (1976) and subsequently by Martin and Briggs (1986). Factors that influence satisfaction are reinforcement and feedback, intrinsic rewards, and cognitive evaluation.

The uses of reinforcement schedules to shape and maintain desired behaviors will help sustain motivation for a task. These conditioning systems, if applied properly, insure that the learner receives rewards predictably, and this helps the learner develop a sense of security in the consistency between behavior and outcomes. As long as the rewards are important to the learner, then the learner's motivation will remain high.

In some cases, an extrinsically applied system of rewards can decrease motivation, especially when the rewards are not a natural consequence of the learning, and are under the obvious control of someone else (Condry, 1977; Deci, 1975). If a person is intrinsically interested in a task, then extrinsic rewards can direct attention away from the task and to the rewards. In part, this is because intrinsic satisfaction is related to successful, self-determined effort (Cross, 1981). Deci and Ryan (1985), and Wlodkowski (1985) explain the complex relationships among instrinsically vs. extrinsically motivated behavior in relation to satisfaction.

The third element of satisfaction is that of equity, or cognitive evaluation. It is related to the notions of intrinsic satisfaction, but refers more specifically to the internal processes of evaluating outcomes in terms of expectations. This can be at a purely affective level, or at a cognitive level. That is, a person's initial "gut level" emotional response to a situation can be altered upon reflection. For example, you may have worked so hard on a project, been so ego-involved, and had such high expectation, that you are incapable of feeling good about the final product immediately after finishing it. But, a few positive comments from an objective observer who is not just trying to please you can cause you to reorient your perspective and feel much better. Adams (1965) and Deci and Porac (1978) deal with these issues.

To summarize, the ARCS Model contains four categories of factors that influence individual motivation. The process of motivation includes getting and sustaining the learner's attention, establishing the relevance of the instruction, building or maintaining the learner's confidence, and providing satisfying consequences.

ISSUES

In applying the ARCS model, or using any other approach to motivational design, there are many issues to consider in relation to the nature of motivation, the conditions that influence it, and its influence on learning and performance. Three issues that are important are the specification of motivational objectives, entry characteristics of the audience, and motivation vs. hygiene effects in strategy selection.

Motivational Objectives

Typically, motivational effects are measured in one of two ways. The first is at an *affective reaction* level. Learners are given a simple rating scale or semantic differential which measures the degree to which they liked the instruction and felt good about it. The second is at the achievement level. Measures are taken to see whether the motivational strategy had an effect on improved *learning performance*. Both of these are inadequate if not inappropriate.

In designing and testing motivational strategies, it is better to determine what type of motivational effect is desired, and to then write a corresponding objective. General affective reaction can be very useful, but motivational objectives can also be written in terms of increased persistence, more consistent levels of persistence, improved confidence, increases in perceived relevance, level of excitement, and voluntary engagement in the task (continuing motivation, Maehr, 1976), to mention but a few.

In some cases, motivation may be improved, especially in terms of continuing motivation, without noticeable improvements on measured learning performance. The criterion tests used for learning might not measure important aspects of motivation and long range performance. Therefore, when working with motivation, especially in an experimental or validational setting, it is best to have motivational objectives that state the desired motivational behavior in addition to the learning objectives.

Audience Analysis

The second issue of concern is audience analysis. The possibilities for introducing creative strategies for improving the motivational appeal of instruction are endless. Audience analysis based on a model of the major factors in motivation helps to answer questions about how many and what type of strategies to use. In using the ARCS Model, the designer assesses the motivational profile of the audience. This can be a rigorous process of measurement, or it can be an informal determination based on the designer's knowledge of the audience.

For example, if most of the students in a given audience have a high need to learn a given body of material, and if they are confident in their ability to succeed, then few motivational strategies would be needed for relevance and confidence. With regard to attention and satisfaction, only a few specific strategies would be needed to stimulate their attention from time to time, and to maintain intrinsic satisfaction with accomplishments. In contrast, if a group of learners who are nervous about working on computers are going to begin their first lesson of computer assisted instruction, there will be a higher than normal requirement for a "friendly" program to build confidence. These examples illustrate that it is possible to determine in advance where the greatest emphasis needs to be in terms of motivational enhancements, and whether a moderate amount of motivational emphasis vs. a heavy emphasis might be needed. The four factors of the ARCS Model help to make judgments as to the area of emphasis when designing courseware.

Motivation Vs. Hygiene

The third issue concerns the motivational vs. hygienic properties of motivational strategies. This concept, in the general sense established by Hertzberg (1966), helps to distinguish features of courseware design that will be demotivating and irritating if they are not done well, but will not motivate the students to learn even if they are done well. For example, it is irritating to sit through a long animated graphic at the beginning of a program after you have seen it once or twice, and it is irritating to have to sit and wait if you are using a program that has to make frequent trips to the disk to run subroutines. These irritations will decrease a person's motivation to work with the given piece of software. Software evaluation criteria often consist of such hygiene factors, but high ratings on these characteristics does not mean that the person will want to study the lesson on the disk. Motivation to learn is enhanced by features that relate directly to the instructional content and methods of teaching. In the next section, which describes some of the strategies in each of the four parts of the ARCS Model, the emphasis is on motivational strategies, but hygienic strategies are also included.

MOTIVATIONAL STRATEGIES

As described in the preceding sections, the ARCS Model contains four categories of variables, and is used in the motivational design process to assist in profiling learner motivation and to generate motivational objectives. Another of its major functions is to assist in generating motivational strategies.

As presently constituted, the ARCS Model has three major subcategories of strategies under each of the major categories (Fig. 16.2). The method of deriving and field testing the model was reported in earlier publications (Keller, 1979, 1983). Based on this earlier work, and the work of Kopp (1982, 1983), Keller and Kopp (1987), Malone (1981), McCombs (1984), and Wlodkowski (1985), further refinements have been made in the strategy subcategories. The remainder of this section contains a brief overview of each strategy and how it can apply to courseware design.

Attention

Strategy A.1.

Perceptual arousal. Gain and maintain student attention by the use of novel, surprising, incongruous, or uncertain events in instruction.

This is roughly equivalent to Berlyne's (1965) concept of "perceptual curiosity," and to the activation of the orienting reflex as defined by Hebb (1955). People respond easily, or even automatically, to unexpected stimuli in their

Attention	A.1.	Perceptual Arousal
	A.2.	Inquiry Arousal
	A.3.	Variability
Relevance	R.1.	Familiarity
	R.2.	Goal Orientation
	R.3.	Motive Matching
Confidence	C.1.	Learning Requirements
	C.2.	Success Opportunities
	C.3.	Personal Control
Satisfaction	S.1.	Natural Consequences
	S.2.	Positive Consequences
	S.3.	Equity

FIG. 16.2. Subcategories of motivational design strategies in the ARCS Model.

environment. The audio and visual capabilities of the computer can be particularly effective in getting attention at this level. Animation, inverse, flash, and sound are all effective attention getters. Also effective are unusual ways of presenting information, such as progressive disclosure of a list of items that begins at the bottom left of the screen and moves upward to the right.

The screens in Fig. 16.3 illustrate a "before and after" condition of an effective use of flash, sound, and animation. In this example from the "Carrying" program in the Guildmaster™ series,[1] the numeral to be carried flashes for a moment then moves around the screen to its new location at the top of the tens column. It is accompanied by a beeping sound as it moves.

Unusual content is also attention getting. Presenting two facts that seem contradictory, a fact that contradicts most people's experience, or a bizarre fact will stimulate attention. For example, books of "believe it or not" facts, and unusual statistics are almost always popular with adolescents.

An important caution in this category is to avoid disfunctional attention-getting effects. Having a word flashing on one part of the screen makes it very difficult to concentrate on other parts of the screen. Adding attention-getting animation can be very irritating if it is time consuming and the learner has no choice but to sit through it.

---

[1]Guildmaster™ is a product of Renaissance Learning Systems, Copyright 1985. The examples in this article have been chosen selectively from the program called "Carrying."

FIG. 16.3. Audiovisual enhancements. This example is from the *Carrying* program produced by Renaissance Learning Systems, Copyright 1985.

Strategy A.2.

Inquiry arousal. Stimulate information seeking behavior by posing, or having the learner generate, questions or a problem to solve.

Suchman (1966) and others have demonstrated the motivating effect of having the learner pose questions, and generate problem-solving activities to answer the questions. This category is similar to Berlyne's (1965) "epistemic curiosity" which refers to the type of curiosity that results in information seeking and problem-solving behaviors. Once you have gotten people's attention through perceptual arousal, you will activate a much deeper level of curiosity by engaging them in an inquiring frame of mind.

There are many things that can be done effectively with the computer that would be difficult with many other media. For example, the popularity of verbal and graphic adventure games on the computer illustrates the potential for stimulating learner curiosity by presenting problem-solving situations accompanied by an air of mystery. Mystery can be evoked in a problem-solving environment when the availability of information is suggested but hidden from view, and there is a promise of obtaining the information as a result of a change in vantage point (Kaplan, 1973; Kaplan & Kaplan, 1978). The use of foreshadowing in literature and drama, or a graphic that shows a path disappearing into a forest can create a sense of mystery.

In an instructional setting, learners can be led toward the ultimate answer by working through a succession of problem-solving activities combined with partial revelations of knowledge. With graphics and animation, the learner can "move" through a series of scenes and situations.

410

At a simpler level, engage the learner's interest by using question-response-feedback interactions that require active thinking, not just verbal recall. Course-ware can also stimulate inquiry attitudes by allowing learners to create their own problems to solve. For example, present a scientific experiment in a manner that allows the student to make choices about variables and quantities, and have the computer present the consequences.

Strategy A.3.

Variability. Maintain student interest by varying the elements of instruction.

From a purely theoretical point-of-view, variability could probably come under perceptual arousal (Strategy A.1). However, it is included as a separate category for pragmatic reasons. The primary factors under perceptual arousal, such as novelty, imply something new and "catchy," perhaps even trendy. Variation refers more to an occasional change in the sequences of instructional events (Gagné, 1985), or other aspects of the way in which information is formatted and presented.

In computer assisted instruction it is usually best to keep instructional segments short, and to intermingle information presentation screens with interactive screens. There should be a consistent pattern for screen layout, but vary it from time to time. Also, use audio and visual enhancements sparingly and functionally. Even though people like variety, they also like to have a sense of stability and structure. Consequently, too much variation is as bad as not enough, especially when it detracts from the content of the instruction.

In the "Carrying" program, there is variability in the tutorial in that a demonstration sequence is followed by an interactive sequence, and each of these sequences has a characteristic format. At the end of the tutorial the learner experiences a pleasant variation in style as a 3-dimensional graphic depicting a castle room is constructed on the screen, and is then overlaid with a question and a menu (Fig. 16.4).

The cartoon character, named Enki, in Figs. 16.3 and 16.4 is present at intervals throughout the entire program. He adds continuity and stability during

FIG. 16.4. Posttutorial menu. This example is from the *Carrying* program produced by Renaissance Learning Systems, Copyright 1985.

the various phases of the tutorial and the game. With respect to functional integration, he is not functionally related to the specific math skills being taught, but he contributes to the unifying theme of a guild, he looks like a wizard, and he helps sustain attention.

Relevance

Strategy R.1.

Familiarity. Use concrete language, and use examples and concepts that are related to the learner's experience and values.

People like moderate doses of strange and unexpected events, but they feel the closest affinity to things they already have some familiarity with, or can relate to through specific images. For example, people prefer stories about specific people rather than statements about mankind in general. They like anecdotes and examples that make a situation seem familiar. And, they like to hear more about things they already know something about. That is one reason why people have hobbies or specialties, and why people will choose to listen to speakers on a controversial topic who represent the point of view they already agree with.

In courseware, the use of first person to request the student's name, and the continued use of personal pronouns and the student's name help to make the lesson *friendly* and familiar. Notice the use of the student's name and the personal pronouns in Figs. 16.3 and 16.4. Even though this bit of anthropomorphizing might be regarded as *contrived* by some, most learners seem to respond positively to this feature. It is even more effective when the computer keeps individual records, and can refer back to the student's history.

Even though he is a fantasy figure, the wizard (Figs. 16.3 and 16.4) in the "Carrying" program adds an element of familiarity for the intended age group (ages 6–10). He serves as somewhat of a surrogate teacher. At times he points to specific points on the screen, and his facial expression changes to give feedback on right or wrong answers.

The use of graphic illustrations and animation can also be used to embed abstract or unfamiliar concepts in a familiar setting. In some cases, instructional examples could be embedded in a variety of contexts. For example, math word problems which are equivalent in terms of mathematical properties could be embedded in contexts such as sewing, auto mechanics, earth science, literature, or music and the learner could choose among them. Ross (1983) found that students were more motivated and effective in learning statistical concepts that were taught in a context related to their major area of study.

Strategy R.2.

Goal Orientation. Provide statements or examples that present the objectives and utility of the instruction, and either present goals for accomplishment or have the learner define them.

FIG. 16.5. Goal statement. This example is from the *Carrying* program produced by Renaissance Learning Systems, Copyright 1985.

People tend to be purposive (Tolman, 1949) in their behavior. If they know where they are going, and see a reason for getting there, they are more likely to want to get there, and to exert energy in that regard. This is the most commonly used form of motivation. We have all seen the power of a strongly desired goal on a person's behavior. Sometimes it is fairly easy to stimulate goal orientation. A clear statement of purpose in terms of the importance or utility of the lesson combined with a statement of the learning objective can help the learner develop a focused goal orientation.

Often, however, it is difficult to produce utilitarian goals that a student can relate to in a learning situation. Vocabulary and trigonometry exercises seem far removed from the goals of most adolescents. In these situations, games, simulations, and other activities can provide a meaningful goal orientation. Games and simulations have built-in goals that provide a sense of purpose to the learner. Games are particularly effective in adding relevance to drill and practice courseware which can otherwise become boring. Simulations, by virtue of being based on actual situations or processes, provide an even more effective level of relevance.

Learners can also be allowed to choose among goal options. By being allowed to choose or bypass a game option, or to choose the subject area of examples as described earlier (Strategy R.1.), students can develop a stronger goal orientation.

Still another way to create goal orientation is to make the learning activity prerequisite to participating in a game or simulation that requires the skill (Keller, 1979). This strategy is illustrated in one of the introductory frames in the "Carrying" program (Fig. 16.5). Students are not allowed access to "The Speed Game" until they have mastered the skill taught in the tutorial part of the lesson.

Strategy R.3.

Motive Matching. Use teaching strategies that match the motive profiles of the students.

The methods, or process aspects, of instruction can have an influence on relevance. For example, it is much easier to motivate a high achiever, independently of the utility of the instruction, if the teaching strategies provide the opportunity for the learner to set standards, be personally responsible for success, and to receive frequent feedback concerning progress toward goal accomplishment. Computer courseware which allows the learner to choose among goals of varying difficulty level, provides a scoring system, and presents feedback on performance will help stimulate the need for achievement. Games usually have these features, and can be built into many types of courseware.

However, a person with a high need for affiliation enjoys noncompetitive, cooperative situations. Consequently, courseware that *requires* participation in an embedded competitive game rather than making it an option will demotivate some students. An option could also be provided that would allow two or more students to work together on a program. This could be as simple as asking for each student's name, and then including plural rather than singular requests for input such as, for example, "Discuss the choices and come to an agreement before you enter your response." At a more complex level, the computer could receive multiple responses, compare them, and give feedback to individuals and to the group.

The important point in this strategy is that the factors involved in the process of instruction, such as teaching strategies and classroom environment, affect motivation in addition to the motivating aspects of the outcomes of instruction.

Before leaving the topic of relevance, a few special comments are in order. Games, simulations, and even fantasies can be used to create a heightened sense of relevance, but they also incorporate many other motivational strategies. Orbach (1980) has documented some of the motivational properties of games and simulations, and Malone (1981) found that an arcade type game (darts) embedded in a math drill was appealing, at least to the boys in the sample. Malone called this a fantasy, but his use of the term is slightly different than in the present context.

When used to refer to a created situation that is presented to an audience, the word fantasy describes an event, process, or situation that has deliberate departures from reality, as in the use of animated make-believe creatures, adventures involving dungeons and dragons, and some genres of science fiction. Any of these fantasy elements can be used to create a microworld in which the learner can imaginatively play a role, and can perform the kinds of activities that are required for survival and success in the real world. The fantasy might include the features of a game, but it also includes an invented situation that, like a simulation, goes beyond a game. This can create a very high level of perceived relevance.

When we move away from descriptions of the stimulus materials, and describe learner behavior, then games, simulations, and fantasies all facilitate fantasy behavior. All of these devices make it easy for the learner to make imaginative flights of fancy, to create a perceived role to fulfill. This is why all three of these techniques were mentioned under relevance, but they typically employ other motivational strategies as well. A well-designed simulation or adventure fantasy will incorporate almost all of the strategies in the ARCS Model, which is why they are mentioned under several different categories.

This means that a game, simulation, or fantasy cannot be viewed as a simple 1-dimensional motivational device, but as a complex strategy that has to be designed and used with all of the motivational elements in mind. In using these strategies, as with all motivational strategies, it is important to weigh the benefits against the added development cost of the instruction, the added length, and the possibility of distracting attention from the learning objectives to the point that the motivational devices become ends in themselves.

Confidence

Strategy C.1.

Learning Requirements. Help students estimate the probability of success by presenting performance requirements and evaluative criteria.

The simple act of making the learners aware of the learning objectives, including the criteria for evaluation and the conditions under which they will be evaluated, helps them develop confidence. When learners know what to expect, they are more likely to be confident in their estimate of success than when a high degree of ambiguity surrounds the testing and evaluation process. This principle also applies to the instructional process. If the instruction is confusing due to the language, internal inconsistency, inappropriate exercises, etc., the student's opportunity to learn is diminished, and the confidence in one's likelihood of success will also diminish.

There are several ways that learning requirements can be made clear within the courseware. First is to clearly present the objective and the overall structure of the lesson. Second, explain the evaluative criteria, and provide opportunities for practice with feedback. Third, mention the prerequisite knowledge, skills, or attitudes that will help the learner succeed at the task. Finally, tell the learner how many items are going to be in a test, or in a drill. This simple bit of information helps the learner anticipate the performance requirements.

Many programs do one or more of the above, but they are not always specific. A good example is provided by the "Carrying" program. Just before beginning the problem exercise, Enki tells the student, "You must do 8 of 10 problems correctly to be able to advance to the Speed Dome."

Strategy C.2.

Success Opportunities. Provide challenge levels that allow meaningful success experience under both learning and performance conditions.

In considering challenge, a distinction needs to be made between conditions of learning vs. performance. For example, people high in need for achievement prefer a moderate level of risk, and Malone (1981) describes the uses of uncertain outcomes, randomness, and variable difficulty levels in relation to challenge. These characteristics would apply more to conditions of practice than to learning.

When people are learning new knowledge or skills, they usually want a fairly high degree of assurance that they will be successful, that their efforts will pay-off in terms of accomplishment. If they find that success comes at too high a cost, they will tend to move on to other activities, unless they have an extremely high motive to succeed at the particular activity. When people like math better than social studies, or guitar better than trumpet, it usually reflects, at least in part, that they find one easier than the other. In courseware design, organize the tutorial part of a program or the early stages of practice so that the content and the practice exercises go from easy to difficult, and provide a continuous (100%) reinforcement schedule. This is very much like the concept of shaping a response in operant conditioning. Such an arrangement would provide the student with opportunities for success, and the experience of success has been identified as a critical condition for any affective learning (Martin & Briggs, 1986).

To help prevent excessive challenge for the less capable learners, and boredom among the more capable ones, use instructional management strategies that match learning requirements to prerequisite knowledge and skills. If there is going to be wide variation in the entry level knowledge of people using the program, then provide a pretest and multiple entry points into the instructional sequence.

After people have achieved some degree of mastery with a skill or knowledge area, they are more likely to be stimulated by competition and other sources of uncertainty. This is why gaming activities can be motivating in drill and practice programs and in simulations and fantasies. The insertion of random events that either benefit or punish the player add an element of uncontrollable challenge, but should be at a level that will not ultimately override the influences of skill on performance.

The difficulty level can be controlled by many features such as adding a clock and shortening the response time, varying the speed of the stimulus, or varying the complexity of the situation. Adding these features to the performance activities can help the learner establish a personally meaningful level of challenge, and develop both confidence and self-esteem.

Strategy C.3.

Personal Control. Provide feedback and opportunities for control that support internal attributions for success.

Success, by itself, does not always increase confidence and self-esteem, especially when a person attributes success to luck or the easiness of the task

(Weiner, 1980). Evaluation and feedback methods that provide feedback on performance, and personal control over program features can help a person develop internal attributions of success. These internal attributions, which can be to ability or effort, help build confidence and self-esteem.

However, total control over a learning situation, like total absence of control, can be either very frightening or very frustrating and demotivating to a learner. Merrill (1975) found that giving learners complete control over building their own sequences of instructional events did not improve performance, nor was it motivating. However, a degree of control can both reduce frustration and increase confidence.

Many people find it very annoying when a piece of courseware locks them into a sequence of instruction from which they cannot escape. It is best if the learner can page backwards through a program, or escape and return to the menu at any time. The learner should also have control over pacing. Allowing the learner to hit any key, or a designated key, to go from one screen to the next is the usual way of providing this aspect of learner control. Finally, it is good to give the learner access to the menu immediately after booting the courseware. It is very demotivating to have to sit through a long introduction after you have become familiar with a particular program. All of these features are hygienic in that they help prevent the learner from becoming irritated with the lesson.

Motivation to learn is more likely to be enhanced by providing learner control over access to different parts of the courseware, and over the difficulty level. A menu-driven structure is the ideal way to provide this feature. The student who is motivated to learn may want to move from a tutorial part of the lesson to the practice part at a different time, and in a different sequence than the instructional designer had in mind. This student will also be more motivated when working at a challenge level that is personally satisfying. Providing these options will enhance the motivation to learn of some students, and may help to create it in others.

Finally, use words and phrases that help attribute accomplishment to student effort and ability. This can be done by stating things as you would like the student to be thinking. For example, the first option in Fig. 16.4 is stated in student terms. The inclusion of the word "myself" makes a tremendous difference in personalizing this phrase and putting the emphasis on student effort.

Also, do not require students to keep trying to succeed at a task when success is impossible. Some programs will present a sequence of a given number of problems, and the learner has to work through the entire sequence even through he or she may have missed too many to achieve mastery before finishing half of them. This can be avoided by automatically terminating the program sequence when mastery is impossible. In the "Carrying" program, for example, mastery is 8 correct out of 10 problems. As soon as a student misses 3 problems, the exercise is interrupted and the student is encouraged to start over.

Satisfaction

Strategy S.1.

Natural Consequences. Provide opportunities to use newly acquired knowledge or skill in a real or simulated setting.

One of the best ways to develop or sustain intrinsic motivation for learning is to provide opportunities for the learner to use newly acquired knowledge and skill in a meaningful way. If it is not possible for the learner to do this on the job or in a hobby or other personally satisfying activity, then such things as games, simulations, case study exercises, or role plays can be used. These activities can be very close to an actual area of application in terms of the conditions that are presented, and the knowledge and skills that are required for successful performance. Through the use of imagination and fantasy, the learner can ''enter'' into the world of the simulation.

The use of these approaches is not greatly different from their use in the learning process to develop relevance. The difference is in the end rather than the means. When trying to establish a sense of relevance, these strategies are used to help the learner see the utility of the learning objectives. When used to produce or maintain satisfaction, they are used after the initial learning experience to provide an opportunity for meaningful application. Thus, it would be most effective to use an instructional game or simulation that requires application of previously learned skills as the last part of the instruction (a strategy for satisfaction), and to inform the student of the game or simulation at the outset of the courseware (a strategy for relevance).

This approach was used in the ''Carrying'' program. After achieving mastery, the student is given a menu that includes choices for additional examples or practice, or to begin the Speed Game.

Strategy S.2.

Positive Consequences. Provide feedback and reinforcements that will sustain the desired behavior.

This strategy refers to the use of positive motivational feedback or rewards for success. It is usually administered continuously after each success in the process of acquiring a new skill, and on a schedule thereafter. The use of feedback after every response in a tutorial, and after a series of responses in practice exercises usually fulfills this strategy.

Motivational feedback, in contrast to corrective feedback, may consist of a simple affirmation, ''Correct,'' or a more enthusiastic comment such as ''Great!'' Sometimes, however, this is overdone. The use of statements such as ''That's terrific! What an accomplishment!!'' has no positive motivational effect on a learner who perceived the exercise as being rather simple. In fact, it could dilute the motivational benefits of other aspects of the program.

In the "Carrying" program, for example, students receive a simple smile from Enki for correct answers, and they see the results on the scoreboard. For incorrect answers they receive hints and corrective feedback. After achieving mastery the student is given the simple compliment that he or she did very well.

Designers also include extrinsic rewards such as balloons being popped by arrows, boxcars being added to a railroad train, or animated characters jumping up and down, waving their arms, and smiling. Sometimes the rewarding properties of a wrong answer exceed a correct one. For example, a cannon might roll in from edge of the screen and fire a shot that hits the wrong answer which explodes and disappears. Obviously, the rewards for wrong answer should never exceed those for correct answers. Also since these extrinsic rewards can become more interesting than the instruction itself, it is usually best to use them judiciously.

In some cases, people do not care to be distracted by extrinsic rewards, especially since there is a cost associated with the reward. The cost is the time it takes to wait while the rewarding activities are being executed. Hence, there is an element of external control in this situation. People who are intrinsically motivated by the learning activity do not like to feel that they are being manipulated or controlled (Condry, 1977), or that the learning activity is a means to getting an extrinsic reward. They tend to prefer verbal recognition for their accomplishments in the form of praise when appropriate, and informative feedback that helps them improve. Consequently, for some learners it would be good to make the external reward package a user selected option. Learners could select it and use it until the novelty effect wore off, then exclude it.

Strategy S.3.

Equity. Maintain consistent standards and consequences for task accomplishment.

An otherwise successful learning experience can turn sour if a person believes that his or her performance was not judged fairly, or that the rewards or other opportunities that were supposed to accompany success are not delivered. People evaluate outcomes against their own expectations, against the stated or implied promises by the instructor or courseware, and against the outcomes attained by other people. The person's perceived sense of equity does not require that exceptions never be made, but it does require good communication, and consistent application of the standards and consequences that are announced.

In courseware design, this is another reason for having clearly presented expectations and consequences at the beginning of the learning activity. This can take the form of formally stating the objectives, or informal descriptions of what the learner can expect to achieve. Then, the practice exercises and performance tests should be consistent with the objectives and instructional content.

APPLYING ARCS TO COURSEWARE

The specific application of the ARCS Model will vary for each item of courseware, but there is a typical pattern that is time-based. In the early parts of a program, there is more of a focus on strategies to arouse and sustain attention. Features to establish relevancy and support learner confidence are also included early in the program. As the learner progresses, satisfaction producing strategies are included, along with attention sustaining strategies. The degree to which additional relevance and confidence strategies are included will depend on the audience analysis and motivational objectives.

To illustrate the motivational properties of courseware, a case example is included in this section. Because it was not possible to include examples of all the major types of courseware in one chapter of a book, we chose one which illustrates the more or less generic architecture of a tutorial program. Regardless of the instructional design model that is used in the courseware design, the resulting program tends to include (1) title page, (2) introduction, (3) menu, (4) information presentation, (5) practice and feedback, and (6) assessment and closure. We chose a tutorial rather than a drill and practice or a simulation because it usually combines teaching with practice, and it provides the structure into which a game or simulation would be designed.

The case example used here was designed and programmed in a graduate level introductory computer course using Apple BASIC. The courseware, entitled "Leadership" is intended to introduce five types of leadership style and to provide some case studies in applied settings. Figure 16.6 shows the overall flow of the courseware.

1. Title Page

The title page introduces the content of the courseware in a very compressed manner, and may contain other information such as copyright, author, and a short description of the courseware. Sometimes the title page has the most sophisticated graphic, which might be an animation, of all parts of the courseware.

From a motivational design point of view, the title page is very significant because it is the first screen the student sees. At the very least, the attention getting properties of the title page should stimulate perceptual arousal (A.1), and it is even better if it stimulates the student's information seeking behavior (A.2: inquiry arousal). Graphics are a useful tool for gaining attention, and they do not need to be fancy. Normally, however, they should be related to what the courseware is all about.

The Leadership courseware begins with a screen showing its title using color and graphic capability (Fig. 16.7). This use of graphics, which can be high or low resolution, to create a boldface title in color is a more effective way to gain

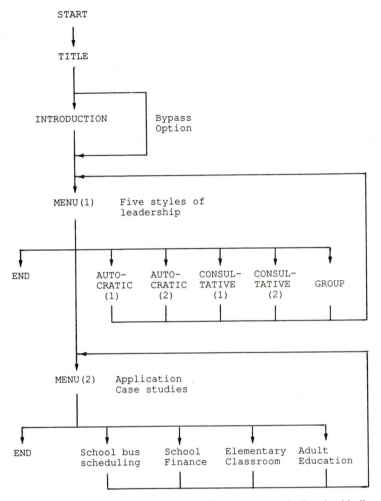

FIG. 16.6. Overall courseware flow of the case example "Leadership."

FIG. 16.7. Use of low resolution graphic for the title.

student attention than a regular sized title in text mode. Fancier graphics such as an animation and a human model may be added to the title page, but they seem not to be necessary for the college audience for this courseware.

2. Introduction

It has become common for computer courseware to include an introductory screen that contains a statement of the terminal learning objective. This should help the student concentrate on the information that is necessary to attain the instructional goal. Since the student knows what should be accomplished, it would also give the student an immediate notice of accomplishment when the goal is attained. Other introductory information may include an overview of the courseware, how to use the courseware, a description of the target audience, and the significance of studying the content of the courseware.

A primary motivational concern in the introduction is to establish relevance. After the student's attention is gained, he or she needs to feel that the courseware is "for me." This feeling may be obtained if the student perceives that the courseware content is familiar (R.1: familiarity) or important (R.2: Goal orientation). Thus, the objective should be stated using concrete terminology that the student can easily comprehend. The inclusion of examples using student language are likely to contribute to an increase in the perceived relevance of the introduction.

Although the statement of the objective may sometimes be enough to establish relevance, an explicit statement of why the courseware is important may enhance the perceived relevance. When the utility of the target skills or knowledge is not obvious to the student, or when the learning task is not in itself entertaining, it should be clearly stated how the accomplishment of the goal relates to further learning or to a future career. A simple sentence such as, "Being able to convert fractions into decimals is necessary to solve the word problems in the next lesson," may help the student attach more importance to a lesson on fraction-decimal conversion.

Along with the statement of the objective, a description of the target audience deserves special attention for its motivational attributes, particularly in regard to confidence building. A description of the target audience (e.g., grade level, prerequisite competencies) can help build the student's confidence if he or she fits the category. Along with the description of target audience, a statement such as, "Having completed the prior section, this section should be readily achievable," may assist the student to form a positive expectation for success with the courseware (C.1: learning requirements). An optional section that reviews prerequisite material can help build learner confidence, and make the new goal seem easier and more attainable.

As shown in Fig. 16.8, the Leadership courseware introduces the concept of leadership as "the key to success." Following the short pause at "READY . . .,"

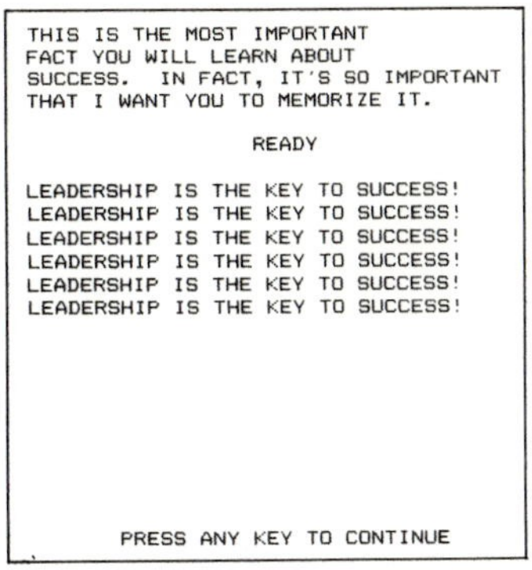

```
                              THIS IS THE MOST IMPORTANT
                              FACT YOU WILL LEARN ABOUT
                              SUCCESS.   IN FACT, IT'S SO IMPORTANT
                              THAT I WANT YOU TO MEMORIZE IT.

                                        READY

                              LEADERSHIP IS THE KEY TO SUCCESS!
                              LEADERSHIP IS THE KEY TO SUCCESS!
                              LEADERSHIP IS THE KEY TO SUCCESS!
                              LEADERSHIP IS THE KEY TO SUCCESS!
                              LEADERSHIP IS THE KEY TO SUCCESS!
                              LEADERSHIP IS THE KEY TO SUCCESS!




                                  PRESS ANY KEY TO CONTINUE
```

FIG. 16.8. Attention getting techniques in the introduction section.

the key sentence "Leadership is the key to success!" is presented using a slower speed of text display. When the student presses any key at the end of this screen, everything is erased except for the last of the key sentences. This illustrates a good use of various attention getting techniques that are available. It also enhances relevance by connecting the learning of leadership styles with "success." The headline helps build relevance by stating that this is the most important fact that the student will learn.

3. Menu Page

Computer courseware typically includes a menu page that serves as the branching point from where the student can select a section to study. The menu page is also the returning point after the completion of each of the sections. Finally, the student can choose to quit the courseware by selecting an <E>xit or <Q>uit option on the menu page. No menu page may be included if the courseware is linearly structured, or relatively short as in drill and practice type courseware. However, the menu-driven structure can improve the utility of the courseware by allowing partial usage of the courseware depending upon a local need for its use. For example, a tutorial may be utilized as a drill and practice if it has a way to use only the practice portions via a menu structure.

The menu page is important motivationally since it gives the student more control over the learning process (C.3: personal control). It is always recommended to have a menu-driven structure in any type of computer courseware except for very short drills. First, the menu-driven structure makes the courseware a set of smaller chunks, or sections. This is likely to help the student to have a sense of where he or she is in relation to the completion of the courseware (C.1: learning requirements), to maintain attention to the instruction by leaving a section and going into another (A.3: variability), and to feel rewarded by finishing a section when the student sees a "star" attached to the completed section on the menu (S.1: positive consequences). Therefore, even if the structure of the

```
WHICH OF THE FOLLOWING LEADERSHIP
STYLES WOULD YOU LIKE TO KNOW MORE
ABOUT? (PRESS A LETTER).

      <A> AI - AUTOCRATIC

      <B> AII - AUTOCRATIC

      <C> CI - CONSULTATIVE

      <D> CII - CONSULTATIVE

      <E> GII - GROUP

      <F> CONTINUE THE PROGRAM

      <Q> QUIT FOR NOW.
```

FIG. 16.9. The first MENU of the case example.

learning task is hierarchical, which prohibits optional sequences among the subsections, the use of a menu-driven structure has some benefits. In this case, the menu can be used not to allow the student a free choice of subsections, but only to indicate the completion of subsections with a predetermined forced sequence, and to provide convenient points to exit and reenter the lesson.

In our case example, there are two menu structures built into the courseware (Fig. 16.6). The first menu (Fig. 16.9) has options for choosing any of the five leadership styles to study, an option for going on to the application case studies, and an option to quit the courseware. At the end of each of the five subsections that teach the basic concepts of five leadership styles, the student is branched back to the menu screen. Compared with a linear structure, shown in Fig. 16.10, the case example is flexible and allows learner control over multiple entry and exit points. In this program, an inflexible linear sequence would lock the learner into a long sequence of instruction and practice, and would have a negative effect on motivation, at least in a hygienic sense.

With respect to motivational strategies, the flexible menu provides the student an opportunity to structure his or her learning environment (C.3: personal control). The student is allowed to choose which section to do first, or even to omit some of the sections and take the posttest. On another occasion, if the student wants to go over a section once again, he or she can choose to do so. The student's control over the learning environment may also contribute to the need for achievement by making the student responsible for sequencing the learning (R.3: motive matching), and to the development of internal attributions for success (C.3: personal control).

Finally, the menu structure may be used to provide more frequent and precise guidance for learning for those who do not wish to have complete control. Recommendations as to which section should be taken first may be given to the student in a form of suggestion on the menu page. This might be helpful for students who are anxious or low in need for achievement (R.3: motive matching).

424

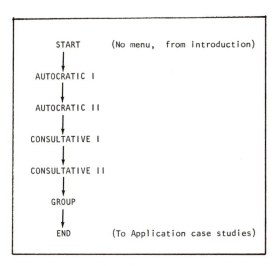

FIG. 16.10. Linear structure as an alternative to the first MENU of the case example.

4. Information Presentation and Learning Guidance

Tutorial instruction usually begins by presenting information to the student. When the learning task involves intellectual skills, rather than just knowledge, a general statement of a concept, rule, or procedure may be introduced first, and be followed by some examples of the application of the generality. After presenting information, an analogy or mnemonic device may be given for remembering factual information, and critical features may be compared with nonexamples to improve discrimination.

The interactiveness of the information presentation portion of the courseware is a strong motivational element. In order to have the student involved in the learning process, posing questions and having the student respond can help stimulate curiosity (A.2: inquiry arousal). As soon as a generality and an example are presented to the student, it is feasible to have him or her complete a part of another example. For example, if the task is to perform a four-step procedure, you may ask the student to recognize which is the correct procedure, then break the procedure into four steps and introduce each of them with some interactive question-answer-feedback process. In a discovery learning approach, the student might be asked for a response even before the generality and an example are presented.

Figures 16.11 and 16.12 show two consecutive screens from the case example, which illustrate a computer-student interaction and the interplay of computer control vs. student control over information. In the first screen, progressive

```
IF YOU CHOOSE TO USE THE 'AI'
LEADERSHIP STYLE, YOU WILL SOLVE THE
PROBLEM OR MAKE THE DECISION YOURSELF,
USING INFORMATION AVAILABLE TO YOU
AT THE TIME.




REMEMBER - THE AI STYLE IS A
VARIATION OF THE AUTOCRATIC APPROACH.


PRESS ANY KEY TO CONTINUE'
```

FIG. 16.11.   Progressive disclosure in information presentation section.

disclosure is used to present the opening statement followed by the second statement. Progressive disclosure provides variation in pacing (A.3: variability) and can create positive suspense about what is going to happen next (A.2: inquiry arousal). After the information is presented, the learner is allowed to take control, and press a key to continue. The second screen requires learner input in the form of an active response to the question. This interactive process helps prevent page after page of "Press any key to continue," with which the student would get bored or become inattentive.

The main point here is to incorporate as many student-computer interactions as possible and as early as possible. Not only does this strategy enhance the Attention property of the courseware, but the use of an easier to more difficult sequence may affect the student's Confidence with the courseware (C.1: learning requirements) and more precise learning guidance may direct the student behavior in the desired direction (S.2: positive consequences). Moreover, the interactions that come before the practice exercise may match the student's need for practice in a psychologically risk-free environment (i.e., not embarrassing, not judged as failure) to build up his or her Confidence (C.3: personal control).

```
WHICH WOULD YOU LIKE TO DO IF YOU
DECIDE TO USE THE 'AI' LEADERSHIP
STYLE?  TYPE 1 OR 2.


1. HAVE A MEETING TO DISCUSS WITH
   YOUR SUBORDINATES.

2. MAKE THE DECISION YOURSELF.


?1

NO, REMEMBER AI STYLE IS A VARIATION
OF THE AUTOCRATIC APPROACH.

PRESS ANY KEY TO CONTINUE'
```

FIG. 16.12.   Student-computer interaction in information presentation section.

5. Practice and Feedback

Tutorial courseware usually has a practice and feedback section after the information presentation section to utilize computer's capability of response judging and conditional branching. In drill and practice courseware, the practice and feedback section is the main body of the program. The practice and feedback section usually starts with an introductory page telling the student how the practice exercise works (e.g., how many questions, how to answer, how to get a point, the mastery criterion, and how to complete/quit the exercise, etc.). The introductory page is followed by a set of practice items, which are sometimes selected from an item pool by using a random generator or by adjusting for the student's progress along the difficulty levels. Depending upon the student's answer to each question, feedback is given and a correct answer is scored as such. Finally, a closure page informs the student of his or her performance, which completes the instructional part of the courseware and leads the student into the assessment or posttest.

The construction of the practice and feedback section can have a large effect on the motivational attributes of the courseware. First of all, the practice and feedback section can be seen as an opportunity for the student to build up his or her Confidence about what is being learned (C.2: success opportunities). Therefore, feedback for the student's responses should be carefully constructed. Instructional feedback that corrects student's mistakes should be given for wrong responses, whereas motivational feedback (i.e., praises) may be given for the correct responses (S.2: positive consequences). Threats, negative comments, critical or embarrassing statements for wrong responses should never be used (e.g., "Where did you get that number?").

The case example utilizes highlighting techniques such as sized text, exclamation marks, and color for motivating feedback following correct answers (S.2: positive consequences), but not for wrong responses. When the student answers a question incorrectly, corrective feedback is given, which is followed by another chance to try the same question. In the process of learning, it possibly may be that a student intentionally selects a wrong stem to examine why it is wrong if he or she knows corrective feedback is given for the wrong choices. On the other hand, it may also be possible that another student intentionally selects a wrong stem to see if anything interesting happens for a wrong response. Thus, it is advised to make feedback for wrong responses informative but not salient to avoid arousing student attention inappropriately.

Second, allowing the student control over his or her practice strategy may positively affect the motivational property of the courseware. Not only providing the goal to be attained, but the structure by which the student can define his or her own goal for the day is possible (C.3: personal control). For example, the student may be asked how many words he or she wants to include in the spelling practice from the item pool; or, given the ideal standard of 90% correct, what percentage of the multiplication problems he or she wants to aim at today within

```
WOULD YOU LIKE TO APPLY WHAT YOU HAVE
LEARNED SO FAR TO A SHORT CASE STUDY?

              PRESS A LETTER

1 <A>   BUS SCHEDULING CASE

2 <B>   THE FINANCE CASE

3 <C>   THE SCHOOL DATA SYSTEM

4 <D>   THE ADULT EDUCATION CASE

  <Q>   NO.  I WOULD PREFER TO QUIT NOW.



THE DIFFICULTY LEVEL IS INDICATED
BY THE NUMBER FOR EACH CASE STUDY
(1: EASIEST, 4: HARDEST).
```

FIG. 16.13.   The second MENU for application case studies.

how many minutes per item? This process would also enhance the perceived relevance of the courseware (R.2: goal orientation) since the student is helping to define the goal.

On the second menu of the Leadership courseware, the student can choose among four short case studies to apply the leadership concepts (Fig. 16.13). It is assumed that the potential users of the courseware would have diverse academic backgrounds. Thus, providing a wide range of application practices, one of which may better fit student interest, would enhance Relevance property of the courseware. In addition, the difficulty level is indicated for each case study on this menu. The student can set his or her own level of challenge (C.3: personal control) from the easiest case to the most difficult case, depending upon his or her perception of the ability or the confidence.

At the closure of the practice and feedback section, the student's accomplishments should be adequately mentioned. When the student finishes a set of practice exercises, he or she should be informed of which goals were accomplished. For the accomplished goals, the student should also be given a word of encouragement, and a comment that ability and effort have determined the success (C.3: personal control) could be included on the closure page (e.g., "Congratulations! You must have studied very carefully. You have passed this practice exercise. Press <RETURN> to go back to the menu to keep up with your good work."). This helps mold internal attributions for success.

On the other hand, if a goal has not been met, then support the student's effort and provide directions for the next activity that would help the student attain the goal. It may also be a good idea to stress the importance of the task at hand in a wider scope (R.2: goal orientation), to point out the progress the student is making compared with the previous tries, and/or to suggest a break before the next try.

6. Assessment and Closure

Sometimes courseware includes not only an instructional function, but an assessment function as a separate section. Typical construction of the assessment

428

section, or the posttest, is the same as that of practice and feedback except for the absence of feedback. In some courseware, the assessment function is built into the practice and feedback section using the computer's capability of keeping scores before giving any feedback messages.

The main motivational design concern for assessment is to maintain consistent standards for the learning task (S.3: equity). When a certain standard is required for the posttest, then it should have been incorporated in the previous practice exercises. For example, if all of the fractions should be reduced to be judged as correct on the posttest, unreduced fractions should be judged as incorrect in the practice, and corrective feedback specific to the reduction of the fraction to the lowest terms should be included. The standards of the assessment such as the mastery criterion and the use of time limits, should be indicated to the student prior to the posttest.

At the closure of the assessment section, which is usually the closure of the entire courseware, it is recommended to stress the relationship between the student's effort and success with the courseware (C.3: personal control), to position the success within a larger context of more relevant tasks (R.2: goal orientation), and to provide rewards for the completion of the courseware if the task was not intrinsically interesting (S.2: positive consequences). If directions to go on to more advanced courseware are given, or an optional instructional game is available at the closure of the courseware, the newly learned skills or knowledge may readily utilized in such follow-through activities. This would enhance the motivational property of the courseware by stimulating the student's Satisfaction with the courseware and what has been learned (S.1: natural consequence).

SUMMARY

After introducing the ARCS Model and several issues related to its use in instructional design, the next section of this chapter contained many suggestions for motivational strategies to use in computer courseware. This was followed by a case example based on a tutorial on leadership. It illustrated how motivational strategies can be used selectively in each major component of the tutorial.

The remainder of this summary consists of four tables (see Tables 16.1 through 16.4) that contain a complete listing of the strategies that were described earlier in this paper. These should not be construed as comprehensive sets of rules for producing motivating courseware, but only as a sampling of possibilities. Keep in mind that these strategies should never be incorporated in their totality or arbitrarily. An audience analysis combined with the formulation of motivational objectives will help you determine which strategies and how many to include. The use of these lists to stimulate ideas, when combined with a systematic design approach, should result in courseware that is appealing as well as effective and efficient.

TABLE 16.1
A Sampler of Attention Getting Strategies

A.1. Perceptual Arousal

<u>Audio-visual effects</u>: Use animation, inverse, flash, sound and other audio and visual capabilities of the computer as attention getters.

<u>Unusual content or events</u>: Use unusual, contradictory, or bizarre content to stimulate attention, but use them judiciously.

<u>Absence of distractions</u>: Avoid disfunctional attention-getting effects such as a flashing word that distracts learner's concentration, or a long conpulsory animation.

A.2. Inquiry Arousal

<u>Active responding</u>: Engage the learner's interest by using question-response-feedback interactions that require active thinking.

<u>Problem creation</u>: Allow learners to create their own problems to solve and have the computer judge their solutions or present the consequences.

<u>Sense of mystery</u>: Present problem solving situations in a context of exploration and partial revelations of know-ledge.

A.3. Variability

<u>Brief instructional segment</u>: Keep instructional segments relatively short and make effective use of screen display to facilitate ease of reading.

<u>Interplay of instruction and response</u>: Intermingle information presentation screens with interactive screens.

<u>Format variation</u>: Use a consistent screen format, but include occasional variations.

<u>Functional integration</u>: Use audio and visual enhancements sparingly and functionally to support the instruction and general theme of the lesson.

REFERENCES

Adams, J. S. (1965). Inequity in social exchange. In L. Berkowitz (Ed.), *Advances in experimental social psychology* (Vol. 2). New York: Academic Press.

Alschuler, A. S. (1973). *Developing achievement motivation in adolescents: Education for human growth.* Englewood Cliffs, NJ: Educational Technology Publications.

Bandura, A. (1977). Self efficacy: Toward a unifying theory of behavioral change. *Psychological Review, 84,* 191–215.

Berlyne, D. E. (1965). Motivational problems raised by exploratory and epistemic behavior. In S. Koch (Ed.), *Psychology: A study of a science* (Vol. 5). New York: McGraw-Hill.

Brophy, J. (1983). Conceptualizing student motivation. *Educational Psychologist, 18,* 200–215.

Brophy. J., & Kher, N. (in press). Teacher socialization as a mechanism for developing student

TABLE 16.2
A Sampler of Relevance Generating Strategies

R. 1. Familiarity

<u>Human interest language and graphics</u>: Use personal pronouns and the learner's name, and use illustrations with people or cartoon characters when appropriate.

<u>Illustrations for concreteness</u>: Use graphic illustrations and animation to embed abstract or unfamiar concepts in a familiar setting.

<u>Familiar examples and contexts</u>: Use examples from content areas and situations that are familiar to the learner.

R.2. Goal Orientation

<u>Importance or utility</u>: Clearly state the objective in terms of the importance or utility of the lesson.

<u>Built-in Goals</u>: Use goal oriented games, simulations, and fantasies to provide a sense of purpose.

<u>Goal type options</u>: Allow learners to choose among different types of goals with respect to learning methods or learning outcomes.

R.3. Motive Matching

<u>Goal level options</u>: Allow the learner to choose among goals of varying difficulty level to stimulate the need for achievement.

<u>Scoring system</u>: Provide a scoring system and present feedback on performance to stimulate the need for achievement.

<u>Noncompetitive options</u>: Make participation in a competitive game an option to avoid demotivating students high in the need for affiliation.

<u>Multiple participant opportunities</u>: Provide options to allow two or more students to work cooperatively.

---

motivation to learn. In R. Feldman (Ed.), *Social psychology applied to education*. Cambridge, England: Cambridge University Press.

Condry, J. (1977). Enemies of exploration: Self-initiated versus other-initiated learning. *Journal of Personality and Social Psychology, 35*, 459–477.

Cross, K. P. (1981). *Adults as learners: Increasing participation and facilitating learning*. San Francisco: Jossey-Bass.

deCharms, R. (1976). *Enhancing motivation change in the classroom*. New York: Irvington.

Deci, E. L. (1975). *Intrinsic motivation*. New York: Plenum Press.

Deci, E. L., & Porac, J. (1978). Cognitive evaluation theory and the study of human motivation. In M. R. Lepper & D. Greene (Eds.), *The hidden costs of reward*. Hillsdale, NJ: Lawrence Erlbaum Associates.

Deci, E. L., & Ryan, R. M. (1985). *Intrinsic motivation and self-determination in human behavior*. New York: Plenum Press.

Gagné, R. M. (1985). *The conditions of learning and theory of instruction* (4th Ed.). New York: Holt, Rinehart, & Winston.

Hebb, D. O. (1955). Drives and C.N.S. (Conceptual Nervous System). *Psychological Review, 62*, 243–254.

TABLE 16.3
A Sampler of Confidence Building Strategies

C.1. Learning Requirements

Objective and structure: Clearly present the objective and
the overall structure of the lesson.

Criteria and feedback: Explain the evaluative criteria and
provide opportunities for practice with feedvack.

Prerequisites: Mention the prerequisite knowledge, skills,
or attitudes that will help the learner succeed at the
task.

Test conditions: Tell the learner how many items are going
to be in a test or drill, and whether it will be timed.

C.2. Success Opportunities

Easy to difficult: During the initial learning phase, organize
the courseware from easy to difficult and provide a frequent or continuous reinforcement schedule.

Appropriate difficulty level: Match learning requirements to
prerequisite knowledge and skills to prevent excessive
challenge or boredom.

Multiple entry points: Provide a pretest and multiple entry
points into the instructional sequence.

Random, uncontrollable events: Insert random events during
practive or application, but not during initial learning,
to add a degree of uncontrollable challenge.

Variable difficulty level: Control difficulty level by adding
a time-limit, varying the speed of the stimulus, or varying
the complexity of the situation.

C.3. Personal Control

Exit control: Allow the learner to escape and return to the
menu at any time, and if feasible, to page backwards.

Pacing control: Give the learner control over pacing by hitting
a key to go from one screen to the next.

Quick access: Give the learner access to the menu immediately
after booting the courseware, or make the introductory
material optional.

Menu structure: Use a menu-driven structure to provide learner
control over access to different parts of the courseware.

Attributional language: Use words and phrases that help attribute
success to the learner's effort and ability.

Hertzberg, F. (1966). *Work and the nature of man.* New York: World Publishing.

Jones, R. A. (1977). *Self-fulfilling prophecies: Social psychological and physiological effects of expectancies.* New York: Halsted Press.

Kaplan, R. (1973). Predictors of environmental preference: Designers and clients. In W. Preiser (Ed.), *Environmental design research.* Stoudsburg, PA: Dowden, Hutchinson and Russ.

Kaplan, S., & Kaplan, R. (1978). *Humanscape: Environments for people.* North Scituate, MA: Duxbury Press.

Keller, J. M. (1975). *Effects of instructions and reinforcement contingencies in the development of learned helplessness.* Unpublished Doctoral Dissertation, Indiana University.

TABLE 16.4
A Sampler of Satisfaction Producing Strategies

S.1. Natural Consequences

Application exercises: Include exercises that require the
application of the newly acquired knowledge and skills.

Transfer to subsequent tasks: Built the courseware so that
the newly acquired knowledge or skills are immediately
utilized in subsequent parts of the program.

Simulated applications: Include an instructional game or
simulation at the end of course ware that requires
application of previously learned skills or knowledge.

S.2. Positive Consequences

Appropriate reinforcement schedule: Use positive motivational
feedback or other rewards for success after every response
in a tutorial, and after a series of responses in practice
exercises.

Meaningful reinforcement: Avoid diluting the motivational
benefits of feedback by providing too much praise for a
rather simple task.

Rewards for correct responses: Use extrinsic rewards for correct responses and do not provide rewarding consequences
after wrong answers.

Judicious rewards: Use extrinsic rewards judiciously so that
the rewards are not more interesting than the instruction
itself.

Optional reward package: Make the external reward package a
user selected option to avoid negative effects of external
control.

S.3. Equity

Purpose and content consistency: Keep the structure and content
of the lesson consistent with its stated purpose and outline.

Exercise and test consistency: Make the exercises and tests
consistent with each other and with the objectives.

Keller, J. M. (1979). Motivation and instructional design: A theoretical perspective. *Journal of Instructional Development, 2*(4), 26–34.

Keller, J. M. (1983). Motivational design of instruction. In C. M. Reigeluth (Ed.), *Instructional-design theories and models: An overview of their current status.* Hillsdale, NJ: Lawrence Erlbaum Associates.

Keller, J. M. (1984). The use of the ARCS model of motivation in teacher training. In K. E. Shaw (Ed.), *Aspects of educational technology, Volume XVII: Staff development and career updating.* London: Kogan Page.

Keller, J. M., & Kopp, T. (1987). Application of the ARCS model of motivational design. In C. M. Reigeluth (Ed.), *Instructional theories in action: Lessons illustrating selected theories and models.* Hillsdale, NJ: Lawrence Erlbaum Associates.

Kopp, T. W. (1982). Designing boredom out of instruction. *NSPI Journal,* May, 23–27, 32.

Kopp, T. W. (1983). *Boredom in college lecture instruction.* Unpublished Doctoral Dissertation, Syracuse University.

Maehr, M. L. (1976). Continuing motivation: An analysis of a seldom considered educational outcome. *Review of Educational Research, 46,* 443–462.

Malone, T. W. (1981). Toward a theory of intrinsically motivating instruction. *Cognitive Science, 4,* 335–369.

Martin, B. L., & Briggs, L. J. (1986). *The affective and cognitive domains: Integration for instruction and research.* Englewood Cliffs, NJ: Educational Technology Publications.

Maw, W. H., & Maw, E. W. (1968). Self appraisal of curiosity. *Journal of Educational Research, 61,* 462–466.

McCombs, B. L. (1984). Processes and skills underlying continuing intrinsic motivation to learn: Toward a definition of motivational skills training. *Educational Psychologist, 4,* 190–218.

Merrill, M. D. (1975). Learner control: Beyond aptitude-treatment interactions. *AV Communications Review, 23,* 217–226.

Orbach, E. (1980). Simulations games and motivation for learning: A theoretical framework. *Simulation and Games, 4,* 440–453.

Papert, S. (1980). *Mindstorms: Children, computers and powerful ideas.* New York: Basic Books.

Pulos, S., Fisher, S., & Spage, E. K. (1985, September). *A child's-eye view of computer.* Paper presented at the annual meeting of the American Psychological Association, Los Angeles.

Raynor, J. O. (1974). Relationships between achievement-related motives, future orientation, and academic performance. In J. W. Atkinson, & J. O. Raynor (Eds.), *Motivation and achievement.* Washington, DC: V. H. Winston.

Ross, S. M. (1983). Increasing the meaningfulness of quantitative material by adapting context to student background. *Journal of Educational Psychology, 75,* 519–529.

Rotter, J. B. (1966). Generalized expectancies for internal versus external control of reinforcement. *Psychological Monographs, 80* (Whole No. 609).

Seligman, M. E. (1975). *Helplessness.* San Francisco: Freeman.

Suchman, J. R. (1966). A model for the analysis of inquiry. In H. J. Klausmeier, & C. W. Harris (Eds.), *Analysis of concept learning.* New York: Academic Press.

Tolman, E. C. (1949). *Purposive behavior in animals and men.* Berkeley: University of California Press.

Weiner, B. (1980). *Human motivation.* New York: Holt, Rinehart and Winston.

White, R. W. (1959). Motivation reconsidered: The concept of competence. *Psychological Review, 66,* 297–323.

Wlodkowski, R. J. (1985). *Enhancing adult motivation to learn.* San Francisco: Jossey-Bass.

Zuckerman, M. (1971). Dimensions of sensation seeking. *Journal of Consulting and Clinical Psychology, 36,* 45–52.

Author Index

Numbers in italics indicate pages with complete bibliographic information.

Subject Index

441